Scott Foresman · Addison Wesley
enVisionMATH® 2.0

Volume 1 Topics 1-8

Authors

Randall I. Charles
Professor Emeritus
Department of Mathematics
San Jose State University
San Jose, California

Janet H. Caldwell
Professor of Mathematics
Rowan University
Glassboro, New Jersey

Juanita Copley
Professor Emerita, College of
Education
University of Houston
Houston, Texas

Warren Crown
Professor Emeritus of Mathematics
Education
Graduate School of Education
Rutgers University
New Brunswick, New Jersey

Francis (Skip) Fennell
L. Stanley Bowlsby Professor
of Education and Graduate and
Professional Studies
McDaniel College
Westminster, Maryland

Stuart J. Murphy
Visual Learning Specialist
Boston, Massachusetts

Kay B. Sammons
Coordinator of Elementary
Mathematics
Howard County Public Schools
Ellicott City, Maryland

Jane F. Schielack
Professor of Mathematics
Associate Dean for Assessment
and Pre K-12 Education,
College of Science
Texas A&M University
College Station, Texas

Mathematicians

Roger Howe
Professor of Mathematics
Yale University
New Haven, Connecticut

Gary Lippman
Professor of Mathematics and
Computer Science
California State University East Bay
Hayward, California

Glenview, Illinois   Boston, Massachusetts   Chandler, Arizona   Upper Saddle River, New Jersey

Contributing Authors

Zachary Champagne
District Facilitator, Duval County
Public Schools
Florida Center for Research in
Science, Technology, Engineering,
and Mathematics (FCR-STEM)
Jacksonville, Florida

Jonathan A. Wray
Mathematics Instructional
Facilitator
Howard County Public Schools
Ellicott City, Maryland

ELL Consultants

Janice Corona
Retired Administrator
Dallas ISD, Multi-Lingual
Department
Dallas, Texas

Jim Cummins
Professor
The University of Toronto
Toronto, Canada

Texas Reviewers

Theresa Bathe
Teacher
Fort Bend ISD

Chrissy Beltran
School Wide Project Coordinator
Ysleta ISD

Renee Cutright
Teacher
Amarillo ISD

Sharon Grimm
Teacher
Houston ISD

Esmeralda Herrera
Teacher
San Antonio ISD

Sherry Johnson
Teacher
Round Rock ISD

Elvia Lopez
Teacher
Denton ISD

Antoinese Pride
Instructional Coach
Dallas ISD

Joanna Ratliff
Teacher
Keller ISD

Courtney Jo Ridehuber
Teacher
Mansfield ISD

Nannie D. Scurlock-McKnight
Mathematics Specialist
A.W. Brown Fellowship-Leadership
Academy
Dallas, TX

Brian Sinclair
Math Instructional Specialist
Fort Worth ISD

ISBN-13: 978-0-328-76724-3
ISBN-10: 0-328-76724-7

11 12 13 14 15 V011 20 19 18 17 16

Digital Resources

> Look for these digital resources in every lesson!

Go to PearsonTexas.com

 Solve
Solve & Share problems plus math tools

 Learn
Visual Learning Animation Plus with animation, interaction, and math tools

A-Z **Glossary**
Animated Glossary in English and Spanish

 Tools
Math Tools to help you understand

 Check
Quick Check for each lesson

 Games
Math Games to help you learn

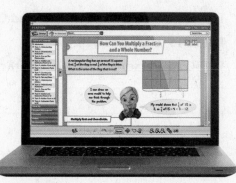

eText
The pages in your book online

PearsonTexas.com
Everything you need for math anytime, anywhere

Key

Number and Operations

Algebraic Reasoning

Geometry and Measurement

Data Analysis

Personal Financial Literacy

> **Mathematical Process Standards** are found in all lessons.

Digital Resources at PearsonTexas.com

Solve   Learn   Glossary

Check   Tools   Games

And remember, the pages in your book are also online!

Contents

Topics

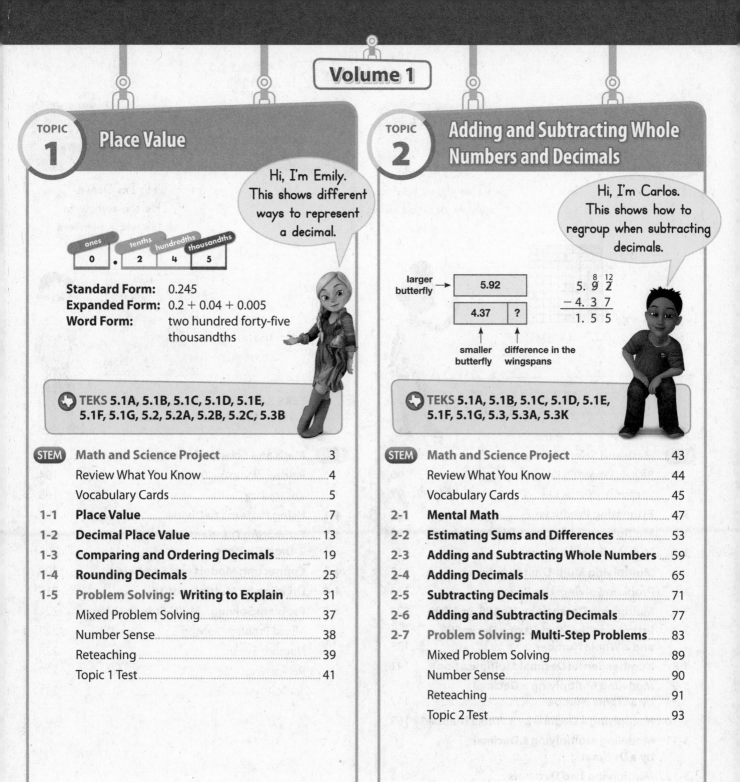

Volume 1

TOPIC 1
Place Value

Hi, I'm Emily. This shows different ways to represent a decimal.

ones	tenths	hundredths	thousandths
0 .	2	4	5

Standard Form: 0.245
Expanded Form: $0.2 + 0.04 + 0.005$
Word Form: two hundred forty-five thousandths

TEKS 5.1A, 5.1B, 5.1C, 5.1D, 5.1E, 5.1F, 5.1G, 5.2, 5.2A, 5.2B, 5.2C, 5.3B

TOPIC 2
Adding and Subtracting Whole Numbers and Decimals

Hi, I'm Carlos. This shows how to regroup when subtracting decimals.

larger butterfly — 5.92

smaller butterfly — 4.37 ?

difference in the wingspans

$$5.\overset{8}{9}\overset{12}{2}$$
$$-\ 4.\ 3\ 7$$
$$\overline{1.\ 5\ 5}$$

TEKS 5.1A, 5.1B, 5.1C, 5.1D, 5.1E, 5.1F, 5.1G, 5.3, 5.3A, 5.3K

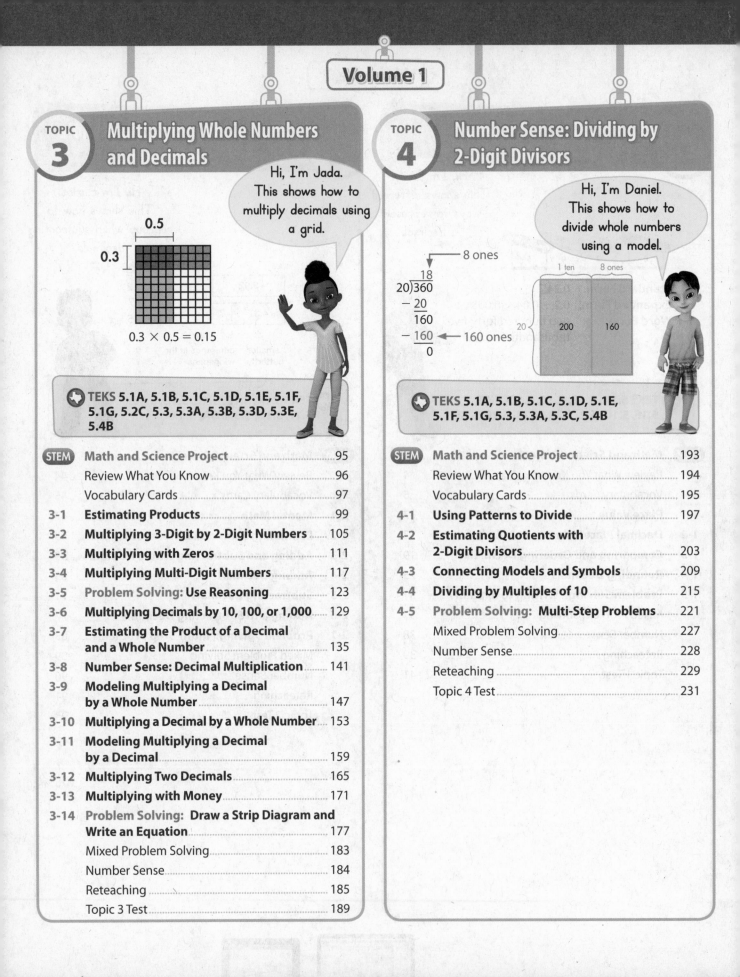

TOPIC 3 Multiplying Whole Numbers and Decimals

Hi, I'm Jada. This shows how to multiply decimals using a grid.

0.5

0.3

$0.3 \times 0.5 = 0.15$

TEKS 5.1A, 5.1B, 5.1C, 5.1D, 5.1E, 5.1F, 5.1G, 5.2C, 5.3, 5.3A, 5.3B, 5.3D, 5.3E, 5.4B

TOPIC 4 Number Sense: Dividing by 2-Digit Divisors

Hi, I'm Daniel. This shows how to divide whole numbers using a model.

8 ones

160 ones

1 ten 8 ones

20 200 160

TEKS 5.1A, 5.1B, 5.1C, 5.1D, 5.1E, 5.1F, 5.1G, 5.3, 5.3A, 5.3C, 5.4B

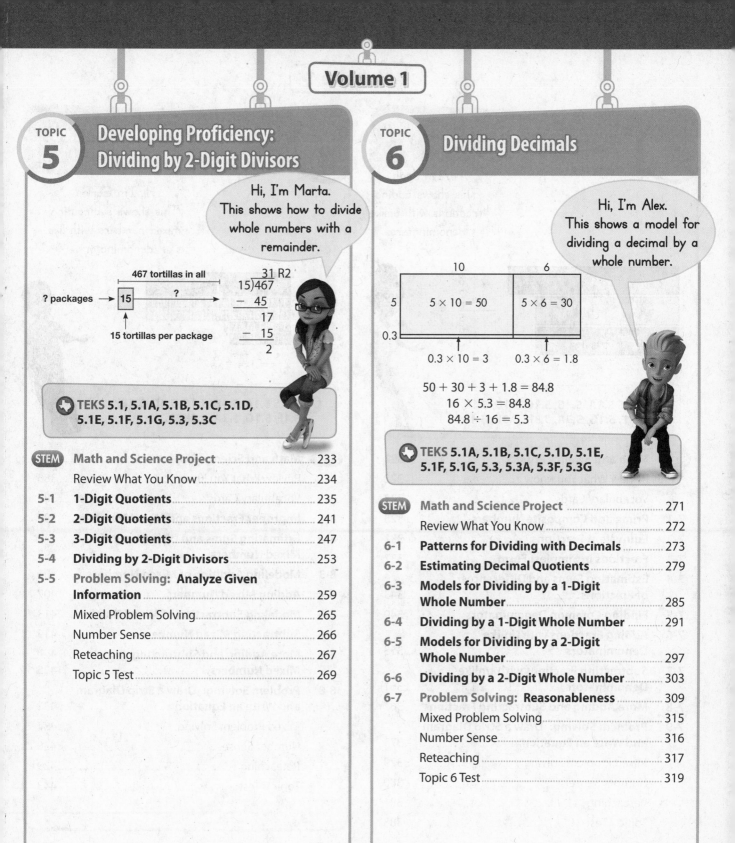

Volume 1

TOPIC 5 — Developing Proficiency: Dividing by 2-Digit Divisors

Hi, I'm Marta. This shows how to divide whole numbers with a remainder.

467 tortillas in all

? packages → 15 — ? — 15 tortillas per package

$$31 \text{ R2}$$
$$15\overline{)467}$$
$$-\ 45$$
$$\ 17$$
$$-\ 15$$
$$\ 2$$

⭐ TEKS 5.1, 5.1A, 5.1B, 5.1C, 5.1D, 5.1E, 5.1F, 5.1G, 5.3, 5.3C

TOPIC 6 — Dividing Decimals

Hi, I'm Alex. This shows a model for dividing a decimal by a whole number.

	10	6
5	5 × 10 = 50	5 × 6 = 30
0.3	0.3 × 10 = 3	0.3 × 6 = 1.8

$$50 + 30 + 3 + 1.8 = 84.8$$
$$16 \times 5.3 = 84.8$$
$$84.8 \div 16 = 5.3$$

⭐ TEKS 5.1A, 5.1B, 5.1C, 5.1D, 5.1E, 5.1F, 5.1G, 5.3, 5.3A, 5.3F, 5.3G

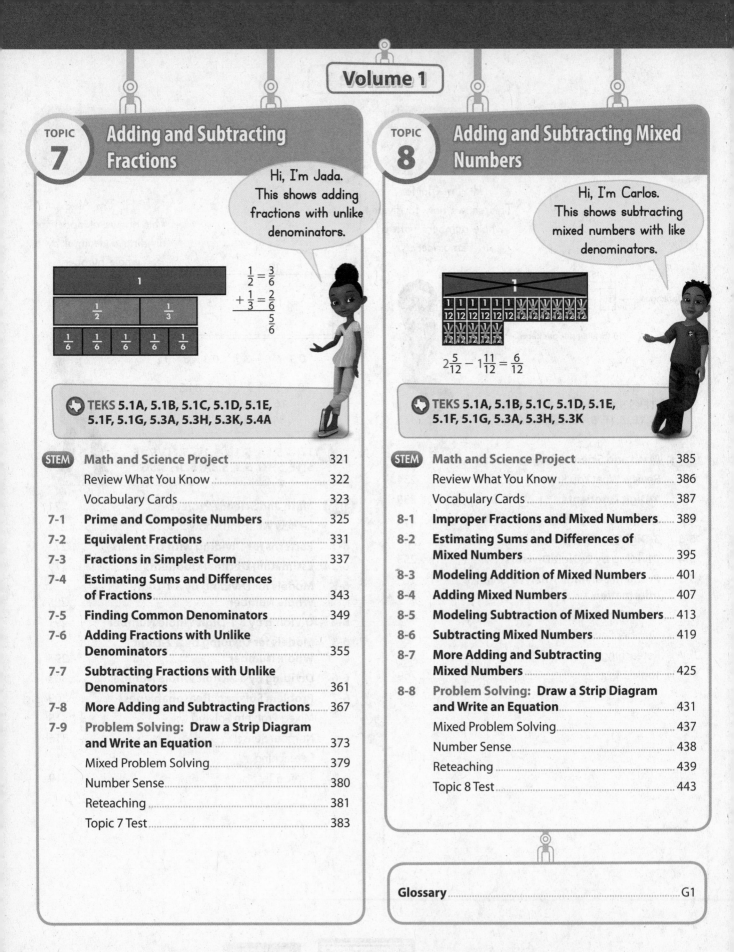

Volume 1

TOPIC 7 — Adding and Subtracting Fractions

Hi, I'm Jada. This shows adding fractions with unlike denominators.

$$\frac{1}{2} = \frac{3}{6}$$
$$+ \frac{1}{3} = \frac{2}{6}$$
$$\frac{5}{6}$$

TEKS 5.1A, 5.1B, 5.1C, 5.1D, 5.1E, 5.1F, 5.1G, 5.3A, 5.3H, 5.3K, 5.4A

TOPIC 8 — Adding and Subtracting Mixed Numbers

Hi, I'm Carlos. This shows subtracting mixed numbers with like denominators.

$$2\frac{5}{12} - 1\frac{11}{12} = \frac{6}{12}$$

TEKS 5.1A, 5.1B, 5.1C, 5.1D, 5.1E, 5.1F, 5.1G, 5.3A, 5.3H, 5.3K

TOPIC 9 — Multiplying and Dividing Fractions

Hi, I'm Emily. This shows how to divide a whole number by a unit fraction using a model.

$$3 \div \frac{1}{4} = 3 \times \frac{4}{1} = 12$$

⭐ TEKS 5.1A, 5.1B, 5.1C, 5.1D, 5.1E, 5.1F, 5.1G, 5.3, 5.3I, 5.3J, 5.3L

TOPIC 10 — Expressions and Equations

Hi, I'm Jackson. This shows how to evaluate an algebraic expression.

$23 + n$

$23 + 3 = 26$

DATA	n	$23 + n$
	3	$23 + 3$
	5	$23 + 5$
	7	$23 + 7$

⭐ TEKS 5.1A, 5.1B, 5.1C, 5.1D, 5.1E, 5.1F, 5.1G, 5.4, 5.4B, 5.4D, 5.4E, 5.4F

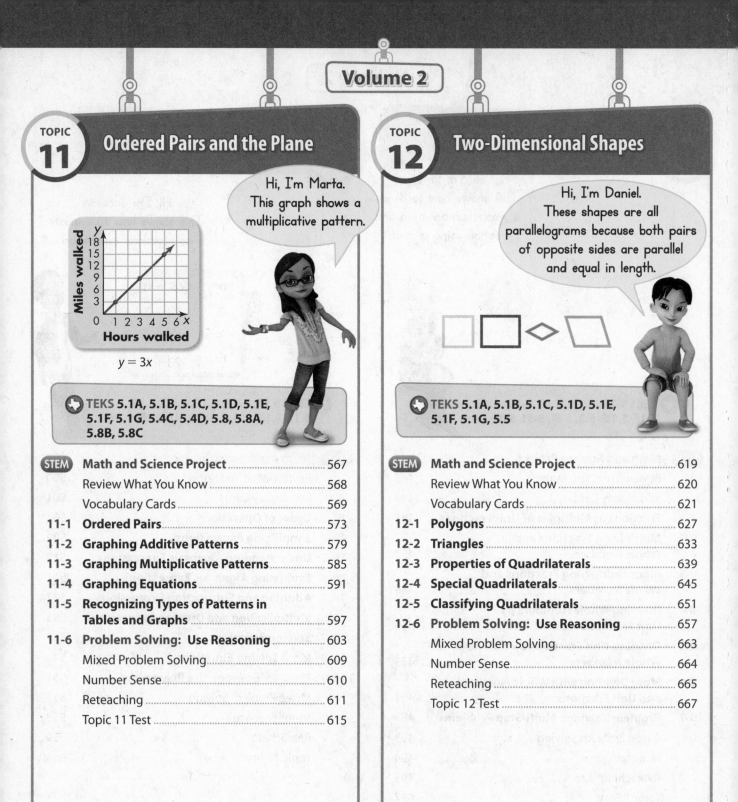

Volume 2

TOPIC 11 — Ordered Pairs and the Plane

Hi, I'm Marta. This graph shows a multiplicative pattern.

$y = 3x$

TEKS 5.1A, 5.1B, 5.1C, 5.1D, 5.1E, 5.1F, 5.1G, 5.4C, 5.4D, 5.8, 5.8A, 5.8B, 5.8C

TOPIC 12 — Two-Dimensional Shapes

Hi, I'm Daniel. These shapes are all parallelograms because both pairs of opposite sides are parallel and equal in length.

TEKS 5.1A, 5.1B, 5.1C, 5.1D, 5.1E, 5.1F, 5.1G, 5.5

Volume 2

TOPIC 13 — Perimeter, Area, and Volume

Hi, I'm Emily. This shows one way to find the volume of a rectangular prism.

$$V = B \times h$$
$$V = 56 \times 6$$
$$V = 336 \text{ cubic cm}$$

6 cm

Area of base: 56 square cm

TEKS 5.1, 5.1A, 5.1B, 5.1C, 5.1D, 5.1E, 5.1F, 5.1G, 5.4B, 5.4G, 5.4H, 5.6, 5.6A, 5.6B

TOPIC 14 — Measurement Units and Conversions

Hi, I'm Carlos. This shows how customary units of length are related.

1 foot (ft) = 12 inches (in.)
1 yard (yd) = 3 ft = 36 in.
1 mile (mi) = 1,760 yd = 5,280 ft

TEKS 5.1A, 5.1B, 5.1C, 5.1D, 5.1E, 5.1F, 5.1G, 5.4H, 5.7

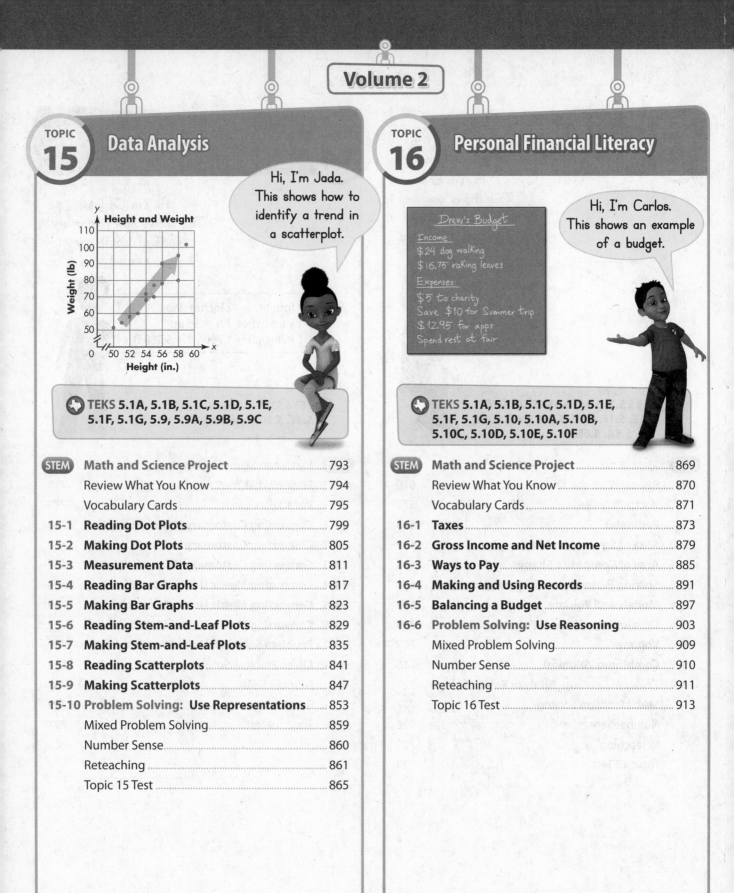

Volume 2

TOPIC 15 — Data Analysis

Height and Weight

Hi, I'm Jada. This shows how to identify a trend in a scatterplot.

TEKS 5.1A, 5.1B, 5.1C, 5.1D, 5.1E, 5.1F, 5.1G, 5.9, 5.9A, 5.9B, 5.9C

TOPIC 16 — Personal Financial Literacy

Drew's Budget

Income:
$24 dog walking
$16.75 raking leaves
Expenses:
$5 to charity
Save $10 for Summer trip
$12.95 for apps
Spend rest at fair

Hi, I'm Carlos. This shows an example of a budget.

TEKS 5.1A, 5.1B, 5.1C, 5.1D, 5.1E, 5.1F, 5.1G, 5.10, 5.10A, 5.10B, 5.10C, 5.10D, 5.10E, 5.10F

Volume 2

Step Up to Grade 6

These lessons help you prepare for Grade 6.

⭐ TEKS 6.2B, 6.2C, 6.3A, 6.4C, 6.4E, 6.4G, 6.5A, 6.8B, 6.11

Have a great year!

✪ Problem-Solving Handbook

Applying Math Processes

Analyze
- How does this problem connect to previous ones?
- What am I asked to find?
- What information do I know?

Plan
- What is my plan?
- What strategies can I use? (See the list of some helpful strategies.)
- How can I use tools?
- How can I organize and record information?

Solve
- How can I use number sense?
- How can I estimate?
- How can I communicate and represent my thinking?

Justify
- How can I explain my work?
- How can I justify my answer?

Evaluate
- Have I checked my work?
- Is my answer reasonable?

Use this Problem-Solving Handbook throughout the year to help you solve problems.

Some Helpful Strategies

- Represent the Problem
  - Draw a Picture or Strip Diagram
  - Write an Equation
  - Make a Table or List
- Look for a Pattern
- Use Reasoning
- Analyze Given Information
- Analyze Relationships

Problem-Solving Tools

Real Objects

$\frac{1}{6}$	$\frac{2}{6}$	$\frac{3}{6}$
$\frac{4}{6}$	$\frac{5}{6}$	$\frac{6}{6}$

Manipulatives

Distance swam

Bob	$\frac{5}{6}$ mile	
June	$\frac{7}{8}$ mile	
Tina	$\frac{3}{4}$ mile	

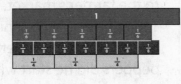

Paper and Pencil

$$\begin{array}{r} \$40.00 \\ -\$25.98 \\ \hline \$14.02 \end{array}$$

Technology

Problem-Solving Techniques

Mental Math

Sale!

T-shirt........$19.98
Jeans..........$48.50
Sweater.....$29.50

$19.98 + 48.50 + 29.50 = ?$
$20 + 50 + 30 = 100$
$100 - 2.02 = 97.98$

Estimation

The hummingbird's heart beats 597 times in a minute.

There are 60 minutes in an hour.
$597 \times 60 = ?$
About $600 \times 60 = 36,000$ heartbeats in an hour.

Number Sense

Soccer Attendance

DATA		
Game 1	550
Game 2	675
Game 3	642
Game 4	588

Each number is between 500 and 700. The total attendance will be between 2,000 and 2,800.

Strip Diagrams

You can draw a **strip diagram** to show how the quantities in a problem are related. Then you can write an equation to solve the problem.

Part-Part-Whole: Addition and Subtraction

Draw this **strip diagram** for situations that involve joining parts of a whole or separating a whole into parts.

Whole → | 875
| 225 | 650 |

Part   Part

Problem 1

David saved $125.50. Then he spent $102.25 on a new bicycle. Now how much money does David have?

$125.50 → | $125.50
| $102.25 | ? |

$102.25   ? dollars
for bicycle   left

$125.50 − $102.25 = ? or
$125.50 − ? = $102.25

He has $23.25 after buying the bicycle.

Problem 2

A farmer brought some peppers to the farmer's market. He sold 150 peppers. At the end of the day, he had 165 peppers left. How many peppers did he start with?

? peppers → | ?
| 150 | 165 |

150 peppers   165 peppers
sold   left

150 + 165 = ? or ? − 150 = 165

He started with 315 peppers.

Pictures help you understand.
Don't trust key words in a problem.

Comparison: Addition and Subtraction

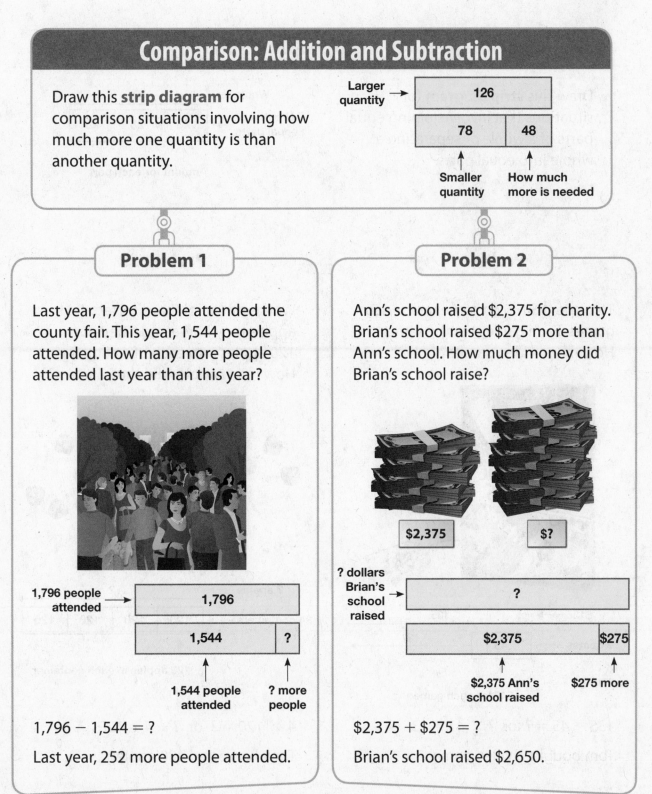

Draw this **strip diagram** for comparison situations involving how much more one quantity is than another quantity.

Larger quantity →

| 126 |
| 78 | 48 |

↑ Smaller quantity ↑ How much more is needed

Problem 1

Last year, 1,796 people attended the county fair. This year, 1,544 people attended. How many more people attended last year than this year?

1,796 people attended →

| 1,796 |
| 1,544 | ? |

↑ 1,544 people attended   ↑ ? more people

1,796 − 1,544 = ?

Last year, 252 more people attended.

Problem 2

Ann's school raised $2,375 for charity. Brian's school raised $275 more than Ann's school. How much money did Brian's school raise?

$2,375 $?

? dollars Brian's school raised →

| ? |
| $2,375 | $275 |

↑ $2,375 Ann's school raised   ↑ $275 more

$2,375 + $275 = ?

Brian's school raised $2,650.

More Strip Diagrams

The **strip diagrams** on these pages can help you solve problems involving multiplication and division.

Equal Parts: Multiplication and Division

Draw this **strip diagram** for situations that involve joining equal parts of a whole or separating a whole into equal parts.

Whole → 84

Number of equal parts → | 28 | 28 | 28 |

↑ Amount for each part

Problem 1

Tom spent $135 on some new video games. Each game cost the same. How many video games did he buy?

VIDEO GAME SPORTS

$45

$135 → 135

? games → | 45 | ?

↑ $45 for each game

$135 \div 45 = ?$ or $? \times 45 = 135$

Tom bought 3 video games.

Problem 2

Workers at an orchard sorted the apples they harvested. They put 120 apples into each of 4 containers. How many apples did they harvest?

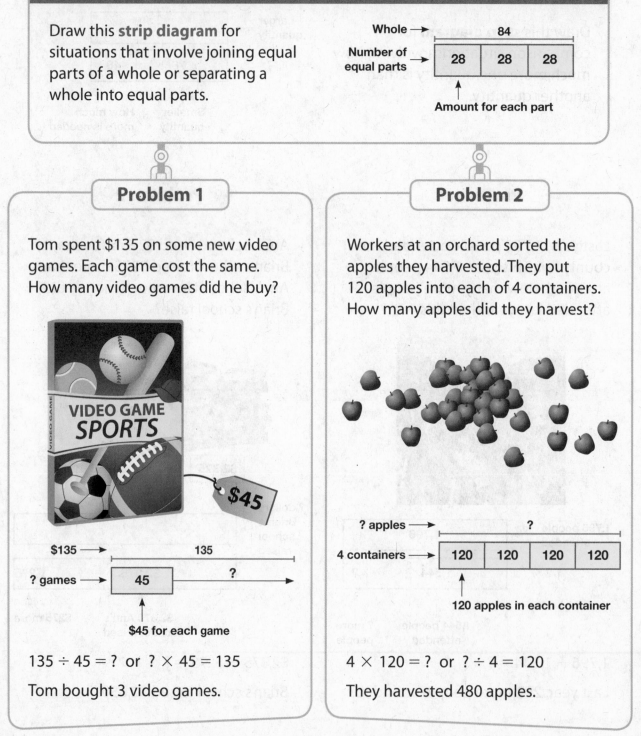

? apples → ?

4 containers → | 120 | 120 | 120 | 120 |

↑ 120 apples in each container

$4 \times 120 = ?$ or $? \div 4 = 120$

They harvested 480 apples.

Multiplication and division are similar to addition and subtraction.

Comparison: Multiplication and Division

Draw this **strip diagram** for comparison situations involving how many times one quantity is of another quantity.

78		
Larger quantity → | 26 | 26 | 26 | 3 times as many

Smaller quantity → | 26 |

Problem 1

Joe buys a new tent and sleeping bag. The tent costs 4 times as much as the sleeping bag. How much does the sleeping bag cost?

$?

$160

160			
$160 cost of tent → | ? | ? | ? | ? | 4 times as much

$? price of sleeping bag → | ? |

$160 ÷ 4 = ?$ or $4 \times ? = 160$

The sleeping bag costs $40.

Problem 2

Linda biked 175 miles last summer. Kendra biked 3 times as far as Linda. How many miles did Kendra bike?

?		
? miles Kendra biked → | 175 | 175 | 175 | 3 times as many

175 miles Linda biked → | 175 |

$3 \times 175 = ?$ or $? \div 3 = 175$

Kendra biked 525 miles.

More Problem-Solving Strategies

Creating a solution plan involves choosing and trying a strategy and then sometimes trying a different strategy.

Strategy	Example	When I Use It
Draw a Picture	Martin has a garden behind his house. The garden is 50 feet long and 20 feet wide. What is the perimeter of Martin's garden? 50 ft 20 ft ⬜ 20 ft 50 ft The perimeter of Martin's garden is 140 feet.	A **representation** of the problem can help you visualize the facts and identify relationships.
Write an Equation	Monica made 144 ounces of punch for a party. If she pours the punch into 6-ounce glasses, how many glasses can she fill? Find $144 \div 6 = n$. $n = 24$, so Monica can fill 24 glasses.	You can **communicate ideas** by writing an equation to describe a situation involving an operation or operations.
Make a Table and Look for a Pattern	Barbara is making salsa at a restaurant. For every 3 tomatoes she uses, she also uses 2 jalapeños. If she uses 30 tomatoes, how many jalapeños does she use? <table><tr><td>Tomatoes</td><td>3</td><td>6</td><td>15</td><td>30</td></tr><tr><td>Jalapeños</td><td>2</td><td>4</td><td>10</td><td>20</td></tr></table> Barbara uses 20 jalapeños.	Make a table and look for a number **relationship** when there are 2 or more quantities that change in a predictable way.

There's almost always more than one way to solve a problem.

Strategy	Example	When I Use It
Use Reasoning	Sue's train leaves at 7:30 A.M. She takes $\frac{1}{2}$ hour to get from home to the train station. She also takes an hour to get ready. She wants to arrive $\frac{1}{2}$ hour before the train leaves. What is the latest time she should get up? Time Sue needs to get up ← $1\frac{1}{2}$ hours — Time to arrive at station ← 30 minutes — Time train leaves 7:30 Sue should get up by 5:30 A.M.	**Reason** with the facts you know to find what actions cause the end result.
Analyze Given Information	Suzanne spent $8 on two items for lunch. What did she buy? $6.75 + $2.50 > $8 Too much $2.50 + $1.25 < $8 Not enough $6.75 + $1.25 = $8 Perfect! Suzanne bought a sandwich and a juice bottle.	**Analyze given information** to help find a solution. <table><tr><th>Item</th><th>Cost</th></tr><tr><td>Sandwich</td><td>$6.75</td></tr><tr><td>Chips</td><td>$2.50</td></tr><tr><td>Juice Bottle</td><td>$1.25</td></tr></table>
Analyze Relationships	A zoo has 75 animals. There are 25 mammals. The rest are reptiles and birds. There are 4 birds for every 1 reptile. How many birds and reptiles are there? There are 50 birds and reptiles in all. If there are 4 birds, then there will be 1 reptile. So, there are 40 birds and 10 reptiles: 40 + 10 = 50. There are 40 birds and 10 reptiles.	You can **analyze relationships** in information you are given to find unknown information.

Problem-Solving Recording Sheet

> This sheet helps you organize your work and make sense of problems.

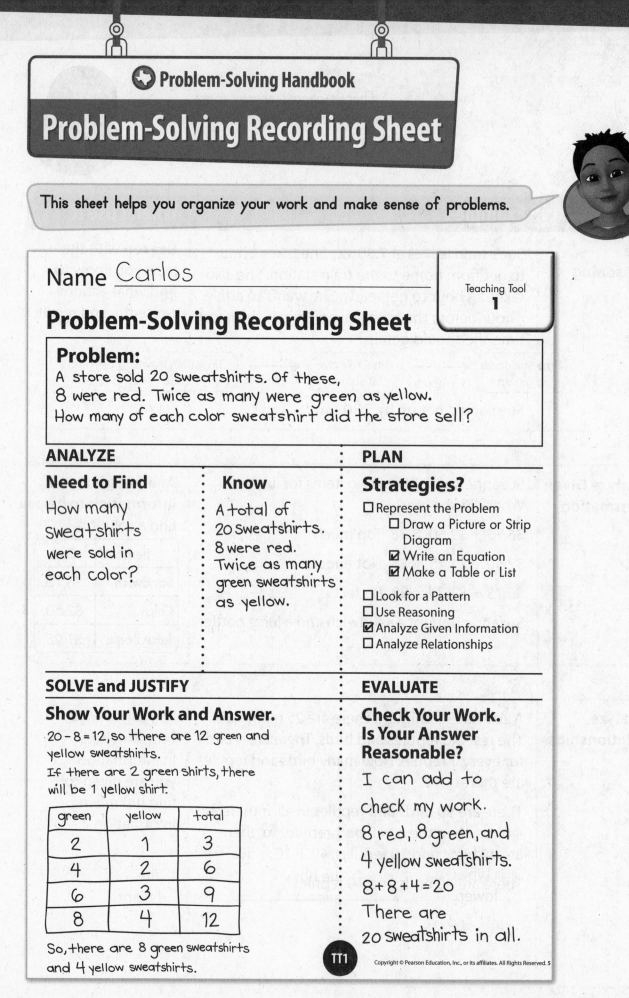

Name **Carlos**

Teaching Tool
1

Problem-Solving Recording Sheet

Problem:
A store sold 20 sweatshirts. Of these,
8 were red. Twice as many were green as yellow.
How many of each color sweatshirt did the store sell?

ANALYZE

Need to Find

How many sweatshirts were sold in each color?

Know

A total of 20 Sweatshirts. 8 were red. Twice as many green sweatshirts as yellow.

PLAN

Strategies?
- ☐ Represent the Problem
  - ☐ Draw a Picture or Strip Diagram
  - ☑ Write an Equation
  - ☑ Make a Table or List

- ☐ Look for a Pattern
- ☐ Use Reasoning
- ☑ Analyze Given Information
- ☐ Analyze Relationships

SOLVE and JUSTIFY

Show Your Work and Answer.

20 – 8 = 12, so there are 12 green and yellow sweatshirts.

If there are 2 green shirts, there will be 1 yellow shirt.

green	yellow	total
2	1	3
4	2	6
6	3	9
8	4	12

So, there are 8 green sweatshirts and 4 yellow sweatshirts.

EVALUATE

Check Your Work. Is Your Answer Reasonable?

I can add to check my work.
8 red, 8 green, and 4 yellow sweatshirts.
8 + 8 + 4 = 20
There are 20 sweatshirts in all.

TT1

My Word Cards

Use the examples for each word on the front of the card to help complete the definitions on the back.

value

5,318

The value of the 3 is 300.

standard form

5,318

expanded form

5,000 + 300 + 10 + 8

word form

five thousand, three hundred eighteen

thousandth

0.629

9 is in the thousandths place.

equivalent decimals

0.7 = 0.7

rounding

To the nearest tenth, 1.34 rounds to 1.3.

Complete the definition. Extend learning by writing your own definitions.

_____ is a common way of writing a number with commas separating groups of three digits starting from the right.

The place of a digit in a number tells you its _____.

_____ is a way to write a number using words.

_____ is a way to write a number that shows the place value of each digit.

Decimals that name the same amount are called _____.

A _____ is one out of 1,000 equal parts of a whole.

_____ is a process that determines which multiple of 10, 100, 1,000 and so on, a number is closest to.

Name _____

☆ ✦ ☆
Solve & Share

The population of a country many years ago was in the millions. Today, the same country has grown to over one billion people. How many millions are there in one billion? *Show your work here and use digital tools to solve the problem.*

⬥ **TEKS 5.2** Represent, compare, and order positive rational numbers and understand relationships as related to place value.
Mathematical Process Standards 5.1A, 5.1B, 5.1C, 5.1D, 5.1E, 5.1F

You can **create** and use **representations**. How can you use what you know about ones, thousands, and millions to write numbers in the billions? *Show your work!*

Digital Resources at PearsonTexas.com

Solve   Learn   Glossary   Check   Tools   Games

Look Back!

Connect How are numbers in the billions similar to numbers in the millions, thousands, and ones?

A-Z

A

The place of a digit in a number tells you its value. A place-value chart is helpful in reading and writing a number such as 1,600,000,000.

What are the different ways to write this large number?

The digits 0, 1, 2, 3, 4, 5, 6, 7, 8, and 9 are used to represent numbers.

It would take about 1,600,000,000 quarters laid end-to-end to circle the world at the equator one time.

How can you write a number in a place-value chart?

B

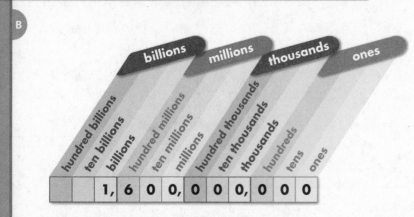

1 is in the billions place.
Its value is 1,000,000,000.

Standard form:
1,600,000,000

Expanded form:
1,000,000,000 + 600,000,000

Word form:
one billion, six hundred million

Do You Understand?

Convince Me! What pattern do you see in the names of the place values for each period (ones, thousands, millions, billions)?

Name _____

Another Look!
Place-Value Chart

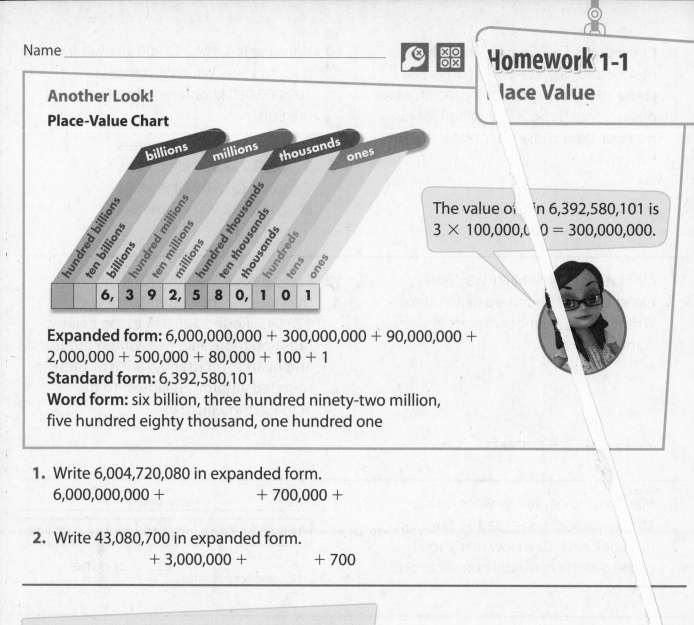

The value of 3 in 6,392,580,101 is
3 × 100,000,000 = 300,000,000.

Expanded form: 6,000,000,000 + 300,000,000 + 90,000,000 +
2,000,000 + 500,000 + 80,000 + 100 + 1
Standard form: 6,392,580,101
Word form: six billion, three hundred ninety-two million,
five hundred eighty thousand, one hundred one

1. Write 6,004,720,080 in expanded form.
   6,000,000,000 + _____ + 700,000 +

2. Write 43,080,700 in expanded form.
   _____ + 3,000,000 + _____ + 700

In **3** and **4**, write each number in standard form.

3. Four hundred two million
   seventy-three thousand
   one hundred eighty

4. Eight hundred forty-three billion,
   two hundred eight million,
   seven hundred thirty-two thousand,
   eight hundred thirty-three

5. Write 12,430,090 in expanded form.

6. What number is 10,000 less than 337,676?

7. What number is 1,000,000 greater than
   337,676?

8. Write the word form for 3,1_5_2,308,726.

   What is the value of the underlined digit?

9. Communicate Sue and Jonah chose numbers for a place-value game. Sue chose the number one hundred fifty-two million. Jonah chose five billion for his number. Who chose the greater number? Explain.

10. ⭐ Neptune is 4,498,252,900 kilometers from the Sun. Which distance is 200,000,000 kilometers closer to the Sun?

A 6,498,252,900 kilometers

B 4,698,252,900 kilometers

C 4,298,252,900 kilometers

D 2,498,252,900 kilometers

11. Mental Math The Milky Way Galaxy has at least two hundred billion stars. Write half this number of stars in standard form.

12. Extend Your Thinking One day, the state fair total attendance was 126,945. Round 126,945 to the nearest hundred thousand, nearest ten thousand, and nearest thousand. Which of these rounded amounts is closest to the actual attendance?

13. Maricko and her family went on a 10-day vacation. She read 12 pages in her book each day. How many total pages did she read while on vacation?

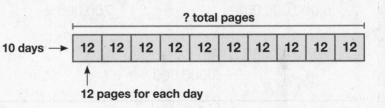

? total pages

10 days → | 12 | 12 | 12 | 12 | 12 | 12 | 12 | 12 | 12 | 12 |

12 pages for each day

14. Analyze Information Which state's population is greater than Florida's population but less than Texas's population? Explain how you found your answer.

2010 U.S. Populations

Top 5 States

DATA		
California	:	37,253,956
Florida	:	18,801,310
Illinois	:	12,830,632
New York	:	19,378,102
Texas	:	25,145,561

15. Number Sense Is the population of California greater than or less than twice the population of New York? Use number sense to explain how you know.

Name _____

Solve & Share

A runner won a 100-meter race with a time of 9.85 seconds. How can you use place value to explain this time? Draw a place-value chart to show the value of this time.

⭐ **TEKS 5.2A** Represent the value of the digit in decimals through the thousandths using expanded notation and numerals. Also, 5.2.
Mathematical Process Standards 5.1A, 5.1B, 5.1C, 5.1D, 5.1F, 5.1G

Digital Resources at PearsonTexas.com

Solve   Learn   Glossary   Check   Tools   Games

You can **connect ideas** and use what you know about whole-number place value to help you understand decimal place value.

Look Back!

Number Sense How can you write 9.85 in expanded form?

A

Jo picked a seed from her flower. The seed has a mass of 0.245 gram. What are some different ways you can represent 0.245?

Did you know that a single seed from an orchid such as this one can have a mass of 0.245 gram?

What are some ways decimals can be represented?

A place-value chart can help you write decimals in standard form, expanded form, expanded notation, and word form.

B

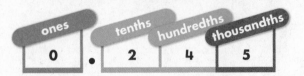

ones		tenths	hundredths	thousandths
0	.	2	4	5

Standard Form: 0.245 — The 5 is in the thousandths place. Its value is 0.005.

Expanded Form: 0.2 + 0.04 + 0.005

Expanded Notation: $\left(2 \times \frac{1}{10}\right) + \left(4 \times \frac{1}{100}\right) + \left(5 \times \frac{1}{1,000}\right)$

Word Form: two hundred forty-five thousandths

Do You Understand?

Convince Me! How many hundredths are in one tenth? How many thousandths are in one hundredth? Tell how you know.

Name _____

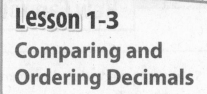
☆ ☆
Solve & Share
The lengths of three ants were measured in a laboratory. The lengths were 0.521 centimeter, 0.498 centimeter, and 0.550 centimeter. Which ant was the longest? Which ant was the shortest?

TEKS 5.2B Compare and order two decimals to thousandths and represent comparisons using the symbols >, <, or =. Also, 5.2.
Mathematical Process Standards 5.1A, 5.1C, 5.1D, 5.1E, 5.1G

How can **number sense** help you compare and order the decimals? *Tell how you decided.*

Digital Resources at PearsonTexas.com

Solve   Learn   Glossary   Check   Tools   Games

Look Back!

Connect What are the lengths of the ants in order from least to greatest?

How Can You Compare and Order Decimals?

Scientists collected and measured the lengths of different cockroach species. Which cockroach had the greater length, the American or the Oriental cockroach?

Comparing decimals is like comparing whole numbers!

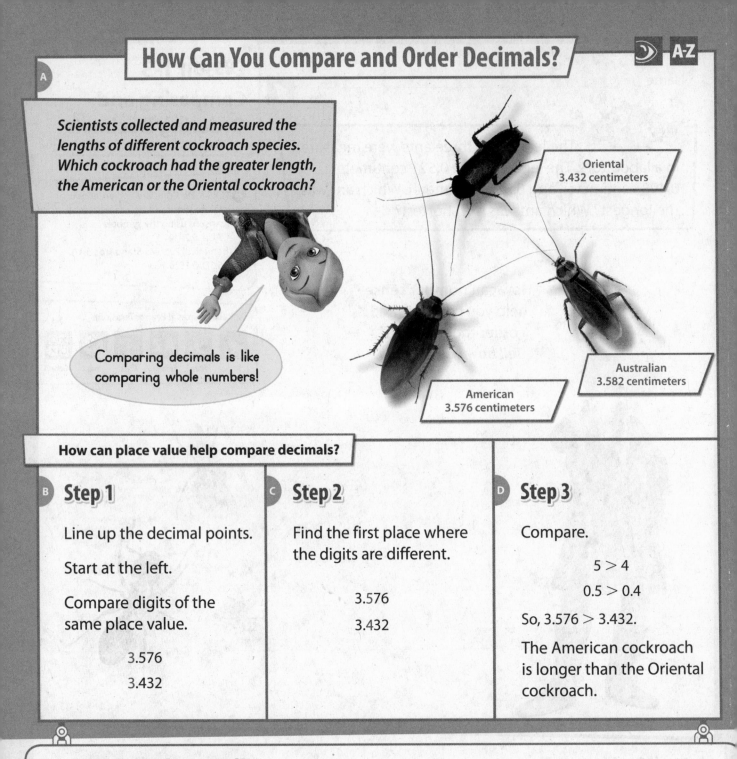

Oriental
3.432 centimeters

Australian
3.582 centimeters

American
3.576 centimeters

How can place value help compare decimals?

B **Step 1**

Line up the decimal points.

Start at the left.

Compare digits of the same place value.

3.576
3.432

C **Step 2**

Find the first place where the digits are different.

3.576
3.432

D **Step 3**

Compare.

$5 > 4$

$0.5 > 0.4$

So, $3.576 > 3.432$.

The American cockroach is longer than the Oriental cockroach.

Do You Understand?

Convince Me! Valerie said, "12.68 is greater than 12.8 because 68 is greater than 8." Is she correct? Explain.

Name _____

Solve & Share

In science class, Marci recorded numbers from an experiment as 12.87, 12.13, 12.5, and 12.08. Which numbers are closer to 12? Which are closer to 13? How can you tell?

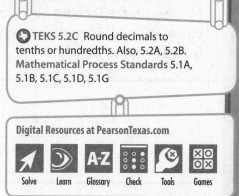

TEKS 5.2C Round decimals to tenths or hundredths. Also, 5.2A, 5.2B. Mathematical Process Standards 5.1A, 5.1B, 5.1C, 5.1D, 5.1G

Digital Resources at PearsonTexas.com

Solve   Learn   Glossary   Check   Tools   Games

You can **select and use tools**, such as a number line, to help determine what number is half way between two whole numbers. *Show your work!*

12 ————————————————————————— 13

Look Back!

Justify What is the halfway point between 12 and 13? Is that point closer to 12 or 13?

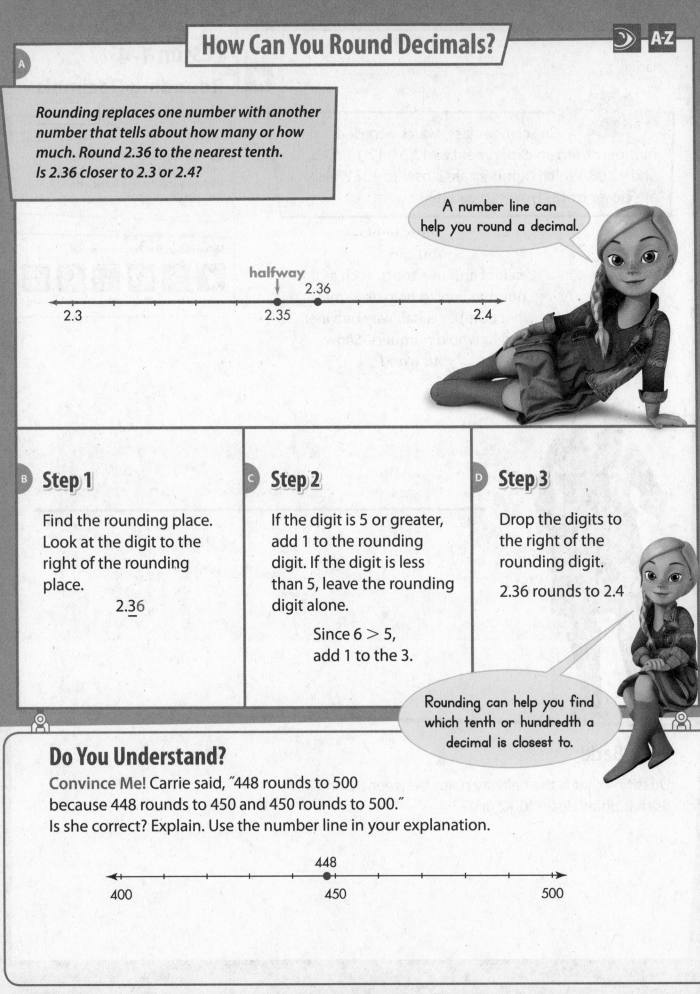

Rounding replaces one number with another number that tells about how many or how much. Round 2.36 to the nearest tenth. Is 2.36 closer to 2.3 or 2.4?

A number line can help you round a decimal.

halfway

2.36

2.3   2.35   2.4

B Step 1

Find the rounding place. Look at the digit to the right of the rounding place.

2.36

C Step 2

If the digit is 5 or greater, add 1 to the rounding digit. If the digit is less than 5, leave the rounding digit alone.

Since $6 > 5$, add 1 to the 3.

D Step 3

Drop the digits to the right of the rounding digit.

2.36 rounds to 2.4

Rounding can help you find which tenth or hundredth a decimal is closest to.

Do You Understand?

Convince Me! Carrie said, "448 rounds to 500 because 448 rounds to 450 and 450 rounds to 500." Is she correct? Explain. Use the number line in your explanation.

448

400   450   500

Another Example

Round 3.2 to the nearest whole number.

Is 3.2 closer to 3 or 4?

Step 1

Find the rounding place. Look at the digit to the right of the rounding place.

3.2

Step 2

If the digit is 5 or greater, add 1 to the rounding digit. If the digit is less than 5, leave the rounding digit alone. Since 2 < 5, leave 3 the same.

Step 3

Drop the digits to the right of the decimal point. Drop the decimal point.

3.2 rounds to 3

☆ Guided Practice ☆

In **1** through **8**, round each number to the place of the underlined digit.

1. 16.5

2. 56.1

3. 1.32

4. 42.78

5. 1.652

6. 582.04

7. 80,547.645

8. 135,701.949

9. To round 74.58 to the nearest tenth, which digit do you look at? What is 74.58 rounded to the nearest tenth?

10. Connect A car-rental service charges customers for the number of miles they travel, rounded to the nearest whole mile. George travels 40.8 miles. For how many miles will he be charged? Explain.

☆ Independent Practice ☆

In **11** through **14**, round each decimal to the nearest whole number.

11. 4.5

12. 57.3

13. 34.731

14. 215.39

In **15** through **18**, round each number to the place of the underlined digit.

15. 7.158

16. 0.758

17. 6.4382

18. 84.732

Problem Solving

19. The picture at the right shows the length of an average American alligator. What is the length of the alligator rounded to the nearest tenth?

A 4.0 meters
B 4.3 meters
C 3 meters
D 4.4 meters

4.39 meters

20. Reason Name two different numbers that round to 8.21 when rounded to the nearest hundredth.

21. Number Sense To the nearest hundred, what is the greatest whole number that rounds to 2,500? the least whole number?

22. Draw all of the lines of symmetry in the figure shown below.

23. Extend Your Thinking Emma needs 2 pounds of ground meat to make a meatloaf. She has one package with 2.36 pounds of ground meat and another package with 2.09 pounds of ground meat. She uses rounding and finds that both packages are close to 2 pounds. Explain how Emma can choose the package closer to 2 pounds.

24. Robert slices a large loaf of bread to make 12 sandwiches. He makes 3 turkey sandwiches and 5 veggie sandwiches. The rest are ham sandwiches. What fraction of the sandwiches Robert makes are ham? Write the fraction in simplest form.

25. Analyze Information After buying school supplies, Ruby had $32 left over. She spent $4 on notebooks, $18 on a backpack, and $30 on a new calculator. How much money did Ruby start with? Write an equation to show your work.

26. The Andersons took the family dog to the vet. The dog weighed 35.45 pounds. What is this decimal rounded to the nearest tenth? nearest whole number? nearest ten? Which of these rounded numbers is closest to the actual weight?

Remember, when rounding look at the digit to the right.

© Pearson Education, Inc. 5

Name _____

Another Look!

An African Watusi steer's horn measures 95.25 centimeters around. What is 95.25 rounded to the nearest tenth?

On a number line, 95.25 is halfway between 95.2 and 95.3.

halfway

95.2   95.25   95.3

Step 1

Find the rounding place. Look at the digit to the right of the rounding place.

95.2<u>5</u>

Step 2

If the digit is 5 or greater, increase the rounding digit by 1. If the digit is less than 5, the rounding digit stays the same.

The digit to the right is 5, so increase the 2 in the tenths place to 3.

Step 3

Drop the digits to the right of the rounding digit.

95.25 rounded to the nearest tenth is 95.3.

1. Ian mailed a package that weighed 5.63 pounds. What is his first step to find the weight of the package rounded to the nearest tenth of a pound? What is the next step? What is 5.63 rounded to the nearest tenth?

In **2** through **5**, round each decimal to the nearest whole number.

2. 6.7   3. 12.1   4. 30.92   5. 1.086

In **6** through **13**, round each number to the place of the underlined digit.

6. 32.6<u>5</u>   7. 3.2<u>4</u>6   8. 41.<u>0</u>73   9. 0.42<u>4</u>

10. 6.<u>0</u>99   11. 6.1<u>3</u>   12. 183.<u>9</u>2   13. 905.2<u>5</u>5

14. Does the blue line appear to be a line of symmetry? Explain.

15. ★ Sean lives about 15.5 miles from the airport. Which number rounds to 15.5 when rounded to the nearest tenth?

    A 15.0

    B 15.49

    C 15.04

    D 15.55

16. What is three and sixty-two thousandths rounded to the nearest hundredth? to the nearest tenth? to the nearest whole number?

17. **Number Sense** If the area of a park is exactly halfway between 2.4 and 2.5 acres, what is the area of the park?

18. **Connect** One year, the price of wheat was $8.87 per bushel. The next year, the price was $9.60. Round the price per bushel of wheat for each year to the nearest tenth of a dollar.

19. **Extend Your Thinking** Explain how you can round 25.691 to the greatest place.

20. **Number Sense** A professional baseball team won 84 games this season. The team won 14 more games than it lost. There were no ties. How many games did the team lose? How many did it play?

?	
84	?

21. **Explain** If rounded to the nearest dime, what is the greatest amount of money that rounds to $105.40? What is the least amount of money that rounds to $105.40? Explain your answers.

22. The students in Mr. Bhatia's class measure the length of four bees. The students round the lengths to the nearest tenth. Whose bee has a length that rounds to 0.5 inch? 0.8 inch?

DATA	Student	Bee Lengths
	Isabel	0.841 inch
	Pablo	0.45 inch
	Wendi	0.55 inch
	Brett	0.738 inch

Name _____

⭐ **Solve & Share**

Ann has two pieces of ribbon. One is 0.3 meter long and the other is 0.09 meter long. Which is longer? Write and explain to a classmate how you know which ribbon is longer.

TEKS 5.1G Display, explain, and justify mathematical ideas and arguments using precise mathematical language in written or oral communication. Also, 5.2B, 5.3B. Mathematical Process Standards 5.1A, 5.1B, 5.1C, 5.1D, 5.1E, 5.1G

Digital Resources at PearsonTexas.com

Solve Learn Glossary Check Tools Games

You can **communicate** math ideas using words, pictures, numbers, and symbols. *Show your work in the space below!*

Look Back!

Explain Is there any part of your explanation that might be difficult for a classmate to understand? Tell why.

How Can You Write a Good Math Explanation?

A Analyze

There are 24 teams in a basketball league. Each team has 13 players. How many players are on all of the teams?

Write to explain your answer.

A good math explanation should be:
- correct
- simple
- complete
- easy to understand

Math explanations can use words, pictures, numbers or symbols.

B Plan and Solve

I drew a picture with 13 rows. Each row has 2 tens and 4 ones.

13 × 2 tens = 26 tens, or 260 ones

13 × 4 = 52 ones

Then I added to find the total numbers of players.

260 + 52 = 312 Players

This is a good explanation! Way to go!

Do You Understand?

Convince Me! Do you think the explanation above could be better? Tell why.

☆ Guided Practice ☆

1. **Represent** Use expanded form to show the value of the digits in 2,467,809,300.

2. **Communicate** The numbers below follow a pattern. Write and explain the pattern and how to find the next number.

   700   70   7   0.7

3. Explain how to write the number that is one million more than 458,610,008.

4. **Justify** Jared said, "7.48 rounds to 7.5 and 7.5 rounds to 8. So, 7.48 rounds to 8." Write and explain if Jared's reasoning is correct.

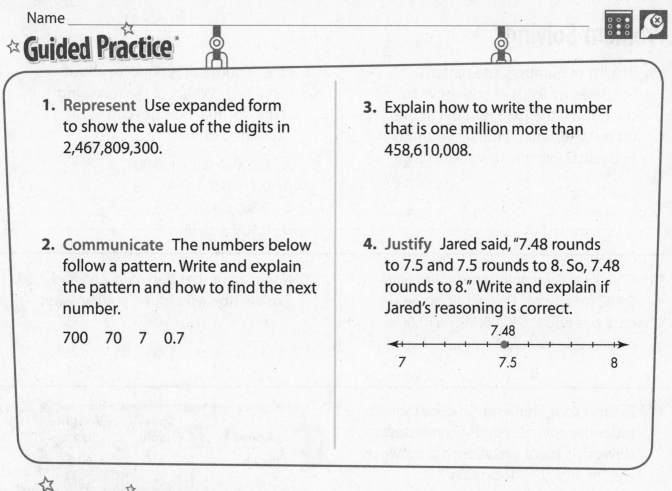

Independent Practice ☆

5. Explain how to write the number that is 0.02 less than 1.423.

6. Use expanded form to show the value of the digits in 1.059.

In **7** and **8**, use the data table.

7. Write and explain why it might be easier to place the numbers in Set A in order from least to greatest than it is for the numbers in Set B.

8. Order all six of the numbers in the data table from least to greatest.

DATA	Set A	Set B
	2.56	0.56
	4.76	0.09
	1.02	0.84

Problem Solving

9. In a list of numbers, the pattern increases by 0.001 as you move to the right. If the third number in the list is 0.046, what is the first number in the list? Explain how you know.

10. One centimeter is equal to about 0.394 inch. Which of the following is the decimal number written in expanded form?

   A $0.300 + 0.09 + 0.004$

   B $0.3 + 0.9 + 0.4$

   C $0.30 + 0.9 + 4$

   D $0.300 + 0.94$

11. Check for Reasonableness Jim paid $9.82 for a book. He told Nora the cost was about $10.00. Was $10.00 a reasonable rounded amount? Explain.

12. Name a number between 2.65 and 2.66. Explain how you found your answer.

13. Extend Your Thinking Use the table to order the animal speeds from fastest to slowest. Is there a relationship between weight and speed? Explain.

DATA	Animal	Speed (kph)	Weight (kg)
	Cheetah	110	60.5
	Giraffe	52.5	1,250
	Hippopotamus	28.9	3,900
	Zebra	55.5	415

14. Formulate a Plan Justin gets a sandwich and a bottle of juice for lunch. His sandwich options are tuna, veggie, or chicken. He can have either orange juice or apple juice. How many different possible lunches can Justin choose from? Make a list to help you solve this problem.

15. Maria and her family went to a movie. They bought 2 adult tickets for $8 each and 3 student tickets for $5 each. They paid with two $20 bills. How much change did they get back?

> Which part of the problem should you find first?

16. The greatest distance of Mercury from Earth is 138,000,000 miles. The greatest distance of Mars from Earth is 249,000,000 miles. Write these numbers in expanded form.

Homework 1-5
Writing to Explain

Another Look!

Tony bought three items for his new puppy from the Doggy Discount Store. Order the prices from least expensive to most expensive. Draw a chart to help.

Dollars	Dimes	Pennies
$2 .	0	9
$2 .	5	0
$2 .	5	7

$ 2.09

$ 2.57

$ 2.50

You can use place value to explain how to order numbers including amounts of money.

---

1. Ryan started the baseball season with new equipment. Order the prices from most expensive to least expensive. Explain how you solved the problem.

$11.09

$12.01

$11.99

2. If Ryan had bought a new baseball glove for $12.50, how would the order of the prices from most expensive to least expensive change?

---

3. Lee and Ernesto each have 1 ten dollar bill and some coins in their wallet. Ernesto has 5 quarters and 6 dimes. Lee has 4 quarters, 8 dimes, and 10 pennies. Who has more money? Explain.

4. What is the value of the blue digit in the number below? Describe two ways to find the value.

5,670,249,114

5. The picture at the right shows the length of a
⭐ car. What is the length of the car rounded to
   the nearest tenth of a meter?

   A 4 meters
   B 4.1 meters
   C 4.2 meters
   D 5 meters

4.12 meters

6. **Explain** Liam arranges his coins in the
   following pattern: $0.37, $0.39, $0.41,
   $0.43. Explain his pattern, and then tell
   what the next amount of coins would be.

7. Marta wrote six and eighty hundredths.
   Nicky wrote six and eight tenths. Who
   wrote the greater number? Explain.

8. **Personal Financial Literacy** Hal gets $20
   🐷 a week allowance. He spends $15, shares
   $2, and saves the rest. How much does
   he save in 4 weeks? Tell how you found
   the answer.

9. **Extend Your Thinking** Rick wants
   to compare 87.421 and 91.396.
   What might happen if he compares
   the 421 thousandths and the
   396 thousandths first?

10. **Number Sense** On a backpacking trip,
    Darcy took 43 photographs. Eva also took
    some photographs. Together they took
    116 photographs. How many photos
    did Eva take? Write an equation using a
    variable to show your work.

11. **Estimation** Pierre owns a bike shop. He
    needs to order 12 replacement parts that
    each cost $9.75. The factory offers free
    shipping for orders greater than $100.
    Will Pierre need to pay a shipping cost?
    Use estimation to explain your answer.

12. Susan is starting a change jar. She puts
    in $0.25 each week. The table shows
    how much money is in her jar at the
    end of each week. Complete the table
    to find out how much she will have
    after 10 weeks. What patterns do you
    notice in the table?

Week:	1	2	3	4	5	10
Amount saved ($)	0.25					

Add $\frac{3}{6} + \frac{2}{6}$

You can **select tools** like real objects, manipulatives, technology, and paper and pencil to solve problems.

I chose fraction strips to show how to add $\frac{3}{6}$ and $\frac{2}{6}$. Manipulatives such as fraction strips make it easy to see that the sum of $\frac{3}{6} + \frac{2}{6}$ is $\frac{5}{6}$.

You could select digital tools to solve this problem too.

1
$\frac{1}{6}$ $\frac{1}{6}$ $\frac{1}{6}$

$\frac{1}{6}$ $\frac{1}{6}$

Tell whether you would select real objects, manipulatives, technology, or paper and pencil to solve each problem.

1. The perimeter of a rectangular patio is 36 feet. The length is 10 feet. What is the width of the patio?

2. A wall was divided into 8 equal parts. Pete and Jon each painted $\frac{1}{4}$ of the wall. What fraction of the wall did they paint? How many parts is this?

3. Samantha rides her bike 26 kilometers each week. How many kilometers did Samantha ride last year if she did not ride for 4 weeks during bad weather?

4. How is 54×16 like 16×54?

Error Search

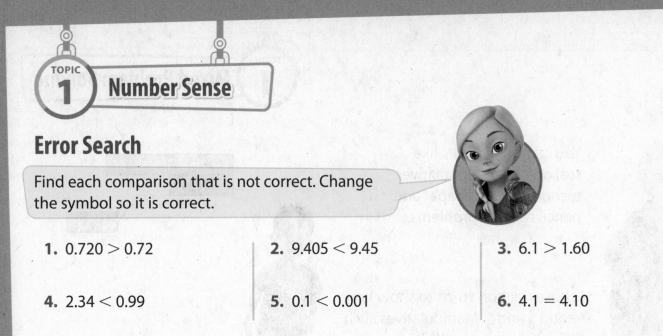

Find each comparison that is not correct. Change the symbol so it is correct.

1. 0.720 > 0.72

2. 9.405 < 9.45

3. 6.1 > 1.60

4. 2.34 < 0.99

5. 0.1 < 0.001

6. 4.1 = 4.10

Reasoning

Write whether each statement is true or false. If you write false, change the numbers or words so that the statement is true.

7. The number 456,721,000 is one million more than 455,721,000.

8. The number 7,423,091,144 is two billion less than 5,423,091,144.

9. The hundred thousands digit in 123,021,455 is changed to form 223,021,455.

10. The number 0.907 in expanded form is 0.9 + 0.007.

11. The number 1.825 is four thousandths less than 1.865.

12. There are 80 hundredths in 8 tenths.

13. Ten 10s equal one thousand.

Name _____

Set A pages 7–12

Write the word form and tell the value of the underlined digit for 930,365.

Nine hundred thirty thousand, three hundred sixty-five.

Since the 0 is in the thousands place, its value is 0 thousands or 0.

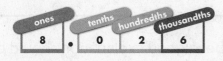
Use digital tools to solve these and other Reteaching problems.

Remember you can find the value of a digit by its place in a number.

Reteaching

Write the word form and tell the value of the underlined digit.

1. 9,000,009

2. 3,485,002,000

3. 25,678

4. 17,874,000,000

Set B pages 13–18

A place-value chart can help you write decimals in standard form, expanded form, and word form.

ones	.	tenths	hundredths	thousandths
8	.	0	2	6

Standard form: 8.026
Word form: Eight and twenty-six thousandths
Expanded form: 8 + 0.02 + 0.006

Remember the word *and* is written for the decimal point.

Write each number in standard form.

1. eight and fifty-nine hundredths
2. seven and three thousandths
3. six and eight hundred thirty-seven thousandths
4. 2 + 0.2 + 0.05 + 0.001
5. 3 + 0.2 + 0.004
6. 0.6 + 0.03 + 0.006

Set C pages 19–24

Compare. Write >, <, or =.

8.45 ◯ 8.47

Line up the decimal points. Start at the left to compare. Find the first place where the digits are different.

8.4**5**
8.4**7**

0.05 < 0.07 So, 8.45 < 8.47.

Remember that equivalent decimals, such as 0.45 and 0.450, can help you compare numbers.

Compare. Write >, <, or =.

1. 0.584 ◯ 0.58
2. 9.327 ◯ 9.236
3. 5.2 ◯ 5.20
4. 5.643 ◯ 5.675
5. 0.07 ◯ 0.08

Round 12.087 to the place of the underlined digit.

12.0<u>8</u>7   Look at the digit following the underlined digit. Look at 7.

Round to the next greater number of hundredths because 7 > 5.

12.087 is about 12.09.

Round 9.073 to the place of the underlined digit.

<u>9</u>.073   Look at the digit following the underlined digit. Look at 0.

Since 0 < 5 the digit in the ones place remains the same.

9.073 is about 9.

Remember that rounding a number means replacing it with a number that tells about how many or how much.

Round each number to the place of the underlined digit.

1. 10.2<u>4</u>5   **2.** <u>7</u>3.4

3. 9.1<u>4</u>5   **4.** 3.9<u>9</u>9

5. 13.0<u>2</u>3   **6.** 45.3<u>9</u>8

7. 0.1<u>5</u>3   **8.** 0.6<u>2</u>5

9. <u>8</u>.978   **10.** 5.7<u>3</u>9

11. Raul mails three packages. The packages weigh 13.09 ounces, 13.16 ounces, and 13.8 ounces. Which package's weight is closest to 13 ounces?

When you solve problems, you write to explain your answers. You can use words, pictures, or numbers to communicate your reasoning to others.

Megan practiced the long jump for the field day competition. First, she jumped 3.20 meters. Then she jumped 3.09 meters. Which jump was her better jump? Explain.

A number line shows 3.20 to the right of 3.09. Since 3.20 is greater than 3.09, her better jump is 3.20 meters.

Remember a good explanation should be correct, simple, and easy to understand.

1. Mr. Wilson's odometer shows that he has driven 216,784 miles. Explain how to write the number for the odometer reading after he drives 10,000 more miles.

2. The heights of Sara's tomato plants are 1.15 meters, 1.05 meters, and 1.1 meters. Explain how to order the heights from tallest to shortest.

3. Jake's height is 4.5 feet. Explain how to round Jake's height to the nearest foot.

Name _____

1. About 885,000,000 people speak Mandarin Chinese. How is 885,000,000 written in words?

  A eight hundred million, eighty-five thousand

  B eight hundred eighty-five million

  C eight billion, eighty-five million

  D eight hundred eighty-five billion

4. In the year 2010, the population of New York was about 19,300,000. Which of the following is **NOT** another way to write this number?

  A 10,000,000 + 9,000,000 + 300,000

  B 19 million, 3 hundred thousand

  C 19,000,000 + 300,000

  D 10,000,000 + 9,000,000 + 30,000

2. A national park has eighty thousand, nine-hundred twenty-three and eighty-six hundredths acres of non-federal land. Which shows this number in standard form?

  A 80,923.68

  B 80,923.86

  C 80,923.086

  D Not here

5. A certain machine part must be between 2.73 and 3.55 inches. Which number is greater than 2.73 and less than 3.55?

  A 3.73

  B 3.6

  C 2.55

  D 2.75

3. The circumference of a bowling ball is less than 27.002 inches. Which of the following numbers is less than 27.002?

  A 27.02

  B 27.2

  C 27.004

  D 27.001

6. Luke shaded 20 squares on his hundredths decimal model. Tim shaded an equivalent amount on his tenths decimal model. Which decimal represents the amount Tim shaded?

  A 20.0

  B 2.0

  C 0.2

  D 0.02

7. The weight of Darrin's phone is 3.475 ounces. What is 3.475 written in expanded form?

A $3 + 0.4 + 0.07 + 0.005$

B $3 + 0.47 + 0.05$

C $3 + 0.4 + 0.7 + 0.005$

D $3 + 0.4 + 0.7 + 0.5$

8. Mrs. Martin has $7,000 in her savings account. Alonzo has $\frac{1}{10}$ as much money in his account as Mrs. Martin. How much money does Alonzo have in his account?

9. Pablo has a piece of wire that is 2.15 meters long. If Pablo rounds this length to the nearest tenth of a meter, what number will be in the tenths place?

10. In basketball, Dimitri is averaging 12.375 rebounds per game. If Dimitri improves his average by 1 rebound per game, what is his improved average in word form?

11. The numbers below follow a pattern. Which statement can explain the pattern?

0.006   0.06   0.6   6   _____

A Add 6 to find the next number.

B Subtract zero to find the next number.

C Move the 6 one place to the right to find the next number.

D Move the 6 one place to the left to find the next number.

12. Kendra and her horse completed the barrel racing course in 15.839 seconds. If she rounds her score to the nearest hundredth of a second, what number will she write in the hundredths place?

Adding and Subtracting Whole Numbers and Decimals

Essential Questions: How can sums and differences of decimals be estimated? What are standard procedures for adding and subtracting whole numbers and decimals? How can sums and differences be found mentally?

All creatures in the animal kingdom have special structures that help them survive.

Did you know that lobsters, butterflies, horses, mice, ants and manatees all have 'feelers' in common?

I hope we're on the same wavelength! Here's a project on whiskers and antennae. Maybe that will give us a feel for adding and subtracting whole numbers and decimals.

Math and Science Project: Whiskers and Antennae

Do Research Use the Internet or other sources to find out more about whiskers and antennae. Which species have them? What is their function? How are whiskers and antennae alike? How are they different?

Journal: Write a Report Include what you found. Also in your report:

- Find out how many types of animals have feelers and how they use them.

- Compare two animals to find the length, number, and function of their whiskers or antennae.

- Make up and solve addition and subtraction problems based on your findings.

Name _____

Review What You Know

Vocabulary

Choose the best term from the box. Write it on the blank.

> - the Associative Property of Addition
> - the Commutative Property of Addition
> - compensation
> - compatible numbers

1. Using _____ you can add two numbers in any order.

2. When you adjust one number to make subtraction easier and change the other number, you use _____.

3. When you can change the grouping of numbers when adding you are using _____.

Rounding

Round each number to the nearest hundred.

4. 748   **5.** 293   **6.** 139

Round each number to the nearest thousand.

7. 3,857   **8.** 2,587   **9.** 2,345

Round each number to the underlined digit.

10. 84.59   **11.** 2.948   **12.** 3.812

Adding and Subtracting with Regrouping

Find each sum or difference.

13. 829 + 276   **14.** 9,536 + 495

15. 612 − 357   **16.** 5,052 − 761

17. Vivica sees that a printer costs $679 and a computer costs $1,358. What is the total cost of the printer and the computer?

18. The Pecos River is 926 miles long, and the Brazos River is 1,280 miles long. How many miles longer is the Brazos River than the Pecos River?

A 2,206 miles   **C** 364 miles
B 1,206 miles   **D** 354 miles

Estimating

19. Select the appropriate tool - objects or paper and pencil - to solve this problem. Show your work.
Explain How do you use rounding when estimating a sum?

My Word Cards

Use the examples for each word on the front of the card to help complete the definitions on the back.

A-Z

compatible numbers

547 is close to 550.

294 is close to 300.

compensation

Find $648 + 325$.

↓ Add 2

$650 + 325 = 975$

↓ Subtract 2

So, $648 + 325 = 973$.

My Word Cards

Complete the definition. Extend learning by writing your own definitions.

_____ is adjusting one number to make a computation easier and balancing the adjustment by changing another number.

_____ are numbers that are easy to compute with mentally.

Name _____

Solve & Share

Three pieces of software for sale cost $20.75, $10.59, and $18.25. What is the total cost of the software? *Use mental math to solve.*

TEKS 5.3K Add and subtract positive rational numbers fluently. Also, 5.3. Mathematical Process Standards 5.1A, 5.1B, 5.1C, 5.1D, 5.1G

Digital Resources at PearsonTexas.com

Solve | Learn | Glossary | Check | Tools | Games

You can use **number sense** to help you. What do you know about adding three numbers that will make it easier to solve this problem?

Look Back!

Number Sense Which two numbers above were easy to add in your head? Why?

A

Properties of addition can help you find the total cost of these three items.

The Commutative Property and Associate Property make it easy to add $11.45 + $3.39 + $9.55.

Associative Property lets you change the grouping of addends.
($11.45 + $3.39) + $9.55 = $11.45 + ($3.39 + $9.55)

Commutative Property lets you add two decimals in any order.
$11.45 + $3.39 = $3.39 + $11.45

$11.45

$3.39

$9.55

B Use the Commutative Property to change the order.

$11.45 + ($3.39 + $9.55) = $11.45 + ($9.55 + $3.39)

Use the Associative Property to change the grouping.

$11.45 + ($9.55 + $3.39) = ($11.45 + $9.55) + $3.39

C Add $11.45 and $9.55 first because they are easy to compute mentally.

$11.45 + $9.55 = $21

$21 + $3.39 = $24.39

The three items cost a total of $24.39.

Compatible numbers are numbers that are easy to compute mentally.

Do You Understand?

Convince Me! Use mental math to find the sum. Explain your thinking.

Jim earns $22.50, $14.75, and $8.50 on three different days. How much did he earn in all?

Another Example

With compensation, adjust one or both numbers to make the calculation easier. Then adjust the difference or sum to get the final answer.

Use compensation to subtract.

Find 4.25 − 3.08 mentally.

4.25 − 3.10 = 1.15

0.02 too much was subtracted → Compensate, add back 0.02

4.25 − 3.08 = 1.17

Use compensation to add.

Find $3.47 + $4.35 mentally.

$3.50 + $4.35 = $7.85

Add 0.03 → Compensate, take away 0.03

$3.47 + $4.35 = $7.82

☆ Guided Practice *

In **1** through **4**, use mental math to add or subtract.

1. 12.72 + 3.04 + 8.28

2. 6.97 + 4.15

3. 9.04 − 6.98

4. 4.02 + 3.19 + 16.48

5. **Communicate** In the addition example above, why is the answer $0.03 less than $7.85?

6. Which numbers are easier to subtract, 15.50 − 8.75 or 15.75 − 9? Explain.

Independent Practice ☆

Leveled Practice In **7** through **12**, use mental math to add or subtract.

7. 7.1 + 5.4 + 2.9 =
   _____ + 5.4 =
   _____

8. 373.4 − 152.9 =
   373.4 − _____ = 220.4
   _____ + 0.1 = _____

9. $18.25 + $7.99 + $4.75

10. 1.05 + 3.72 + 4.28 + 2.95

11. 2,504 + 140 + 160

12. 35.7 − 14.8

Problem Solving

13. Connect Joanne bought three books that cost $3.95, $4.99, and $6.05. How much did she spend in all? Use mental math to find the sum.

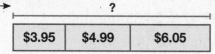

? spent →

	?	
$3.95	$4.99	$6.05

14. Explain Use compensation to find each difference mentally. Explain how you found each difference.

A 67 − 29

B 456 − 198

15. Mental Math The table shows how many points a team scored during a football game. Use mental math to find how many points the team had scored after the first three quarters.

Quarter	Points
1	14
2	9
3	6
4	10

DATA

16. On three different days at her job, Sue earned $27, $33, and $49. She needs to earn $100 to buy a desk for her computer. If she buys the desk, how much money will she have left over?

17. Analyze Information A shelf can hold 50 DVDs. Jill has 27 DVDs. She plans to buy 5 new ones. Each DVD costs $9. After she buys the new ones, how many more DVDs will the shelf hold?

18. Three different gymnasts had scores of 8.903, 8.827, and 8.844. Order the scores from greatest to least.

A 8.827, 8.844, 8.903

B 8.844, 8.903, 8.827

C 8.903, 8.844, 8.827

D 8.827, 8.903, 8.844

19. Which of the following is true?

A 3.4 + 7.6 = 7.6 + 4.3

B 3.14 + 0 = 0

C (4.5 + 9.7) + 6.5 = 4.5 + (9.7 + 6.5)

D (1.1 + 10.9) − 7.5 = (10.9 − 1.1) + 7.5

20. Explain When finding the difference of two numbers mentally, can you use the Commutative Property? Explain.

21. Extend Your Thinking Daria bought a skein of alpaca yarn for $47.50, a skein of angora yarn for $32.14, a skein of wool yarn for $16.50, and a pair of knitting needles for $3.86. How much did she spend in all? Describe how you calculated your answer.

Another Look!

You can use properties of addition, compatible numbers, or compensation to help you find the answers.

Use properties of addition to find $5.7 + 6.1 + 4.3$.	Use compensation to find $12.7 + 3.9$.	Use compensation to find $18.3 - 6.9$.
$5.7 + 6.1 + 4.3$ ↓ Use the Commutative Property. $5.7 + 4.3 + 6.1$ ↓ Add. $10 + 6.1 = 16.1$	$12.7 + 3.9$ ↓ Add 0.1 to 3.9. $12.7 + 4 = 16.7$ ↓ Subtract 0.1. $12.7 + 3.9 = 16.6$	$18.3 - 6.9$ ↓ Add 0.1 to 6.9. $18.3 - 7 = 11.3$ ↓ 0.01 too much was subtracted. Add 0.1. $18.3 - 6.9 = 11.4$

1. $275 + 180 + 120 =$

$275 +$ _____ $=$

_____

2. $19.5 + 24.7 + 7.5 =$

$19.5 +$ _____ $+ 24.7 =$

_____ $+ 24.7 =$ _____

3. $87.2 - 25.9 =$

$87.2 -$ _____ $= 61.2$

_____ $+ 0.1 =$ _____

For **4** through **15**, use mental math to solve.

4. $8.4 + 6.21 + 2.6$

5. $7.35 + 1.47 + 9.65$

6. $12.32 - 8.79$

7. $75.25 - 11.92$

8. $34.76 + 170.1 + 16.24$

9. $54.3 - 19.74$

10. $192.63 - 7.95$

11. $201.96 + 38.7 + 3.84$

12. $100.6 + 296.5$

13. $421.2 - 305.8$

14. $1,050 + 815 + 250$

15. $\$5.40 + \$8.70 + \$6.30$

16. Connect James is buying school supplies. He buys a notebook for $2.45, a package of mechanical pencils for $3.79, and an eraser for $1.55. Use mental math to find how much he spent in all.

? spent ⟶

?		
$2.45	$3.79	$1.55

17. Explain How is using mental math to add with decimals like using mental math to add whole numbers? How is it different?

18. Analyze Information Isabel made the following graph to show the daily share price for Company XYZ. What was the change in the price from Monday to Friday?

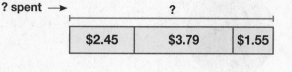

What is the scale on the graph?

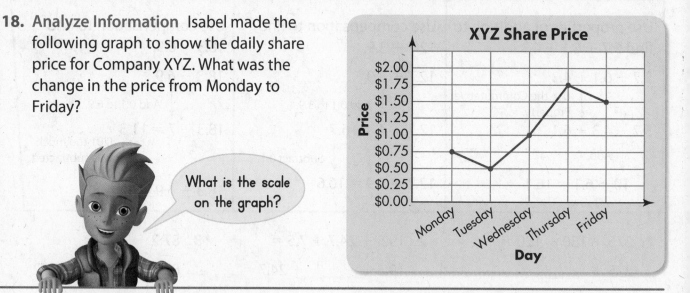

19. A restaurant bought 48.5 pounds of apples from a local orchard. The next month, the restaurant bought another 65.3 pounds of apples and 24.5 pounds of pears. How many pounds of fruit did the restaurant buy?

A 73 pounds
B 113.8 pounds
C 138.3 pounds
D 143.8 pounds

20. Explain As part of his workout, Jamal does 2 sets of 25 push-ups. If he does this 10 times each month, how many push-ups does he do each month? Write an equation to show your work.

21. Extend Your Thinking Julia went to the supermarket and bought a dozen eggs, two pounds of bananas, and a jar of tomato sauce. A store coupon for $0.70 off any purchase does not appear on the receipt. If Julia used the coupon, how much did she spend in all?

eggs 1 dozen $2.51

bananas 2 lb @
$0.99/lb $1.98

tomato sauce $1.49

Name _____

☆ **Solve & Share** ☆

An amusement park has two roller coasters. One is 628 feet long, and the other is 485 feet long. If you ride both roller coasters, about how many feet will you travel in all? *Use estimation to solve.*

⬧ **TEKS 5.3A** Estimate to determine solutions to mathematical and real-world problems involving addition, subtraction, multiplication, or division. **Mathematical Process Standards 5.1A, 5.1C, 5.1D, 5.1G**

You can use **reason** to decide what you are asked to find. Is the problem looking for an exact answer? How can you tell?

Digital Resources at PearsonTexas.com

Solve   Learn   Glossary   Check   Tools   Games

Look Back!

Number Sense About how much longer is the one coaster than the other? Show your work.

A

Students are collecting cans of dog food to give to an animal shelter. Estimate the sum of the cans collected in Weeks 3 and 4.

There is more than one way to find an estimate.

Week	Cans of dog food
1	172
2	298
3	237
4	345
5	338

DATA

B ## One Way

Round each addend to the nearest hundred.

$$237 \longrightarrow 200$$
$$+\ 345 \longrightarrow +\ 300$$
$$\overline{\ 500}$$

$237 + 345$ is about 500.

The students collected about 500 cans of dog food in Weeks 3 and 4.

C ## Another Way

Substitute compatible numbers.

$$237 \longrightarrow 250$$
$$+\ 345 \longrightarrow +\ 350$$
$$\overline{\ 600}$$

$237 + 345$ is about 600.

The students collected about 600 cans of dog food in Weeks 3 and 4.

Compatible numbers are easy to add!

Do You Understand?

Convince Me! Tomás said, "We did great in Week 4! We collected just about twice as many cans as in Week 1!"

Use estimation to decide if he is right. Explain your thinking.

Another Example

You can estimate differences.

Estimate $22.8 - 13.9$.

One Way

Round each number to the nearest whole number.

$$
\begin{array}{rcr}
22.8 & \longrightarrow & 23 \\
-\ 13.9 & \longrightarrow & -\ 14 \\
\hline
& & 9
\end{array}
$$

$22.8 - 13.9$ is about 9.

Another Way

Substitute compatible numbers.

$$
\begin{array}{rcr}
22.8 & \longrightarrow & 25 \\
-\ 13.9 & \longrightarrow & -\ 15 \\
\hline
& & 10
\end{array}
$$

$22.8 - 13.9$ is about 10.

☆ Guided Practice*

In **1** through **8**, estimate the sums and differences.

1. $49 + 22$
2. $86 - 18$

3. $179 + 277$
4. $232 - 97$

5. $23.8 - 4.7$
6. $87.2 + 3.9$

7. $389 - 214$
8. $576 + 94$

9. **Explain** In the example above, which estimate is closer to the actual difference? How can you tell without subtracting?

10. In the example on the previous page, the students collected more cans of dog food in Week 4 than in Week 3. Estimate about how many more.

Independent Practice ☆

In **11** through **18**, estimate each sum or difference.

11.
$$
\begin{array}{r}
79 \\
+\ 32 \\
\hline
\end{array}
$$

12.
$$
\begin{array}{r}
788 \\
-\ 572 \\
\hline
\end{array}
$$

13.
$$
\begin{array}{r}
837 \\
+\ 488 \\
\hline
\end{array}
$$

14.
$$
\begin{array}{r}
385,600 \\
-\ 235,700 \\
\hline
\end{array}
$$

15.
$$
\begin{array}{r}
2.9 \\
+\ 3.9 \\
\hline
\end{array}
$$

16.
$$
\begin{array}{r}
\$12.99 \\
-\ \$\ 3.95 \\
\hline
\end{array}
$$

17.
$$
\begin{array}{r}
8.1 \\
3.7 \\
+\ 7.9 \\
\hline
\end{array}
$$

18.
$$
\begin{array}{r}
3.8 \\
4.1 \\
+\ 3.3 \\
\hline
\end{array}
$$

Problem Solving

19. Reason The cost of one DVD is $16.98, and the cost of another DVD is $9.29. Ed estimated the cost of the two DVDs to be about $27. Is his estimate higher or lower than the actual cost? Explain.

20. Three rock samples have masses of 74.05 g, 9.72 g, and 45.49 g. A scientist estimates the total mass of the samples by rounding each mass to the nearest whole number. What numbers will he add?

    A 75, 10, and 46   **C** 74, 10, and 45

    B 74.1, 9.7, and 45.5   **D** 75, 10, and 50

21. Use a Strip Diagram Amy has a large farm with a stable of horses. Her horses eat 30 bales of hay each week. How many weeks will it take her horses to eat 360 bales of hay?

```
|<----------------- 360 ----------------->|
                      ?
| 30 | - - - - - - - - - - - - - - - - - ->
```

22. Javier bought two books that cost a total of $18.60. He paid for them with a $20 bill. The cashier gave him 2 $1 bills and 4 dimes as change. Was this the correct amount? Explain your reasoning.

23. The size and shape of Golden Gate Park is often compared to the size and shape of Central Park. About how many more acres does Golden Gate Park cover than Central Park?

Do you need an exact answer or an estimate?

Central Park in New York City has an area of 843 acres.

Golden Gate Park in San Francisco, California, has an area of 1,017 acres.

24. Extend Your Thinking A teacher is organizing a field trip. Each bus can seat up to 46 people. Is it better to estimate higher or lower than the actual number of people going on the field trip? Why?

25. Connect Umberto buys a game for $7.89 and some batteries for $5.49. He pays with a $20 bill. Estimate how much change he should get, to the nearest dime.

Another Look!

During one week, Mr. Graham drove a truck to four different towns to make deliveries. Estimate how far he drove in all. About how much farther did he drive on Wednesday than on Monday?

Mr. Graham's Mileage Log

Day	Cities	Mileage
Monday	Mansley to Mt. Hazel	243
Tuesday	Mt. Hazel to Perkins	303
Wednesday	Perkins to Alberton	279
Thursday	Alberton to Fort Maynard	277

DATA

Round each number to the nearest hundred.

$$243 \longrightarrow 200$$
$$303 \longrightarrow 300$$
$$279 \longrightarrow 300$$
$$+\,277 \longrightarrow +\,300$$
$$1{,}100$$

Mr. Graham drove about 1,100 miles.

Estimate the difference to the nearest ten.

$$279 \longrightarrow 280$$
$$-\,243 \longrightarrow -\,240$$
$$40$$

Mr. Graham drove about 40 more miles on Wednesday than on Monday.

---

1. Marisol rode her bicycle each day for five days. Estimate how far she biked in all. Round each number to the nearest whole number.

   $12 + $ ____ $ + 18 + $ ____ $ + $ ____ $ = $ ____

   She biked about ____ miles.

2. About how much farther did she bike on Wednesday than on Thursday?

   $18 - $ ____ $ = $ ____

   She biked about ____ more miles on Wednesday.

Marisol's Bike Rides

Day	Mileage
Monday	12.3
Tuesday	14.1
Wednesday	17.7
Thursday	11.8
Friday	15.2

DATA

Estimate each sum or difference.

3. $19.7 - 6.9$ **4.** $59 + 43 + 95$ **5.** $582 + 169 + 23$ **6.** $87.99 - 52.46$

7. About how many more inches of rain did Asheville get than Wichita? About how many more days did it rain in Asheville than Wichita?

DATA

Average Yearly Precipitation of U.S. Cities		
City	Inches	Days
Asheville, North Carolina	47.71	124
Wichita, Kansas	28.61	85

8. Analyze Information ★ Four friends made a bar graph to show how many baseball cards they collected over the summer.

About how many cards did they collect in all?

A 160
B 140
C 120
D 40

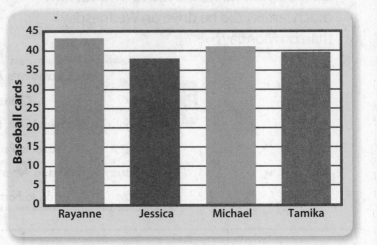

9. Explain Estimate the total weight of two boxes that weigh 9.4 pounds and 62.6 pounds using rounding and compatible numbers. Which estimate is closer to the actual total weight? Why?

10. Extend Your Thinking A gardener is estimating the amount of mulch needed for two garden beds. There is no room to store extra mulch. Is it better to overestimate or underestimate how much mulch he needs? Why?

11. Cory is building a rectangular sandbox with a length of 8.75 feet and a width of 4.2 feet. How can you estimate the perimeter of the sandbox?

12. A book club is reading three books. The first has 260 pages, the second 175 pages, and the third 120 pages. Rachel reads the first book and Kerry reads the other two. Use compatible numbers to estimate how many more pages Kerry read than Rachel. Show your work.

Name _____

☆ ⚡ ☆
Solve & Share

In June, 26,945 people hiked a trail. In July, 13,628 people hiked the same trail. How many people in all hiked the trail in these two months? *Solve anyway you choose.*

⭐ TEKS 5.3K Add and subtract positive rational numbers fluently. Also, 5.3. Mathematical Process Standards 5.1C, 5.1D, 5.1G

You can **select and use tools** to help you. What tool can you use to help you add large numbers?

Digital Resources at PearsonTexas.com

Solve Learn Glossary Check Tools Games

Look Back!

Check for Reasonableness How can you check that your answer to the problem above is reasonable?

How Can You Add and Subtract Whole Numbers?

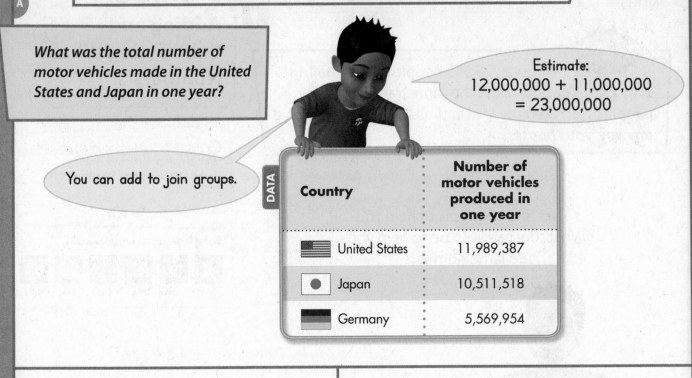

What was the total number of motor vehicles made in the United States and Japan in one year?

Estimate:
12,000,000 + 11,000,000
= 23,000,000

You can add to join groups.

DATA

Country	Number of motor vehicles produced in one year
United States	11,989,387
Japan	10,511,518
Germany	5,569,954

B ## Step 1

Line up numbers by place value. Add the ones, tens, and hundreds.

$$
\begin{array}{r}
\overset{1\,1}{11{,}989{,}387} \\
+\ 10{,}511{,}518 \\
\hline
905
\end{array}
$$

C ## Step 2

Continue adding. Regroup if needed. Insert commas in the sum to separate periods.

$$
\begin{array}{r}
\overset{1\,11\ \ 11}{11{,}989{,}387} \\
+\ 10{,}511{,}518 \\
\hline
22{,}500{,}905
\end{array}
$$

In one year, a total of 22,500,905 vehicles were made.

The sum is reasonable since the estimate was 23,000,000.

Do You Understand?

Convince Me! For the example above, Sandra said, "The United States made over 1,000,000 more cars than Japan."

How do you think she estimated this number? Use subtraction to find the exact answer.

Another Example

A factory made 5,002 bicycles this year.
Last year, they made only 2,684 bicycles.
How many more bicycles did they make this year than last year?

Subtract the ones. Think of 5,000 as
500 tens. Regroup.

$$
\begin{array}{r}
\overset{4\ \ 9\ \ 9\ \ 12}{5{,}0\,0\,2} \\
-\ 2{,}6\,8\,4 \\
\hline
8
\end{array}
$$

Subtract the tens, hundreds, and
thousands.

$$
\begin{array}{r}
\overset{4\ \ 9\ \ 9\ \ 12}{5{,}0\,0\,2} \\
-\ 2{,}6\,8\,4 \\
\hline
2{,}3\,1\,8
\end{array}
$$

So, 2,318 more bicycles were made this year.

☆ Guided Practice *

For **1** through **4**, add or subtract.

1.
$$
\begin{array}{r}
5{,}741 \\
+\ 31{,}018 \\
\hline
\end{array}
$$

2.
$$
\begin{array}{r}
7{,}110 \\
+\ 499 \\
\hline
\end{array}
$$

3.
$$
\begin{array}{r}
9{,}234 \\
-\ 2{,}387 \\
\hline
\end{array}
$$

4.
$$
\begin{array}{r}
110{,}652 \\
-\ 8{,}600 \\
\hline
\end{array}
$$

5. Explain In Step 1 of the example on page 60, explain how you regrouped the tens place.

6. In the example on the previous page, how many cars did the United States and Germany make in all?

☆ Independent Practice ☆

In **7** through **18**, add or subtract. Check the answer to subtraction exercises by adding.

7. 7,469 + 8,374

8. 19,335 + 24,281

9. 40,742 + 22,597

10. 102,369 + 60,320

11. 18,269 + 109,347

12. 75,977 + 24,683

13. 4,002 − 3,765

14. 58,005 − 1,098

15. 113,300 − 1,774

16. 454,900 − 33,870

17. 31,483 − 29,785

18. 103,558 − 64,671

Problem Solving

19. Reason Why should you estimate before you find the sum or difference of large numbers?

20. About 36,100,000 households in the U.S. have cats and about 43,300,000 households have dogs. About how many more households have dogs than cats?

The table at the right shows the amount of time (rounded to the nearest hour) that astronauts have spent in space for several space programs.

21. For the five space programs listed, what ⭐ is the total number of hours astronauts spent in space?

A 14,608 hours   C 19,988 hours

B 17,621 hours   D 20,038 hours

DATA

Program	Years	Total Hours
Mercury	1961–1963	54
Gemini	1965–1966	970
Apollo	1968–1972	2,502
Skylab	1973–1974	4,105
Space Shuttle	1981–1995	12,407

22. How much longer did astronauts in the ⭐ Space Shuttle program spend in space than all of the other programs combined?

A 631 hours   C 4,776 hours

B 2,194 hours   D 12,407 hours

23. Extend Your Thinking Lisa has a basket of 17 tomatoes. She makes sauce with 9 tomatoes. If Lisa wants to split up the rest between 3 friends and herself, how many tomatoes does each person get?

24. Suppose that there are about 48,000 farms in Florida and about 36,000 farms in New York. Are the total number of estimated farms in Florida and New York greater or less than 100,000?

25. Humans are born with 350 bones. Some of these bones fuse together as we age. Adults only have 206 bones. How many more bones does a baby have than an adult?

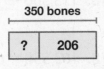

350 bones

?	206

26. Personal Financial Literacy Jorge has $8. He wants to buy a hamburger for $4.98, fries for $0.99, and a drink for $1.39. Tax is $0.52. Does he have enough money? Tell how to use estimation to decide.

Name _____

Another Look!

Find 35,996 + 49,801.		Find 35,996 − 17,902.	

Write the numbers, lining up places. Add the ones and then the tens.

```
   35,996
 + 49,801
       97
```

Write the numbers, lining up places. Subtract the ones, tens, and hundreds.

```
   35,996
 − 17,902
      094
```

When the sum of the column is greater than 9, you need to regroup.

Continue by subtracting thousands and ten thousands. Regroup as needed.

```
   2 15
   3̶5̶,996
 − 17,902
   18,094
```

Continue adding hundreds, thousands, and ten thousands. Regroup as needed.

```
     11
   35,996
 + 49,801
   85,797
```

The 3 in the ten thousands place is regrouped to 2 ten thousands and 10 thousands.

So, 35,996 + 49,801 = 85,797.

So, 35,996 − 17,902 = 18,094.

1.
```
     1
   7,502
 + 9,909
      11
```

2.
```
      7 12
  64,78̶2̶
 − 33,925
      57
```

3.
```
  835,029
 − 26,332
```

4.
```
  570,624
+ 129,588
```

5.
```
  258,000
−  79,455
```

6.
```
  $38,945
+  $7,256
```

Find each sum and difference. Write >, <, or = for each ◯.

7. 1,233 + 486 ◯ 2,220 − 481

8. 193 + 233 ◯ 309 + 118

9. 544 + 4,732 ◯ 2,512 + 1,930

10. 9,491 − 6,230 ◯ 7,020 − 3,759

11. 5,845 + 6,155 ◯ 7,985 + 4,025

12. 742 + 2,868 ◯ 4,000 − 390

13. Myronville School District has 12,081 students, and Saddleton School District has 45,035 students. How many more students are there in Saddleton than in Myronville?

14. Number Sense Is 4,000 a reasonable estimate for the difference of 9,215 − 5,022? Explain.

For **15** through **17**, use the table at the right.

15. How many people were employed as public officials and natural scientists?

16. How many more people were employed as university teachers than as lawyers and judges?

DATA	**People Employed in the U.S. by Occupation in 2000**	
	Occupation	**Workers**
	Public Officials	753,000
	Natural Scientists	566,000
	University Teachers	961,000
	Lawyers and Judges	926,000

17. Which is smallest?

⭐

A the difference between university teachers and natural scientists

B the difference between university teachers and public officials

C the difference between natural scientists and public officials

D the difference between lawyers and judges and public officials

Can you use estimation to help you?

18. Extend Your Thinking Corey earned $3,200 working over the summer. If he made $400 each week, how many weeks did he work? How many weeks would he need to work to earn $6,400? $8,800?

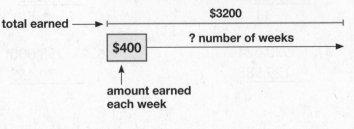

total earned ⟶ | $3200 |
| $400 | ? number of weeks |
↑
amount earned each week

---

19. A sequoia known as Tall Tree measures about 368 feet. Another sequoia known as General Grant measures about 267 feet. How much would General Grant have to grow to be as tall as Tall Tree?

368	
267	x

Name _____

☆ ☆
Solve & Share

Mr. Davidson has two sacks of potatoes. The first sack weighs 11.39 pounds. The second sack weighs 14.27 pounds. How many pounds of potatoes does Mr. Davidson have in all? *Solve this problem any way you choose.*

🔄 TEKS 5.3K Add and subtract positive rational numbers fluently. Also, 5.3. Mathematical Process Standards 5.1B, 5.1C, 5.1F, 5.1G

Digital Resources at PearsonTexas.com

| Solve | Learn | Glossary | Check | Tools | Games |

Analyze Relationships
How can you use what you know about adding whole numbers to help you add decimals?

11.39 lb   14.27 lb

Potatoes   Potatoes

Look Back!

Connect Ideas How is adding decimals like adding whole numbers?

How Can You Add Decimals?

A

A swim team participated in a relay race. The swimmer's times for each leg of the race were recorded in a table. What was the combined time for Caleb and Bradley's legs of the relay race?

You can find 21.49 + 21.59, but first estimate: 21 + 22 = 43.

DATA

Swimmers in Relay	Time in Seconds
Caleb	21.49
Bradley	21.59
Vick	20.35
Matthew	19.03

B **Step 1**

Write the numbers.

Line up the decimal points.

$$21.49$$
$$+\ 21.59$$

Adding decimals is just like adding whole numbers!

C **Step 2**

First, add the hundredths.

Regroup if necessary.

$$\overset{1}{21.49}$$
$$+\ 21.59$$
$$8$$

D **Step 3**

Add the tenths, ones, and tens. The decimal point in the sum is aligned with the decimal point in the addends. Check the sum with your estimate.

$$\overset{1\ 1}{21.49}$$
$$+\ 21.59$$
$$43.08$$

The combined time for Caleb and Bradley was 43.08 seconds.

Do You Understand?

Convince Me! André said the last two legs of the race took 3,938 seconds. What mistake did he make?

☆ Guided Practice *

In **1** through **6**, use hundredths grids to help add.

1. 0.82
     + 4.21

2. 9.1
     + 7.21

3. 9.7 + 0.24

4. 3.28 + 6.09

5. 0.26 + 8.3

6. 4.98 + 3.02

7. **Check for Reasonableness** How do you know that the combined time for the first two legs of the race in the example on page 66 is reasonable?

8. In the example on page 66, what was the combined time for the middle two legs of the relay race?

You can estimate first to check that your answers are reasonable.

☆ Independent Practice ☆

Leveled Practice In **9** through **26**, use hundredths grids to help add.

9. 1.03
     + 0.36
     ▢.3▢

10. 6.9
      + 2.8
      ▢.7

11. 45.09▢
      + 2.005
      7.▢9

12. 2.02
      + 0.78

13. 13.094
      + 4.903

14. 356.2
      + 12.45

15. 4.298
      + 0.65

16. 9.001
      + 1.999

17. $8.23
      + $64.10

18. $44.00
      + $91.46

19. 17.49
      + 9

20. 42.89
      + 8.2

21. $271.90 + $34.22

22. 658.2 + 0

23. 0.922 + 6.4

24. 8.02 + 9.07

25. 13.9 + 0.16

26. 0.868 + 15.973

Problem Solving

27. A mural of the Chicago skyline measures 17.6 meters on two sides and 26.21 meters on the other two sides. What is the perimeter of the mural?

    A 38.81 m

    B 48.21 m

    C 55.74 m

    D 87.62 m

28. Explain Juan adds 3.8 + 4.6 and gets a sum of 84. Is his answer correct? Tell how you know.

29. A frog jumped 0.34 meter, 0.68 meter, and 0.51 meter in three jumps. How far did it jump in all?

30. A farmer sold 53.2 pounds of carrots and 29.4 pounds of asparagus to a restaurant. How many pounds of vegetables did the restaurant buy?

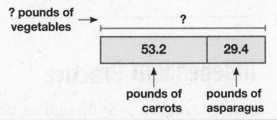

For **31** and **32**, use the table.

31. Which two cities have the greatest combined rainfall for a typical year?

    A Caribou and Boise

    B Springfield and Macon

    C Macon and Boise

    D Caribou and Springfield

32. Mental Math Which location had less than 45 inches of rain but more than 40 inches of rain?

DATA	Location	Rainfall Amount in a Typical Year (in inches)
	Macon, GA	45
	Boise, ID	12.19
	Caribou, ME	37.44
	Springfield, MO	44.97

33. Extend Your Thinking Tim earned $16 babysitting and $17.50 mowing a lawn. He paid $8.50 for a movie and bought a small popcorn. Write an expression to show how much money he has left.

DATA	Popcorn Prices	
	Size	Cost
	Small	$1.95
	Medium	$3.45
	Large	$4.95

Name _____

Another Look!

A scientist used a solution for two experiments. For the first experiment, he used 0.62 milliliter of solution. For the second experiment, he used 0.56 milliliter of solution. How much solution did he use for the two experiments?

You can estimate first to check that your answer is reasonable.

Write the numbers, lining up the decimal points. Include the zeros to show place value.	Add the hundredths and the tenths. Remember to write the decimal point in your answer.
0.62 + 0.56	$\overset{1}{0.62}$ + 0.56 1.18 The scientist used 1.18 milliliters of solution.

1. Find 55.25 + 2.987 + 16.3

```
  5 5 . 2 5
      2 . 9 8 7
+  1 6 . 3
  _____
      7  .   3
```

_____

For 2 through 9, find the sum.

2.   2.97
      + 0.35

3.   5.62
      + 7.99

4. 13.88 + 7.694

5. 41.5 + 12.619

6. 39.488 + 26.7

7. 67.55 + 0.83

8. 88.8 + 4.277 + 78.95

9. 2.94 + 45.6 + 58.418

10. How much combined snowfall was there in Milwaukee and Oklahoma City?

11. What is the combined snowfall total for all three cities?

	City	Snowfall (inches) in 2000
	Milwaukee, WI	87.8
	Baltimore, MD	27.2
	Oklahoma City, OK	17.3

In science class, students weighed different amounts of clay. Carmen weighed 4.361 ounces, Kim weighed 2.704 ounces, Simon weighed 5.295 ounces, and Angelica weighed 8.537 ounces.

12. How many ounces of clay did Carmen and Angelica have combined?

13. How many ounces of clay did Kim and Simon have combined?

14. **Use a Strip Diagram** Carmen has 3 bags of marbles. They have masses of 10.3 grams, 5.23 grams, and 3.74 grams. What is the total mass of all the marbles?

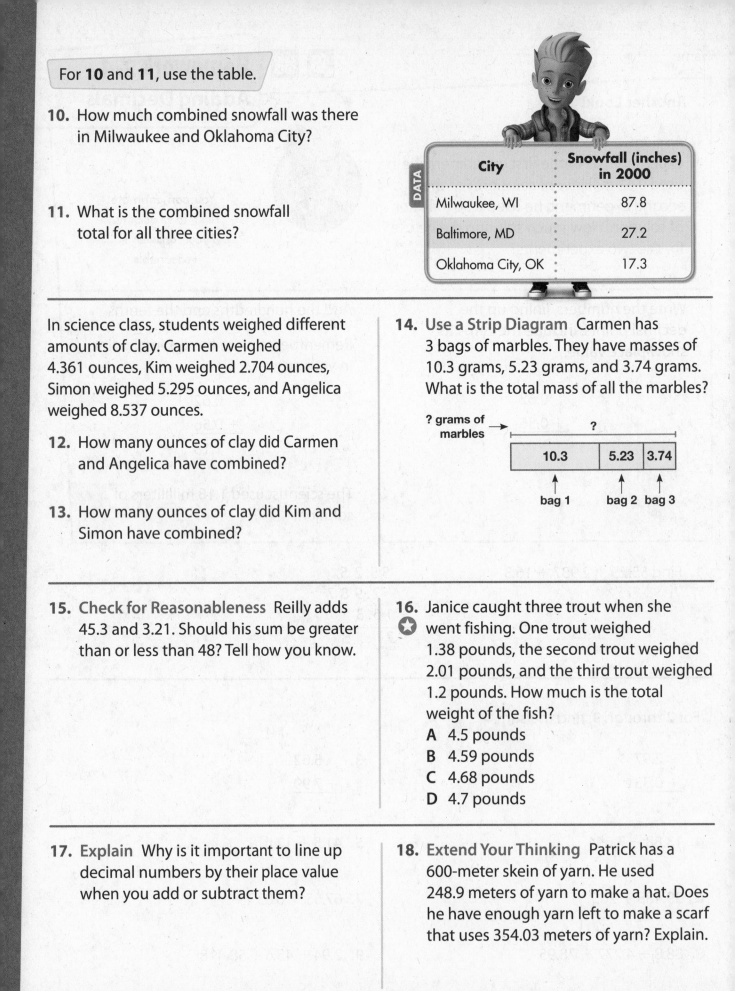

? grams of marbles →

?

| 10.3 | 5.23 | 3.74 |

bag 1   bag 2 bag 3

15. **Check for Reasonableness** Reilly adds 45.3 and 3.21. Should his sum be greater than or less than 48? Tell how you know.

16. Janice caught three trout when she went fishing. One trout weighed 1.38 pounds, the second trout weighed 2.01 pounds, and the third trout weighed 1.2 pounds. How much is the total weight of the fish?
    A 4.5 pounds
    B 4.59 pounds
    C 4.68 pounds
    D 4.7 pounds

17. **Explain** Why is it important to line up decimal numbers by their place value when you add or subtract them?

18. **Extend Your Thinking** Patrick has a 600-meter skein of yarn. He used 248.9 meters of yarn to make a hat. Does he have enough yarn left to make a scarf that uses 354.03 meters of yarn? Explain.

Name _____

Solve & Share

Ms. Garcia is an electrician and has a length of wire that is 32.7 meters long. She has another length of wire that is 15.33 meters long. How much longer is the one wire than the other? *Solve this problem any way you choose.*

TEKS 5.3K Add and subtract positive rational numbers fluently. Also, 5.3. Mathematical Process Standards 5.1B, 5.1C, 5.1F, 5.1G

Digital Resources at PearsonTexas.com

Solve   Learn   Glossary   Check   Tools   Games

Connect Ideas You can use what you know about whole number subtraction to subtract decimals. *Show your work in the space below!*

Look Back!

Number Sense How can you use addition to check the problem about Ms. Garcia's wires?

How Can You Subtract Decimals?

What is the difference in the wingspans of the two butterflies?

5.92 cm

4.37 cm

You can estimate 6 – 4 before you find the exact answer.

larger butterfly → | 5.92 |

| 4.37 | ? |

↑ smaller butterfly   ↑ difference in the wingspans

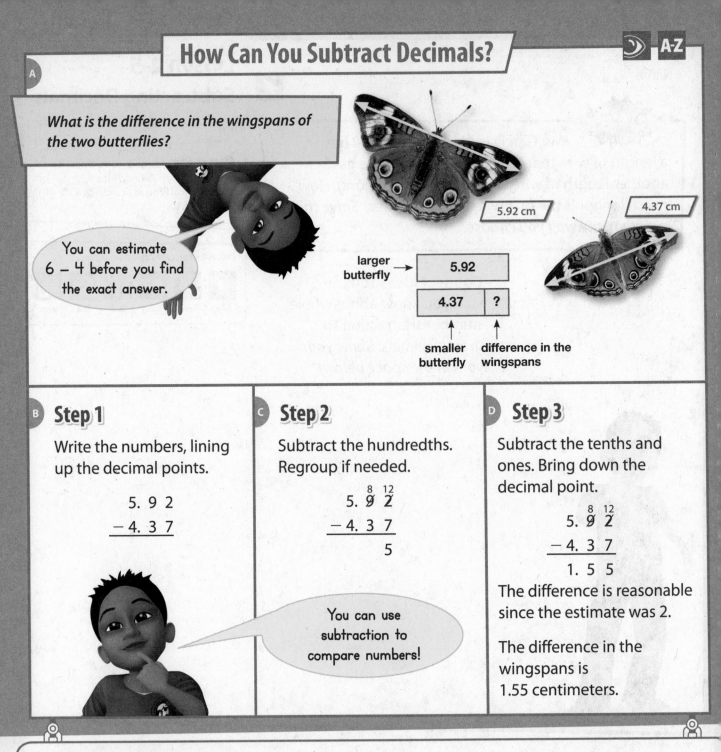

B Step 1

Write the numbers, lining up the decimal points.

```
  5. 9 2
– 4. 3 7
```

C Step 2

Subtract the hundredths. Regroup if needed.

```
    8 12
  5. 9̷ 2̷
– 4. 3 7
        5
```

You can use subtraction to compare numbers!

D Step 3

Subtract the tenths and ones. Bring down the decimal point.

```
    8 12
  5. 9̷ 2̷
– 4. 3 7
  1. 5 5
```

The difference is reasonable since the estimate was 2.

The difference in the wingspans is 1.55 centimeters.

Do You Understand?

Convince Me! An average person's upper leg bone measures 19.88 inches and the lower leg bone measures 16.94 inches. How much longer is the upper leg bone than the lower leg bone? Use a strip diagram to help.

upper leg bone | 19.88 in. |

lower leg bone | ? | 16.94 in. |

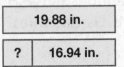

☆ Guided Practice *

In **1** through **8**, subtract the decimals.

1. 16.82
− 5.21

2. 7.21
− 6.1

3. 23.06
− 8.24

4. $4.08
− $2.12

5. 56.8 − 2.765

6. $43.80 − $16.00

7. 22.4 − 10.7

8. $36.40 − $21.16

9. Check for Reasonableness Explain why 1.55 centimeters is a reasonable answer for the difference in the wingspans of the two butterflies.

10. Maria rewrote 45.59 − 7.9 as 45.59 − 7.90. Is the value of 7.9 changed by annexing a zero after 7.9? Why or why not?

Independent Practice ☆

Leveled Practice In **11** through **26**, subtract to find the difference.

11. 7.8
− 4.9
▢ .9

12. $20.60
$14.35
$ ▢ .2

13. 43.905
− 7.526
3 ▢ . ▢ 7 ▢

14. 65.29 ▢
− 28.038
3 ▢ .2 ▢ ▢

15. 15.03 − 4.121

16. 13.9 − 3.8

17. 65.18 − 12.005

18. $52.02 − $0.83

19. 7.094 − 3.657

20. 34.49 − 12.619

21. 85.22 − 43.548

22. $10.05 − $4.50

23. 5.271 − 3.4

24. 23.6 − 8.27

25. 8.04 − 0.339

26. $21.37 − $10.95

Problem Solving

27. The Pyramid of Khafre measured 143.5 meters high. The Pyramid of Menkaure measured 65.5 meters high. What was the difference in the heights of these two pyramids?

  A 68.8 meters

  B 69.3 meters

  C 78 meters

  D 212.3 meters

Menkaure
65.5 meters high

Khafre
143.5 meters high

28. Explain Why is it necessary to line up decimal points when subtracting decimals?

29. Check for Reasonableness Sue subtracted 2.9 from 20.9 and got 1.8. Explain why this is not reasonable.

30. Damaris had $20. She bought some postcards for $5.97. How much money did she have left?

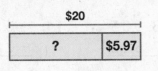

31. Extend Your Thinking Jonah bought a 1.5-liter bottle of seltzer. He used 0.8 liter of seltzer in some punch. Which is greater, the amount he used or the amount he has left?

32. Personal Financial Literacy Abe had $156.43 in his bank account at the beginning of the month. He made the two withdrawals shown in his check register. How much money does he have left in his bank account? He must have at least $100 in his account by the end of the month or he will be charged a fee. How much money does he need to deposit to avoid being charged a fee?

Date	Deposit	Withdrawal	Balance
9/1	17.85		156.43
9/8		24.97	
9/10		39.41	

Name _____

Another Look!

Mr. Montoya bought 3.5 pounds of ground beef. He used 2.38 pounds to make hamburgers. How much ground beef does he have left?

Had 3.5 pounds of ground beef →

3.5 lb	
2.38 lb	?

ground beef used ↑   ground beef left ↑

Write the numbers, lining up the decimal points. Include the zero to show place value.	Subtract the hundredths. Regroup if you need to.	Subtract the tenths and the ones.
3.50 − 2.38	$3.\overset{4\ 10}{\cancel{5}\cancel{0}}$ − 2.38 2	$3.\overset{4\ 10}{\cancel{5}\cancel{0}}$ − 2.38 1.12

Remember to write the decimal point in your answer.

So, Mr. Montoya has 1.12 pounds of ground beef left over.

---

1. Anya bought 1.4 pounds of peaches. She used 0.37 pound in a fruit salad. How much is left? Use the strip diagram to help you.

Pounds of peaches →

1.4 pounds	
0.37	?

peaches used ↑   peaches left ↑

For **2** through **7**, find the difference.

2. 82.7
  − 5.59

3. 43.3
  − 12.82

4. 7.28
  − 4.928

5. $72.35
  − 6.19

6. 1.248
  − 0.92

7. 6.04
  − 3.487

8. Number Sense Kelly subtracted 2.3 from 20 and got 17.7. Explain why this answer is reasonable.

9. Explain Describe the steps you would use to subtract 7.6 from 20.39.

For **10**, use the table.

10. In 2000, how much greater was Miami's rainfall ⭐ than Albany's?

A 107.97 in.
B 54.31 in.
C 14.93 in.
D 14.13 in.

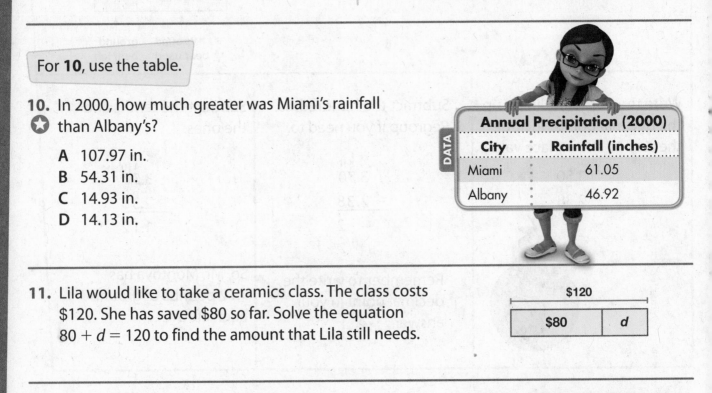

Annual Precipitation (2000)	
City	**Rainfall (inches)**
Miami	61.05
Albany	46.92

11. Lila would like to take a ceramics class. The class costs $120. She has saved $80 so far. Solve the equation 80 + d = 120 to find the amount that Lila still needs.

$120
| $80 | d |

12. Extend Your Thinking The first-place swimmer's time in the 100-meter freestyle at a local swim meet was 1.32 seconds faster than the second-place swimmer. What was the time for the first-place swimmer? What was the difference in time between the second- and third-place swimmers?

100-m Freestyle	
Finish	**Time (seconds)**
First	?
Second	9.33
Third	13.65

13. The distance from Carlo's house to the library is 5.6 miles. He rode his bike 3.85 miles, then took a break at the park. How much farther is it to the library?

14. Nadia deposited $8 into her online account, then downloaded one MP3 for $1.99 and another for $0.98. How much money does she have left in her account?

Name _____

Solve & Share

Julie and Paulo are building a tree house. Julie has a wood board that is 1.15 meters long and Paulo has a board that is 0.7 meter long. What is the total length of the two boards? *Solve this problem any way you choose.*

TEKS 5.3K Add and subtract positive rational numbers fluently. Also, 5.3. Mathematical Process Standards 5.1B, 5.1C, 5.1E, 5.1G

Digital Resources at PearsonTexas.com

Solve	Learn	Glossary	Check	Tools	Games

How can you **create and use representations** to model the problem?

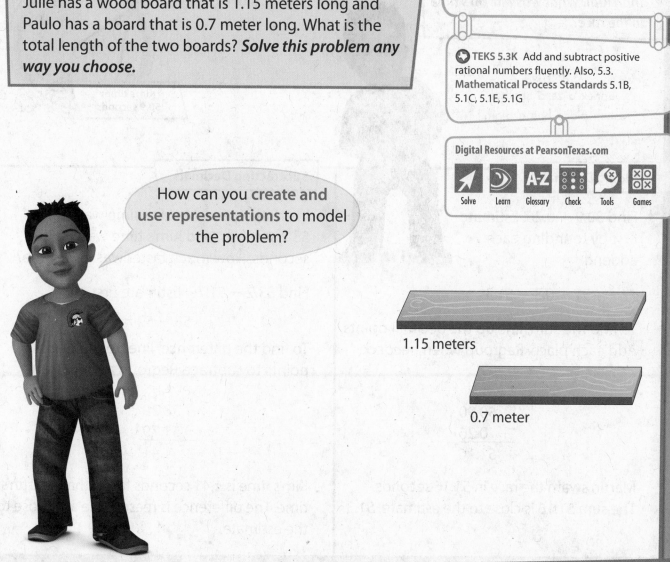

1.15 meters

0.7 meter

Look Back!

Create and Use Representations How much longer is one board than the other? Use a strip diagram to find your answer.

A

Kim and Martin swam 50 meters. Martin took 0.26 second longer than Kim. What was Martin's time in the race?

If needed, annex a zero so that each place has a digit.

Martin's time: 0.26 second longer

Kim's time: 50.9 seconds

Adding Decimals

B Find $50.9 + 0.26$. Estimate first by rounding each addend.

$$51 + 0.3 = 51.3$$

To find the sum, line up the decimal points. Add each place. Regroup when needed.

$$
\begin{array}{r}
\overset{1}{5}0.90 \\
+\ \ 0.26 \\
\hline
51.16
\end{array}
$$

Martin swam the race in 51.16 seconds. The sum 51.16 is close to the estimate, 51.3.

Subtracting Decimals

C In another race, Martin's time was 53.2 seconds, and Kim's time was 51.79 seconds. How much faster was Kim's time?

Find $53.2 - 51.79$. Estimate first.

$$53 - 52 = 1$$

To find the difference, line up the decimal points to subtract. Regroup as necessary.

$$
\begin{array}{r}
\overset{2\ 11}{5}\overset{\cancel{1}0}{3.20} \\
-\ 51.79 \\
\hline
1.41
\end{array}
$$

Kim's time is 1.41 seconds faster than Martin's time. The difference is reasonable and close to the estimate.

Do You Understand?

Convince Me! In a race the next day, Kim's time was 51.7 seconds and Martin's time was 0.79 second slower than Kim's time. Estimate Martin's time and then find the exact answer.

☆ Guided Practice ☆

In **1** through **8**, find each sum or difference.

1. 5.9
  + 2.7

2. 4.01
  − 2.95

3. 2.57 + 7.706

4. 1.5 − 1.056

5. 10 + 3.284

6. 15 − 6.108

7. 3.45 − 1.6

8. 9.124 + 2.06

9. Communicate How are adding and subtracting decimals similar to and different from adding and subtracting whole numbers?

10. Explain Describe how you know whether to add or subtract to solve a decimal problem.

Independent Practice ☆

Leveled Practice In **11** through **26**, find each sum or difference.

11.   2.1 7
  − 0.8☐
  ───────
  1.☐

12.   4. 3☐
  + 4. 1 6
  ───────
  8.☐6

13.   7.62☐
  − 3.86 7
  ───────
  ☐5☐

14.   4.81 5
  + 2.17☐
  ───────
  ☐.9☐

15. 5.187 − 0.48

16. 5.78 + 16.597

17. 9.501 − 9.45

18. 14 + 9.8

19. 46.91 − 28.7

20. 5.61 + 2.4

21. 27 + 0.185

22. 0.46 − 0.333

23. 32 − 23.07

24. 219.501 + 127.2

25. 104.31 − 85.042

26. 40.957 + 312.49

Remember to line up the decimal points.

Problem Solving

27. The U.S. Census Bureau tracks the time people take to travel to work.

How does the average travel time in New York compare to the time in Chicago?

A 4.8 minutes longer
B 5.2 minutes longer
C 5.6 minutes longer
D 10.4 minutes longer

Location	Average Travel Time to Work (minutes)
United States	25.5
Los Angeles, CA	29.6
Chicago, IL	35.2
New York, NY	40.0

28. Explain Mr. Smith gave a cashier a $50 bill for a purchase of $38.70. The cashier gave him a $10 bill, two $1 bills, and three dimes back. Did Mr. Smith get the correct change? Why or why not?

29. Estimation Minh wrote the following number sentence: $2.6 + 0.33 = 5.9$. Use estimation to show that Minh's answer is incorrect.

30. Number Sense Becky is counting backwards from 18.5. Identify the pattern she is using and complete the sequence of numbers.

18.5, 17.25, 16, _____, _____

31. Connect The price of one share of a company at the end of the day Monday was $126.38. The price of a share decreased $7.95 the next day. What was the price of the share at the end of the day Tuesday?

32. Extend Your Thinking A visitor to the Grand Canyon hiked down the South Kaibab Trail and along the River Trail on one day. The next day, she hiked up the Bright Angel Trail. How far did she hike the first day? How much farther did she hike the first day than the second day? How much longer was her total route than if she had hiked the North Kaibab Trail?

Trails in Grand Canyon National Park	
Trail	Length (kilometers)
South Kaibab	10.1
River	2.7
Bright Angel	12.6
North Kaibab	22.9

Name _____

Another Look!

Find 1.93 + 41.6.

Estimate by rounding to the nearest whole number.
2 + 42 = 44

Write the numbers, lining up the decimal points. Annex zeros so all numbers have the same number of decimal places.

$$\begin{array}{r} \overset{1}{1.93} \\ +\ 41.60 \\ \hline 43.53 \end{array}$$ ⟵ Annex a zero.

Add the numbers. Regroup if necessary. Write the decimal point in your answer.

43.53 is close to 44, so the answer is reasonable.

Find 18.5 − 7.82.

Estimate using compatible numbers.
18.5 − 8 = 10.5

Write the numbers, lining up the decimal points. Annex zeros so all numbers have the same number of decimal places.

$$\begin{array}{r} \overset{7\ \ \overset{14}{\cancel{4}}10}{1\cancel{8}.\cancel{5}\cancel{0}} \\ -\ 7.82 \\ \hline 10.68 \end{array}$$ ⟵ Annex a zero.

Subtract. Regroup if necessary. Write the decimal point in your answer.

10.68 is close to 10.5, so the answer is reasonable.

For **1** through **12**, find the sum or difference.

1. $\begin{array}{r} 45.6 \\ +\ 26.3 \\ \hline \end{array}$

2. $\begin{array}{r} 14.25 \\ -\ 5.14 \\ \hline \end{array}$

3. $\begin{array}{r} 17.2 \\ +\ 6.08 \\ \hline \end{array}$

4. 24.84 − 22.7

5. 13.64 − 8.3

6. 0.214 + 15.9

7. 3.652 − 1.41

8. 18.06 + 9.798

9. 8.006 − 6.38

10. 55.5 − 4.56

11. 83.92 + 0.166

12. 57.3 − 42.816

13. Check for Reasonableness Jaime wrote 4.4 − 0.33 = 1.1. Is his answer reasonable? Why or why not?

14. Explain Trey wrote 9.009 − 0.01 = 9.008. Is his answer correct? Why or why not?

15. In a long jump competition, Khaila jumped 3.9 meters. Alicia jumped 3.08 meters. How much farther did Khaila jump?

  A 0.01 meter

  B 0.82 meter

  C 0.98 meter

  D 1.01 meters

16. Number Sense Mrs. Ibara wrote three decimal numbers on the board followed by two blank spaces. Complete the sequence of numbers.

4.15, 6.3, 8.45, _____, _____

Look for number patterns.

For **17** and **18**, use the table.

17. Extend Your Thinking Jane bought three sheets of poster board and a pack of markers. Denise bought two packs of construction paper and a tube of glue. Who spent more? How much more?

DATA	Craft Supplies	
	Poster board	$1.29/sheet
	Markers	$4.50/pack
	Tape	$1.99/roll
	Glue	$2.39/tube
	Construction paper	$3.79/pack

18. If Jane buys two more sheets of poster board, how much does she spend all together?

19. Represent Richard has $107.56 in his checking account. He receives $40 for a graduation present and deposits the entire amount. Then he withdraws $30.60 to pay for new clothes. How much money does he have left in his account? Write an equation to represent this problem and solve.

20. Tools Use the Craft Supplies table above to solve. Julene has $25 to make posters for a school pep rally. She buys two packs of markers, one pack of construction paper, two tubes of glue, and a roll of tape. How many sheets of poster board can she buy with the money she has left over? Explain your answer.

Name _____

⭐ TEKS 5.1A Apply mathematics to problems arising in everyday life, society, and the workplace. Also, 5.3K. Mathematical Process Standards 5.1B, 5.1C, 5.1D, 5.1G

☆ **Solve & Share** ☆

At a baseball game, Sheena bought a pretzel for $2.75 and a sandwich for $6.95. She paid with a $20 bill. How much change did she receive? *Solve this problem any way you choose.*

You can create and use a representation. How can a strip diagram help you find the answer?

Digital Resources at PearsonTexas.com

Solve   Learn   Glossary   Check   Tools   Games

Look Back!

Communicate Is there more than one way to solve this multi-step problem? Explain.

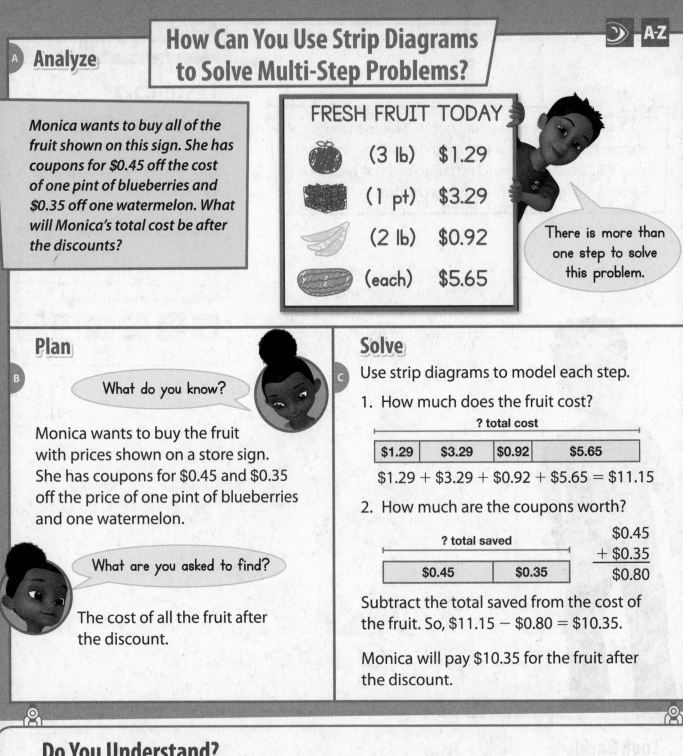
How Can You Use Strip Diagrams to Solve Multi-Step Problems?

A Analyze

Monica wants to buy all of the fruit shown on this sign. She has coupons for $0.45 off the cost of one pint of blueberries and $0.35 off one watermelon. What will Monica's total cost be after the discounts?

FRESH FRUIT TODAY

🍎	(3 lb)	$1.29
🫐	(1 pt)	$3.29
🫛	(2 lb)	$0.92
🍉	(each)	$5.65

There is more than one step to solve this problem.

Plan

B

What do you know?

Monica wants to buy the fruit with prices shown on a store sign. She has coupons for $0.45 and $0.35 off the price of one pint of blueberries and one watermelon.

What are you asked to find?

The cost of all the fruit after the discount.

Solve

C

Use strip diagrams to model each step.

1. How much does the fruit cost?

? total cost			
$1.29	$3.29	$0.92	$5.65

$1.29 + $3.29 + $0.92 + $5.65 = $11.15

2. How much are the coupons worth?

? total saved	
$0.45	$0.35

$0.45
+ $0.35
$0.80

Subtract the total saved from the cost of the fruit. So, $11.15 − $0.80 = $10.35.

Monica will pay $10.35 for the fruit after the discount.

Do You Understand?

Convince Me! Benicio says, "You can subtract the discounts from the prices first and then add to get the answer." Is he correct? Solve this way to check. Which way is easier? Explain.

☆ **Guided Practice** *

Solve.

1. Nate has a $5 bill and a $10 bill. He spends $2.50 for a smoothie and $2 for a muffin. How much money does he have left?

? total $	
$5	$10

? total spent	
$2	$2.50

2. What two questions and answers are needed to solve Problem 1?

3. **Explain** Why do you find and answer two questions before solving Problem 1?

☆ **Independent Practice** ☆

Leveled Practice In **4** through **6**, write and answer two questions needed to solve each problem. Then solve.

4. Lonny planted 15 roses and 6 daisies. His dog digs up 4 roses and 2 daisies. How many flowers are left planted?

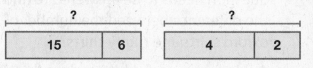

?	
15	6

?	
4	2

5. Paige takes riding lessons 5 days per week for 2 hours each day. Maggie takes guitar lessons twice a week for $2\frac{1}{2}$ hours each day, and piano lessons 3 days per week for 1 hour each day. Which girl spends more hours on lessons? How many more hours?

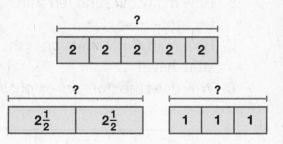

?				
2	2	2	2	2

?	
$2\frac{1}{2}$	$2\frac{1}{2}$

?		
1	1	1

6. Elias saved $30 in July, $21 in August, and $50 in September. He spent $18 on movies and $26 on gas. How much money does Elias have left?

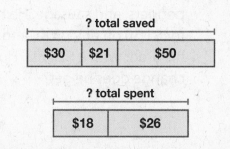

? total saved		
$30	$21	$50

? total spent	
$18	$26

Problem Solving

7. Mr. Smith kept a log of his driving for three days of a trip. How many more miles did he drive for business than for personal use?

Driving Log		
Day	**Business**	**Personal Use**
Monday	48 miles	11 miles
Tuesday	59 miles	8 miles
Wednesday	78 miles	28 miles

8. Tuan has $50. At a craft fair, he spends $12 for food, $19.50 for a small painting, and $6 for a straw hat. How much money does Tuan have left?

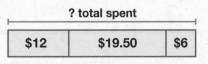

? total spent

$12	$19.50	$6

9. Explain Pull-over shirts cost $24.95 each. Describe how to estimate the cost of 4 shirts. What is the estimate?

10. A men's store has 63 blue oxford shirts and 44 tan oxford shirts. The same store has 39 red rugby shirts. Which question needs to be answered to find the difference between the number of oxford shirts and rugby shirts?

A How many oxford shirts does the store have?

B How many blue and red shirts does the store have?

C How many total shirts does the store have?

D Why does the store sell oxford shirts?

11. Rita budgeted $250 to refurnish her home. She spent $156 on two rugs and $205 on a new lamp. Rita wants to know how much more money she spent than she had budgeted. Which expression can be evaluated to answer this question: How much has Rita spent on the rugs and the lamp?

A $156 + $205

B $250 − $156

C $156 + $250

D $250 + $205

12. Extend Your Thinking Brandon orders a pizza with extra cheese, onions, peppers, and sausage. He has a coupon for $1.50 off any pizza, and he pays for his order with a $20 bill. How much change does he get?

Build Your Own Pizza	Price
Basic pizza	$4.99
Extra cheese	$0.99
Extra vegetables: onions, mushrooms, peppers, eggplant	$0.89 each
Extra meats: chicken, pepperoni, sausage	$1.29 each

Name _____

Another Look!

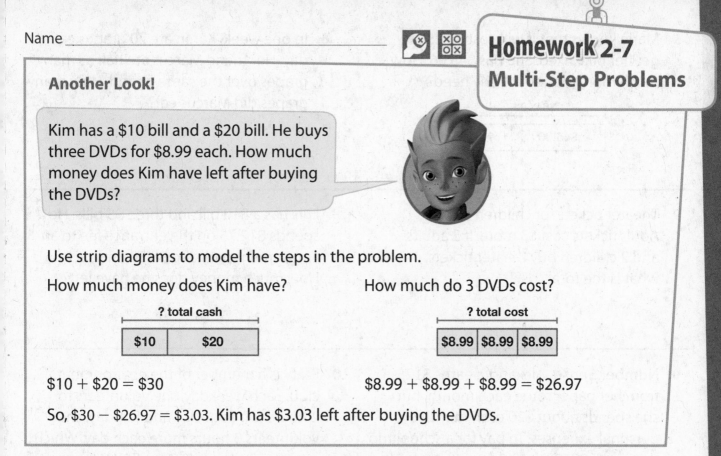

Kim has a $10 bill and a $20 bill. He buys three DVDs for $8.99 each. How much money does Kim have left after buying the DVDs?

Use strip diagrams to model the steps in the problem.

How much money does Kim have?

? total cash

$10	$20

$10 + $20 = $30

How much do 3 DVDs cost?

? total cost

$8.99	$8.99	$8.99

$8.99 + $8.99 + $8.99 = $26.97

So, $30 − $26.97 = $3.03. Kim has $3.03 left after buying the DVDs.

---

1. Brianna has $25 and a $10 gift certificate to a clothing store. She buys two T-shirts for $9.97 each. What are the questions you must answer before you can find how much money she has left?

? total $

$25	$10

? total cost

$9.97	$9.97

2. In Problem 1, how much money does Brianna have left?

---

3. Vincent sold a painting for $35 and a drawing for $5. Then he used the money to buy two paint brushes for $3.50 each. What are the questions you must answer before you can find how much money he has left?

? total made

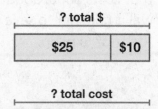

$35	$5

4. In Problem 3, how much money does Vincent have left?

? total spent

$3.50	$3.50

5. Marie knows that it will cost $64.50 to get her bike fixed. She has $45.06. How much more money will she need?

$64.50	
$45.06	?

6. In one week, Karen ate 20 grapes each day. Her friend Marcus ate half as many grapes over the same period. How many grapes did Marcus eat?

7. Theater tickets for children cost $5. Adult tickets cost $3 more. If 2 adults and 2 children buy theater tickets, what is the total cost?

8. Luis has a $10 bill and three $5 bills. He spends $12.75 on the entrance fee to an amusement park and $8.50 on snacks. How much money does he have left?

9. Number Sense Alexandra earns $125 from her paper route each month, but she spends about $20 each month on personal expenses. To pay for a school trip that costs $800, about how many months will it take her to save enough money for the trip? Explain.

10. Patty is a member of the environmental club. Each weekday, she volunteers for 2 hours. On Saturday and Sunday, she volunteers 3 hours more each day. Which expression shows how to find the number of hours she volunteers in one week?

A $2 + 5$

B $2 + 2 + 2 + 2 + 2 + 5 + 5$

C $2 + 2 + 2 + 3 + 3$

D $2 + 3 + 3$

11. Extend Your Thinking One week, Melissa walked to school and back every weekday. She walked from home to the library and back on Saturday, and from home to the mall and back on Sunday. Melissa had a goal of walking 15 miles in one week. Did she meet her goal? Explain.

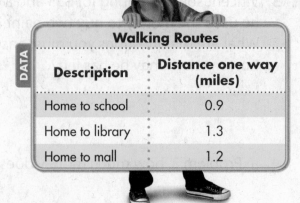

Walking Routes

Description	Distance one way (miles)
Home to school	0.9
Home to library	1.3
Home to mall	1.2

Name _____

1. Estimation In the vault event, the gymnastics team had final scores of 15.300, 14.698, 12.385, and 13.588. About how many points did they earn in all? Tell how you know.

Applying Math Processes
- How does this problem connect to previous ones?
- What is my plan?
- How can I use tools?
- How can I use number sense?
- How can I communicate and represent my thinking?
- How can I organize and record information?
- How can I explain my work?
- How can I justify my answer?

2. Reason Tanya is buying a skateboard for $42.38, a helmet for $17.60, and a set of elbow and knee pads for $12.89. She estimates the total cost to be about $71. Is her estimate higher or lower than the actual cost? Explain.

3. Analyze Information Carie and Wyatt did a weekend fundraising event. Each earned $10 for every kilometer. On Saturday, Wyatt biked 8.5 kilometers more than Carie. Who biked the greatest distance overall? Complete the table to answer the question. About how much money did they raise in all?

Daily Distance (kilometers)				
	Friday	Saturday	Sunday	Total km
Wyatt	91.12		56.3	
Carie	99.78	72.78	62.12	

4. Connect In two months, Sam climbed four mountains. The mountain heights were 14,230 feet, 20,720 feet, 15,945 feet, and 17,159 feet. Use mental math to estimate the total height. Write the expression you used to find your estimate.

5. Extend Your Thinking Marco found an old freestyle BMX bike at the junk yard. To fix the bike, he had to buy the following parts: 1 bike chain for $12.22; 2 wheels for $30.58 each; and 1 set of bike pedals for $19.99. He sold the bike for $161.49. Write an expression to show how much money he made after selling the bike.

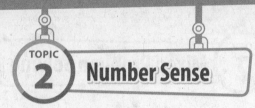

Error Search

Find each group that is not ordered correctly from least to greatest. Circle what is wrong and rewrite the order so that it is correct.

1. 3.009, 3.104, 3.112

2. 7.405, 7.45, 7.008

3. 4.637, 4.652, 4.66, 4.71

4. 0.91, 0.89, 1.035, 1.34

5. 0.622, 0.715, 0.083, 0.85

6. 8.72, 8.726, 8.865, 8.905

7. 9.117, 9.386, 9.42, 1.09

8. 0.725, 7.23, 16.196, 25.002

Compatible Numbers

Draw loops around two or more numbers next to each other, across or down, with a sum of 200 or 1,000. Look for compatible numbers.

9. Find sums of 200.

107	73	160	165	35
93	83	140	43	105
6	44	60	32	85
57	76	84	125	115
137	124	56	49	95

Compatible numbers are numbers that are easy to compute with mentally.

10. Find sums of 1,000.

522	6	472	399	139
453	270	730	281	219
305	630	19	463	513
145	370	251	256	129
97	178	725	275	825

Name _____

Set A | pages 47–52

Add 15.3 + 1.1 + 1.7 using mental math.

Use compatible numbers. These are numbers that are easy to calculate mentally.

15.3 and 1.7 are compatible numbers.

The Commutative Property of Addition allows us to add in any order.

$$15.3 + 1.1 + 1.7 = 15.3 + 1.7 + 1.1$$
$$= 17.0 + 1.1$$
$$= 18.1$$

So, 15.3 + 1.1 + 1.7 = 18.1.

Remember that you can use compatible numbers or compensation to find sums and differences.

Use mental math to add or subtract.

1. 8.6 + 23.4 + 1.4

2. 27 − 9.9

3. 13.5 + 5.7 + 36.5

4. 205.4 − 99.7

5. $12.35 + $25.89 + $19.65

6. 1.29 + 3.72 + 5.15 + 2.85

Set B | pages 53–58

Estimate 19.9 + 17.03.

$$\begin{array}{rl} 19.9 & \longrightarrow \quad 20 \\ + 17.03 & \longrightarrow \underline{+ 17} \\ & \qquad\quad 37 \end{array}$$ Round to the nearest whole number.

19.9 + 17.03 is about 37.

Estimate 22.4 − 16.2.

$$\begin{array}{rl} 22.4 & \longrightarrow \quad 20 \\ - 16.2 & \longrightarrow \underline{- 15} \\ & \qquad\quad 5 \end{array}$$ Use compatible numbers.

22.4 − 16.2 is about 5.

Remember that using compatible numbers to estimate is often easier than rounding.

Estimate each sum or difference.

1. 76 + 23

2. 358 + 293

3. 15.01 − 4.4

4. 80.01 + 2.89

5. 25,003 − 12,900

6. 9.5 + 9 + 8.6

Set C | pages 59–64

Find 6,259 − 2,488.

Line up numbers by place value. Subtract the ones, and then subtract the tens, hundreds, and thousands. As you subtract, regroup if needed.

$$\begin{array}{r} 6,259 \\ - 2,488 \\ \hline 1 \end{array} \qquad \begin{array}{r} {\scriptstyle 5\ \ 11} \\ {\scriptstyle 5\ \cancel{7}\ 15} \\ \cancel{6,2}\cancel{5}9 \\ - 2,488 \\ \hline 3,771 \end{array}$$

Remember to use what you already know about regrouping to help add and subtract with larger numbers.

Add or subtract. Check the answer to subtraction exercises by adding.

1. $\begin{array}{r} 9,371 \\ + 6,059 \end{array}$

2. $\begin{array}{r} 14,506 \\ - 8,759 \end{array}$

Lucy bought 3.12 pounds of pears and 9 pounds of apples. Find how many more pounds of apples than pears Lucy bought.

Write the numbers. Add a decimal point to the whole number. Annex zeros. Line up the decimal points.

$$\begin{array}{r} 9.00 \\ -\ 3.12 \\ \hline \end{array}$$

Subtract the hundredths, tenths, and ones.

$$\begin{array}{r} 9.00 \\ -\ 3.12 \\ \hline 5.88 \end{array}$$

Remember to annex zeros so that each place has a digit.

1. $7.06 + 0.85$

2. $24.07 - 5.316$

3. $51.92 - 28.003$

4. $8.71 - 0.4$

5. $98 + 3.79$

6. Talia measured two strings. The green string was 2.37 cm long. The blue string was 4 cm long. How many centimeters longer was the blue string than the green string?

When you solve multi-step problems, you can use strip diagrams to model the steps.

Gene wants to buy a catcher's mitt for $52.00 and baseball shoes for $95.75. He has a coupon for $8.50 off the price of the catcher's mitt.

How much will Gene have to pay for the catcher's mitt after he uses the coupon?

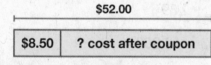

$52.00 − $8.50 = $43.50

How much will Gene owe for his total purchase?

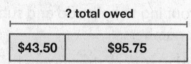

$43.50 + $95.75 = $139.25

Gene will owe $139.25 for his purchase.

Remember to break up the information into smaller parts that can be shown with strip diagrams.

Write and answer the hidden question or questions. Then solve.

DATA	Job	Earnings
	Mowing lawn	$13.50
	Raking leaves	$11.00
	Walking dogs	$14.75

1. Pedro earned money doing different jobs for neighbors. He kept a table of what he earned. If Pedro bought a magazine subscription for $16.95 from his earnings, how much money did he have left?

2. Now Pedro wants to buy two DVDs for $10.99 each. Does he have enough money left over?

Name _____

1. A dollhouse has 15.15 square feet downstairs and 6.25 square feet upstairs. Which of the following is a reasonable estimate of the total square footage in the dollhouse?

   A 9 square feet

   B 21 square feet

   C 90 square feet

   D Not here

2. Lexi went shopping and bought shirts that cost $12.15 and $16.85. She paid $1.74 in taxes. How much she did she pay in all? Use mental math to solve.

   A $29.00

   B $30.74

   C $30.85

   D $32.74

3. Which two trails combined are **NOT** greater than 4 miles?

Trails	Miles
Red	2.75
Blue	3.5
Yellow	2.95
Green	1.2

   A Red and blue

   B Blue and yellow

   C Yellow and green

   D Red and green

4. Beth worked 33.25 hours last week and 23.75 hours this week. How many total hours did she work? Use mental math to solve.

   A 46 hours

   B 47 hours

   C 56 hours

   D 57 hours

5. In a recent city election, 20,542 people voted for the current mayor and 22,797 people voted for the new candidate. What was the total number of votes?

   A 42,249

   B 42,339

   C 43,339

   D 43,349

6. The table shows the areas of two islands. How many more square miles is the area of Greenland than the area of New Guinea?

Island	Area (sq mi)
Greenland	839,999
New Guinea	316,615

   A 1,156,614 square miles

   B 1,145,504 square miles

   C 587,716 square miles

   D 523,384 square miles

7. Eduardo is training for a marathon. He ran his first mile in 12.56 minutes and his second mile in 12.98 minutes. What is his combined time for the first two miles?

8. The Thomas Jefferson Memorial is on 18.36 acres of land and the Franklin Delano Roosevelt Memorial is on 7.5 acres of land. How many more acres is the Jefferson Memorial than the Roosevelt Memorial?

A 9.86 acres

B 10.86 acres

C 11.31 acres

D 17.61 acres

9. Petra uses her computer each weekday for 2 hours. During the weekend, she uses her computer for twice as many hours each day. How many hours a week does Petra use her computer?

10. One year, the precipitation in Dallas measured 35.16 inches. The next year, Dallas received 37.1 inches of precipitation. How many more inches of precipitation did Dallas receive the next year?

A 1.06 inches

B 1.94 inches

C 2.06 inches

D 2.94 inches

11. Shemekia has one basket of fruit that weighs 23.7 pounds. She has another basket of vegetables that weighs 6.912 pounds. What is the combined weight of the two baskets?

12. The dog trainer gives treats to 8 dogs as rewards. The trainer rewards each dog with 3 treats. If the trainer started with a bag of 60 treats, how many treats does he have left?

© Pearson Education, Inc. 5

Multiplying Whole Numbers and Decimals

Essential Questions:
- What are the standard procedures for estimating products of whole numbers and decimals?
- What are the standard procedures for finding products involving whole numbers and decimals?
- How can some products be found mentally?

In one hour, the Sun provides enough energy to power everything on Earth for a whole year.

We can use solar energy for heat and electricity without polluting the air.

Let's see if we can use the Sun to charge my music player. Here's a project about solar energy.

Math and Science Project: Solar Energy

Do Research Use the Internet or other sources to learn about solar energy. Find at least five ways that we use the Sun's energy today.

Journal: Write a Report Include what you found. Also in your report:

- Describe at least one way that you could use solar energy. Could it save you money?

- Estimate how much your family pays on energy costs such as lights, gasoline, heating and cooling.

- Make up and solve problems by multiplying whole numbers and decimals.

Review What You Know

Vocabulary

Choose the best term from the box. Write it on the blank.

- equation
- factors
- overestimate
- partial products
- product
- round
- underestimate
- variable

1. A(n) _____ is another word for a number sentence.

2. One way to estimate a number is to _____ the number.

3. A(n) _____ is the answer to a multiplication problem.

4. In the equation $9 \times 5 = 45$, 9 and 5 are both _____.

5. Using 50 for the number of weeks in a year is a(n) _____.

6. A quantity that is unknown may be represented by a(n) _____.

7. A(n) _____ is greater than the actual number.

Multiplication

Find each product.

8. 12×15 9. 22×40

10. 31×35 11. 24×12

12. 14×41 13. 29×60

Rounding

Round each number to the nearest ten.

14. 864   15. 651

16. 348   17. 985

18. 451   19. 749

Using Estimation

Explain Write an answer to the question.

20. Kayla's birthday is a few days more than 7 months away. How can Kayla estimate the number of days until her birthday?

My Word Cards

Use the examples for each word on the front of the card to help complete the definitions on the back.

A-Z

underestimate

70 × 30 is an underestimate for 72 × 34 since 70 < 72 and 30 < 34.

overestimate

50 × 20 is an overestimate for 45 × 19 since 50 > 45 and 20 > 19.

partial products

57
× 14
228 ← partial products
+ 570 ←
798

variable

25 + n = 37
↑
variable

My Word Cards

Complete the definition. Extend learning by writing your own definitions.

The result of using greater numbers to estimate a sum or product is called an _____.

The result of using lesser numbers to estimate a sum or product is called an _____.

A letter, such as *n*, that represents a number in an expression or an equation is called a _____.

_____ are products found by breaking one of two factors into ones, tens, hundreds, and so on, and then multiplying each of these by the other factor.

Name _____

Solve & Share

A school club wants to buy shirts for each of its 38 members. Each shirt costs $23. About how much money will all the shirts cost? *Solve this problem any way you choose.*

⭐ TEKS 5.3A Estimate to determine solutions to mathematical and real-world problems involving addition, subtraction, multiplication, or division. **Mathematical Process Standards** 5.1A, 5.1C, 5.1D, 5.1G

Digital Resources at PearsonTexas.com

Solve   Learn   Glossary   Check   Tools   Games

You can **communicate** your mathematical ideas. Are you asked for an exact answer or an estimate?

$23

Look Back!

Number Sense How can you use number sense to tell that the exact answer has to be greater than $600? Explain how you know.

How Can You Estimate Products?

A

A store needs at least $15,000 in sales per month to make a profit. If the store is open every day in March and sales average $525 per day, will the store make a profit in March?

You can use rounding to estimate.

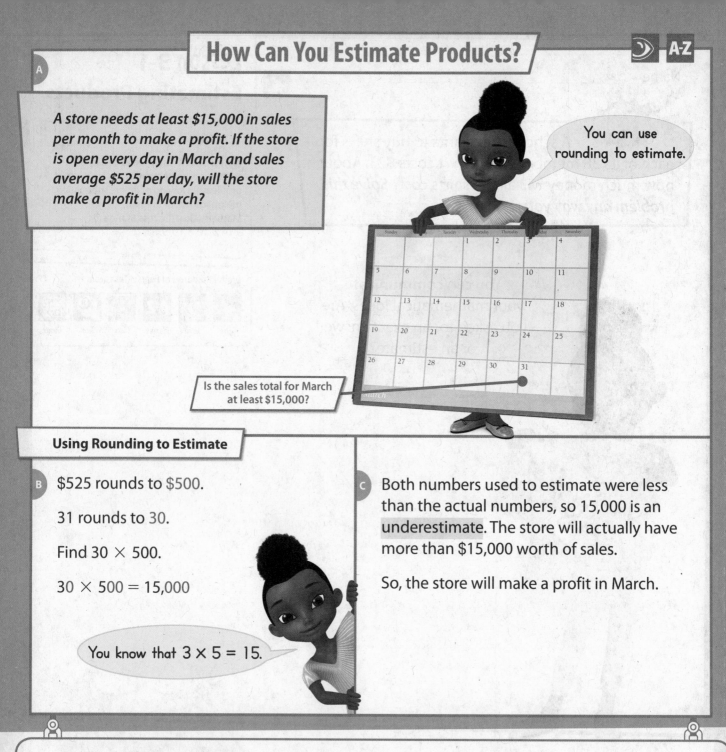

Is the sales total for March at least $15,000?

Using Rounding to Estimate

B

$525 rounds to $500.

31 rounds to 30.

Find 30 × 500.

30 × 500 = 15,000

You know that 3 × 5 = 15.

C

Both numbers used to estimate were less than the actual numbers, so 15,000 is an underestimate. The store will actually have more than $15,000 worth of sales.

So, the store will make a profit in March.

Do You Understand?

Convince Me! A different store needs to make at least $20,000 to make a profit in March. They average $685 a day for the month. James used rounding and estimation to say, "$685 is almost $700. $700 × 30 days is $21,000. I think it is going to be a close call!" What do you think?

Another Example

Estimate 24 × 39.

You can also use compatible numbers to estimate.

25 and 4 are compatible numbers.

25 × 4 = 100

25 × 40 = 1,000

So, 1,000 is a good estimate for 24 × 39.

Both numbers used to estimate were greater than the actual numbers.

So, 1,000 is an **overestimate**.

☆ Guided Practice ☆

In **1** through **5**, estimate.
Then, tell if your estimate is an overestimate or underestimate.

1. 29 × 688

2. 21 × 733

3. 43 × 108

4. 38 × 690

5. 82 × 248

6. **Estimation** Each egg carton holds one dozen eggs. Michael's chicken farm fills 121 egg cartons. He thinks that there were over 1,500 eggs. Is he correct? Use an estimate to find out.

Independent Practice ☆

Leveled Practice In **7** through **14**, estimate each product.

7. 18 × 586

8. 30 × 118

9. 19 × 513

10. 38 × 249

11. 11 × 803

12. 44 × 212

13. 79 × 397

14. 42 × 598

Problem Solving

15. Reason Estimate 53 × 375. Is the estimated product closer to 15,000 or 20,000? Explain.

16. Number Sense Give two factors whose estimated product is 8,000.

17. Communicate Samuel needs to estimate the product of 23 × 395. Explain two different methods Samuel can use to estimate.

18. ★ Lance has 102 packages of sports cards. Each package has 28 cards. Use rounding to estimate. About how many cards does Lance have?

A 3,500

B 3,250

C 3,000

D 2,750

19. A company bought 29 computers for $912 each. Estimate the total cost of the computers.

20. Explain why using either compatible numbers or rounding as a method for estimation would be the same for 32 × 695.

21. Justify Susan used rounding to estimate 24 × 413 and found 20 × 400. Jeremy used compatible numbers and found 25 × 400. The actual product is 9,912. Whose method gives an estimate closer to the actual product? Explain.

22. Extend Your Thinking Abby counts 12 large boxes and 18 small boxes of pencils in the supply cabinet. Each large box contains 144 pencils. Each small box contains 24 pencils. Estimate the total number of pencils. Is your estimate an overestimate or an underestimate? Explain why it might be better to have an underestimate rather than an overestimate.

Is your answer reasonable?

Name _____

Another Look!

Mrs. Carter orders new supplies for Memorial Hospital. About how much will it cost to purchase 14 pulse monitors?

Supplies	
Electronic thermometers	$19 each
Pulse monitors	$189 each
Pillows	$17 each
Telephones	$19 each

DATA

Use rounding to Estimate
Estimate 14 × 189. You can round 14 to 10 and 189 to 200.   10 × 200 = 2,000

Use compatible numbers to Estimate
Estimate 14 × 189. Replace 14 with 15 and 189 with 200.   15 × 200 = 3,000

The 14 pulse monitors will cost between $2,000 and $3,000.

---

1. About how much would it cost to buy 18 MP3 players? About how much would it cost to buy 18 AM/FM radios?

Electronics Prices	
CD player	$74.00
MP3 player	$99.00
CD/MP3 player	$199.00
AM/FM radio	$29.00

DATA

In **2** through **15**, estimate each product.

2. 184 × 21
   Round 184 to _____.
   Round 21 to _____.
   Multiply _____ × _____ = _____.

3. 77 × 412
   Round 77 to _____.
   Round 412 to _____.
   Multiply _____ × _____ = _____.

4. 87 × 403

5. 19 × 718

6. 888 × 30

7. 352 × 20

8. 52 × 797

9. 189 × 46

10. 56 × 396

11. 498 × 47

12. 492 × 22

13. 928 × 89

14. 308 × 18

15. 936 × 41

16. Connect Laura's family is going on a driving vacation. They will drive 4,180 miles over the next two weeks. About how many miles will they drive on average each week?

17. Connect A bus service drives passengers between Milwaukee and Chicago every day. They travel from city to city a total of 8 times each day. The distance between the two cities is 89 miles. In the month of February, there are 28 days. The company's budget allows for 28,000 total miles for February. Is 28,000 miles a reasonable budget mileage amount?

18. A club has a budget for $800 for entertainment. ⭐ Which combination of adults and children below is within their budget?

A 17 adults, 24 children over 5

B 15 adults, 29 children over 5

C 13 adults, 33 children over 5

D 12 adults, 35 children over 5

19. The same number of adults as children (age 5–12) attends the show. A total of 38 tickets was purchased. Can you use compatible numbers to find the total cost for all the tickets?

DATA	Ticket	Price (in $)
	Adult	23
	Child, age 5–12	17
	Under 5	8

20. Communicate A case of 24 pairs of the same kind of sports shoes costs a little more than $800. Explain whether $28 per pair is a good estimate of the price.

21. Extend your Thinking Explain whether rounding or compatible numbers gives a closer estimate for the product below.

$48 \times 123 = 5,904$

Name _____

☆ Solve & Share

A local charity collected 163 cans of food every day for 14 days. How many cans did they collect in the first 10 days? How many did they collect in the remaining 4 days? How many cans did they collect in all? *Solve this problem any way you choose!*

⭐ TEKS 5.3B Multiply with fluency a three-digit number by a two-digit number using the standard algorithm. Also, 5.3. Mathematical Process Standards 5.1A, 5.1B, 5.1E, 5.1G

Digital Resources at PearsonTexas.com

| Solve | Learn | Glossary | Check | Tools | Games |

You can **connect ideas.** You know how to multiply by 10 and by a single-digit number.

FOOD DRIVE

Look Back!

Check for Reasonableness How can you check that your answer is reasonable?

How Do You Multiply 3-Digit Numbers by 2-Digit Numbers?

Last month a bakery sold 389 boxes of bagels. How many bagels did the store sell last month?

You can use multiplication to join equal groups.

12 bagels per box

Using Multiplication to Combine Equal Groups

Step 1

Multiply by the ones, and regroup if necessary.

$$
\begin{array}{r}
{}^{1\,1}\,389 \\
\times\ \ 12 \\
\hline
778
\end{array}
$$

2 × 9 ones = 18 ones or
        1 ten and 8 ones
2 × 8 tens = 16 tens
16 tens + 1 ten = 17 tens
17 tens = 1 hundred 7 tens

2 × 3 hundreds = 6 hundreds
6 hundreds + 1 hundred =
7 hundreds

Step 2

Multiply by the tens, and regroup if necessary.

$$
\begin{array}{r}
389 \\
\times\ \ 12 \\
\hline
778 \\
+\ 3890
\end{array}
$$

10 × 9 ones = 90 ones
10 × 8 tens = 80 tens or
8 hundreds
10 × 3 hundreds =
30 hundreds or
3 thousands

Step 3

Add the partial products.

$$
\begin{array}{r}
389 \\
\times\ \ 12 \\
\hline
778 \\
+\ 3890 \\
\hline
4{,}668
\end{array}
$$

The store sold 4,668 bagels last month.

Do You Understand?

Convince Me! Is 300 × 10 a good estimate for the number of bagels sold at the bakery? Explain.

☆ Guided Practice ☆

In **1** through **4**, find each product. Estimate to check that your answer is reasonable.

1.   236
        × 46

2.   425
        × 61

3.   951
        × 62

4.   185
        × 55

5. **Connect** A theater can seat 540 people at one time. How many tickets are sold if the theater sells out every seat for one 30-day month?

6. **Check for Reasonableness** Is 500 × 30 a good estimate for the number of tickets sold at the theater in one month?

☆ Independent Practice ☆

Leveled Practice In **7** through **22**, find each product. Estimate to check that your answer is reasonable.

7.   451
        × 10

8.   892
        × 18

9.   946
        × 33

10.   735
        × 41

11. 25 × 100

12. 81 × 11

13. 106 × 72

14. 390 × 59

15. 18 × 360

16. 75 × 222

17. 481 × 35

18. 659 × 17

19. 340 × 89

20. 439 × 22

21. 273 × 29

22. 64 × 475

Problem Solving

Remember, there are 60 minutes in 1 hour.

23. Analyze Information Which is the total number of heartbeats in 1 hour for a dog and a rabbit?

A 312

B 6,012

C 18,720

D 27,600

DATA	Animal	Heart Rate (beats per minute)
	Dog	100
	Gerbil	360
	Rabbit	212

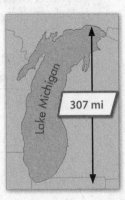

24. Connect The fifth-grade class at Monticello Middle School sold more bags of popcorn than any other class. They ordered 17 cases of popcorn. Each case had 242 bags. How many bags of popcorn did the class sell?

25. Check for Reasonableness Is 3,198 a reasonable product for 727 × 44? Why or why not?

26. Connect The length of the Nile River in Africa is about 14 times the length of Lake Michigan. About how many miles long is the Nile River?

Lake Michigan — 307 mi

27. Connect A store received a shipment of 38 TVs valued at $425 each. What is the total value of the shipment?

28. Extend Your Thinking A garden store sells plants in flats. There are 6 plants in each tray. Each flat has 6 trays. The garden store sold 18 flats on Saturday and 21 flats on Sunday. How many plants did the garden store sell in all?

Name _____

Another Look!

Last year, 23 students in 5th grade were assigned a kindergarten student as a reading buddy. Each student read for 1 hour during each reading session and for a total of 128 sessions. How many hours did all 5th grade students read?

Estimate $130 \times 20 = 2,600$

Step 1
Multiply by the ones. Regroup as needed.

$$
\begin{array}{r}
1\overset{2}{2}8 \\
\times\ \ 23 \\
\hline
384
\end{array}
$$

Step 2
Multiply by the tens. Regroup as needed.

$$
\begin{array}{r}
\overset{2}{1}28 \\
\times\ \ \ \ 3 \\
\hline
384
\end{array}
$$

Step 3
Add the partial products.

$$
\begin{array}{r}
\overset{1}{1}28 \\
\times\ \ 20 \\
\hline
2,560
\end{array}
$$

$$
\begin{array}{r}
384 \\
+\ 2,560 \\
\hline
2,944
\end{array}
$$

All the 5th grade students read for 2,944 hours. The answer is reasonable because it is close to the estimate.

In **1** through **10**, find each product. Estimate to check that your answer is reasonable.

1.
$$
\begin{array}{r}
282 \\
\times\ \ 19 \\
\hline
\end{array}
$$
←— Multiply by the ones.

$+$ _____ ←— Multiply by the tens.

←— Add the partial products.

2.
$$
\begin{array}{r}
538 \\
\times\ \ 46 \\
\hline
\end{array}
$$

3.
$$
\begin{array}{r}
395 \\
\times\ \ 76 \\
\hline
\end{array}
$$

4.
$$
\begin{array}{r}
483 \\
\times\ \ 57 \\
\hline
\end{array}
$$

5.
$$
\begin{array}{r}
628 \\
\times\ \ 33 \\
\hline
\end{array}
$$

6.
$$
\begin{array}{r}
154 \\
\times\ \ 35 \\
\hline
\end{array}
$$

7. 682×25

8. 324×71

9. 158×96

10. 516×29

11. Analyze Information The Parents' Club has $2,500 to invest in printed shirts to sell at their fundraiser. What is the maximum number of shirts that they can buy?

Quantity	Price per Shirt (in $)
101–150	18
151–200	15
over 200	11

A 137 shirts
B 166 shirts
C 227 shirts
D 233 shirts

12. Check for Reasonableness Is 2,750 a reasonable answer for 917 × 33? Explain.

13. Formulate a Plan Which equation shows how you can find the number of minutes in one year?

A 60 × 24 × 365
B 60 × 60 × 24
C 60 × 365
D 60 × 60 × 365

14. Connect The Martin School budgets $10,000 to replace 144 computer monitors. The best price they find is $76 for each monitor. With this price, are they within their budget?

15. Justify In a class of 24 students, 13 students sold over 150 raffle tickets each, and the rest of the class sold about 60 raffle tickets each. The class goal was to sell 2,000 tickets. Did they reach their goal? Explain.

16. Extend Your Thinking The table shows the average speed in kilometers per hour for two different racecars. In 12 hours, how much farther will the yellow car go than the red car? Show your work.

Car	Average Speed (km/h)
Red	217
Yellow	242

Name _____

☆ **Solve & Share** ☆

A school district is replacing all of the desks in its classrooms. There are 103 classrooms and each classroom needs 24 new desks. How many desks will the school district need to buy?

Connect Ideas Use what you know about multiplying 3-digit and 2-digit numbers. *Show your work!*

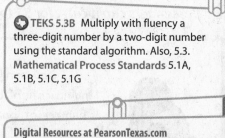

TEKS 5.3B Multiply with fluency a three-digit number by a two-digit number using the standard algorithm. Also, 5.3. Mathematical Process Standards 5.1A, 5.1B, 5.1C, 5.1G

Digital Resources at PearsonTexas.com

Solve   Learn   Glossary   Check   Tools   Games

Look Back!

Reason What is a good estimate for the problem above? Explain.

How Can You Multiply with Zeros?

An antique steam train makes one sight-seeing tour each day. If every seat is filled for each trip, how many passengers can it carry for 31 tours?

You can use multiplication to find the number of passengers.

The train has a total of 208 seats.

Multiplying Numbers with Zero

B Step 1

Find 31 × 208.

Estimate:

30 × 200 = 6,000

? passengers in all

208	31 tours →

↑

Number of seats per tour

C Step 2

Multiply the ones.

Regroup if necessary.

Remember that multiplying with a zero gives a product of zero.

$$\begin{array}{r} 208 \\ \times 31 \\ \hline 208 \end{array}$$

D Step 3

Multiply the tens.

Regroup if necessary.

$$\begin{array}{r} \overset{2}{208} \\ \times 31 \\ \hline 208 \\ +6240 \\ \hline 6,448 \end{array}$$

Add the Partial Products.

The antique steam train can carry 6,448 passengers.

Do You Understand?

Convince Me! Suppose the train fills an average of 102 seats for each tour. What is a reasonable estimate for the number of passengers that the train can carry in 28 tours? Write an equation to show your work.

© Pearson Education, Inc. 5

Guided Practice

In **1** through **4**, multiply to find the product. Estimate to check for reasonableness.

1. 205
    × 23

2. 108
    × 34

3. 410
    × 44

4. 302
    × 30

5. **Connect** There are 104 rows with 24 seats per row for a concert. How many seats are available?

6. **Explain** Why is it important to "estimate to check for reasonableness"?

Independent Practice

Leveled Practice In **7** through **18**, find each product. Estimate to check for reasonableness.

7. 302
    × 17

8. 608
    × 23

9. 109
    × 47

10. 510
    × 72

11. 902
    × 35

12. 207
    × 61

13. 108
    × 58

14. 505
    × 77

15. 407
    × 39

16. 280
    × 66

17. 105
    × 24

18. 360
    × 48

Problem Solving

19. Analyze Information There are 27 students in Mr. Mello's class. Find the total number of pages the students read by the end of November.

20. Estimation Which choice has an estimated product of 24,000?

  A 105 × 24
  B 205 × 12
  C 305 × 78
  D 405 × 45

History Book Progress

Month	Chapter	Pages
September	1	35
October	2	38
November	3	35

DATA

21. Number Sense How much greater is 106 × 23 than 105 × 23?

  A 1
  B 23
  C 105
  D 106

22. Connect The Empire State Building in New York City has 102 stories. The number of windows averages just less than 64 windows per story. What is the maximum number of windows in the Empire State Building?

23. Connect Maria rents a trombone for 9 years (108 months) for $34 per month. How much does she pay?

24. Explain Another music store rents trombones for $30 per month plus a yearly fee of $48. Which deal is better? Should Maria change her rental plan?

25. Robert brought glass bottles and aluminum cans to a recycling center. The total amount of money he received from the center was $8.84. He got $3.46 for all the aluminum cans. How much money did he get for the glass bottles?

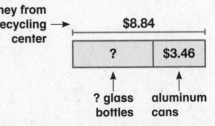

Money from recycling center → $8.84

?	$3.46

? glass bottles   aluminum cans

Another Look!

Find the product of 304 × 23.

$$
\begin{array}{r}
\overset{1}{3}04 \\
\times \quad 23 \\
\hline
912 \\
+ \quad 6080 \\
\hline
6{,}992
\end{array}
$$

Step 1   First, multiply 304 by 3 ones.

Step 2   Then, multiply 304 by 2 tens.

Step 3   Finally, add the partial products.

1. Use the place-value chart at the right to multiply 36 × 405. Record each partial product in the correct place in the chart.

A place-value chart can help keep the numbers in the right place!

thousands period   ones period

hundred thousands	ten thousands	one thousands	hundreds	tens	ones	
			4	0	5	
×				3	6	**What I Multiply**

In **2** through **9**, find each product. Estimate to check for reasonableness.

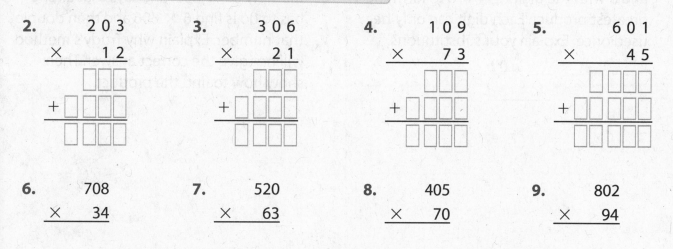

2.
$$
\begin{array}{r}
203 \\
\times \quad 12 \\
\hline
\square\square\square \\
+ \square\square\square\square \\
\hline
\square\square\square\square
\end{array}
$$

3.
$$
\begin{array}{r}
306 \\
\times \quad 21 \\
\hline
\square\square\square \\
+ \square\square\square\square \\
\hline
\square\square\square\square
\end{array}
$$

4.
$$
\begin{array}{r}
109 \\
\times \quad 73 \\
\hline
\square\square\square \\
+ \square\square\square\square \\
\hline
\square\square\square\square
\end{array}
$$

5.
$$
\begin{array}{r}
601 \\
\times \quad 45 \\
\hline
\square\square\square\square \\
+ \square\square\square\square \\
\hline
\square\square\square\square
\end{array}
$$

6.
$$
\begin{array}{r}
708 \\
\times \quad 34 \\
\end{array}
$$

7.
$$
\begin{array}{r}
520 \\
\times \quad 63 \\
\end{array}
$$

8.
$$
\begin{array}{r}
405 \\
\times \quad 70 \\
\end{array}
$$

9.
$$
\begin{array}{r}
802 \\
\times \quad 94 \\
\end{array}
$$

10. Connect The Memorial Middle School Band has 108 members. They want to buy jackets with the name of the band on the back. What is the difference in the total price between the screen-print and the embroidered jackets?

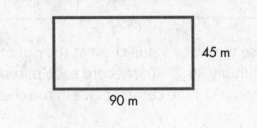

Jackets	Price (in $)
Screen print name	35
Embroidered name	48

DATA

---

11. ⭐ Wildlife protection groups build bat houses to help save bats. One bat house holds about 302 bats. About how many bats could 12 bat houses hold?

A 1,200 bats

B 2,030 bats

C 3,600 bats

D 4,000 bats

12. A soccer field has a length of 90 meters and a width of 45 meters. What is the total area of the soccer field?

45 m

90 m

---

13. Explain A packing crate can hold 205 avocados. There were 7,000 avocados picked at a large grove. The owner has 36 packing crates. Does he have enough crates to ship out the avocados? Explain.

14. Check for Reasonableness Sarah found that the product of 49 and 805 is 3,165. How would finding an estimate help her know that the answer is NOT reasonable?

---

15. Extend Your Thinking Replace the a, b, c, and d with the digits 2, 4, 6, 8 to form the greatest product. Each digit can only be used once. Explain your substitutions.

$$a\,0\,b$$
$$\times \quad c\,d$$

16. Extend Your Thinking Trudy wants to multiply 66×606. She says that all she has to do is find 6×606 and then double that number. Explain why Trudy's method will not give the correct answer. Then show how to find the product.

Name _____

Solve & Share

Write and solve a real-world problem with a question that can be answered by the equation.

$$36 \times 208 = n$$

⭐ TEKS 5.3B Multiply with fluency a three-digit number by a two-digit number using the standard algorithm. Also, 5.3. Mathematical Process Standards 5.1A, 5.1C, 5.1D, 5.1G

Digital Resources at PearsonTexas.com

| Solve | Learn | Glossary | Check | Tools | Games |

You can **connect** mathematics to everyday life. Think about what kind of situations multiplication describes.

Look Back!

Connect Write another problem for the equation. Tell how your two problems are the same and how they are different.

How Can You Use Multiplication to Solve Problems?

How much does the Carson family pay each year for their cell phones?

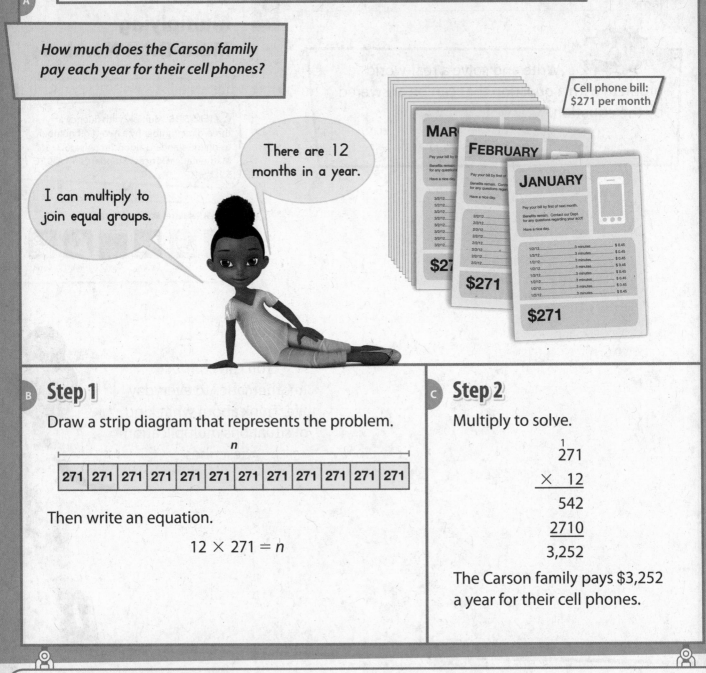

I can multiply to join equal groups.

There are 12 months in a year.

Cell phone bill: $271 per month

B Step 1

Draw a strip diagram that represents the problem.

	n										
271	271	271	271	271	271	271	271	271	271	271	271

Then write an equation.

$$12 \times 271 = n$$

C Step 2

Multiply to solve.

$$
\begin{array}{r}
^{1}271 \\
\times\ \ 12 \\
\hline
542 \\
2710 \\
\hline
3{,}252
\end{array}
$$

The Carson family pays $3,252 a year for their cell phones.

Do You Understand?

Convince Me! Is $3,252 a year a reasonable answer? Explain.

Name _____

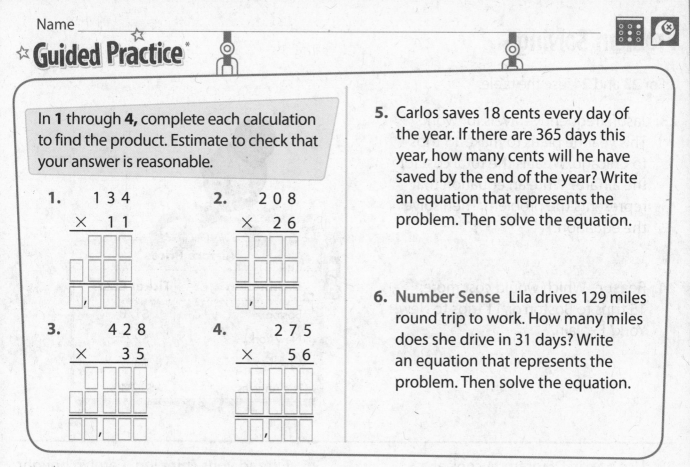

In **1** through **4,** complete each calculation to find the product. Estimate to check that your answer is reasonable.

1.   1 3 4
   × 1 1

2.   2 0 8
   × 2 6

3.   4 2 8
   ×   3 5

4.   2 7 5
   ×   5 6

5. Carlos saves 18 cents every day of the year. If there are 365 days this year, how many cents will he have saved by the end of the year? Write an equation that represents the problem. Then solve the equation.

6. **Number Sense** Lila drives 129 miles round trip to work. How many miles does she drive in 31 days? Write an equation that represents the problem. Then solve the equation.

Independent Practice ☆

Leveled Practice In **7** through **22,** find each product. Estimate to check that your answer is reasonable.

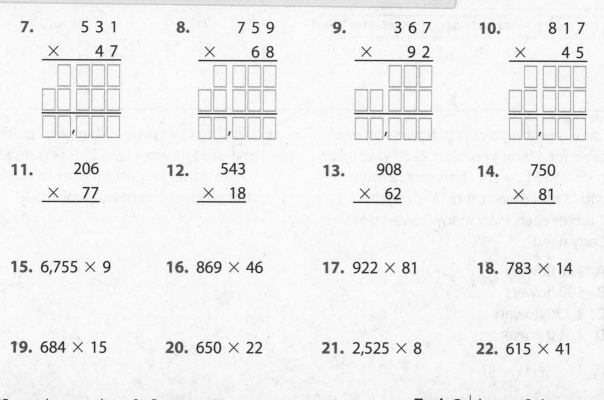

7.   5 3 1
   ×   4 7

8.   7 5 9
   ×   6 8

9.   3 6 7
   ×   9 2

10.   8 1 7
   ×   4 5

11.   206
   ×   77

12.   543
   ×   18

13.   908
   ×   62

14.   750
   ×   81

15. 6,755 × 9

16. 869 × 46

17. 922 × 81

18. 783 × 14

19. 684 × 15

20. 650 × 22

21. 2,525 × 8

22. 615 × 41

Problem Solving

For **23** and **24**, use the table.

23. Jason frequently travels for work. This year he plans to make 15 trips to Chicago. What is the total cost for the airfare? Write an equation that represents the problem. Then solve the equation.

24. **Reason** Which would cost more: 15 trips to Boston or 11 trips to New York? Explain.

These are round-trip prices.

Airfare Prices

Destination	Ticket Cost
Boston	$178
New York	$225
Chicago	$489
Los Angeles	$1,240

---

25. **Use a Strip Diagram** A cook at a restaurant is planning her food order. She expects to use 115 pounds of potatoes each day for 12 days. How many pounds of potatoes will she order?

? number of pounds

| 115 | 115 | 115 | 115 | 115 | 115 | 115 | 115 | 115 | 115 | 115 | 115 |

↑
12 days

26. **Extend your Thinking** Carolyn bought a gallon of paint that covers 250 square feet. She wants to paint a wall that is 16 feet wide and 12 feet high. Explain whether or not she will need more than one gallon of paint.

---

27. Carly is putting a vase of flowers on each ⭐ table for a family reunion. Each vase will contain 15 flowers. There are 12 rows with 8 tables each and 18 rows with 7 tables each. How many flowers does Carly need?

A 222 flowers
B 500 flowers
C 3,330 flowers
D 7,500 flowers

28. **Writing to Explain** When you multiply a 3-digit number by a 2-digit number, what is the greatest number of digits the product can have? Explain.

Another Look!

A sports store sells skateboards for $112. Last month the store sold 45 skateboards. How much money did the store make from selling them?

Use mental math to multiply.
$112 = 100 + 10 + 2$
$100 \times 45 = 4,500$
$10 \times 45 = 450$
$2 \times 45 = 90$
$4,500 + 450 + 90 = 5,040$
So, the store made $5,040 from selling skateboards.

> Rewrite one of the factors in expanded form. Then multiply each addend by the other factor.

1. Find 206×55 using expanded form.

$206 = 200 + 0 +$ _____

$200 \times 55 =$ _____

_____ $\times 55 =$ _____

_____ $+ 330 =$ _____

So, $206 \times 55 =$ _____.

2. Find 240×15 using partial products.

$240 \times 5 =$ _____

$240 \times$ _____ $= 2,400$

$1,200 +$ _____ $=$ _____

So, $240 \times 15 =$ _____.

For **3** through **10**, find each product.

3.   423
   $\times$ 18

4.   914
   $\times$ 12

5.   125
   $\times$ 15

6.   425
   $\times$ 82

7.   185
   $\times$ 24

8.   88
   $\times$ 33

9.   630
   $\times$ 15

10.   440
   $\times$ 75

11. Write a problem that you can solve with multiplication. Use a product greater than 1,000. Solve your problem.

12. Tomika ran 84 miles in 4 weeks. She ran 7 days each week. If she ran the same number of miles each day, how many miles did she run each day?

A 21 miles

B 7 miles

C 4 miles

D 3 miles

---

13. Connect Pete owns several pizza restaurants. Each cheese pizza sells for $8. How much money was made in January at the Westland location?

14. How many more pizzas did the Downtown location sell than the Center City location? Write an equation to show your work.

DATA

Cheese Pizza Sales for January	
Location	**Number Sold**
Downtown	1,356
Center City	998
Westland	1,824

---

15. Extend Your Thinking A farmer grows 128 red tomato plants and 102 yellow tomato plants. Each plant produces about 32 tomatoes. What is a reasonable estimate for the total number of tomatoes?

16. Justify Jane multiplied 825 × 22 and got 3,300. Flynn multiplied the same numbers and got 18,150. Which student is correct? What mistake did the student whose answer is incorrect make?

---

17. Mr. Thompson's fifth-grade class made a dot plot of the number of movies each student watched in the past month. How many more students watched 6 or more movies than watched 2 or fewer movies?

18. How many students in all are in Mr. Thompson's class?

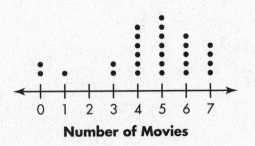

Number of Movies

Name _____

☆ **Solve & Share**

A group of 44 travelers wants to buy tickets for a guided architectural tour. Each ticket costs $12. Is an exact answer needed or is an estimate enough to find the total cost of the tickets? Explain how you know.

You can use the information in the problem to **construct an argument** to support your answer.

⊕ **TEKS 5.1C** Select tools, including real objects, manipulatives, paper and pencil, and technology as appropriate, and techniques, including mental math, estimation, and number sense as appropriate, to solve problems. Also, 5.3A, 5.3B. Mathematical Process Standards 5.1D, 5.1G

Digital Resources at PearsonTexas.com

Solve   Learn   Glossary   Check   Tools   Games

Look Back!

Number Sense The group gets a discount of $2 off each ticket. Will $400 be enough to buy a ticket for everyone? Explain.

A Analyze

Flight 719 carries 39 passengers. Each passenger brings 2 suitcases. The airplane can safely carry 5,000 pounds of luggage. Is an exact answer needed, or is an estimate enough to decide if the luggage for this flight is under the weight limit?

Average weight: 36 pounds per suitcase

You can use multiplication to help you decide.

B Plan

You do not need to know the exact weight of all the luggage. You just need to know if the total weight is less than 5,000 pounds.

You only need an estimate.

C Solve and Justify

Estimate the number of suitcases.
$40 \times 2 = 80$ suitcases

Then estimate the weight of all the suitcases.
80×40 pounds $= 3,200$ pounds

Compare the estimated weight to the limit.
3,200 pounds $<$ 5,000 pounds

The luggage for this flight is under the weight limit.

Do You Understand?

Convince Me! In the example above, would it have been okay to round the average weight of a suitcase to 30 pounds? Explain.

© Pearson Education, Inc. 5

☆ Guided Practice ☆

For **1**, tell whether an exact answer is needed or if an estimate is enough. Then solve.

1. Dario bought two T-shirts for $12 each and a pair of shorts for $18. He paid with a 50-dollar bill. How much change did he get back?

2. Explain In Problem 1, why was an exact answer needed to solve the problem?

3. Estimation Felix is buying shrubs for his garden. He has $200 to spend. Can he buy 5 shrubs that cost $42 each? Explain.

☆ Independent Practice ☆

In **4** and **5**, use the sign. Tell whether an exact answer is needed or if an estimate is enough. Then solve.

4. For a school fundraiser, Jason sold 162 plain pizzas. Milo sold 148 pepperoni pizzas. Who earned more money from selling pizzas?

PLAIN PIZZA............$10
PEPPERONI PIZZA...$12

5. For a school fundraiser, Celia sold 125 plain pizzas and 103 pepperoni pizzas. How much money did Celia collect?

6. A sports store is having a 12-day clearance sale. The goal is to sell at least 700 baseball caps. About how many caps does the store need to sell each day?

7. Khalil bought a new book that has 300 pages. He wants to finish reading it in 8 weeks. He reads the same number of pages each week. About how many pages should he read each week? Use estimation and write an equation to solve.

It's easy to estimate using compatible numbers.

Problem Solving

8. **Number Sense** A sports reporter said that 50,000 fans were at a soccer game. Explain how this number could be both an exact answer and an estimate.

9. A store sells 120 solar-powered tents. Each tent costs between $62 and $76. Which of the following amounts is a reasonable estimate for the total cost of the tents?

   A $9,500   C $7,000
   B $8,100   D $6,500

For **10** through **12**, use the data at right.

10. **Estimation** A 10-pound bag of puppy food has about 920 pieces of food. How many pieces of food are in 20 bags of puppy food?

11. The pet store sold 28 bags of kitty litter on the first day of the sale. How much money did the store receive for this?

12. The store sold 47 bags of kitty litter and 63 bags of puppy food on the second day of the sale. How much money did the store receive for this?

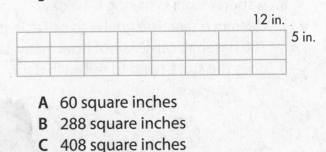

Kitty Litter
Each 50-pound bag: ONLY $14

Puppy Food
Each 10-pound bag: ONLY $19

13. **Extend Your Thinking** Terry has $100 to paint his garage. He buys 4 gallons of paint that cost $23 each. Is he within his budget? Explain.

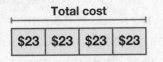

Total cost

| $23 | $23 | $23 | $23 |

14. A garden is divided into equal parts as shown. What is the total area of the garden?

12 in.
5 in.

   A 60 square inches
   B 288 square inches
   C 408 square inches
   D 1,440 square inches

Another Look!

Tell whether an exact answer is needed or if an estimate is enough. Then solve.

Bill drew 36 frames for his comic book. If he wants to put only 4 frames on each page, how many pages long will his comic book be?

The problem gives a limit of 4 frames on each page, so an exact answer is needed.

$36 \div 4 = 9$

So, Bill's comic book will be 9 pages long.

Remember, when the words "about" and "almost" are in the question, an estimate may solve the problem.

In **1** through **6**, tell whether an exact answer is needed or if an estimate is enough. Then solve.

1. Joy is making name tags for the members of the Sunshine Club. She must make tags for 18 girls and 12 boys. How many name tags must she make?

2. On Tuesday, a snack bar sold 309 big pretzels, 286 boxes of popcorn, and 78 bags of peanuts. About how many snacks did the snack bar sell?

3. A theater has 1,024 seats. There will be 92 events at the theater this season. If each seat is filled for each event, how many people will attend in all?

4. Lars wants to earn $70 to buy a camera. He earns $42 mowing lawns and $17 washing cars. Does he earn enough to buy the camera?

5. A diner serves an average of 384 lunches a day. About how many lunches are served in 5 days?

6. A coach buys shin guards for each of 19 players on a soccer team. How many shin guards should the coach buy?

7. A dog walker charges $12 for each dog she walks. In one week, she walked 38 dogs. Which choice gives the best estimate of the amount of money she earned in that week?

   A $10 × 30 = $300
   B $12 × 30 = $360
   C $12 × 40 = $480
   D $20 × 40 = $800

8. **Number Sense** Alexis bought 3 dog crates at the dog show. Each crate cost $87, including tax. How much did Alexis spend in all? Is an estimate or an exact answer needed? Explain.

9. **Extend Your Thinking** Bridgette drew a rectangle. Its length is twice as great as its height. What is the perimeter of her rectangle?

5 in.

10. Jett bought 5 comic books and 2 pens. Each book cost $9, and each pen cost $2. About how much did Jett spend in all?

11. A school district hires a cleaning company to wash all of its playground equipment. The company charges $78 an hour. If it takes 19 hours to finish the job, how much does this job cost?

12. **Justify** A school district needs to order supplies for its science labs. The table shows the prices for the lab items. The district has $14,000 to buy 98 microscopes. Will that be enough money? Explain.

Item	Price
Balance scale	$124
Hot plate	$43
Microscope	$135

13. **Reason** Simon has 148 baseball cards. He sells 62 of them and gives one-half of the remaining cards to his sister. How many cards does Simon have left?

   A 86 baseball cards
   B 74 baseball cards
   C 62 baseball cards
   D 43 baseball cards

You can work backward to double-check your answer!

Name _____

Solve & Share

Javier is helping his parents put up posters in their movie theater. Each poster has a thickness of 0.012 inch. How thick is a stack of 10 posters? 100 posters? 1,000 posters?

TEKS 5.3E Solve for products of decimals to the hundredths, including situations involving money, using strategies based on place-value understandings, properties of operations, and the relationship to the multiplication of whole numbers. Also, 5.3.
Mathematical Process Standards 5.1B, 5.1C, 5.1D, 5.1F, 5.1G

Digital Resources at PearsonTexas.com

Solve   Learn   Glossary   Check   Tools   Games

How can you use what you know about **mental math** and place value to help you? *Show your work!*

Look Back!

Analyze Relationships How does your answer for 1,000 posters compare to 0.012?

What is the Rule for Multiplying Decimals by 10, 100, or 1,000?

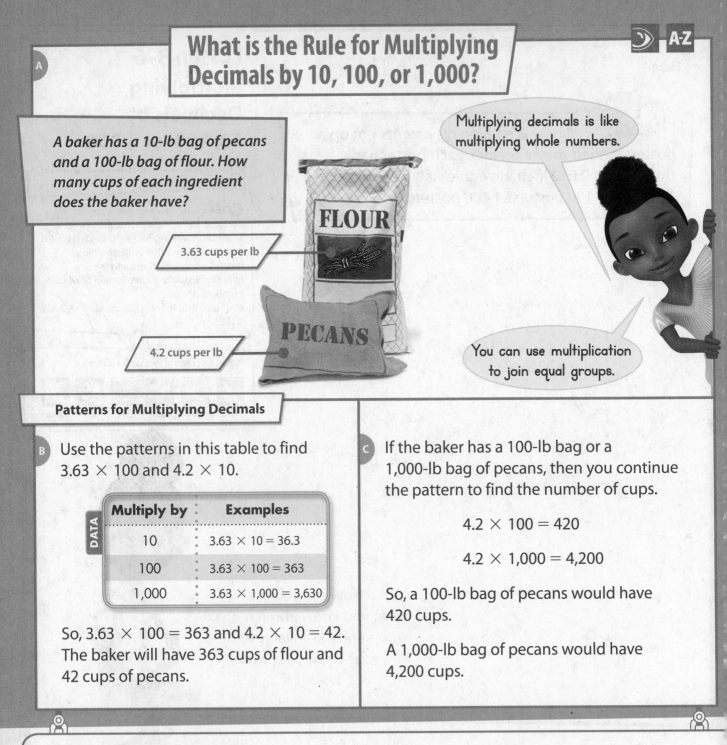

A baker has a 10-lb bag of pecans and a 100-lb bag of flour. How many cups of each ingredient does the baker have?

FLOUR

3.63 cups per lb

PECANS

4.2 cups per lb

Multiplying decimals is like multiplying whole numbers.

You can use multiplication to join equal groups.

Patterns for Multiplying Decimals

B Use the patterns in this table to find 3.63 × 100 and 4.2 × 10.

Multiply by	Examples
10	3.63 × 10 = 36.3
100	3.63 × 100 = 363
1,000	3.63 × 1,000 = 3,630

So, 3.63 × 100 = 363 and 4.2 × 10 = 42. The baker will have 363 cups of flour and 42 cups of pecans.

C If the baker has a 100-lb bag or a 1,000-lb bag of pecans, then you continue the pattern to find the number of cups.

4.2 × 100 = 420

4.2 × 1,000 = 4,200

So, a 100-lb bag of pecans would have 420 cups.

A 1,000-lb bag of pecans would have 4,200 cups.

Do You Understand?

Convince Me! Complete the chart. What patterns do you see in the placement of the decimal point?

	× 10	× 100	× 1,000
1.275			
26.014			
0.4			

☆ Guided Practice *

In **1** through **6**, find each product.

1. 0.009 × 10   **2.** 4.5 × 10

3. 3.1 × 1,000   **4.** 7.4 × 100

5. 0.062 × 100   **6.** 1.24 × 1,000

7. Mental Math Tell how you can use mental math to find the product of 5.8 × 1,000.

8. The baker buys ten 100-lb bags of flour. How many cups of flour are there in ten 100-lb bags? Use the data on page 130.

Independent Practice ☆

Leveled Practice Find each product.

Place-value understanding can help you solve these problems.

9. 4.23 × 1 = _____
   4.23 × 10 = _____
   4.23 × 100 = _____
   4.23 × 1,000 = _____

10. 0.086 × 1 = _____
   0.086 × 10 = _____
   0.086 × 100 = _____
   0.086 × 1,000 = _____

11. 63.7 × 10   **12.** 563.7 × 1,000   **13.** 0.365 × 100   **14.** 5.02 × 1,000

15. 94.6 × 1,000   **16.** 0.9463 × 100   **17.** 0.678 × 10   **18.** 681.7 × 100

19. 4.3 × 10   **20.** 0.32 × 100   **21.** 5.1 × 100   **22.** 1.02 × 1,000

23. 0.004 × 1,000   **24.** 0.001 × 10   **25.** 6.02 × 100   **26.** 5.07 × 10

Problem Solving

For **27** and **28**, use the table.

27. Monroe uses a microscope to observe specimens in science class. The microscope enlarges objects to 100 times their actual size. Complete the table to show the size of each specimen as seen in the microscope.

28. Monroe's teacher wants each student to draw a sketch of the longest specimen. Which specimen is the longest?

DATA	Specimen	Actual Length (cm)	Size Seen in the Microscope (cm)
	A	0.008	
	B	0.011	
	C	0.0025	
	D	0.004	

29. A sporting goods store had a total of 123 football jerseys. Following a weekend sale it has 28 jerseys left in stock. Solve the equation $123 - n = 28$ to find how many jerseys were sold over the weekend.

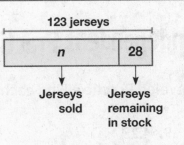

30. **Check for Reasonableness** Is 0.018 a reasonable answer for 1.8×100? Explain.

31. Jon's binoculars enlarge objects to 10 times their actual size. If the length of an ant is 0.43 inch, what is the length as seen up close through his binoculars?

   A 0.043 inch
   B 4.3 inches
   C 43 inches
   D 430 inches

32. **Reason** If you add a ten thousands digit that is 3 times the thousands digit to the number 3,721, what is the new number?

33. **Extend Your Thinking** Jefferson drew a line 9.5 inches long. Brittany drew a line 10 times as long. What is the difference in length between the two lines?

Another Look!

A builder is installing tiles at a restaurant. The area of each tile is 0.25 square meter. What is the area of 1,000 tiles?

$0.25 \times 1 = 0.25$
$0.25 \times 10 = 2.5$
$0.25 \times 100 = 25$
$0.25 \times 1,000 = 250$

So, the area of 1,000 tiles is 250 square meters.

Use patterns and place value to help you multiply a decimal by 10, 100, or 1,000.

For **1** and **2**, use patterns to find the products.

1. $0.057 \times 1 =$ _____
   $0.057 \times 10 =$ _____
   $0.057 \times 100 =$ _____
   $0.057 \times 1,000 =$ _____

2. $13.09 \times 1 =$ _____
   $13.09 \times 10 =$ _____
   $13.09 \times 100 =$ _____
   $13.09 \times 1,000 =$ _____

For **3** through **16**, find each product.

3. 0.62×10

4. 0.0063×100

Each zero in the second factor moves the decimal point one place to the right.

5. $7.25 \times 1,000$

6. 19.212×100

7. 17.07×10

8. 6.1×10

9. 37.96×100

10. $0.024 \times 1,000$

11. 0.418×100

12. $92.3 \times 1,000$

13. 5.001×10

14. $1.675 \times 1,000$

15. 14.04×10

16. 843.5×100

17. Jennifer planted a tree that was 0.17 meter tall. After 10 years, the tree was 100 times as tall as when she planted it. What is the height of the tree after 10 years?

A 0.017 meter
B 1.7 meters
C 17 meters
D 170 meters

18. Justify Marco and Suzi each multiplied 0.721 × 100. Marco got 7.21 for his product. Suzi got 72.1 for her product. Which student multiplied correctly? How do you know?

19. The table shows the distance a truck can travel using one gallon of gasoline. Complete the table to find the number of miles the truck can travel for the given number of gallons of gasoline.

What pattern do you see in the table?

DATA	Gallons	Miles
	1	14.5
	10	
	100	
	1,000	

20. A square chess board has sides measuring 16 inches. What is the area of the chess board? What is the area of each small square in the chess board?

The formula for area of a square is A = s × s.

16 in.

21. Reason Give an example of two numbers that are both 6-digit numbers, but the greater number is determined by the hundreds place.

22. Extend Your Thinking A store has a contest to guess the mass of 10,000 peanuts. If a peanut has a mass of about 0.45 gram, what would be a reasonable guess for the mass of 10,000 peanuts?

☆ ★
Solve & Share

Renee needs 32 strands of twine for an art project. Each strand must measure 1.25 cm long. About how much twine does she need for the project? *Solve this problem any way you choose!*

Connect Ideas You know how to estimate with whole numbers. *Show your work!*

Lesson 3-7
Estimating the Product of a Decimal and a Whole Number

⭐ TEKS 5.3A Estimate to determine solutions to mathematical and real-world problems involving addition, subtraction, multiplication, or division. Also, 5.2C. Mathematical Process Standards 5.1A, 5.1C, 5.1D, 5.1G

Digital Resources at PearsonTexas.com

Solve   Learn   Glossary   Check   Tools   Games

Look Back!

Justify Is your estimate an overestimate or an underestimate? How can you tell?

What Are Some Ways to Estimate Products with Decimals?

A planner for a wedding needs to buy 16 pounds of sliced cheddar cheese. About how much will the cheese cost?

The words *about how much* mean you only need an estimate.

$2.15 per pound

You can use different ways to estimate a product.

B One Way

Round each number to the greatest place that has a non-zero digit.

$$\$2.15 \times 16$$
$$\$2 \quad \times \quad 20$$

$2 × 20 = $40

The cheese will cost about $40.

C Another Way

Use compatible numbers that you can multiply mentally.

$$\$2.15 \times 16$$
$$\$2 \quad \times \quad 15$$

$2 × 15 = $30

The cheese will cost about $30.

Do You Understand?

Convince Me! About how much money would 18 pounds of cheese cost if the price is $3.95 per pound? Use two different ways to estimate the product. Which of your estimates is closer to the actual cost? Explain.

Another Example

Manuel walks 0.75 mile to and from school each day. If there have been 114 school days so far this year, about how many miles has he walked all together?

Round to the nearest whole number.

114×0.75

$\downarrow \qquad \downarrow$

$114 \times 1 = 114$

Use compatible numbers.

114×0.75

$\downarrow \qquad \downarrow$

$100 \times 0.8 = 80$ Be sure to move the decimal point correctly.

Both methods provide reasonable estimates of how far Manuel has walked.

☆ Guided Practice*

In **1** through **6**, estimate each product using rounding or compatible numbers.

1. 0.87×112 **2.** 104×0.33

3. 9.02×80 **4.** 0.54×24

5. 33.05×200 **6.** 0.79×51

7. Explain About how many miles does Manuel walk each month during the school year? Explain your answer.

8. Communicate How can estimating be helpful before finding an actual product?

Independent Practice ☆

Estimate each product.

9. 0.12×105 **10.** 45.3×4 **11.** 99.2×82 **12.** 37×0.93

13. 1.67×4 **14.** 3.2×184 **15.** 12×0.37 **16.** 0.904×75

Problem Solving

Souvenir	Cost
Button	$1.95
T-Shirt	$12.50

17. About how much money does Stan need to buy 5 T-shirts and 10 buttons?

18. Joseph buys a pair of shorts for $17.95 and 4 T-shirts. About how much money does he spend?

19. Marcy picked 18.8 pounds of peaches at the pick-your-own orchard. Each pound costs $1.28. Which is the best estimate for the cost of Marcy's peaches?

A $12
B $26
C $40
D $52

20. Connect Ms. Webster works 4 days a week at her office and 1 day a week at home. The route to Ms. Webster's office is 23.7 miles. The route home is 21.8 miles. About how many miles does she drive for work each week? Explain how you found your answer.

21. The Perez family ranch now covers 13,496 acres. If they buy 2,495 more acres from a neighbor, how large will their ranch be?

22. Extend Your Thinking Jerome needs 26.9 yards of fabric to make bandannas for the Humane Society's pet parade. The fabric costs $7.65 per yard. Find an underestimate and an overestimate for the cost of the fabric.

Find and answer the hidden question to solve the problem.

23. Personal Financial Literacy Joshua has $20. He spends $4.58 and $7.43. He shares $3.50. How much money does he have left? Show how you found the answer.

Another Look!

Zane needs to buy 27 party favors for the family reunion. The favors cost $2.98 each. About how much will the party favors cost?

You can estimate to check the reasonableness of your product.

There are two ways you can estimate.

Round both numbers.

$2.98 × 27

$3 × 30 = $90
The favors will cost about $90.

Replace the factors with compatible numbers and multiply mentally.

$2.98 × 27

$3 × 25 = $75
The favors will cost about $75.

1. Zane needs 0.8 ounce of lime juice per person for the punch he is making. He wants to make about 32 servings of punch. Estimate how much lime juice he needs using rounding. Show how you solved the problem.

2. Jo wants to make 125 servings of the same punch that Zane makes. Estimate how much lime juice she needs. Show how you solved the problem.

Estimate each product.

3. 19.3 × 6

4. 345 × 5.79

5. 9.66 × 0.46

6. 8.02 × 70

7. 1.56 × 48

8. 45.1 × 5

9. 0.13 × 11

10. 99.7 × 92

11. 147 × 10.4

12. 23.7 × 4.76

13. 3 × 0.85

14. 0.35 × 9

15. Can Mrs. Davis and her two sisters get their hair colored for less than $100 if they include a $10 tip? Explain.

16. If Mrs. Davis and her sisters also get haircuts, about how much will they pay all together?

DATA	Treatment	Cost
	Shampoo	$7.95
	Haircut	$14.95
	Coloring	$28.95

---

17. Mrs. Smith bought her three children new raincoats. Each raincoat cost $25.99. Which is the best estimate for the amount Mrs. Smith spent on raincoats?

A $26

B $50

C $75

D $150

18. Dentalia shells were used by some Native American tribes to make jewelry. Each dentalia shell is 1.25 inches long. If a necklace had been made with 18 dentalia shells, about how long was this necklace? Explain your estimate.

---

19. Connect In the football stadium, there are 56,244 seats. There are 48,889 tickets sold for Saturday's game. How many seats will be empty on Saturday?

20. Extend Your Thinking Lana got a tip of 16%, or 0.16 for delivering pizzas for a party. If the total bill for the pizza was $98.19, about how much was Lana's tip?

---

21. Tools A youth hockey league is selling popcorn to raise money for new uniforms. Sidney sold 9 boxes for a total of $72 in sales. Use the strip diagram and write an equation to find the value of c, the cost of each box sold by Sidney.

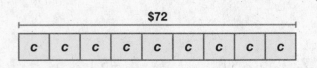

Name _____

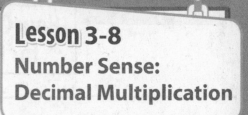

Solve & Share

Three students in Ms. Cho's class wrote the following problems on the board. The correct digits in the products are given, but the decimal point isn't placed yet. Where should the decimal point go in each product?

TEKS 5.3E Solve for products of decimals to the hundredths, including situations involving money, using strategies based on place-value understandings, properties of operations, and the relationship to the multiplication of whole numbers. Also, 5.3. Mathematical Process Standards 5.1A, 5.1B 5.1C, 5.1D, 5.1F

1. $7.85 \times 16 = 1256$

2. $0.98 \times 0.5 = 49$

3. $1.06 \times 1.5 = 159$

Digital Resources at PearsonTexas.com

| Solve | Learn | Glossary | Check | Tools | Games |

You can use **number sense** about the size of each factor to help you. *Show your work!*

Look Back!

Analyze Relationships If both factors are less than 1, what do you know about their product?

How Can You Use Number Sense for Decimal Multiplication?

A-Z

You have learned how to estimate when multiplying with decimals. You can also use number sense to reason about the relative size of factors and the product. Where does the decimal point go?

$$45.20 \times 0.55 = 2486$$

You can use number sense to put the decimal point in the correct place.

B Think about the relative size of the factors.

Multiplying a number by a decimal less than 1 gives a product less than the other factor.

Since 0.55 is less than 1, the product is less than 45.2.

Since 0.55 is about half, the decimal point should be between the 4 and 8.

$$45.2 \times 0.55 = 24.86$$

C Use number sense to think about factors.

What decimal can be written to give the reasonable answer shown?

_____ × 5.1 is about 30.

6.1 × 5.1 is about 30.

6 times 5 equals 30, so the other factor has to be close to 6.

Do You Understand?

Convince Me! The decimal point is missing in the answer for each of these problems. Use number sense to decide where the decimal point should be. Explain your thinking.

$$54.7 \times 0.53 = 28991$$

$$54.7 \times 5.3 = 28991$$

☆ Guided Practice ☆

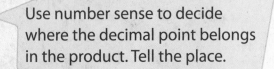

Use number sense to decide where the decimal point belongs in the product. Tell the place.

1. 5 × 3.4 = 17

2. 3.1 × 6.2 = 1922

3. 0.6 × 0.4 = 24

4. Communicate Describe the unknown factor.

_____ × 5.1 is about 300.

5. Number Sense Janelle wrote 23.4 for the product of 7.8 × 0.3. Use number sense to decide if Janelle placed the decimal point in the product in the correct place. If it is incorrect, give the correct product.

☆ Independent Practice ☆

For **6** through **9**, the product is shown without the decimal point. Use number sense to place the decimal point appropriately.

6. 5.01 × 3 = 1503

7. 6.22 × 3 = 1866

8. 0.9 × 0.9 = 81

9. 1.8 × 1.9 = 342

For **10** through **15**, tell whether or not the decimal point has been placed correctly in the product. If not, rewrite the product with the decimal point correctly placed.

10. 12 × 4.8 = 57.6

11. 5.2 × 6.4 = 3.328

12. 6.99 × 21 = 14.679

13. 0.05 × 12.4 = 6.2

14. 18 × 3.38 = 60.84

15. 9.01 × 91 = 81.991

Problem Solving

16. Analyze Information A pig farmer needs 60 square feet to house a sow. Is the pen pictured to the right large enough? Explain.

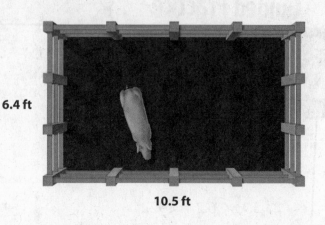

6.4 ft

10.5 ft

17. Communicate Quincey says that 3 is a good estimate for 3.4×0.09. Is he correct? Why?

Think of 0.09 as a fraction.

18. The moving company packed 12 boxes. Each box weighed 14.52 pounds. Which of the following is a reasonable estimate for the total weight of the boxes?

A 15 pounds
B 30 pounds
C 100 pounds
D 150 pounds

19. Connect Ron bought 2 DVDs for $12.95 each. He spent $25 on magazines. Did he spend more on DVDs or magazines? How much more?

20. Extend Your Thinking Given a product of 7.5, find two possible factors and write the multiplication equation.

21. Math and Science You can convert gallons to liters by using a factor of 3.79. About how many liters are in 37 gallons?

22. Extend Your Thinking Find two factors that would give a product of 0.22.

Name _____

Another Look!

Amelia can walk 3.6 miles in one hour.
How far can she walk in 2.1 hours?

$3.6 \times 2.1 = 756$
Use number sense to place the decimal in the product.

75.6 and 756 are not reasonable answers.
Amelia will walk 7.56 miles in 2.1 hours.

Think of a reasonable distance that Amelia can walk in about 2 hours.

1. Jordan enters 3.4×6.8 into his calculator. He writes the digits 2312 from the display and forgets the decimal point. Where should Jordan write the decimal point? Explain.

For **2** through **5**, the product is shown without the decimal point. Use number sense to place the decimal point appropriately.

2. $6 \times 5.01 = 3006$

3. $12.8 \times 3.2 = 4096$

4. $4.06 \times 20.1 = 8161$

5. $24 \times 6.3 = 1512$

For **6** through **11**, tell whether or not the decimal point has been placed correctly in the product. If not, rewrite the product with the decimal point correctly placed.

6. $0.6 \times 0.7 = 0.042$

7. $1.1 \times 13.8 = 1.518$

8. $8.6 \times 3 = 2.58$

9. $19 \times 8.3 = 157.7$

10. $2.8 \times 345.1 = 966.28$

11. $56.2 \times 7.9 = 4,439.8$

For **12** and **13**, use the data table.

12. **Connect** Mrs. Cooper has $20. Can she buy a museum ticket for her 10-year-old daughter, a ticket for herself, and a book that costs $3.99? Explain.

Science Museum	
Ticket	**Price**
Child	$5.75
Adult	$11.25

DATA

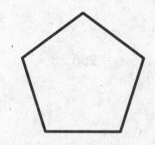

13. A family with 2 adults and 3 children is visiting the science museum. Will $40 be enough for them to get in? Explain how you know.

---

14. **Mental Math** Estimate the product of 3.9 and 4.6 using mental math. Explain the method you used.

15. **Reason** Will the actual product of 7.69×5 be greater than or less than its estimate of 8×5? Why?

---

16. One serving of yogurt has 95 calories. Which of the following is a reasonable estimate for the number of calories in 2.5 servings of yogurt?

    A 100 calories
    B 150 calories
    C 250 calories
    D 350 calories

17. **Extend Your Thinking** Bruce jogs from his house to the library and back again to tutor students. The distance from his house to the library is 0.28 mile. If Bruce tutored at the library 328 days last year, about how many miles did he jog?

---

18. Alicia drew a pentagon with equal side lengths and equal angles. Then she added red lines of symmetry to her drawing. How many lines did she draw? Use the picture to show how you know.

Name _____

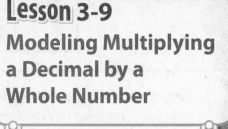

Lesson 3-9
Modeling Multiplying a Decimal by a Whole Number

Solve & Share

Mara has 4 garden plots. Each is 0.7 acre in area. How much area is covered by the garden plots? Use objects or the grids below to show your work.

How can you **use representations** to show decimal multiplication?

TEKS 5.3D Represent multiplication of decimals with products to the hundredths using objects and pictorial models, including area models. Also, 5.3E. Mathematical Process Standards 5.1A, 5.1C, 5.1D, 5.1E, 5.1G

Digital Resources at PearsonTexas.com

Solve   Learn   Glossary   Check   Tools   Games

Look Back!

Construct Arguments Ed says a decimal grid shows 10 tenths. Monica says a decimal grid shows 100 hundredths. Who is correct? Explain.

How Can You Multiply a Decimal by a Whole Number?

Bari displayed four paintings side-by-side in one row. Each painting has the same width. What is the total width of the 4 paintings?

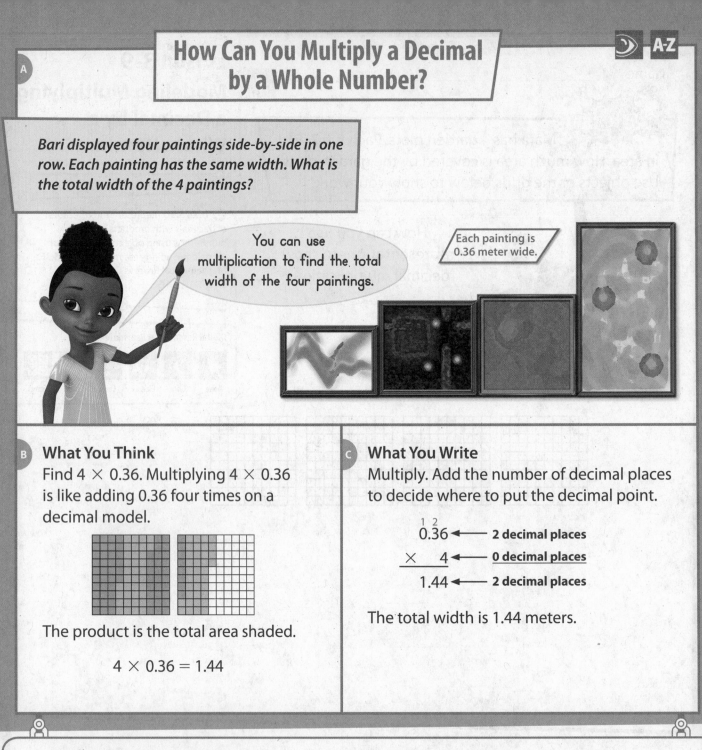

You can use multiplication to find the total width of the four paintings.

Each painting is 0.36 meter wide.

B   What You Think

Find 4 × 0.36. Multiplying 4 × 0.36 is like adding 0.36 four times on a decimal model.

The product is the total area shaded.

$$4 \times 0.36 = 1.44$$

C   What You Write

Multiply. Add the number of decimal places to decide where to put the decimal point.

$$
\begin{array}{r}
\overset{1\ \ 2}{0.36} \leftarrow \textbf{2 decimal places} \\
\times \qquad 4 \leftarrow \underline{\textbf{0 decimal places}} \\
1.44 \leftarrow \textbf{2 decimal places}
\end{array}
$$

The total width is 1.44 meters.

Do You Understand?

Convince Me! Bari also has 5 drawings that are each 0.27 meter wide. If they are set side-by-side, what would the total width be? Use the grids to show your work. Then find the product using an equation and compare the answers.

☆ Guided Practice*

In **1** through **4**, place the decimal point in the product.

1. 2 × 0.32 = 64   **2.** 3 × 1.5 = 45

3. 5 × 0.23 = 115   **4.** 8 × 1.06 = 848

In **5** through **8**, find the product. You may use grids to help.

5. 0.8 × 4   **6.** 0.7 × 21

7. 0.5 × 6   **8.** 0.6 × 5

9. **Tools** In the example on page 148, which method do you prefer to use to find the product, using a model or writing an equation? Explain.

10. **Explain** How can you place the decimal in the product when you multiply with decimals?

Independent Practice ☆

Leveled Practice In **11** through **13**, place the decimal point in the product.

You can use what you know about place value to help you!

11. 0.7 × 12 = 84   **12.** 2 × 2.04 = 408   **13.** 3 × 4.8 = 144

In **14** through **25**, find the product. You may use grids or arrays to help.

14. 5 × 0.5   **15.** 4 × 0.27   **16.** 6 × 0.13   **17.** 0.78 × 5

18. 10 × 0.32   **19.** 6 × 2.03   **20.** 1.35 × 5   **21.** 100 × 0.12

22. 4 × 0.15   **23.** 3 × 2.5   **24.** 0.9 × 7   **25.** 0.35 × 3

Problem Solving

26. Analyze Information Which activity is about 20 times as fast as the top swimming speed?

The abbreviation *mph* stands for miles per hour.

27. Extend Your Thinking Maya's dad tells her his boat can travel 3 times as fast as the fastest rowing speed. About how fast is her dad's boat? How can you tell?

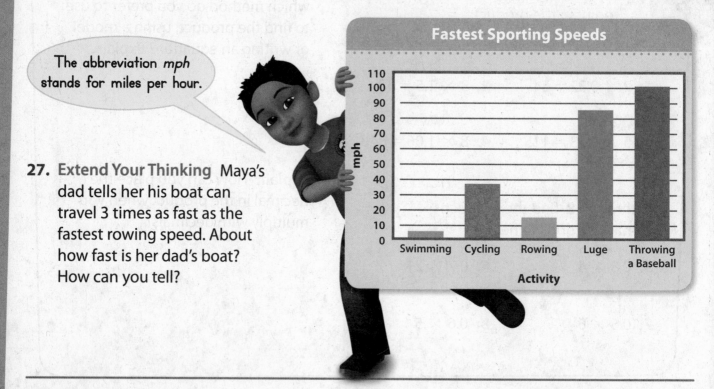

Fastest Sporting Speeds

mph

Activity: Swimming, Cycling, Rowing, Luge, Throwing a Baseball

28. ⭐ Which expression does this decimal model show?

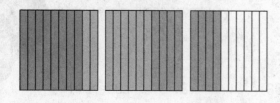

A 3×0.8
B $3 + 0.8$
C $3 \div 0.8$
D $3 - 0.8$

29. Estimation Jen solved the math sentence $9 \times 0.989 = 89.01$. How can you use estimation to show that Jen's answer is wrong? What mistake do you think she made?

30. Connect The distance between Dallas and Houston is 240 miles. In one month, a bus driver makes 14 round trips between the two cities. How far does she drive?

31. Math and Science In one county in Texas, electricity from wind power costs $0.05 per kWh (kilowatt-hour). Electricity from solar power costs $0.15 per kWh. How many times as great is the cost of one kilowatt-hour of solar power as the cost of one kilowatt-hour of wind power?

Name _____

Another Look!

A movie was shown in two parts. Part 1 was 1.3 hours long. Part 2 was twice as long as Part 1. How long was Part 2?

Use an area model and hundredths grids to find the product.

Shade 1.3 two times.

Count the hundredths squares in the shaded area to find the product.

$1.3 \times 2 = 2.6$ So, Part 2 of the movie was 2.6 hours long.

Multiply.

$$1.3 \leftarrow \text{1 decimal place}$$
$$\underline{\times\ 2} \leftarrow + \text{0 decimal places}$$
$$2.6 \leftarrow \text{1 decimal place}$$

Add the number of decimal places in the two factors to find the number of decimal places in the product.

1. Shade the model to find 0.4×3. Then show how to find the product using a multiplication equation.

2. Shade the model to find 0.08×6. Then write the product.

So, $0.08 \times 6 =$

For **3** through **5**, place the decimal point in the product.

3. $12 \times 0.08 = 96$

4. $24 \times 0.17 = 408$

5. $3.42 \times 5 = 171$

For **6** through **9**, find the product.

6. 3×0.33

7. 0.45×100

8. 3×6.89

9. 7.6×2

10. Connect Ryan measures the perimeter of his square painting so he can make a wood frame. Find the perimeter of the painting in centimeters and in meters.

├─── 30.5 centimeters ───┤

11. Which product is represented by the decimal model?

A 5.0
B 0.90
C 0.18
D 0.10

Remember, each small square is 1 hundredth.

12. Draw a Strip Diagram Anthony bikes a long trail near his house. The trail is 16.2 miles long. If he bikes it 4 times, how far will he have traveled? Draw a strip diagram to help you.

13. Estimation The wings of a ruby-throated hummingbird beat an average of 52 times per second. About how many times will its wings beat in a minute?

14. Monica buys 2.6 yards of fabric to make a tablecloth. Then she buys three times that amount of fabric for curtains. How much fabric does Monica buy in all?

15. Extend Your Thinking If $0.36 \times 4 = 1.44$, how would your product be different if the factors were 3.6 and 4?

16. Math and Science A school's 430 square meter rooftop solar panel generates about 1,100 kWh (kilowatt-hours) of electricity each month. What might be the panel's dimensions? Use one dimension that is not a whole number.

17. Connect If 14 giant solar power plants generate 2.6 gigawatts (GW) of energy to power 1.8 million homes, how many homes can 28 solar plants power?

Name _____

Solve & Share

A car travels 1.15 kilometers in 1 minute. If it travels at a constant speed, how far will it travel in 3 minutes? in 5 minutes? *Solve this problem any way you choose!*

🌐 TEKS 5.3E Solve for products of decimals to the hundredths, including situations involving money, using strategies based on place-value understandings, properties of operations, and the relationship to the multiplication of whole numbers. Also, 5.3. Mathematical Process Standards 5.1A, 5.1C, 5.1E, 5.1F, 5.1G

Digital Resources at PearsonTexas.com

| Solve | Learn | Glossary | Check | Tools | Games |

You can **connect** what you know about whole-number multiplication to multiplying a decimal by a whole number.

Look Back!

Connect How can addition be used to answer the questions above?

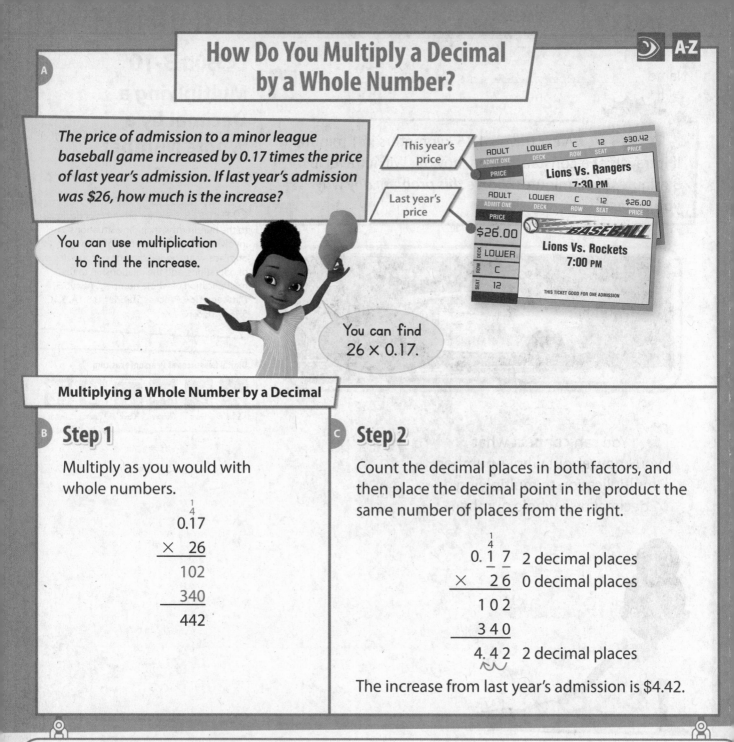

How Do You Multiply a Decimal by a Whole Number?

The price of admission to a minor league baseball game increased by 0.17 times the price of last year's admission. If last year's admission was $26, how much is the increase?

This year's price

Last year's price

ADULT	LOWER	C	12	$30.42
ADMIT ONE	DECK	ROW	SEAT	PRICE
PRICE				

Lions Vs. Rangers
7:30 PM

ADULT	LOWER	C	12	$26.00
ADMIT ONE	DECK	ROW	SEAT	PRICE
PRICE				
$26.00				

BASEBALL
Lions Vs. Rockets
7:00 PM

THIS TICKET GOOD FOR ONE ADMISSION

LOWER
ROW C
SEAT 12

You can use multiplication to find the increase.

You can find 26 × 0.17.

Multiplying a Whole Number by a Decimal

Step 1

Multiply as you would with whole numbers.

```
  1
  4
  0.17
×   26
  102
  340
  442
```

Step 2

Count the decimal places in both factors, and then place the decimal point in the product the same number of places from the right.

```
    1
    4
  0. 1 7    2 decimal places
×     2 6    0 decimal places
    1 0 2
    3 4 0
  4. 4 2    2 decimal places
```

The increase from last year's admission is $4.42.

Do You Understand?

Convince Me! Here are two similar problems:

```
   33        0.33
 × 19      × 19
  297       297
  330       330
  627       627
```

Place the decimal point correctly in each answer. Explain your thinking. How is multiplying decimals like multiplying whole numbers? How is it different?

© Pearson Education, Inc. 5

Name _____

For **1** through **6**, find each product.

1.   9.8
      $\times$ 2

2.   0.67
       $\times$ 8

3. 34 $\times$ 5.3

4. 34.6 $\times$ 21

5. 0.6 $\times$ 15

6. 55 $\times$ 1.1

7. Communicate What is the difference between multiplying a whole number by a decimal and multiplying two whole numbers?

8. Use the admission information on page 154. How much will admission cost to a minor league game this year? Explain how you found your answer.

Independent Practice

For **9** through **24**, find each product.

9.   34.6
      $\times$ 9

10.   56.3
       $\times$ 22

11.   405
       $\times$ 0.47

12.   9.32
       $\times$ 16

13. 64.2 $\times$ 20

14. 38.6 $\times$ 19

15. 40 $\times$ 0.22

16. 57 $\times$ 2.3

17. 5.8 $\times$ 11

18. 56 $\times$ 0.4

19. 170 $\times$ 0.003

20. 0.3 $\times$ 99

21. 26 $\times$ 1.61

22. 50 $\times$ 0.914

23. 10.76 $\times$ 100

24. 2.54 $\times$ 12

Problem Solving

25. Connect The table shows the heights of four boys. If the boys line up according to height from tallest to shortest, who is first in line?

Name	Height (cm)
Raul	145.52
Tim	151
Yuko	159.5
Joe	145.25

26. What is the difference in height between the tallest boy and the shortest boy? Write an equation to show your work.

---

27. To meet peak energy demand, an electric power cooperative buys back electricity generated locally. They pay $0.07 per solar-powered kWh (kilowatt-hour). How much money does a school make when it sells back 956 kWh to the cooperative?

Round and estimate to check for reasonableness.

28. The airline that Vince is using has a baggage weight limit of 41 pounds. He has two green bags, each weighing 18.4 pounds, and one blue bag weighing 3.7 pounds. What is the combined weight of his baggage?

A 22.1 lb
B 38.7 lb
C 40.5 lb
D 41 lb

---

29. Michael keeps track of how much time he uses on his family's computer each week for 10 weeks. He created the frequency table with the data he collected. How many hours in all did Michael spend on the computer?

Number of Hours	Frequency
$3\frac{1}{2}$	2
4	4
$4\frac{1}{2}$	3
5	1

---

30. Justify Sara is multiplying two factors, one with one decimal place and one with two decimal places. She says the product could have two decimal places. Is she correct? Explain.

31. Extend Your Thinking Heather clears a rectangular region in her yard for a garden. If the length is a one-digit whole number and the width is 5.5 meters, what is the least possible area? What is the greatest possible area? Explain how you found your answers.

Another Look!

Travis can read a book chapter in 2.3 hours.
The book has 18 chapters. How long will
it take Travis to read the book?

> 41.4 is a reasonable answer
> because 2 × 20 = 40.

Step 1

Multiply as with whole numbers.

$$
\begin{array}{r}
\overset{2}{2.3} \\
\times\ \ 18 \\
\hline
184 \\
+\ \ 230 \\
\hline
414
\end{array}
$$

Step 2

Count the total decimal places
in both factors.

2.3 1 decimal place
18   0 decimal places

Since there is a total of 1 decimal
place in the factors, there is 1 decimal
place in the product.

41.4

---

1. Each juice bottle contains 8.6 ounces.
How many ounces of juice are there
in a carton with 12 bottles?

2. Leslie is buying cans of diced tomatoes
that weigh 14.5 ounces each. If she buys
8 cans, how many total ounces does
she buy?

> For **3** through **14**, find each product.

3.
$$
\begin{array}{r}
27.4 \\
\times\ \ 7 \\
\hline
\end{array}
$$

4.
$$
\begin{array}{r}
336 \\
\times\ \ 0.4 \\
\hline
\end{array}
$$

5.
$$
\begin{array}{r}
88 \\
\times\ \ 1.8 \\
\hline
\end{array}
$$

6.
$$
\begin{array}{r}
4.02 \\
\times\ \ 9 \\
\hline
\end{array}
$$

7. 71.7 × 12

8. 105 × 0.4

9. 1.4 × 32

10. 0.89 × 21

11. 40.4 × 18

12. 0.3 × 279

13. 95 × 5.7

14. 46 × 0.46

15. Werner's Deli can make 2.2 sandwiches in 1 minute. How many sandwiches can Werner's make in 30 minutes?

A 66 C 22

B 60 D 15

16. Justify Tony's T-shirt Shop is selling 8 T-shirts for $96. Timothy's House of T-shirts sells 6 of the same T-shirts for $78. Which store has the better price? How can you tell?

17. If each month in Rock had the same average rainfall as in August, what would the total amount of rainfall be after 12 months?

18. List the deserts in order from greatest amount of rainfall in August to least amount of rainfall in August.

DATA	Desert Rainfall in August	
	Desert	**Average Rainfall (mm)**
	Lotus	0.1
	Rock	0.19
	Cactus	0.17

19. Number Sense Write two numbers that are greater than 32.467 and less than 32.567. Then find the difference of your two numbers.

20. Personal Financial Literacy Halley spent $35.28 buying supplies to make key chains. She sold 20 key chains for $4 each. What was her profit? That is, how much more money did she get from selling the key chains than she spent to make them? Tell how you found the answer.

21. A 100-watt solar power panel usually costs $146. They are on sale for 0.75 of the regular price. What is the sale price?

22. Extend Your Thinking A family has a huge array of solar panels to make electricity. If each month they sell back 420 kWh for $0.07 per kWh, how much money could they make in a year?

23. Carla had a piece of rope that was $14\frac{7}{8}$ in. long. She used some of the rope for a crafts project. Now there is $14\frac{3}{8}$ in. left. How much rope did she use? Write your answer in simplest form. Use the number line to help you solve.

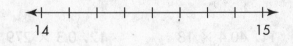

14   15

© Pearson Education, Inc. 5

Name _____

Solve & Share

A rectangle has an area of 0.24 square meter. What is one possibility for the length and width of the rectangle? Tell why. *Solve this problem any way you choose. You may use a hundredths grid if you like.*

TEKS 5.3D Represent multiplication of decimals with products to the hundredths using objects and pictorial models, including area models.
Mathematical Process Standards 5.1A, 5.1B, 5.1C, 5.1D, 5.1E

Digital Resources at PearsonTexas.com

| Solve | Learn | Glossary | Check | Tools | Games |

Create and Use Representations You can draw a picture on a hundredths grid to help you find the answer. *Show your work in the space below!*

0.1

Look Back!

Is there another pair of dimensions that would work? Explain how you know.

How Can You Model Decimal Multiplication?

A carpenter cut two shelves with the dimensions given below. Show how to use a model to find the area of each shelf.

Will each answer be greater or less than 1?

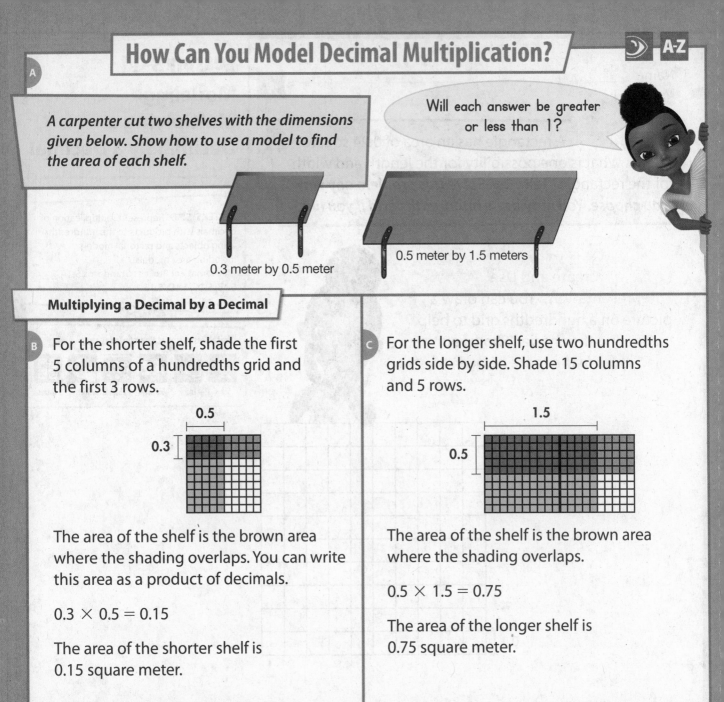

0.3 meter by 0.5 meter

0.5 meter by 1.5 meters

Multiplying a Decimal by a Decimal

B For the shorter shelf, shade the first 5 columns of a hundredths grid and the first 3 rows.

0.5

0.3

The area of the shelf is the brown area where the shading overlaps. You can write this area as a product of decimals.

$0.3 \times 0.5 = 0.15$

The area of the shorter shelf is 0.15 square meter.

C For the longer shelf, use two hundredths grids side by side. Shade 15 columns and 5 rows.

1.5

0.5

The area of the shelf is the brown area where the shading overlaps.

$0.5 \times 1.5 = 0.75$

The area of the longer shelf is 0.75 square meter.

Do You Understand?

Convince Me! Use the hundredths grid to model 0.6×0.7. Explain how to find the product.

160

Name _____

☆ **Guided Practice** *

For **1** and **2**, shade the hundredths grids to find the product.

1. 0.8 × 0.7

2. 2.1 × 0.1

3. Represent Each square shown has a side length of one-tenth unit. What multiplication equation does the drawing model?

4. Check for Reasonableness Explain why 2.7 is not a reasonable answer for 0.3 × 0.9. What is the correct answer?

Independent Practice ☆

For **5** through **8**, shade the hundredths grids to find the product.

Remember that the area where the shading overlaps represents the product.

5. 0.5 × 0.4

6. 0.7 × 0.3

7. 1.7 × 0.5

8. 1.2 × 0.6

For **9** through **16**, find the product. You may use grids to help.

9. 0.2 × 0.8

10. 2.4 × 0.7

11. 3.9 × 0.4

12. 0.5 × 0.7

13. 0.9 × 0.1

14. 0.2 × 1.5

15. 0.6 × 0.6

16. 2.8 × 0.3

For another example, see Set I on page 188. **Topic 3** | Lesson 3-11   **161**

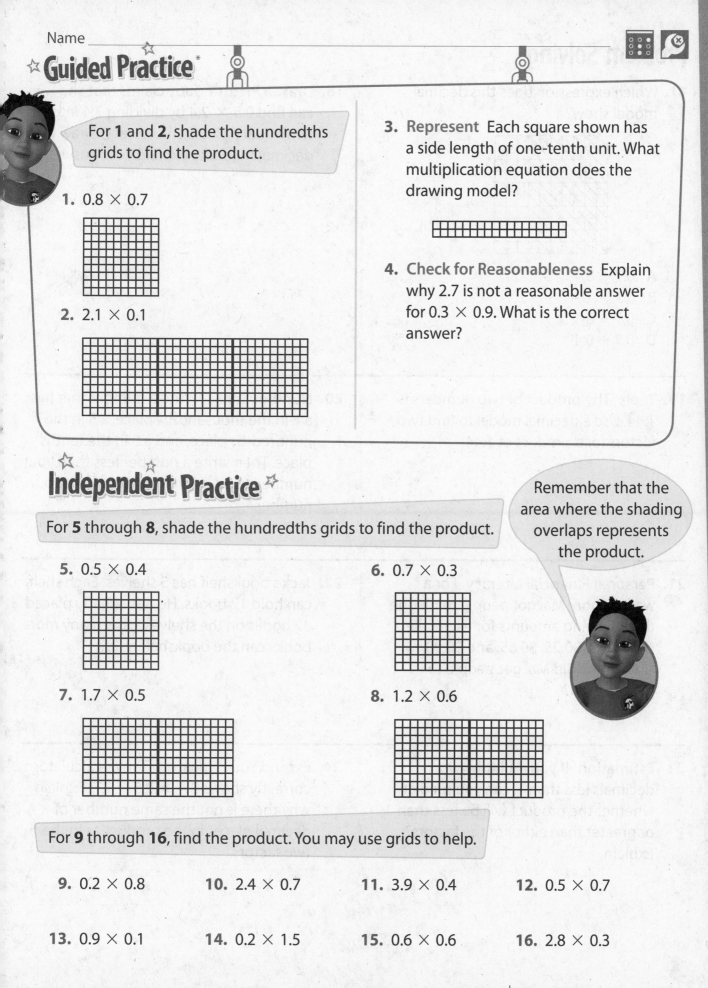

Problem Solving

17. Which expression does this decimal model show?

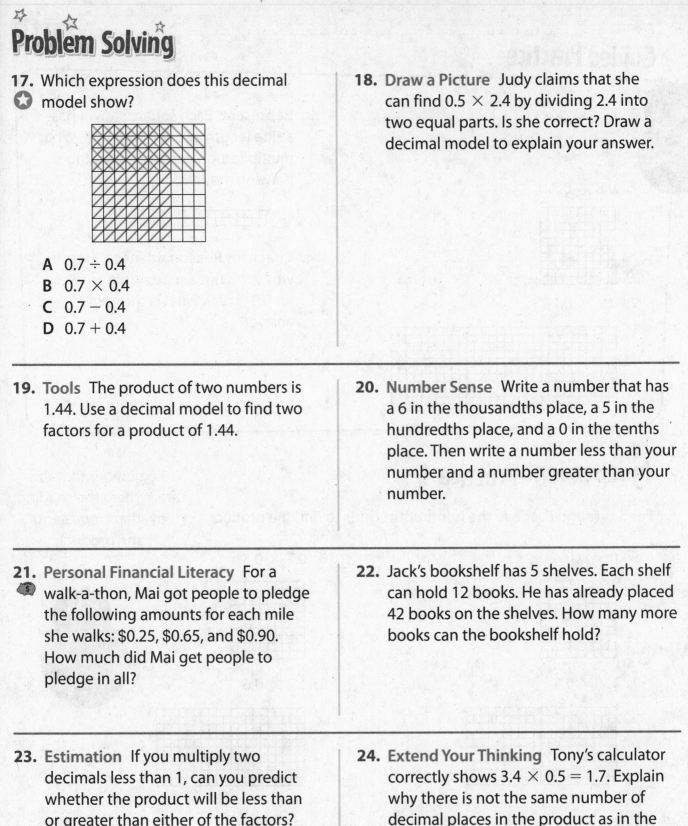

  A 0.7 ÷ 0.4
  B 0.7 × 0.4
  C 0.7 − 0.4
  D 0.7 + 0.4

18. **Draw a Picture** Judy claims that she can find 0.5 × 2.4 by dividing 2.4 into two equal parts. Is she correct? Draw a decimal model to explain your answer.

19. **Tools** The product of two numbers is 1.44. Use a decimal model to find two factors for a product of 1.44.

20. **Number Sense** Write a number that has a 6 in the thousandths place, a 5 in the hundredths place, and a 0 in the tenths place. Then write a number less than your number and a number greater than your number.

21. **Personal Financial Literacy** For a walk-a-thon, Mai got people to pledge the following amounts for each mile she walks: $0.25, $0.65, and $0.90. How much did Mai get people to pledge in all?

22. Jack's bookshelf has 5 shelves. Each shelf can hold 12 books. He has already placed 42 books on the shelves. How many more books can the bookshelf hold?

23. **Estimation** If you multiply two decimals less than 1, can you predict whether the product will be less than or greater than either of the factors? Explain.

24. **Extend Your Thinking** Tony's calculator correctly shows 3.4 × 0.5 = 1.7. Explain why there is not the same number of decimal places in the product as in the two factors.

Homework 3-11
Modeling Multiplying a Decimal by a Decimal

Another Look!

When you multiply the length by the width of a rectangular region, you find the area of the region.

Use area models to multiply a decimal by a decimal.

Find 0.7 × 0.9

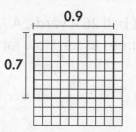

Use each factor as a side of a rectangle on a hundredths grid.

Shade the area of the 0.7 by 0.9 rectangle. Count the squares in the shaded area to find the product.

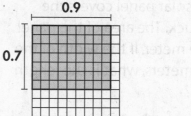

The shaded area contains 63 hundredths squares, so **0.7 × 0.9 = 0.63**.

In **1** through **3**, shade the hundredths grids to find the product.

1. 0.8 × 0.8

2. 0.5 × 0.6

3. 0.7 × 1.6

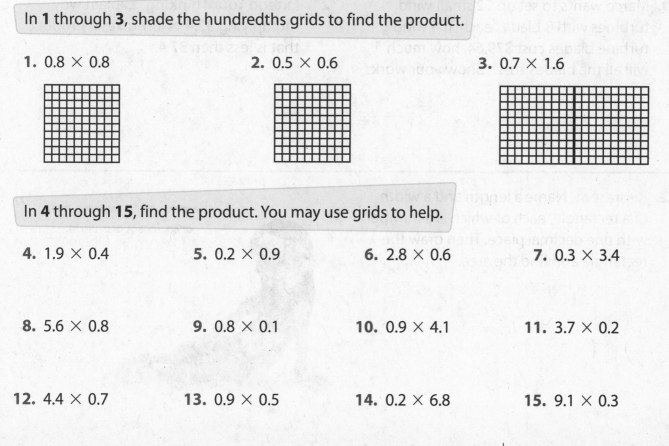

In **4** through **15**, find the product. You may use grids to help.

4. 1.9 × 0.4   **5.** 0.2 × 0.9   **6.** 2.8 × 0.6   **7.** 0.3 × 3.4

8. 5.6 × 0.8   **9.** 0.8 × 0.1   **10.** 0.9 × 4.1   **11.** 3.7 × 0.2

12. 4.4 × 0.7   **13.** 0.9 × 0.5   **14.** 0.2 × 6.8   **15.** 9.1 × 0.3

16. Phil uses the model below to help him multiply decimals. Which product is represented by the decimal model?

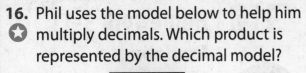

A 0.45
B 0.50
C 0.55
D 0.90

17. Number Sense Write a problem that uses multiplication of two decimals to find the answer. The product must have two decimal places.

18. Connect A solar panel covers the hood of a truck. The area of the panel is 0.8 square meter. If the width of the panel is 1.6 meters, what is the length of the panel?

19. Raul can hit a golf ball 26.4 yards. A.J. can hit a golf ball 10 times as far. How far can A.J. hit the ball?

20. Marco wants to set up 12 small wind turbines with 3 blades each. If 4 wind turbine blades cost $79.64, how much will all the blades cost? Show your work.

21. Extend Your Thinking Explain why multiplying 37.4 × 0.1 gives a product that is less than 37.4.

22. Represent Name a length and a width of a rectangle, each of which is a number with one decimal place. Then draw the rectangle and find the area.

Remember to express the area in square units.

Name _____

Solve & Share

Julie has 0.5 of her backyard set up for growing vegetables. Of the vegetable area, 0.4 has bell peppers in it. What part of the backyard contains bell peppers?

TEKS 5.3D Represent multiplication of decimals with products to the hundredths using objects and pictorial models, including area models. Also, 5.3, 5.3E. Mathematical Process Standards 5.1A, 5.1C, 5.1D, 5.1F, 5.1G

Digital Resources at PearsonTexas.com

Solve   Learn   Glossary   Check   Tools   Games

You can **create and use representations** to solve a problem. Remember, you can use a grid to find products.

Look Back!

Analyze Relationships What do you notice about the factors and their product in the above problem?

How Can You Multiply Two Decimals?

Nancy walked 1.7 miles in 1 hour. If she walks at the same rate, how far will she walk in 1.5 hours?

You can use properties or a model to represent the multiplication.

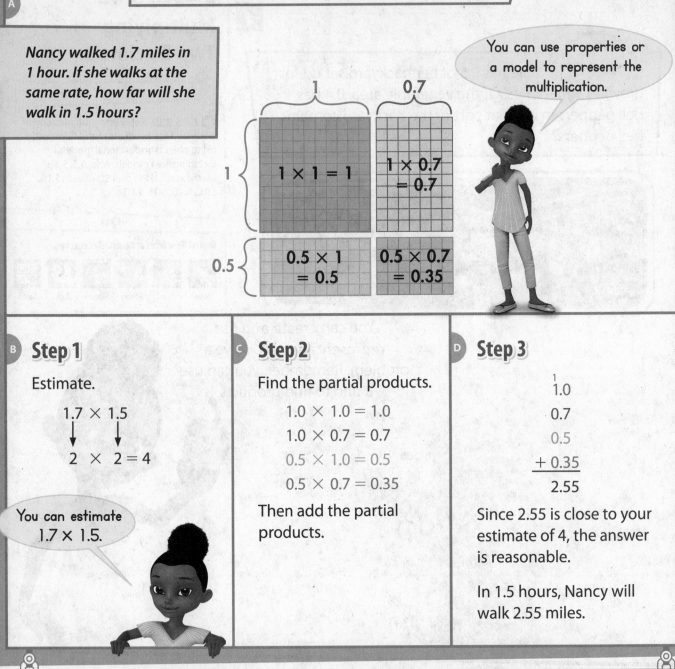

	1	0.7
1	$1 \times 1 = 1$	$1 \times 0.7 = 0.7$
0.5	$0.5 \times 1 = 0.5$	$0.5 \times 0.7 = 0.35$

B Step 1

Estimate.

$$1.7 \times 1.5$$
$$\downarrow \quad \downarrow$$
$$2 \times 2 = 4$$

You can estimate 1.7×1.5.

C Step 2

Find the partial products.

$$1.0 \times 1.0 = 1.0$$
$$1.0 \times 0.7 = 0.7$$
$$0.5 \times 1.0 = 0.5$$
$$0.5 \times 0.7 = 0.35$$

Then add the partial products.

D Step 3

$$\overset{1}{1.0}$$
$$0.7$$
$$0.5$$
$$\underline{+\ 0.35}$$
$$2.55$$

Since 2.55 is close to your estimate of 4, the answer is reasonable.

In 1.5 hours, Nancy will walk 2.55 miles.

Do You Understand?

Convince Me! In the example above, how many miles will Nancy walk in 2.8 hours? Estimate first, then compare your answer to the estimate.

Name _____

For **1** through **4**, estimate first. Then find each product. Check that your answer is reasonable.

1.   9.3
    × 4.1

2.   3.2
    × 0.6

3. 0.7 × 1.9

4. 12.6 × 0.2

5. **Communicate** How is multiplying two decimals different from multiplying one decimal by a whole number?

6. Carter is filling 6.5-ounce bottles with salsa that he made for gifts. He was able to fill 7.5 bottles. How many ounces of salsa did he make?

☆ Independent Practice ☆

For **7** through **22**, estimate first. Then find each product. Check that your answer is reasonable.

7.   5.2
    × 4.6

8.   19.1
    × 8.5

9.   0.5
    × 4.5

10.   8.6
    × 0.8

11. 32.3 × 0.7

12. 3.5 × 0.4

13. 6.8 × 7.2

14. 8.3 × 6.4

15. 9.1 × 11.6

16. 18.1 × 3.7

17. 0.6 × 1.5

18. 2.8 × 3.7

19. 5.5 × 0.6

20. 52.2 × 1.6

21. 3.9 × 26.1

22. 15.8 × 1.3

Problem Solving

23. Math and Science The gravity of Venus is 0.35 times that of Jupiter. What is the gravity of Venus in relation to Earth's gravity?

24. About how many times as great is Jupiter's relative surface gravity as Neptune's relative surface gravity?

Relative (to Earth) Surface Gravity

Planet	Gravity
Mercury	0.39
Neptune	1.22
Jupiter	2.6

25. Joy drinks 4.5 bottles of water per day. Each bottle contains 16.5 fluid ounces. How many fluid ounces of water does she drink per day?

A 20.10 fluid ounces
B 64.00 fluid ounces
C 74.25 fluid ounces
D 82.50 fluid ounces

26. Isaac bought three packages of nuts. He bought one package of peanuts that weighed 3.07 pounds. He also bought two packages of pecans that weighed 1.46 pounds and 1.5 pounds. Did the peanuts or the pecans weigh more? How much more?

27. Explain How does estimation help you place the decimal point in a product correctly?

28. Extend Your Thinking The area of a Dimitri's table top is a whole number of square feet. Could the length and width be decimal numbers each with one decimal place? Explain your answer.

29. Connect One quart of water weighs about 2.1 pounds. If there are 4 quarts in a gallon, how much does a gallon of water weigh?

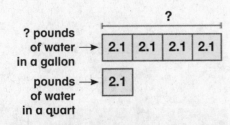

30. One square mile equals 2.6 square kilometers. How many square kilometers are in 14.4 square miles?

Name _____

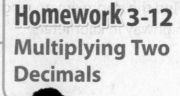
Another Look!

If a semi-truck travels 9.5 miles on 1 gallon of fuel, how many miles will the truck travel on 5.6 gallons of fuel?

Step 1

First, estimate your product so you can check for reasonableness.

$$9.5 \times 5.6$$

$$10 \times 6 = 60$$

Step 2

Find the partial products. Then add.

$$
\begin{array}{r}
9.5 \\
\times\ 5.6 \\
\end{array}
$$

$$
\begin{aligned}
0.6 \times 0.5 &= 0.30 \\
0.6 \times 9 &= 5.4 \\
5 \times 0.5 &= 2.5 \\
5 \times 9 &= \underline{45} \\
& \quad 53.2
\end{aligned}
$$

The truck will travel 53.2 miles on 5.6 gallons of fuel.
Since 53.2 is close to the estimate 60, the answer is reasonable.

---

1. If a truck travels 8.6 miles on 1 gallon of fuel, how many miles will the truck travel on 9.2 gallons of fuel? Estimate. Then find the product. Is your answer is reasonable? Explain.

$$8.6 \times 9.2$$

$$\square \times \square = \square$$

$$
\begin{array}{r}
8.6 \\
\times\ 9.2 \\
\end{array}
$$

For **2** through **13**, estimate first. Then find each product. Check that your answer is reasonable.

2. $\begin{array}{r} 0.2 \\ \times\ 4.6 \\ \hline \end{array}$

3. $\begin{array}{r} 3.9 \\ \times\ 7.1 \\ \hline \end{array}$

4. $\begin{array}{r} 5.4 \\ \times\ 0.1 \\ \hline \end{array}$

5. $\begin{array}{r} 15.3 \\ \times\ 6.4 \\ \hline \end{array}$

6. 9.3×5.8

7. 23.7×4.4

8. 0.8×0.5

9. 13.2×0.3

10. 7.9×6.8

11. 1.6×26.1

12. 0.9×0.6

13. 0.5×96.4

14. Find the approximate length of each highway in kilometers.

DATA	Highway	Length (miles)
	A	11.9
	B	46.2
	C	121

One mile is about 1.6 kilometers.

15. Connect Karly's bedroom measures 13.2 feet long by 10.3 feet wide. Use the formula Area = length × width to determine the number of square feet for the floor of Karly's bedroom.

16. A bag of grass seed weighs 5.8 pounds. ⭐ How many pounds would 2.5 bags weigh?

A 14.5 pounds
B 13.8 pounds
C 8.3 pounds
D 3.3 pounds

17. Adrian bought fruit to make a salad for the picnic. He bought 0.89 pound of grapes, 2.45 pounds of oranges, and 1.49 pounds of apples. What is the weight of the fruit?

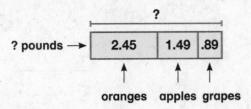

18. Estimation In exercise 17, suppose grapes cost $2.35 per pound, oranges cost $0.99 per pound, and apples cost $1.65 per pound. Rounding to the nearest whole number, about how much did Adrian pay for all the fruit?

19. Extend Your Thinking Why does multiplying numbers by 10 move the decimal point to the right, but multiplying by 0.10 moves the decimal point to the left?

20. Connect A pick-your-own pecan farm charges $1.35 per pound of pecans plus $0.40 per pound to crack the pecans. Amelia picks 20 pounds of pecans. The farm cracks 5 pounds for her. How much does Amelia pay all together?

© Pearson Education, Inc. 5

Name _____

☆ ☆ ☆
Solve & Share

Susan is making sandwiches for a picnic. She needs 1.2 pounds of ham, 1.5 pounds of bologna, and 2 pounds of cheese. How much will she spend? *Solve this problem any way you choose.*

Estimation About how much money can Susan expect to spend? Estimating first helps you check that your exact answer is reasonable.

price per pound	
Ham	$3.40
Bologna	$2.90
Cheese	$4.99

⚡ TEKS 5.3E Solve for products of decimals to the hundredths, including situations involving money, using strategies based on place-value understandings, properties of operations, and the relationship to the multiplication of whole numbers. Also, 5.3. Mathematical Process Standards 5.1A, 5.1B, 5.1C, 5.1D, 5.1E

Digital Resources at PearsonTexas.com

Solve   Learn   Glossary   Check   Tools   Games

Look Back!

Number Sense Does your answer make sense? Is it close to your estimate?

A

Alex is buying vegetables for dinner. He buys 6 ears of corn, 1.4 pounds of green beans, and 2.5 pounds of potatoes. How much money does he spend?

Green Beans	$0.80/lb
Potatoes	$0.60/lb
Corn	$1.20/ear

B

First I'll estimate. I'll round each decimal to the nearest whole number.

Corn
6 × $1 = $6

Green beans
1 × $1 = $1

Potatoes
3 × $1 = $3

Alex spends about 6 + 1 + 3 = $10.

Now I'll find the exact answer.

Multiply with money as you would multiply with decimals.

Corn
$\overset{1}{\$1.20}$
$\times\ \ \ 6$
$\$7.20$

Green beans
$\overset{3}{1.4}$
$\times\ 0.80$
$1.120 = \$1.12$

Potatoes
$\overset{3}{2.5}$
$\times\ 0.60$
$1.500 = \$1.50$

Now add the subtotals:

$7.20
$1.12
+ $1.50
$9.82 Alex spends $9.82 on vegetables.

Money is shown with 2 decimal places.

Do You Understand?

Convince Me! If 7 × 35 = 245, explain how to find 0.7 × $3.50.

☆ Guided Practice *

For **1** through **4**, estimate first. Then find each product. Check that your answer is reasonable.

1. $0.70 × 2.5   **2.** $26.35 × 0.6

3. $3.60 × 12   **4.** $14.90 × 8

5. Reason One of the factors in a multiplication is less than 1. How does the product compare to the other factor?

6. Mary Ann ordered 3 pens and a box of paper on the Internet. Each pen cost $1.65 and the paper cost $3.95 per box. How much did Mary Ann spend?

Estimate first to decide if Mary Ann spent more than $10.

Independent Practice ☆

For **7** through **18**, estimate first. Then find each product. Check that your answer is reasonable.

7. $0.80
     × 14

8. $18.49
     × 4

9. $2.98
     × 21

10. $30.90
     × 6

11. $8.42 × 2.5   **12.** $0.16 × 0.5   **13.** $51.05 × 0.2   **14.** $4.40 × 3.2

15. $3.96 × 1.5   **16.** $0.65 × 1.2   **17.** $9.50 × 0.8   **18.** $0.04 × 3.5

Problem Solving

For **19**, refer to the prices at the right.

$7.55

$15.50

19. Connect Mia is shopping and has $25 in her wallet and a coupon worth $4 off the cost of a dress.

   A How much money will the dress cost if she uses the coupon?

   B Find the total cost of 3 shirts.

   C How much change will Mia get back from $25 after she buys the 3 shirts?

---

20. Analyze Information Charles is at the grocery store to buy 2 loaves of bread. How much will this cost him?

21. Janet has $20.00 in her pocket. Will she be able to buy 11 bars of soap? If so, how much will the 11 bars cost? If not, how much more money does she need?

At the Grocery Store	
Item	**Price**
Bar of soap	$1.60
Bag of chips	$2.75
Loaf of bread	$3.48
Pound cake	$8.95

---

22. ★ To determine the tip for a restaurant server, many people multiply the amount of the check by 0.15. Which would be the amount of tip on a check of $25?

   A $1.25

   B $1.50

   C $2.50

   D $3.75

23. The Parents' Club will need 100 of the same item for International Night. They have a budget of $250. The choices are 100 baseball hats at $2.45 each, 100 sports bottles at $2.50 each, or 100 flags at $2.75 each. Which item(s) can they afford to buy?

---

24. A pound of nails costs $13. Joe buys 2.4 pounds. How much does Joe spend on nails? If there are 200 nails in a pound, how many nails does Joe have?

25. Extend Your Thinking Jason saved $0.02 each day for 1,000 days. How much did he save in all? About how many years did it take him to save this amount? Explain.

Another Look!

Caroline earns $5.40 per hour for babysitting her brother. She babysat for 2.5 hours on Friday and 4 hours on Saturday. How much did Caroline earn?

Estimate.

$5.40 × 2.5
$5 × 3 = $15

$5.40 × 4
$5 × 4 = $20

$15 + $20 = $35

Multiply.

$$\begin{array}{r} \overset{2}{\$5.40} \\ \times\ \ 2.5 \\ \hline 2700 \\ +\ 1080 \\ \hline \$13.500 \end{array}$$

13.500 = $13.50

$$\begin{array}{r} \overset{1}{\$5.40} \\ \times\ \ \ \ 4 \\ \hline \$21.60 \end{array}$$

Add.

$$\begin{array}{r} \overset{1}{\$13.50} \\ +\ \$21.60 \\ \hline \$35.10 \end{array}$$

Caroline earned $35.10.

$35.10 is close to the estimate $35. So, the answer is reasonable.

For **1**, estimate first, then find each product. Check that your answer is reasonable.

1. Rocco sells his used books at a garage sale. He sells paperback books for $1.20 each and hardcover books for $2.25 each. He sells 12 paperback and 9 hardcover books. How much does Rocco earn? Estimate. Then find the answer. Is your answer reasonable? Explain.

2. $0.50
   × 13

3. $22.39
   × 3

4. $1.98
   × 42

5. $40.60
   × 5

6. $7.62 × 1.5

7. $0.08 × 0.5

8. $37.05 × 0.2

9. $6.25 × 3.2

10. $11.24 × 6.5

11. 7 × $0.27

12. 1.4 × $5.85

13. $12.62 × 4.5

14. ⭐ George buys 1.5 pounds of apples, 2.7 pounds of oranges, and 1.9 pounds of grapes. How much change does he get from a $10 bill?

    A $3.05

    B $6.95

    C $7.40

    D $8.50

Apples	$0.30/lb
Grapes	$0.80/lb
Oranges	$0.40/lb

The table shows the coins saved by Tina and her sister for one year.

15. Find the total value of each type of coin the girls have saved.

16. Find the total value for the coins saved by the sisters.

Type of Coin	Number Saved
	1,000
	100
	1,000
	10

17. Represent The fifth-grade planning committee needs to buy items for sandwiches for its annual lunch. Complete the chart to determine the amount of money they'll need to buy each item. Then find the cost to buy all of the items for sandwiches.

Item	Amount	Price	Total
	15.5 pounds	$3.50 per pound	
	10.5 pounds	$2.90 per pound	
	12 packages	$2.50 per package	

18. Analyze Information Reba is making a tablecloth. She needs 3.6 yards of fabric and has $20.00 to spend. Floral fabric costs $4.95 per yard, and striped fabric is $5.75 per yard. Can Reba afford either fabric? Explain.

19. Extend Your Thinking Jackie wants to download songs to her computer. Each song costs $1.99. She has $15 and a coupon for $2.00. How many songs can Jackie download? Explain.

Name _____

Solve & Share

Kevin took 139 standard photos and 109 high-definition photos on a field trip. Marco took 2 times as many standard photos and 3 times as many high-definition photos as Kevin. How many photos did Marco take? *Solve this problem any way you choose.*

Lesson 3-14
Draw a Strip Diagram and Write an Equation

★ TEKS 5.1D Communicate mathematical ideas, reasoning, and their implications using multiple representations, including symbols, diagrams, graphs, and language as appropriate. Also, 5.4B.
Mathematical Process Standards 5.1A, 5.1B, 5.1C, 5.1E, 5.1F, 5.1G

Digital Resources

Solve   Learn   A-Z   Check   Tools   Games
        Glossary

Use a representation How can a strip diagram help you show the problem?

Look Back!
Check for Reasonableness How can you tell if your answer is reasonable?

How Can You Use a Strip Diagram to Solve a Multiplication Problem?

A Analyze

In 1980, a painting was bought for $575. In 2010, the same painting sold for 5 times as much. What was the price of the painting in 2010?

You read the problem and you can draw a strip diagram and use a variable to find the new price of the painting.

B Plan and Solve

What am I asked to find?

The price of the painting in 2010.

Let p = the price of the painting in 2010.

price in 2010 (p)

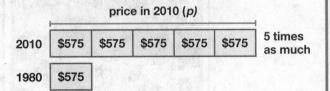

2010	$575 $575 $575 $575 $575 — 5 times as much
1980	$575

$575 \times 5 = p$
$575 \times 5 = \$2{,}875.$
So, $p = \$2{,}875.$

In 2010, the painting sold for $2,875.

C Justify and Evaluate

Justify and explain your work.

The painting cost 5 times as much in 2010. Multiply to combine equal groups. The price, $2,875, is 5 times $575. The answer is correct.

Evaluate the problem-solving process.

My problem-solving process is complete. I analyzed the problem, made a plan, solved the problem, and justified my answer.

Do You Understand?

Convince Me! How can you use estimation to justify that the answer $2,875 is reasonable?

☆ Guided Practice *

Complete the labels for the strip diagram and write an equation. Solve.

1. Sharon's Stationery Store has 219 boxes of cards. May's Market has 3 times as many boxes of cards. How many boxes of cards does May's Market have?

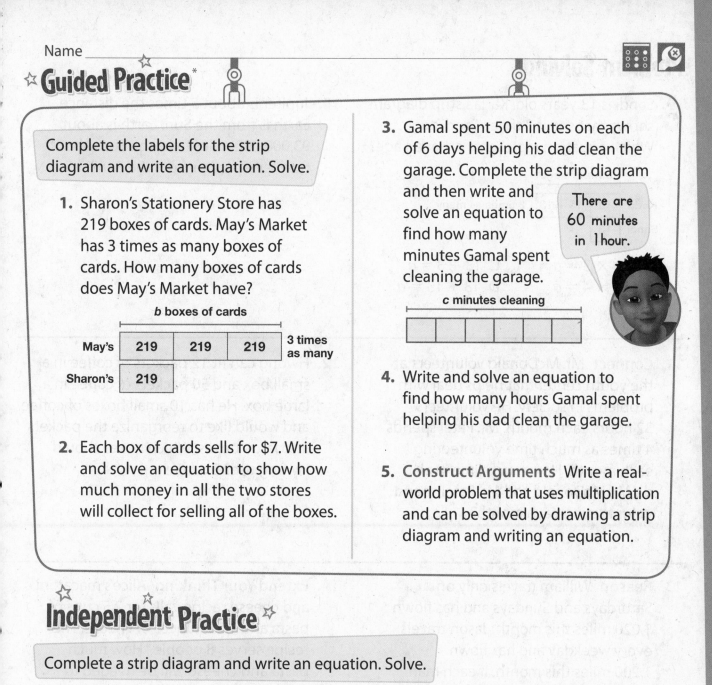

b boxes of cards

| May's | 219 | 219 | 219 | 3 times as many |
| Sharon's | 219 | | | |

2. Each box of cards sells for $7. Write and solve an equation to show how much money in all the two stores will collect for selling all of the boxes.

3. Gamal spent 50 minutes on each of 6 days helping his dad clean the garage. Complete the strip diagram and then write and solve an equation to find how many minutes Gamal spent cleaning the garage.

> There are 60 minutes in 1 hour.

c minutes cleaning

4. Write and solve an equation to find how many hours Gamal spent helping his dad clean the garage.

5. Construct Arguments Write a real-world problem that uses multiplication and can be solved by drawing a strip diagram and writing an equation.

☆ Independent Practice ☆

Complete a strip diagram and write an equation. Solve.

6. There are 8 theaters at the mall. Each of 7 theaters has 175 seats. The mall's theaters have 1,550 seats in all. How many seats are in the eighth theater?

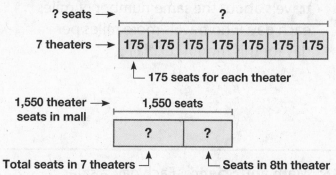

? seats →
?

7 theaters → | 175 | 175 | 175 | 175 | 175 | 175 | 175 |

└─ 175 seats for each theater

1,550 theater → seats in mall   1,550 seats

| ? | ? |

Total seats in 7 theaters ┘   └ Seats in 8th theater

7. Brad lives 12 times as far away from Dallas as Jennie. If Jennie lives 48 miles from Dallas, how many miles from Dallas does Brad live?

8. A hardware store ordered 9 packs of screws from a supplier. Each pack contains 155 screws. How many screws did the store order?

Problem Solving

9. Sandi is 13 years old. Karla's strip diagram shows that she is 3 times Sandi's age. Which equation represents *a*, Karla's age?

	a Karla's age			
Karla	13	13	13	3 times as many
Sandi	13			

    A $13 \times 3 = a$ **C** $13 + 3 = a$
    B $13 \times 4 = a$ **D** $13 + 13 = a$

10. Jupiter is about 5 times the distance Earth is from the Sun. Earth is about 93,000,000 miles from the Sun. About how far is Jupiter from the Sun?

11. **Connect** Mr. McDonald volunteers at the youth center that helps deal with problems in society. He volunteers 32 hours each month. Mr. Patel spends 4 times as much time volunteering each month. How much time in all do Mr. McDonald and Mr. Patel spend volunteering each month?

12. Hwong can fit 12 packets of coffee in a small box and 50 packets of coffee in a large box. He has 10 small boxes of coffee and would like to reorganize the packets into large boxes. Which boxes should Hwong use? Explain.

13. **Reason** William travels only on Saturdays and Sundays and has flown 1,020 miles this month. Jason travels every weekday and has flown 1,200 miles this month. If each man travels about the same number of miles each day, who travels more miles per day for this month? Explain.

14. **Extend Your Thinking** Alice's macaroni and cheese recipe calls for 2.5 cups of pasta and 1.25 ounces of cheese. The recipe serves 8 people. How much pasta and cheese will be needed to serve 24 people?

How many groups of 8 are in 24?

15. **Math and Science** Each day, a solar panel in Austin, Texas, produces 5.26 kWh (kilowatt per hour) per square meter. How many kWh can 9 times as many solar panels produce?

16. **Estimation** A laptop uses about 0.18 kWh. Sabra uses her laptop about 4 hours each day. Her family pays $0.17 per kWh. About how much does it cost Sabra to use her computer for a month? a year?

Name _____

Another Look!

Hailey sleeps from 10:15 P.M. until 6:30 A.M. each day. How many hours does Hailey sleep each week?

> The variable *h* represents the total number of hours of sleep each week.

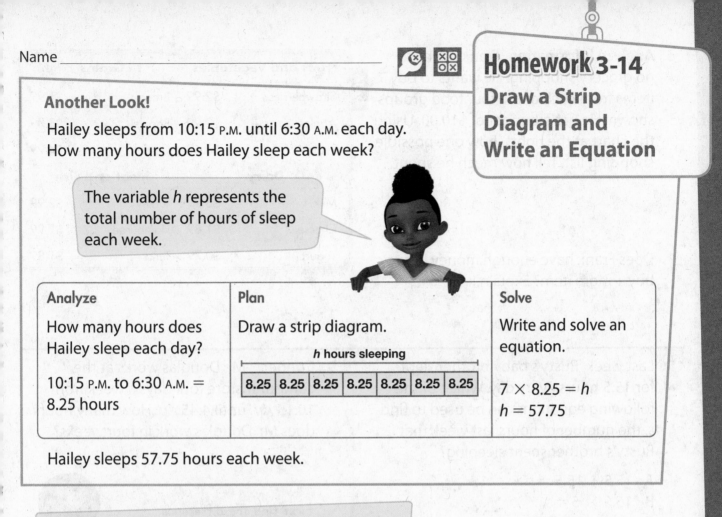

Analyze	Plan	Solve
How many hours does Hailey sleep each day? 10:15 P.M. to 6:30 A.M. = 8.25 hours	Draw a strip diagram. *h* hours sleeping 8.25 | 8.25 | 8.25 | 8.25 | 8.25 | 8.25 | 8.25	Write and solve an equation. $7 \times 8.25 = h$ $h = 57.75$

Hailey sleeps 57.75 hours each week.

For **1** through **5**, draw a strip diagram and write an equation. Solve.

1. Maria sleeps 9.5 hours each school night. If there are 5 school nights in a week, how many hours of sleep does Maria get? Complete the strip diagram and write an equation. Solve.

   h hours sleeping

2. An aquarium has display tanks that each contain 75 fish. How many fish are on display in 6 tanks?

   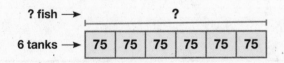

3. Each elephant at the zoo eats 125 pounds of food per day. How many pound of food will 8 elephants eat?

4. Joy can swim at a pace of 5.6 miles per hour. If a dolphin swims 4 times as fast as Joy, how fast does a dolphin swim?

5. Jerry weighs 96 pounds. If a male brown bear weighs 12 times as much, what is the brown bear's weight?

6. Analyze Information Frank needs to go grocery shopping. He wants to buy items from each of the four food groups shown. He has a budget of $10.00. Using the chart at the right, show one possible shopping list. Tell how much he spent.

DATA

Fruits and Vegetables		Grains	
Strawberries	$2.99	Bread	$1.99
Apples	$3.99	Bagels	$3.49
Pears	$1.69	Cereal	$4.29
Dairy		**Meat and Fish**	
Milk	$3.29	Turkey	$2.99
Cheese	$1.89	Hamburger	$2.99
Yogurt	$0.79	Tuna	$1.89

7. Does Frank have enough money left to buy 1 more item? Explain.

---

8. Last week, Rusty's baby brother slept for 15.5 hours every day. Which of the following equations can be used to find s, the number of hours last week that Rusty's brother spent sleeping?

- **A** $15.5 + 15.5 = s$
- **B** $15.5 \times 5 = s$
- **C** $15.5 \times 7 = s$
- **D** $15.5 + 7 = s$

9. Connect Mr. Douglas works at the computer store four days a week from 10:15 A.M. until 4:45 P.M. How many hours does Mr. Douglas work in four weeks?

> First find the difference between 10:15 A.M. and noon and then between noon and 4:45 P.M.

---

10. Lora is thinking of a number. She told her friend that if she subtracts 87 from the number and then divides by 2, she will get 15. Use the strip diagram to help you find Lora's number.

Lora's number →

?	
87	?

11. There are 500 sheets of paper in a book. Each sheet is 0.01 cm thick. The book's front and back cover are each 0.1 cm thick. What is the total thickness of the book and its covers? Use a strip diagram or equation to help you solve.

---

12. Mental Math When Mary was born, she weighed 8.2 pounds. When she was 10 years old, she weighed 10 times as much. How much did Mary weigh when she was 10 years old?

13. Extend Your Thinking Daniel has 12 tennis balls. Manuel has twice as many tennis balls as Daniel. Kendra has twice as many balls as Manuel. How many tennis balls do they have in all?

Name _____

1. **Connect** A flea measures 0.06 inch in length. The length of a caterpillar is 33 times the length of the flea. What is the length of the caterpillar?

2. **Mental Math** Lisa bought 23 books of stamps. Each book cost $9. How much did Lisa spend in all? Explain how you solved the problem using mental math.

Applying Math Processes
- How does this problem connect to previous ones?
- What is my plan?
- How can I use tools?
- How can I use number sense?
- How can I communicate and represent my thinking?
- How can I organize and record information?
- How can I explain my work?
- How can I justify my answer?

3. **Analyze Information** The table shows the number of miles 3 runners ran last week. Order the numbers from least to greatest. Which runner ran the farthest? How do you know?

DATA	Name	Miles
	Darla	15.2
	Casey	15.25
	Juan	15.03

4. Erin has 35 quarters. She uses the Distributive Property to find how much money she has in all. Which of the following could be the equation that Erin wrote? Use coins or objects to help.

A 30($0.20) + 5($0.05) = $6.25
B 35($0.20 + $0.05) = $8.75
C 35($0.20 + $0.50) = $24.50
D Not here

5. **Represent** A window is divided into 12 equal parts. One-third of the window is blue and one-fourth of the window is red. The remaining parts of the window are green. What fraction of the window is green?

6. **Extend Your Thinking** Carolina has enough pumpkin seeds to cover 350 square feet. Her garden measures 18 feet by 22 feet. Does she have enough pumpkin seeds to fill the garden? Explain.

Error Search

For **1** through **4**, find each answer that is not correct. Change what is wrong and rewrite the answer so it is correct.

1.	215	2.	158	3.	8.7	4.	0.65
	× 18		× 0.3		× 1.9		× 13
	1,935		2,054		16.53		0.845

Over or Under

Estimation For **5** through **16**, circle the better estimate.

5. 132 × 12
over 1,000
under 1,000

6. 887 × 98
over 90,000
under 90,000

7. 18 × 56
over 1,200
under 1,200

8. 220 × 21
over 4,000
under 4,000

9. 28 × 190
over 6,000
under 6,000

10. 45 × 381
over 20,000
under 20,000

11. 28 × 18
over 600
under 600

12. 742 × 11
over 7,400
under 7,400

13. 128 × 25
over 2,500
under 2,500

14. 81 × 55
over 4,000
under 4,000

15. 32 × 94
over 2,700
under 2,700

16. 254 × 9
over 3,000
under 3,000

Name _____

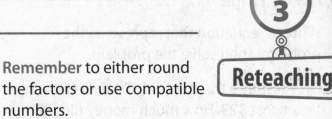

Set A pages 99–104

Estimate 37 × 88.

Step 1
Round both factors.

37 is about 40 and
88 is about 90.

Step 2
Use mental math and
multiply the rounded
factors.

40 × 90 = 3,600

Remember to either round
the factors or use compatible
numbers.

Estimate each product.

1. 7 × 396   **2.** 17 × 63

3. 91 × 51   **4.** 70 × 523

5. 256 × 16   **6.** 45 × 806

7. 27 × 89   **8.** 8 × 415

Set B pages 105–110

A store received a shipment of 38 TVs
valued at $425 each. What is the total value
of the shipment? Find 425 × 38.

Step 1	**Step 2**	**Step 3**
Multiply the ones.	Multiply the tens.	Add the partial products.

$$
\begin{array}{r}
\overset{2\,4}{425} \\
\times\ \ 38 \\
\hline
3400
\end{array}
\qquad
\begin{array}{r}
\overset{1}{425} \\
\times\ \ 38 \\
\hline
3400 \\
12750
\end{array}
\qquad
\begin{array}{r}
425 \\
\times\ \ 38 \\
\hline
3400 \\
+\ 12750 \\
\hline
16,150
\end{array}
$$

Remember to regroup if necessary. Estimate
to check that your answer is reasonable.

Find each product.

1. 54 × 9   **2.** 92 × 6

3. 67 × 48   **4.** 81 × 19

5. 51 × 605   **6.** 32 × 871

Set C pages 111–116

Find 53 × 406.
Estimate: 50 × 400 = 20,000

Multiply the ones. Multiply the tens. Then
add the partial products.

$$
\begin{array}{r}
\overset{\overset{3}{1}}{406} \\
\times\ \ \ 53 \\
\hline
1218 \leftarrow 3 \times 406 \\
+\ 20300 \leftarrow 50 \times 406 \\
\hline
21,518
\end{array}
$$

Remember to add any regrouped numbers
after multiplying by zero.

Find each product.

1. 34 × 108   **2.** 76 × 504

3. 47 × 302   **4.** 83 × 206

5.
$$
\begin{array}{r}
604 \\
\times\ \ 55
\end{array}
$$
     6.
$$
\begin{array}{r}
708 \\
\times\ \ 94
\end{array}
$$

Set D pages 117–122

Write an equation that represents the problem. Then solve the problem.

On Tuesday a theater sold 309 tickets. Each ticket cost $29. How much money did the theater make from the sale of the tickets?

309 × $29 = n

n = $8,961

The theater made $8,961.

Remember to estimate to check that your answer is reasonable.

Write an equation that represents the problem. Then solve.

The first 15 rows of an auditorium have 108 seats in each row. How many seats are there in all?

 Set E pages 123–128

Decide whether an exact answer is needed or an estimate is enough.

Don made hotel reservations. The room costs $128 each night. How much is Don's hotel bill if he stays for 12 nights?

The hotel needs to know exactly how much Don has to pay, so an exact answer is needed.

$128 × 12 = 1,536

Don's hotel bill is $1,536.

Remember When you are asked to find total costs and amounts of change, an exact answer is usually required.

Decide whether an exact answer is needed or an estimate is enough.

1. A freight elevator can hold up to 5,000 pounds. Jackson wants to load 28 boxes onto the elevator. Each box weighs 150 pounds. Is the total weight of all the boxes under the elevator weight limit?

Set F pages 129–134 and 135–140

Use the patterns in this table to find 8.56 × 10 and 0.36 × 100.

	Multiply by	Move the decimal point to the right
DATA	10	1 place
	100	2 places
	1,000	3 places

8.56 × 10 = 85.6 = 85.6

0.36 × 100 = 36.0 = 36

Remember when you need to move the decimal point beyond the number of digits in the number you are multiplying, you can annex one or more zeros.

Use mental math to solve 1 and 2. Estimate the products of 3 and 4.

1. 10 × 4.5   3. 24 × 3.67

2. 1,000 × 4.5   4. 8 × 56.7

Set G pages 141–146 and 147–152

Find 52.5×1.9 Estimate: $50 \times 2 = 100$

Step 1

Multiply as you would with whole numbers.

$$\begin{array}{r} 525 \\ \times\ 19 \\ \hline 9975 \end{array}$$

Step 2

Since 1.9 is greater than 1, the product will be greater than 52.5. Since 1.9 is about 2, the decimal point should be between the 9 and the 7.

$$\begin{array}{r} 52.5 \\ \times\ 1.9 \\ \hline 99.75 \\ \uparrow \end{array}$$

So, $52.5 \times 1.9 = 99.75$

Remember to compare each factor to 1 in order to determine the relative size of the product. Use area models or arrays if necessary.

Find each product.

1. 5×98.2 **2.** 4×0.21

3. 4.4×6 **4.** 7×21.6

5. 12.5×163.2 **6.** 16×52.3

7. 0.8×0.1 **8.** 0.05×0.4

9. 6.4×3.2 **10.** 315×0.01

Set H pages 153–158

Find 12×0.15.

Step 1

Multiply as you would with whole numbers.

$$\begin{array}{r} 12 \\ \times\ 0.15 \\ \hline 60 \\ +\ 120 \\ \hline 180 \end{array}$$

Step 2

Count the decimal places in both factors. Then, place the decimal point in the product the same number of places from the right.

$$\begin{array}{r} 12 \\ \times\ 0.15 \quad \text{2 places} \\ \hline 60 \\ +\ 120 \\ \hline 1.80 \end{array}$$

So, $12 \times 0.15 = 1.8$.

Remember to count the decimal places in both factors before you place the decimal point in the product.

Find each product.

1. 50×3.67 **2.** 5.86×5

3. 14×9.67 **4.** 8×56.7

5. 11×0.06 **6.** 2.03×6

7. 25×1.63 **8.** 5.62×75

Set I pages 159–164 and 165–170

Find 0.9 × 0.1

Shade the area created by the factors on a hundredths grid. Count the squares to find the product.

0.1

0.9

So 0.9 × 0.1 = 0.09

Remember to use area models and arrays to help you find the product if needed.

Find each product.

1. 2.4 × 3.6   **2.** 5.8 × 5.2

3. 8.3 × 10.7   **4.** 3.42 × 4.5

5. 1.4 × 6.7   **6.** 11.2 × 9.7

7. 23.3 × 60.5   **8.** 9.2 × 67.5

Set J pages 171–176

Ami wants to buy 2 tickets to a ballgame. Each ticket costs $28.75. Ami has $60.00. Is that enough money to buy tickets?

Find the total cost of the tickets.

$28.75 × 2 = $57.50

Determine whether she has enough money.

$60.00 > $57.50

Ami has enough money to buy the tickets.

Remember Check that your answer is reasonable by estimating.

Solve.

1. Selma is buying 3.5 pounds of grapes. Each pound costs $1.80. How much money does Selma spend?

2. Jeff buys 2 sandwiches for $3.95 each and 3 drinks for $1.25 each. He pays for the food with a $20-bill. How much change does he receive?

Set K pages 177–182

Draw a picture and write an equation. Solve.

The length of James's pool is 16 ft. The length of the pool at Wing Park is 4 times as long. How long is the pool at Wing Park?

Let ℓ = the length of Wing Park pool.

ℓ **length of Wing Park Pool**

| 16 | 16 | 16 | 16 |

↑

length of James's pool in feet

16 × 4 = ℓ
ℓ = 64 ft

The length of Wing Park pool is 64 ft.

Remember that a picture can help you visualize an equation.

Solve.

1. Mia has a collection of 34 dolls. A toy store has 15 times as many dolls. How many dolls are in the store?

2. Lea takes 23 surveys at school. She needs to take twice this amount before the end of the week. How many more surveys does Lea need to take?

Name _____

1. Dr. Peterson works about 178 hours each month. Which of the following can **NOT** be used to find a reasonable estimate of the number of hours he works in a year?

A 200 × 20

B 200 × 12

C 200 × 10

D 180 × 10

2. A banana contains 105 calories. Last week, Brendan and Lea ate a total of 14 bananas. How many calories does this represent?

A 525

B 1,450

C 1,470

D 4,305

3. The latest mystery novel costs $24. The table shows the sales of this novel by a bookstore. What is the total amount of sales on Saturday?

Day	Books Sold
Thursday	98
Friday	103
Saturday	157
Sunday	116

DATA

A $3,768

B $3,748

C $2,784

D $942

4. There are 36 large fish tanks at the zoo. Each tank holds 205 gallons of water. How many gallons of water would it take to fill all of the tanks?

A 7,380

B 7,210

C 6,380

D 6,361

5. On Monday, 115 delivery trucks were loaded with packages. Each truck carried between 58 and 63 packages. Which of the following amounts is a reasonable estimate for the total number of packages loaded for delivery on Monday?

A 12,000

B 10,000

C 7,000

D 5,000

6. There are 45 cans of mixed nuts. If each can has 338 nuts, what is the total number of nuts, n, in all of the cans? Solve for n.

$45 \times 338 = n$

A $n = 16,900$

B $n = 15,210$

C $n = 13,770$

D $n = 13,520$

7. Credit cards are 0.76 mm thick. How thick is a stack of 1,000 credit cards piled one on top of the other?

A 760 mm

B 76 mm

C 0.076 mm

D 0.00076 mm

8. Leo has 59 bricks each measuring 0.19 m wide. He stacks the bricks to make a tower. Which of the following provides the best estimate of the height of Leo's tower?

A $100 \times 0.15 = 15$

B $60 \times 0.2 = 12$

C $60 \times 0.1 = 6$

D $70 \times 0.2 = 14$

9. Susan colored in the decimal grid shown below. Which expression shows the area of the grid Susan colored?

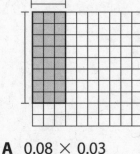

A 0.08×0.03

B 0.8×0.3

C 0.7×0.2

D 0.4×0.6

10. Sue bought 4.6 meters of fabric that cost $3.55 per meter. What was her total cost?

A $160.30

B $16.33

C $14.20

D $12.33

11. A farmer plants 0.4 of a field with wheat. The field is 3.45 acres. How many acres are planted with wheat?

A 0.126

B 0.138

C 1.26

D 1.38

12. Lucia scores 8.65 points on her first gymnastics event at a meet. If she gets the same score on each of four events, what will be her total score?

A 32.48

B 34.6

C 34.8

D 346

13. Alyssa is painting her bedroom blue. Each of four walls has dimensions 12.9 ft by 9.9 ft. How much area will she paint?

A 127.71 sq. ft   **C** 510.84 sq. ft

B 432.81 sq. ft   **D** 520.18 sq. ft

14. If the product of 12.51 and 30 is 375.3, what is the product of 125.1 and 30?

A 3.753

B 37.53

C 375.3

D Not here

15. One glass of lemonade has 115 calories. What is a reasonable estimate for the number of calories in 3.5 glasses of lemonade?

_____

16. Victoria draws the model below to find the amount of trim she will need to make a frame. Which product is represented by Victoria's decimal model?

A 0.8

B 1.4

C 2.0

D 2.8

17. Bradley walks 0.65 mile each Friday to his friend's house. He takes a different route home that is 1.2 miles. About how many miles will Bradley walk to his friend's house and back in a year?

A 50 miles

B 100 miles

C 120 miles

D 400 miles

18. The area of one fabric square is 4.8 square inches. What is the area of a quilt made with 100 fabric squares?

_____

19. Kai has 112 baseball cards. Sharon has 6 times as many cards as Kai. Which equation represents *b*, the number of baseball cards Sharon has?

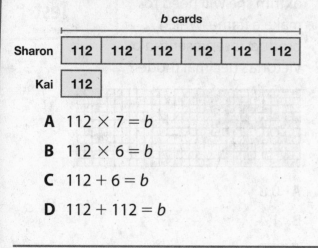

A $112 \times 7 = b$

B $112 \times 6 = b$

C $112 + 6 = b$

D $112 + 112 = b$

20. How much greater is 260×43 than 250×43?

A 10

B 43

C 410

D 430

21. Procter has pictures on his computer organized into 11 folders. He has 76 pictures in each folder. Round each factor to the nearest ten to estimate the total number of pictures.

22. Leticia wants to buy one dozen bagels. How much will this cost?

Bagel	$2.39
Donut	$1.99
Fruit Pie	$3.29

A $28.68

B $27.55

C $24.78

D $23.88

23. Alex buys 3 slices of pizza for $3.49 each and a beverage for $1.98. How much change will he get from $20?

A $14.53

B $12.45

C $7.55

D $4.53

24. Rosanne has 142 songs on her MP3 player. Teresa has 7 times as many songs as Rosanne. How many songs does Teresa have?

Number Sense: Dividing by 2-Digit Divisors

Essential Questions: How can quotients be estimated? How can quotients be found using basic facts, patterns, and models?

One of the hottest summers ever in Texas was in 2011. The average temperature was about 87°F.

It broke a record set in 1934, when the average was about 85°F.

More iced tea, anybody? Here's a project on finding the average temperature using division.

Math and Science Project: Average Temperature

Do Research Use a weather site from the Internet or another source of daily weather reports to find the average daily temperature for your city or town for every day of one month. The average daily temperature is the average temperature for a whole 24-hour period.

Journal: Write a Report Include what you found about daily temperatures. Also in your report:

- Find the average daily high temperature for the month. Which day had the greatest high temperature?

- Find the average daily low temperature for the month. Which day had the least low temperature?

- Make up and solve division problems based on your data.

Review What You Know

Vocabulary

Choose the best term from the box.
Write it on the blank.

> • dividend
>
> • divisor
>
> • quotient
>
> • remainder

1. In the equation $80 \div 10 = 8$, the number 80 is the _____.

2. The number used to divide another number is the _____.

3. The result of dividing two numbers is the _____.

Place Value

Complete using place-value terms.

4. 7,896 is the same as 7 _____
   $+ 8$ _____ $+ 9$ _____
   $+ 6$ _____.

5. 36,000 is the same as 36
   _____.

6. 75,800 is the same as 75
   _____ $+ 8$ _____.

Multiplying and Dividing

Multiply or divide.

7. $63 \div 9$ 8. $48 \div 6$

9. 57×13 10. 71×109

11. For the state fair next month, 132 people volunteered to plan the fair's activities. The volunteers put themselves into 12 equal groups. How many volunteers were in each group?

12. A town is holding a competition for various athletic games. Each community has 14 players. There are 112 communities competing in the games. What is the total number of players competing?

    A   1,676
    B   1,568
    C   126
    D   98

Estimating

13. **Writing to Explain** A county has a goal to build 12,000 bus stop shelters in 48 months. If the county builds 215 bus shelters each month, will it reach its goal? Explain one way to estimate the answer.

My Word Cards

Use the examples for each word on the front of the card to help complete the definitions on the back.

A-Z

remainder

$$43 \div 5 = 8 \text{ R}3$$

↑
remainder

My Word Cards

Complete the definition. Extend learning by writing your own definitions.

The number that remains after the division is complete is called the

_____.

Name _____

Solve & Share

A bakery sells muffins to local grocery stores in boxes that hold 20 muffins each. How many boxes are used if 60 muffins are sold? 600 muffins? 6,000 muffins? *Solve this problem any way you choose.*

TEKS 5.3C Solve with proficiency for quotients of up to a four-digit dividend by a two-digit divisor using strategies and the standard algorithm. Also, 5.3 Mathematical Process Standards 5.1A, 5.1B, 5.1C, 5.1D, 5.1E, 5.1G

Digital Resources at PearsonTexas.com

Solve   Learn   Glossary   Check   Tools   Games

Connect Find the answer for 60 muffins. Then use number sense to find the answers for 600 and 6,000 muffins. *Show your work!*

Look Back!

Connect How can you use multiplication to help you divide 6,000 by 20?

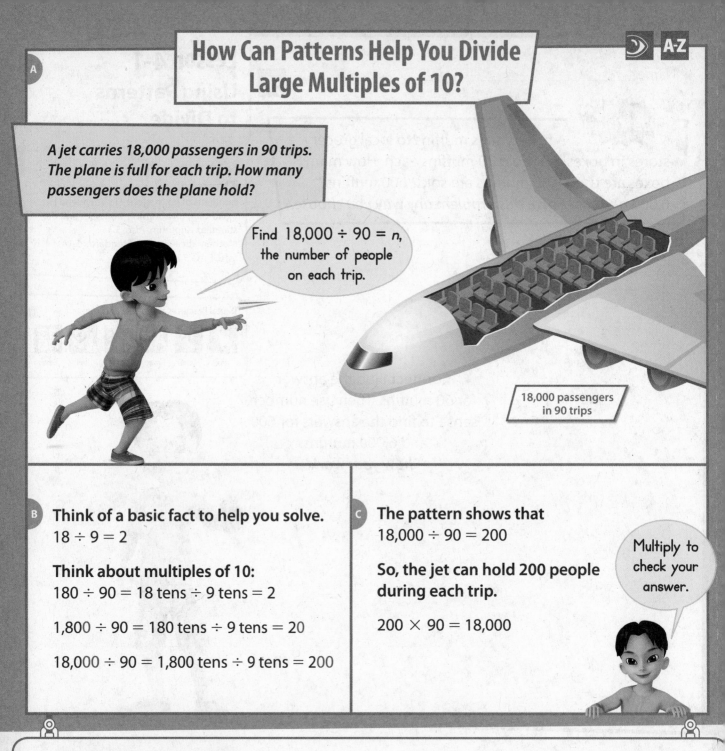
How Can Patterns Help You Divide Large Multiples of 10?

A

A jet carries 18,000 passengers in 90 trips. The plane is full for each trip. How many passengers does the plane hold?

Find $18,000 \div 90 = n$, the number of people on each trip.

18,000 passengers in 90 trips

B Think of a basic fact to help you solve.
$18 \div 9 = 2$

Think about multiples of 10:
$180 \div 90 = 18 \text{ tens} \div 9 \text{ tens} = 2$

$1,800 \div 90 = 180 \text{ tens} \div 9 \text{ tens} = 20$

$18,000 \div 90 = 1,800 \text{ tens} \div 9 \text{ tens} = 200$

C The pattern shows that
$18,000 \div 90 = 200$

So, the jet can hold 200 people during each trip.

$200 \times 90 = 18,000$

Multiply to check your answer.

Do You Understand?

Convince Me! Solve. Show your work.
If the jet above carried 10,000 people in 50 trips, how many people did it carry in each trip?

What basic fact helped you find the answer?

© Pearson Education, Inc. 5

☆ Guided Practice*

In **1** through **7**, find each quotient. Use mental math.

1. 210 ÷ 30 = 21 tens ÷ 3 tens = ____

2. 480 ÷ 60 = 48 tens ÷ 6 tens = ____

3. 15,000 ÷ 30 = 1,500 tens ÷ 3 tens = ____

4. 8,100 ÷ 90 = ____   **5.** 2,800 ÷ 70 = ____

6. 30,000 ÷ 50 = ____   **7.** 1,800 ÷ 60 = ____

8. Reason In Exercise 1, why is 210 ÷ 30 the same as 21 tens ÷ 3 tens?

9. A large jet carried 10,000 people in 20 trips. If the jet was full each trip, how many people did it carry for each trip?

Use a basic fact to help you find the answer.

Independent Practice ☆

Leveled Practice In **10** through **25**, use mental math to find the missing numbers.

10. 560 ÷ 70 = 56 tens ÷ 7 tens = ____   **11.** 360 ÷ 60 = 36 tens ÷ 6 tens = ____

12. 6,000 ÷ 50 = 600 tens ÷ 5 tens = ____   **13.** 24,000 ÷ 60 = 2,400 tens ÷ 6 tens = ____

14. 2,000 ÷ 20 = ____   **15.** 6,300 ÷ 90 = ____   **16.** 240 ÷ 10 = ____

17. 21,000 ÷ ____ = 700   **18.** 2,500 ÷ 50 = ____   **19.** 72,000 ÷ ____ = 800

20. 56,000 ÷ ____ = 800   **21.** 10,000 ÷ 100 = ____   **22.** 45,000 ÷ 90 = ____

23. 42,000 ÷ 70 = ____   **24.** 64,000 ÷ ____ = 800   **25.** 32,000 ÷ ____ = 80

Problem Solving

26. Analyze Information The table shows the number of passengers who flew on airplane flights in or out of one airport. Each flight had the same number of passengers. How many passengers were on each flight?

DATA		
Total passengers	:	27,000
Number of flights	:	90
Bottles of water	:	6,000

27. Represent A truck delivers 478 dozen eggs to stores in one day. Write an expression that finds the number of eggs the truck delivers in one day.

There are 12 in one dozen.

28. Paula wants to divide 480 tomatoes equally among 60 baskets. Which of the following equations can be used to help find t, the number of tomatoes that Paula should put in each basket?

A $48 \div 6 = t$
B $480 \div 6 = t$
C $4,800 \div 6 = t$
D $4,800 \div 60 = t$

29. Connect Ernesto measured the width of each of the three coins below.

| 0.7 inch | 0.84 inch | 0.74 inch |

He used pennies to help measure the length of a pencil. He lined up pennies side-by-side below the pencil. The pencil was 5 pennies long. What was the length of the pencil?

30. Extend Your Thinking A baker uses 30 grams of sea salt for each batch of bread. Sea salt comes in an 18-kilogram package or an 800-gram package. Which size package should the baker buy so that there will be no sea salt left over after making batches? Explain.

1 kilogram = 1,000 grams

Name _____

Another Look!

A school spends $12,000 on 20 new computers. Each computer costs the same amount. How much does each computer cost?

Step 1

Find a basic fact.

A basic fact that can be used for 12,000 ÷ 20 is 12 ÷ 2 = 6.

Step 2

Use a pattern.
12,000 ÷ 20

↓   ↓

1,200 ÷ 2

Solve.
1,200 ÷ 2 = 600
So, 12,000 ÷ 20 = 600

Step 3

Multiply to check.

600 × 20 = 12,000

Each computer costs $600.

In **1** through **16**, use a basic fact and a pattern to help solve.

1. 720 ÷ 90 = 72 tens ÷ 9 tens = ____

2. 4,800 ÷ 60 = 480 tens ÷ 6 tens = ____

3. 1,200 ÷ 30 = ____ tens ÷ ____ tens = ____

4. 25,000 ÷ 50 = _____ tens ÷ ____ tens = ____

5. 320 ÷ 40

6. 9,000 ÷ 30

7. 1,800 ÷ 90

8. 2,000 ÷ 40

9. 24,000 ÷ 80

10. 32,000 ÷ 40

11. 36,000 ÷ 900

12. 40,000 ÷ 50

13. 42,000 ÷ 60

14. 54,000 ÷ 600

15. 49,000 ÷ 70

16. 56,000 ÷ 80

17. Communicate A carton of staples has 50 packages. The carton contains 25,000 staples in all. Each package has an equal number of staples. How many staples are in each package? Explain.

18. Estimation A club collected $3,472 to buy computers. If each computer costs $680, estimate the number of computers that the club can buy.

---

19. Extend Your Thinking A railroad car container can hold 42,000 pounds. Mr. Evans wants to ship 90 ovens and some freezers in the same container. How many freezers could be shipped in the container? Explain.

Chefs & Company
RESTAURANT EQUIPMENT

Weight: 200 lb each

Weight: 600 lb each

---

20. Justify There are 50 communities in Kalb County. Each community has about the same number of people. Marty estimates there are about 300 people living in each community. Is his estimate correct? Justify your answer.

Population of Counties

Number of People vs County Name (Brook, Cobb, Corbin, Kalb, Kent)

---

21. Ms. Grover buys a medium-size package ⭐ of gemstones. She uses 50 gemstones for each jewelry making class that she teaches. She teaches two classes each day. How many days of classes will the package last?

A 10 days   **C** 100 days

B 50 days   **D** 500 days

SMALL 1,000 STONES   MEDIUM 5,000 STONES   LARGE 10,000 STONES

Name _____

Solve & Share

Kyle's school needs to buy posters for a fundraiser. The school has a budget of $147. Each poster costs $13. About how many posters can his school buy? **Solve this problem any way you choose.**

TEKS 5.3A Estimate to determine solutions to mathematical and real-world problems involving addition, subtraction, multiplication, or division. Mathematical Process Standards 5.1A, 5.1B, 5.1C, 5.1D, 5.1G

Digital Resources at PearsonTexas.com

Solve   Learn   Glossary   Check   Tools   Games

Mental Math You can use compatible numbers to estimate quotients. **Show your work!**

Look Back!

Estimation What numbers are close to 147 and 13 that would be easy to divide using mental math?

How Can You Use Compatible Numbers to Estimate Quotients?

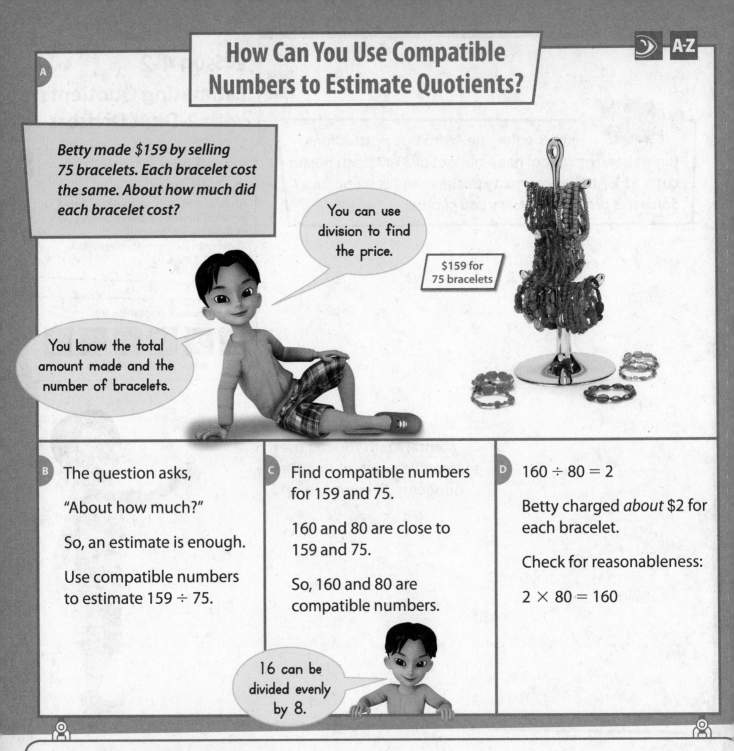

Betty made $159 by selling 75 bracelets. Each bracelet cost the same. About how much did each bracelet cost?

You can use division to find the price.

$159 for 75 bracelets

You know the total amount made and the number of bracelets.

B The question asks,

"About how much?"

So, an estimate is enough.

Use compatible numbers to estimate 159 ÷ 75.

C Find compatible numbers for 159 and 75.

160 and 80 are close to 159 and 75.

So, 160 and 80 are compatible numbers.

16 can be divided evenly by 8.

D $160 \div 80 = 2$

Betty charged *about* $2 for each bracelet.

Check for reasonableness:

$2 \times 80 = 160$

Do You Understand?

Convince Me! Suppose Betty made $230 selling the 75 bracelets. Estimate the cost of each bracelet. What compatible numbers did you use?

☆ Guided Practice *

In **1** through **8**, estimate using compatible numbers.

1. 287 ÷ 42   **2.** 320 ÷ 11

3. 208 ÷ 72   **4.** 554 ÷ 62

5. 815 ÷ 23   **6.** 2,491 ÷ 48

7. 1,220 ÷ 59   **8.** 3,390 ÷ 42

9. **Reason** If you use rounding to estimate in the example at the top of page 204, can you divide easily? Explain.

10. **Justify** Betty has 425 more bracelets to sell. She wants to store these in plastic bags that hold 20 bracelets each. She estimates she will need about 25 bags. Is she correct? Why or why not?

Independent Practice ☆

In **11** through **25**, estimate using compatible numbers.

11. 412 ÷ 84   **12.** 288 ÷ 37   **13.** 2,964 ÷ 73

14. 228 ÷ 19   **15.** 1,784 ÷ 64   **16.** 7,260 ÷ 83

17. 2,280 ÷ 12   **18.** 485 ÷ 92   **19.** 540 ÷ 61

20. 1,710 ÷ 32   **21.** 2,740 ÷ 67   **22.** 4,322 ÷ 81

23. 5,700 ÷ 58   **24.** 7,810 ÷ 44   **25.** 6,395 ÷ 84

Problem Solving

26. Analyze Information The sign shows the price of baseball caps for different pack sizes. Coach Lewis will buy the medium-size pack of caps. About how much will each cap cost?

Packs of Baseball Caps

Do you need an exact answer or an estimate?

20 Small Caps	32 Medium Caps	50 Large Caps
$180.00	$270.00	$360.00

27. Connect Leon bought 8 CDs on sale for $88. The regular price for 8 CDs is $112. How much did Leon save per CD by buying them on sale?

28. A school has 617 students. Each class has between 28 and 32 students. Which of the following is a reasonable estimate of the number of classes in the school?

A 14 classes   C 30 classes

B 20 classes   D 60 classes

29. Construct Arguments There are 91 days until the craft sale. Autumn needs to make 817 rings before the sale. She wants to make the same number of rings each day. About how many rings should she make each day? Explain how Autumn can use compatible numbers to make a reasonable estimate.

30. Extend Your Thinking A rescue group got a shipment of 3,128 bottles of water to help citizens after a natural disaster. Each rescue team needs 55 bottles. Which pair of compatible numbers gives a better estimate for the number of teams that can get the bottles needed — 3,000 ÷ 60 or 3,000 ÷ 50? Explain. Then make the estimate.

31. Personal Financial Literacy Rita saved $5.85 each week for 8 weeks. How much money did she save? Use the strip diagram to solve the problem. Show your work.

? total savings

8 weeks → | 5.85 | | | | | | | |

↑ $ saved each week

Homework 4-2
Estimating Quotients with 2-Digit Divisors

Another Look!

Frog Trail is 1,976 meters long. Shondra walks 43 meters of the trail in one minute. If she walks an equal number of meters each minute, about how many minutes would it take Shondra to walk the trail?

Step 1

Find compatible numbers. Think of a basic fact.

1,976 ÷ 43
↓   ↓
20   ÷ 4 = 5

Step 2

Rewrite the division with compatible numbers using the basic fact. Match place values.

1,976 ÷ 43
↓   ↓
2,000 ÷ 40

Step 3

Solve. Use a pattern to help.

2,000 ÷ 40
↓   ↓
200 ÷ 4 = 50

So, 2,000 ÷ 40 = 50.

It would take Shondra about 50 minutes.

In **1** through **12**, estimate using compatible numbers.

1. 1,769 ÷ 23
↓   ↓
1,800 ÷ □
□

2. 516 ÷ 48
↓   ↓
500 ÷ □
□

3. 891 ÷ 32
↓   ↓
□ ÷ □
□

4. 231 ÷ 34

5. 705 ÷ 9

6. 8,968 ÷ 11

7. 5,624 ÷ 72

8. 1,043 ÷ 23

9. 986 ÷ 11

10. 642 ÷ 94

11. 4,870 ÷ 58

12. 5,721 ÷ 79

13. There are 8 uniforms at a fire station. Their total weight is 538 pounds. About how many pounds does each uniform weigh? Would you use paper and pencil or mental math to solve the problem? Explain. Then solve. Show your work.

14. Estimation A gray whale traveled 152 kilometers in one day. The whale swam between 7 and 8 kilometers each hour. About how many hours did it take the whale to swim the distance? Show two different ways that you can use compatible numbers to find an answer. Then solve.

Remember to check your answer for reasonableness.

15. Use a Strip Diagram Mr. Crane's farm is 413 acres. He divides the farm into 52 equal parts. About how many acres are in each part? Draw a strip diagram to show the basic fact you used. Then solve.

16. A scientist counted 3,921 total eggs in 49 sea turtle nests. There were about the same number of eggs in each nest. Which is a reasonable estimate of the number of eggs she counted in each nest?

A 800 eggs

B 100 eggs

C 80 eggs

D 10 eggs

17. Communicate The table shows data about a new phone company and its customers. Meg wants to find about how many phones the company activated in one minute. Explain why Meg can use 1,500 ÷ 5 to find the answer.

DATA

Clear Connect Company
Number of phones activated: 1,427 in 5 minutes
Number of calls made: 59,835
Number of text messages sent: 2,063

18. Extend Your Thinking Ester's choir wants to learn a new song for the school concert in 7 weeks. The song has 3,016 lines. The choir learns an equal number of lines each day. About how many lines do they need to learn each day to learn the song in time for the concert? Explain.

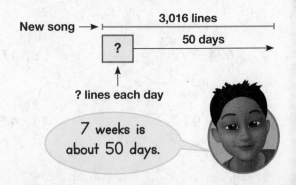

New song → 3,016 lines

? → 50 days

? lines each day

7 weeks is about 50 days.

Name _____

☆ ☆
Solve & Share

A parking lot holds 270 cars. Each row holds 18 cars. How many rows are in this parking lot? *Solve this problem any way you choose.*

⊗ TEKS 5.3C Solve with proficiency for quotients of up to a four-digit dividend by a two-digit divisor using strategies and the standard algorithm.
Mathematical Process Standards 5.1A, 5.1B, 5.1D, 5.1E, 5.1G

Digital Resources at PearsonTexas.com

➚	👁	A-Z	⠿	🔧	⊠
Solve	Learn	Glossary	Check	Tools	Games

Connect Think about the relationship between multiplication and division. *Show your work!*

Look Back!

Create and Use Representations How can multiplication be used to find the length of the missing side?

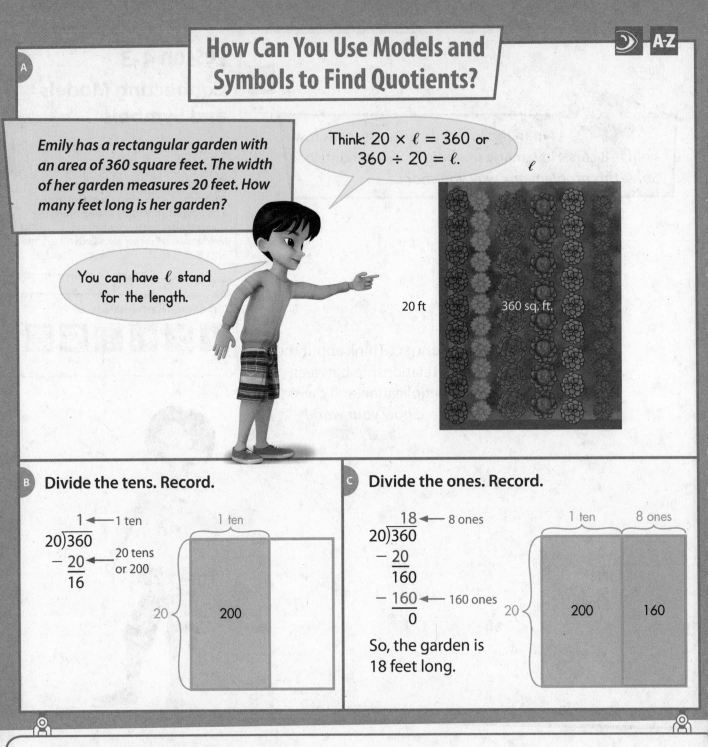

How Can You Use Models and Symbols to Find Quotients?

A

Emily has a rectangular garden with an area of 360 square feet. The width of her garden measures 20 feet. How many feet long is her garden?

You can have ℓ stand for the length.

Think: $20 \times \ell = 360$ or $360 \div 20 = \ell$.

ℓ

20 ft   360 sq. ft.

B Divide the tens. Record.

$$
\begin{array}{r}
1 \leftarrow \text{1 ten} \\
20\overline{)360} \\
-20 \leftarrow \text{20 tens} \\
\hline
16 \quad \text{or 200}
\end{array}
$$

1 ten

20 { | 200

C Divide the ones. Record.

$$
\begin{array}{r}
18 \leftarrow \text{8 ones} \\
20\overline{)360} \\
-20 \\
\hline
160 \\
-160 \leftarrow \text{160 ones} \\
\hline
0
\end{array}
$$

So, the garden is 18 feet long.

1 ten   8 ones

20 { | 200 | 160

Do You Understand?

Convince Me! Use the model to find the quotient of $408 \div 12$.
Hint: Find the value of ℓ and solve.

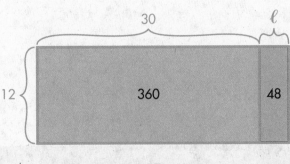

30   ℓ

12 { | 360 | 48

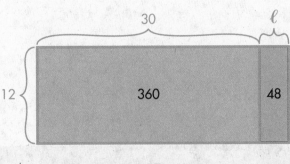

☆ Guided Practice ☆

Use a model to find the quotient.

1. 12)288

X
12	288

For **2** and **3**, use grid paper or draw a picture to find each quotient.

2. 22)682

3. 11)143

4. Reason What is the missing dimension? Tell how you decided.

	42
X	756

5. Represent Write a multiplication equation and a division equation that represent the model shown below. Then solve.

	X
32	672

Independent Practice ☆

Leveled Practice For **6** through **14**, use grid paper or draw a picture to find each quotient.

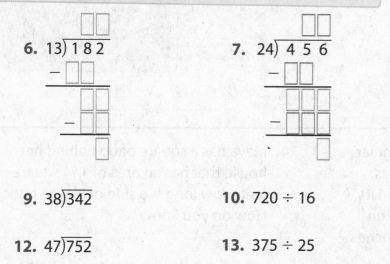

6. 13)1 8 2

7. 24)4 5 6

8. 32)2 5 6

9. 38)342

10. 720 ÷ 16

11. 608 ÷ 19

12. 47)752

13. 375 ÷ 25

14. 576 ÷ 24

Problem Solving

15. Connect Angelo is training for a long-distance bicycle ride. Angelo rides his bicycle at a constant speed of 15 miles each hour. How many hours would it take him to ride 210 miles?

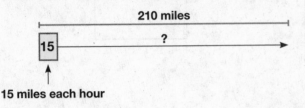

16. Mari needs to make one label for each chair in the school auditorium. There are 16 rows of chairs with the same number of chairs in each row. There are 512 chairs in all. Mari already made labels for 9 of the rows. How many more labels does she need to make?

A 25 labels   C 224 labels
B 32 labels   D 288 labels

17. Analyze Information Use the map. How much longer is the distance from the library to the park to the train station than the distance from the library straight to the train station?

18. If you walk from the train station to the library, then to the park, and then back to the train station, how many miles would you walk in all? Write an equation to show your work.

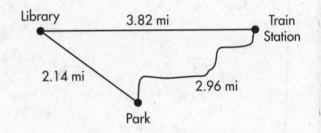

19. Communicate Explain how you can use the picture to show that $391 \div 23 = 17$.

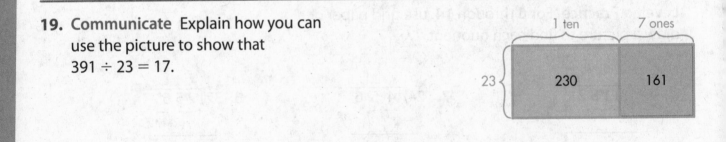

20. Extend Your Thinking A rectangular doormat is 21 inches long and has an area of 714 square inches. Find its width. Is the doormat wide enough to cover an entryway that is 36 inches wide? Show your work.

21. Maya has a square patio behind her house that has an area of 144 square feet. How long is a side of Maya's patio? How do you know?

Another Look!

Hal's store just got a shipment of 195 cans of soup. Hal wants to divide the cans equally on 13 shelves. How many cans should go on each shelf?

> Is there enough for 1 ten to go in each group? Is there enough for 2 tens to go in each group?

Step 1

Divide the tens. Record.

```
        1 ← 1 ten
   13)1 9 5
   − 1 3 0 ← 13 tens or 130
       6 5
```

Step 2

Divide the ones. Record.

```
        1 5 ← 5 ones
   13)1 9 5
   − 1 3 0
       6 5
     − 6 5
         0
```

15 cans should go on each shelf.

For **1** through **9**, find each quotient.

1. 12)168

2. 16)208

3. 17)391

4. 14)420

5. 11)385

6. 24)744

7. 27)675

8. 18)558

9. 19)228

10. Communicate Explain the mistakes in the division below. Show the correct division.

$$
\begin{array}{r}
2\ 1\ 1 \\
19\overline{)5\ 8\ 9} \\
-3\ 8 \\
\hline
2\ 0\ 9 \\
-2\ 0\ 9 \\
\hline
0
\end{array}
$$

11. A 208-meter-long road is divided into 16 parts of equal length. Mr. Ward paints a 4-meter-long strip in each part. How many total meters are not painted in the 208 meters of road?

A	13 meters	C	117 meters
B	64 meters	D	144 meters

What steps do you need to solve to find the answer?

---

12. Explain Use the table. What is the total amount of electricity a computer, a television, and a heater use in 1 hour?

Electricity Used

Appliance	Kilowatts Per Hour
Computer	0.09
Heater	1.5
Light bulb	0.1
Television	0.3

DATA

---

13. Make a Graph Use the bar graph. Astronauts installed 15 new tiles on the outside of the space station. They spent 390 minutes on the task. Each tile took the same amount of time to install. Draw a bar in the graph to show the time needed to install a tile. Explain.

14. Analyze Information How much longer does it take an astronaut to install a light than to install a cable?

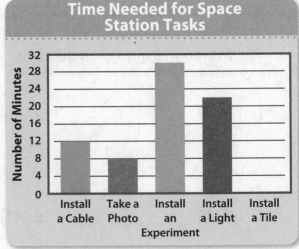

---

15. Extend Your Thinking A rectangular poster has an area of 504 square centimeters. The width of the poster is 14 centimeters. How long is the poster? Finish the model to find the quotient of 504 ÷ 14. Explain how you found the value of *a* in the model. Then solve.

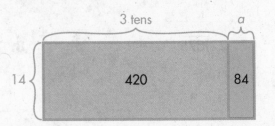

Name _____

Solve & Share

Cameron's soccer team has $168 to buy uniforms that cost $20 each. How many uniforms can his team buy? *Solve this problem any way you choose.*

TEKS 5.3C Solve with proficiency for quotients of up to a four-digit dividend by a two-digit divisor using strategies and the standard algorithm. Also 5.3 Mathematical Process Standards 5.1B, 5.1C, 5.1D, 5.1G

Digital Resources at PearsonTexas.com

| Solve | Learn | Glossary | Check | Tools | Games |

Number sense. Think how estimation and multiplication might be used. *Show your work!*

Look Back!

Number Sense How much more money is needed to buy an additional uniform?

What Are the Steps in Dividing by a Multiple of Ten?

This year, a group of 249 students is taking a field trip. One bus is needed for every 20 students. How many buses are needed?

You can divide to find how many 20s are in 249.

20 students per bus

B Step 1

Find 249 ÷ 20.

Estimate: 240 ÷ 20 = 12

$$\begin{array}{r} 1 \\ 20\overline{)249} \\ -20 \\ \hline 4 \end{array}$$

Divide   24 ÷ 20 = 1

Multiply   1 × 20 = 20

Subtract   24 − 20 = 4

Compare   4 < 20

C Step 2

Bring down the ones. Divide the ones.

$$\begin{array}{r} 12 \text{ R9} \\ 20\overline{)249} \\ -20\downarrow \\ \hline 49 \\ -40 \\ \hline 9 \end{array}$$

Divide   49 ÷ 20 = 2

Multiply   2 × 20 = 40

Subtract   49 − 40 = 9

Compare   9 < 20

Since the remainder is 9, one more bus is needed. A total of 13 buses is needed.

The answer is reasonable because 13 is close to the estimate.

Do You Understand?

Convince Me! For the example above, show how you can check that the quotient is correct. Explain your answer.

☆ Guided Practice ☆

In **1** and **2**, divide. Write the missing numbers.

1.
```
       □□ R □
  20) 2 8 2
     − □□
       8 □
     − 8 0
         2
```

2.
```
        □ R 46
  80) 7 6 6
     − □□□
        □□
```

An estimate tells you if the your answer is reasonable.

3. In the example at the top of page 216, if only 137 students were going on the trip, how many buses would be needed?

4. Reason In the example at the top of page 216, why is 12 buses a reasonable estimate?

☆ Independent Practice ☆

Leveled Practice In **5** through **7**, divide. Write the missing numbers.

5.
```
       □ 5 R 1
  20) 3 1 8
     − 2 □
       □ 1
     − 1 □□
       1 □
```

6.
```
        □ R □
  60) 5 9 3
     − □□□
        □□
     − □
       □ 3
```

7.
```
       □□ R □
  30) 3 2 6
     − □□
        □
     − □
       □□
```

In **8** through **13**, divide.

8. 40)453

9. 50)261

10. 70)867

11. 60)728

12. 80)492

13. 40)375

Problem Solving

14. Estimation Rita's family is moving from Grand Junction to Dallas. The moving van averages 60 miles each hour. About how many hours does it take the van to reach Dallas?

DATA	
Dallas, TX, to Grand Junction, CO	980 miles
Nashville, TN, to Norfolk, VA	670 miles
Charleston, SC, to Atlanta, GA	290 miles
Denver, CO, to Minneapolis, MN	920 miles
Little Rock, AR, to Chicago, IL	660 miles

15. Extend Your Thinking A scientist is working on 15 samples. She needs 70 milliliters of distilled water for each sample. She has a bottle that contains 975 milliliters of distilled water. Is there enough water in the bottle for all 15 samples? Explain.

16. The Port Lavaca fishing pier is 3,200 feet long. If there is one person fishing for every ten feet of length, how many people are fishing from the pier?

17. Mrs. Otis needs 40 tacks to make each picture frame. She needs to make 9 frames. Based on the information at right, which of the following statements is true?

A With Box A, Mrs. Otis can make 9 frames, with 15 tacks left over.

B With Box B, Mrs. Otis can make 9 frames, with 60 tacks left over.

C With Box C, Mrs. Otis can make 9 frames, with 30 tacks left over.

D With Box D, Mrs. Otis can make 11 frames, with none left over.

Box A
375 tacks

Box B
400 tacks

Box C
350 tacks

Box D
445 tacks

18. Number Sense Todd made a table to show different plans he can use to save $500. Complete the table. Which plan can Todd use to save $500 in less than 16 weeks and have $20 extra? Explain how you found your answer.

	Savings Plans for Goal Amount of $500	
Plan	Amount to Save Each Week	Number of Weeks Needed to Make Goal
A	$20	25
B	$30	
C	$40	
D	$50	

Another Look!

Bo has 623 bottle caps to divide equally between 40 friends. How many caps will each friend get? Will there be any caps left over?

Step 1	**Step 2**	**Step 3**	**Step 4**
Divide the tens.	Subtract the tens. Bring down the ones.	Divide the ones.	Subtract the ones. Write the remainder.

Step 1

Divide the tens.

$$\begin{array}{r} 1 \\ 40\overline{)623} \\ 40 \end{array}$$ ◄— 62 tens ÷ 40 groups

40 × 1 ten = 40 tens

Step 2

Subtract the tens. Bring down the ones.

$$\begin{array}{r} 1 \\ 40\overline{)623} \\ -40\downarrow \\ \hline 223 \end{array}$$

Step 3

Divide the ones.

$$\begin{array}{r} 15 \\ 40\overline{)623} \\ -40 \\ \hline 223 \\ 200 \end{array}$$ ◄— 223 ones ÷ 40 groups

40 × 5 ones = 200 ones

Step 4

Subtract the ones. Write the remainder.

$$\begin{array}{r} 15 \text{ R }23 \\ 40\overline{)623} \\ -40 \\ \hline 223 \\ -200 \\ \hline 23 \end{array}$$

Each friend will get 15 caps. There will be 23 caps left over.

In **1** through **8**, find the quotient.

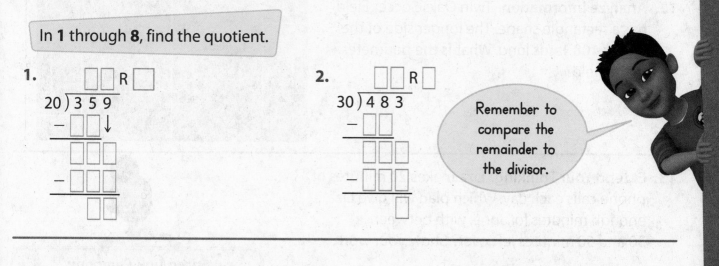

1.
$$\begin{array}{r} \square\square \text{ R }\square \\ 20\overline{)3\ 5\ 9} \\ -\square\square\downarrow \\ \hline \square\square \\ -\square\square \\ \hline \square\square \end{array}$$

2.
$$\begin{array}{r} \square\square \text{ R }\square \\ 30\overline{)4\ 8\ 3} \\ -\square\square \\ \hline \square\square \\ -\square\square \\ \hline \square \end{array}$$

Remember to compare the remainder to the divisor.

3. $40\overline{)7\ 4\ 6}$

4. $50\overline{)8\ 4\ 5}$

5. $70\overline{)6\ 3\ 2}$

6. $60\overline{)7\ 7\ 9}$

7. $40\overline{)9\ 3\ 6}$

8. $30\overline{)3\ 3\ 2}$

9. **Communicate** Why can the calculations in red be thought of as simpler problems? Describe the simpler problems.

$$
\begin{array}{r}
12\ R13 \\
80\overline{)973} \\
\end{array}
$$

12 R 13
80)973 ← 97 tens ÷ 80 groups
－80 ← 80 × 1 ten
173 ← 173 ones ÷ 80 groups
－160 ← 80 × 2 ones
13

10. **Explain** A county has 90 schools. Each school needs 11 computers. The county received 992 new computers. Are there enough computers so that each school gets the number of computers it needs? Explain.

---

11. Ms. Lopez has 60 tables for a party. Each table needs 14 chairs. The sign shows the number of chairs that come in each rental package. Based on this information, which of the following statements is **NOT** true?

   A With Package A, Ms. Lopez does not have enough chairs.
   B With Package B, Ms. Lopez does not have enough chairs.
   C With Package C, Ms. Lopez has enough chairs, with 10 chairs left over.
   D With Package D, Ms. Lopez has enough chairs, with 40 chairs left over.

DATA

Party Furniture Rental

Package	Number of Chairs
A	580
B	775
C	850
D	900

---

12. **Analyze Information** Twin Oaks Soccer Field has a rectangle shape. The longer side of the field is 108 yards long. What is the perimeter of the field?

56 yd

---

13. **Extend Your Thinking** Liza makes 20 minutes of phone calls each day. Which plan will give Liza enough minutes for June, with between 30 and 50 minutes left over? Show your work.

14. Mark and his brother signed up for the Catch Up phone plan. They share the minutes every month equally. How many minutes can Mark use each day without going over his share of minutes?

DATA

Speed Link Company Phone Plans

Plan Name	Number of Minutes Per Month
Connect	550
Chat	625
Share	650
Catch Up	700

Name _____

Solve & Share

Trey signed up for 120 hours of flute lessons. He meets with his music teacher for the same amount of time each Monday and Wednesday for 30 weeks. How long is each lesson? *Solve this problem any way you choose.*

TEKS 5.1A Apply mathematics to problems arising in everyday life, society, and the workplace. Also, 5.3C, 5.4B. Mathematical Process Standards 5.1B, 5.1C, 5.1D, 5.1G

Digital Resources at PearsonTexas.com

Solve   Learn   Glossary   Check   Tools   Games

CALENDAR

S	M	T	W	TH	F	S
	1 Flute Lesson	2	3 Flute Lesson	4	5	6
7	8 Flute Lesson	9	10 Flute Lesson	11	12	13
14	15 Flute Lesson	16	17 Flute Lesson	18	19	20
21	22 Flute Lesson	23	24 Flute Lesson	25	26	27
28	29 Flute Lesson	30	31 Flute Lesson			

Analyze Information You can solve multiple-step problems by finding the hidden question. *Show your work!*

Look Back!

Communicate What hidden question do you need to answer to help you solve the problem?

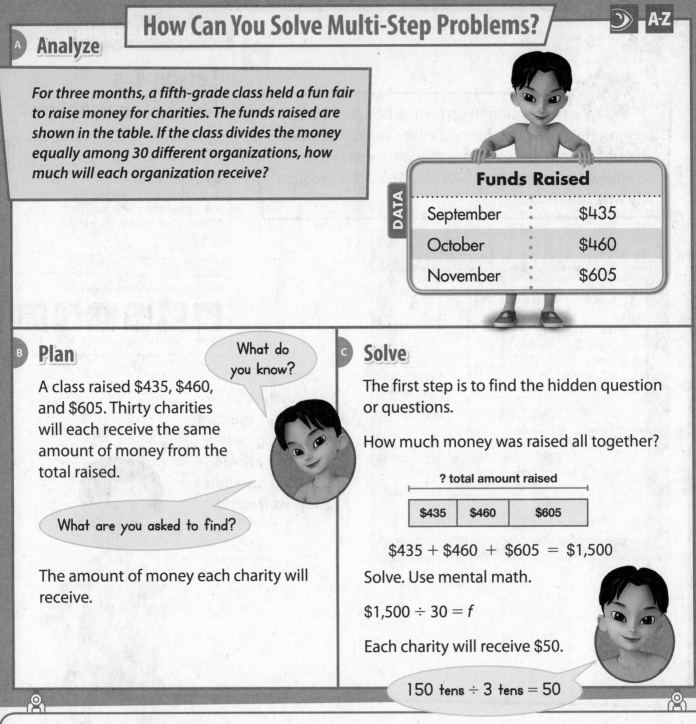
How Can You Solve Multi-Step Problems?

A **Analyze**

For three months, a fifth-grade class held a fun fair to raise money for charities. The funds raised are shown in the table. If the class divides the money equally among 30 different organizations, how much will each organization receive?

DATA

Funds Raised

September	$435
October	$460
November	$605

B **Plan**

What do you know?

A class raised $435, $460, and $605. Thirty charities will each receive the same amount of money from the total raised.

What are you asked to find?

The amount of money each charity will receive.

C **Solve**

The first step is to find the hidden question or questions.

How much money was raised all together?

? total amount raised

| $435 | $460 | $605 |

$$\$435 + \$460 + \$605 = \$1,500$$

Solve. Use mental math.

$$\$1,500 \div 30 = f$$

Each charity will receive $50.

150 tens ÷ 3 tens = 50

Do You Understand?

Convince Me! Using the above example, how much money will each charity receive if the total amount raised is shared equally among 50 charities? Justify your answer.

☆ Guided Practice ☆

1. Nancy wants to transfer 11 pictures to her 256 megabyte (MB) memory card. Each picture is 4 MB and she has already used 28 MB. How much memory will be free on the card after she transfers the pictures?

2. **Formulate a Plan** What is the hidden question Exercise 1? What is its answer?

3. **Draw a Picture** Draw a strip diagram to show the hidden question in Exercise 1.

4. Write a real-world multi-step problem that can be solved by using multiplication.

☆ Independent Practice ☆

In **5** and **6**, solve the multi-step problems. Begin by writing and answering the hidden question or questions.

5. A store is having a sale on bookcases. Three bookcases cost $375. Two bookcases cost $258. If Mrs. Dell wants to spend as little as possible to buy 6 bookcases, how should she buy them?

Hidden Questions

_____

_____

_____

Answers to Hidden Questions

_____

Solve

_____

_____

6. Trent is growing 3 banana plants in his yard. Each plant grows 1 bunch of bananas. A bunch usually has 15 hands. Each hand usually has 7 fruits. How many fruits in all should Trent expect from his banana plants?

Hidden Question

_____

_____

Answer to Hidden Question

_____

Solve

_____

Problem Solving

7. **Analyze Information** Use the table. Compare the amount of fat contained in 2 slices of pizza, 1 cup of macadamia nuts, and 6 cups of popcorn. Which quantity of food contains the most fat? How much more fat does it contain than the quantity with the least fat?

Fat in Food	
Food Description	**Grams of Fat**
1 slice pepperoni pizza	55
1 cup macadamia nuts	101
3 cups popcorn	1

DATA

8. **Explain** Mrs. Ruth drives her car about 575 miles each month. Her odometer shows 13,298 miles. How many miles would the odometer show after 12 months? Explain how you found your answer.

9. **Connect** Ariane is selling jewelry at the state fair. She sells bracelets for $8 each, rings for $5 each, and earrings for $11 per pair. How much will Ariane make if she sells 9 bracelets, 14 rings, and 10 pairs of earrings?

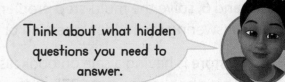

Think about what hidden questions you need to answer.

10. **Extend Your Thinking** Julian buys 13 packages of screws with 75 screws in each package. He needs to use 40 screws to make one bench. How many benches can he make? Draw a strip diagram and write an equation for the hidden question. Then write an equation that helps to solve the problem. Solve.

11. Which question does **NOT** need to be answered to solve the problem?

A rectangular bulletin board is 36 inches long and 24 inches wide. There are 9 sheets of paper posted in rows and columns on the board. Each sheet of paper is 10 inches long and 8 inches wide. What is the area of the board that is not covered with paper?

A What is the perimeter of the board?
B What is the area of the board?
C What is the difference between the areas of the board and the papers?
D What is the area of the papers?

Another Look!

Dex works at a dog adoption shelter. He has 4 large boxes of dog treats with 34 treats in each box and 3 small boxes with 28 treats in each box. How many bags of 20 treats can Dex make from all the treats?

Does the information give you all the values to solve? Or do you need to find some values?

Step 1

Find the hidden questions.

How many treats are in the large boxes?

ℓ total treats in large boxes

34	34	34	34

How many treats are in the small boxes?

s total treats in small boxes

28	28	28

How many treats are there in all?

Step 2

Answer the hidden questions.

$4 \times 34 = \ell$,
$\ell = 136$ treats

$3 \times 28 = s$, $s = 84$ treats

$\ell + s = a$,
$136 + 84 = 220$ treats in all

Step 3

Solve the problem.

$220 \div 20 = b$

$b = 11$

Dex can make 11 bags of treats.

In **1** and **2**, write and answer the hidden question or questions. Then solve.

1. A tropical storm has been moving at 15 miles per hour in the past two days. Bess recorded that the storm moved 135 miles yesterday and 75 miles today. For how many hours has Bess been keeping track of the storm? Draw a strip diagram to help you solve.

2. An online store sells 40 games on Wednesday and 45 on Thursday. On Friday, it sells as many games as it sold on Wednesday and Thursday. How many games were sold from Wednesday to Friday?

3. Use a Strip Diagram Draw a diagram to show the hidden question. Then solve. One gallon of paint will cover 80 tiles. Tariq wants to paint the tiles on the back wall, the side wall, and the front wall. How many gallons of paint does Tariq need to buy?

Surface	Number of Tiles
Back Wall	193
Floor	418
Front Wall	235
Side Wall	547

4. Formulate a Plan Mrs. Scott bought 24 tree seedlings on sale. The total cost of the seedlings would have been $360 at the original price. Mrs. Scott saved a total of $3 on the price of each seedling. What was the total cost of the 24 seedlings at the sale price? Write and answer the hidden question. Then solve. Show your work.

5. Dana has 505 stamps left to put into her stamp book. She had 1,075 stamps to begin. Dana put 30 stamps on each page. Which of the following pairs of equations can be used to find x, the number of pages that Dana has completed?

A $505 + 1,075 = b, b \div 2 = x$
B $505 \div 30 = b, b + 1,075 = x$
C $1,075 - 505 = b, b - 30 = x$
D $1,075 - 505 = b, b \div 30 = x$

6. Number Sense Each small square on the chessboard is equal. The length of a side of a small square is 1 inch. What is the area of the chessboard?

7. Extend Your Thinking Use the data. Suppose a panda eats the least amount of bamboo listed each day. Another panda eats the greatest amount of bamboo listed each day. How many pounds of bamboo would the two pandas eat in one month? Explain.

Animal Facts	
Black Bears	can live to the age of 32 years
Pandas	can eat between 20 and 40 lb of bamboo each day
Polar Bears	can weigh up to 1,400 lb

Name _____

1. Use a Strip Diagram Ms. Wilson has 11 rolls of ribbon. Each ribbon is 2 inches wide and 9 feet long. What is the total length, in inches, of ribbon on the 11 rolls? Draw a strip diagram to help.

Applying Math Processes

- How does this problem connect to previous ones?
- What is my plan?
- How can I use tools?
- How can I use number sense?
- How can I communicate and represent my thinking?
- How can I organize and record information?
- How can I explain my work?
- How can I justify my answer?

2. Communicate A bag of granola has a mass of 0.375 kilogram. What is the value of the digit 5 in 0.375?

3. Analyze Information Use the table.

DATA	Swimmer	Time in Seconds
	1	48.49
	2	47.54
	3	48.52
	4	48.04

What is the combined time for Swimmers 1 and 4?

A 96.03 seconds **C** 96.56 seconds
B 96.53 seconds **D** 192.59 seconds

4. Justify Look at the figures below.

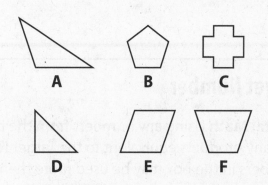

List all the figures that appear to have at least 2 obtuse angles. Justify your answer.

5. Math and Science A biologist measured the height of a Laughing Kookaburra bird. It was 45.8 centimeters tall. What was the height of the bird rounded to the nearest centimeter? Explain.

6. Extend Your Thinking The distance from Everton to Carpenter is 751 miles. The distance from Mitchell to Lincoln is 283 miles. Carl estimated the difference in distances to be about 500 miles. Is his estimate greater or less than the actual distance? Explain. What numbers might Carl have used to estimate?

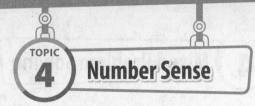

TOPIC 4 Number Sense

Error Search

Find each problem that is not correct. Circle what is wrong and rewrite the problem so it is correct.

1. 2.084 + 53.7

$$\begin{array}{r} \overset{1}{}20.84 \\ +\ 53.70 \\ \hline 74.54 \end{array}$$

2. 0.61 + 17.943

$$\begin{array}{r} \overset{1\ 1}{}06.100 \\ +\ 17.943 \\ \hline 24.043 \end{array}$$

3. 0.48 − 0.325

$$\begin{array}{r} \overset{7\ 10}{0.48\cancel{0}} \\ -\ 0.325 \\ \hline 0.155 \end{array}$$

4. 29.6 − 8.72

$$\begin{array}{r} \overset{16\ 10}{29.6\cancel{0}} \\ -\ 8.72 \\ \hline 21.98 \end{array}$$

Target Number

Mental Math Using any numbers from the box as factors, list as many products equivalent to the Target Number as you can. Numbers in the box may be used more than once.

5.

0.2	0.3	0.4
0.5	0.6	2
3	4	6

6.

2	0.2	0.25	0.5
5	20	40	50

Name _____

Set A pages 197–202

Find 32,000 ÷ 80 using mental math.

Use basic facts and patterns to help.

$32 \div 8 = 4$
$320 \div 80 = 4$
$3,200 \div 80 = 40$
$32,000 \div 80 = 400$

Remember to look for a basic division fact in the numbers. Check your answer by multiplying.

Find each quotient. Use mental math.

1. $360 \div 40$ **2.** $270 \div 90$

3. $2,100 \div 30$ **4.** $4,800 \div 80$

5. $72,000 \div 80$ **6.** $81,000 \div 90$

Set B pages 203–208

Estimate $364 \div 57$.

Use compatible numbers and patterns to divide.

$364 \div 57$
$\downarrow \quad \downarrow$
$360 \div 60 = 6$

So, $364 \div 57$ is about 6.

Remember that compatible numbers are numbers that are easy to work with.

Estimate using compatible numbers.

1. $168 \div 45$ **2.** $525 \div 96$

3. $379 \div 63$ **4.** $234 \div 72$

5. $\$613 \div 93$ **6.** $\$748 \div 92$

Set C pages 209–214

Find $13\overline{)195}$.

Draw a model to help.

1 ten   5 ones

$13\begin{cases} 130 & 65 \end{cases}$

Step 1 Divide the tens.

$\begin{array}{r} 1 \\ 13\overline{)195} \\ -13 \\ \hline 6 \end{array}$

Step 2 How many ones are in each of 13 groups?

$\begin{array}{r} 15 \\ 13\overline{)195} \\ -13 \\ \hline 65 \\ -65 \\ \hline 0 \end{array}$

Remember to separate the dividend into tens and ones before dividing it.

Use a model to find each quotient.

1. $15\overline{)180}$ **2.** $14\overline{)154}$

3. $27\overline{)351}$ **4.** $16\overline{)192}$

5. $11\overline{)143}$ **6.** $31\overline{)217}$

7. $26\overline{)130}$ **8.** $18\overline{)270}$

Set D pages 215–220

Find 461 ÷ 50.

Estimate to decide where to put the first digit in the quotient.

Use compatible numbers. 450 ÷ 50 = 9

So, write 9 in the ones place of the quotient.

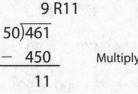

```
        9 R11
  50)461
  −   450      Multiply 9 × 50 = 450
       11
```

Remember that you can multiply to check your estimate of the first digit in the quotient.

1. 20)428   **2.** 30)547

3. 40)387   **4.** 50)653

5. Ivan uses 30 craft sticks to make each toy cabin. He has a box of 342 craft sticks. How many toy cabins can Ivan make? How many sticks will be left over?

Set E pages 221–226

The football coach spent a total of $890 including $50 tax for 35 shirts for the team. Each shirt cost the same. What was the price of one shirt before tax was added?

You can use a problem-solving process with **five steps.**

Analyze Information: The coach spent $890 including $50 tax for 35 shirts. Each shirt cost the same.

Formulate a Plan: What am I asked to find? How much did each shirt cost before tax.

Solve: $890 − $50 = $840; $840 ÷ 35 = $24. Each shirt cost $24 before tax was added.

Justify the Solution: I subtracted the tax, and then divided to find the cost of each shirt. I can multiply and then add to see that the answer matches the problem information.

Evaluate the Problem-Solving Process: I analyzed the problem, formulated a plan, solved the problem, and justified the solution.

Remember to use the problem-solving process to solve the problem.

For Problem 1, analyze the information, formulate a plan, solve the problem, justify your solution, and evaluate the problem-solving process.

1. At a triathlon, athletes bike 110 miles, run a 23-mile marathon, and swim. If the total distance of the triathlon is 135 miles, how far do the athletes swim?

© Pearson Education, Inc. 5

1. It took 5 weeks for Harry to complete his science project. He worked a total of 140 hours. Harry worked on the project 4 days each week. He worked on the project the same number of hours each day. Which two equations help find k, the number of hours Harry worked on the project each day?

A $5 \times 4 = j$; $140 \div j = k$

B $5 \times 140 = j$; $140 \div j = k$

C $140 \div 5 = j$; $j \times 4 = k$

D $140 - 5 = j$; $j \div r = k$

4. A rectangular living room has an area of 425 square feet. The width of the room is 17 feet. How many feet long is the room? Use the model to help.

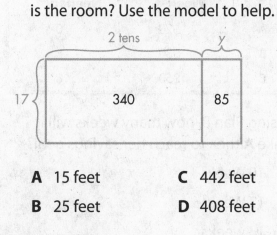

A 15 feet

B 25 feet

C 442 feet

D 408 feet

2. Which of the following is the best choice of compatible numbers to estimate $487 \div 67$?

A 480 divided by 70

B 485 divided by 60

C 490 divided by 60

D 490 divided by 70

5. Which of the following expressions is **NOT** equal to $27,000 \div 30$?

A 270 tens $\div$ 3

B 2,700 tens $\div$ 3 tens

C 2,700 $\div$ 3

D 2,700 tens $\div$ 30 tens

3. The carnival committee has purchased 985 small prizes. If the prizes are to be divided equally among the 20 game booths, how many prizes will each booth have, and how many prizes will be left over?

A 44 per booth with 5 left over

B 49 per booth with none left over

C 49 per booth with 5 left over

D 490 per booth with 5 left over

6. Five Star Farm purchased 2,400 apple trees. If 80 trees can be planted on each acre of land, how many acres will be needed to plant all the trees?

7. Use the table.

Savings Plans for Goal Amount of $384		
Plan	**Amount to Save Each Week**	**Number of Weeks Needed**
A	$20	20
B	$30	
C	$50	8

Using Plan B, how many weeks will it take Althea to reach her savings goal?

A 10 Weeks

B 12 Weeks

C 13 weeks

D 30 weeks

8. The rover *Curiosity* can travel 450 feet per hour on the surface of Mars. How many inches can it travel in 1 minute?

A 5,400 in.   **C** 150 in.

B 900 in.   **D** Not here

9. Use the table. Which equation gives the best estimate of how many times as long as the Chesapeake and Delaware Canal the Erie Canal is?

Canal	Length (in kilometers)
Chesapeake and Delaware Canal	23
Erie Canal	584

A $600 \div 20 = t$ **C** $500 \div 15 = t$

B $500 \div 30 = t$ **D** $60 \div 20 = t$

10. Mrs. Reiss has 264 crayons for her art class of 22 students. How many crayons, c, will each student get if the crayons are divided equally? Use the model.

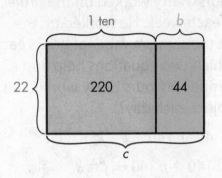

_____

11. Dan divides $16\overline{)608}$. In which place should he write the first digit of the quotient?

_____

12. Mrs. Delgado needs to buy 160 begonias. One plant costs $2. One flat with 20 plants costs $30. How many dollars will she save if she buys them by the flat instead of separately?

			•		
⓪	⓪	⓪		⓪	⓪
①	①	①		①	①
②	②	②		②	②
③	③	③		③	③
④	④	④		④	④
⑤	⑤	⑤		⑤	⑤
⑥	⑥	⑥		⑥	⑥
⑦	⑦	⑦		⑦	⑦
⑧	⑧	⑧		⑧	⑧
⑨	⑨	⑨		⑨	⑨

Developing Proficiency: Dividing by 2-Digit Divisors

Essential Question: What is the standard procedure for dividing with two-digit divisors?

Water is the only substance on Earth that exists in nature as a solid, as a liquid, and as a gas.

Solid water is ice. Water as a gas is water vapor. The same water molecules that we find in liquid water are also in water vapor and ice: H_2O.

Cool! I can skate on water — solid water, not liquid water! Here's a project on states of water.

Math and Science Project: States of Water

Do Research Use the Internet or other sources to learn about the states of water. Find at least 5 examples of water in nature as a solid, as a liquid, and as a gas. At what temperature does liquid water change to ice? At what temperature does liquid water change to water vapor?

Journal: Write a Report Include what you found. Also in your report:

- Explain how liquid water changes to ice and to water vapor.

- At −5°C, 1 inch of rain equals 10 inches of snow. Convert 2 inches of rainfall to snowfall.

- Make up and solve division problems.

Review What You Know

Vocabulary

Choose the best term from the box.
Write it on the blank.

> - divisor
> - factor
> - dividend
> - remainder

1. When you find $418 \div 8$, there are 2 left, called the _____.

2. When you multiply to check your quotient, you can use the number that divided the other number as a _____.

3. The whole that is divided into equal parts is called the _____.

Estimation

Write an expression using compatible numbers that can be used to estimate the quotient.

4. $629 \div 86$

5. $243 \div 51$

6. $713 \div 94$

7. $1,492 \div 65$

8. $1,308 \div 34$

9. $4,163 \div 57$

Multiplying and Dividing

Multiply or divide.

10. $340 \div 20$

11. $156 \div 12$

12. 49×3

13. 7×38

14. Mr. Landers paid \$546 to rent a parking space in a garage for 14 months. Each month of parking cost the same. What was the cost for each month?

    A $39

    B $40

    C $218

    D $560

15. A passenger train has 812 people seated. Each train car seats 70 people. How many train cars are filled? How many people are in the car that is not full?

Estimating

16. **Writing to Explain** If you use $480 \div 80$ to estimate $472 \div 83$, will your estimate be greater than or less than the actual answer? Justify your answer using precise mathematical language.

Name _____

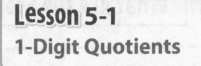

Solve & Share

Darlene needs 250 yards of string to fly kites at a festival. String comes in balls of 80 yards. How many balls of string does she need to buy? *Solve this problem any way you choose.*

How can you **connect** this problem with other problems you have done previously? *Show your work!*

⭐ TEKS 5.3C Solve with proficiency for quotients of up to a four-digit dividend by a two-digit divisor using strategies and the standard algorithm. Also 5.3. Mathematical Process Standards 5.1A, 5.1C, 5.1D, 5.1G

Digital Resources at PearsonTexas.com

Solve   Learn   Glossary   Check   Tools   Games

Look Back!

Check for Reasonableness A classmate said that the answer is 3 not 4. Why is 3 not a reasonable answer?

What Are the Steps for Dividing by 2-Digit Numbers?

A-Z

A theater sold 428 tickets for a show. Each section in this theater has 64 seats. How many sections will be used to seat all the ticket holders?

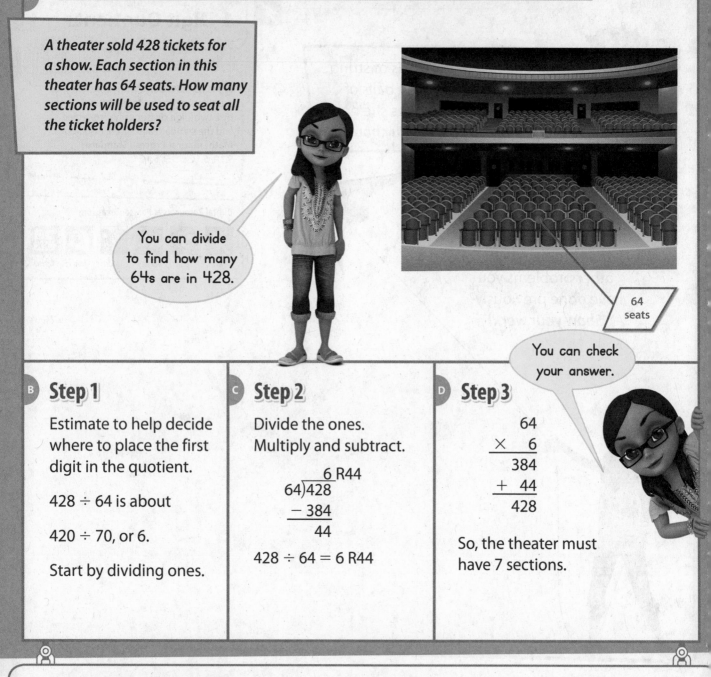

You can divide to find how many 64s are in 428.

64 seats

You can check your answer.

B **Step 1**

Estimate to help decide where to place the first digit in the quotient.

428 ÷ 64 is about

420 ÷ 70, or 6.

Start by dividing ones.

C **Step 2**

Divide the ones. Multiply and subtract.

$$\begin{array}{r} 6 \text{ R44} \\ 64\overline{)428} \\ -384 \\ \hline 44 \end{array}$$

428 ÷ 64 = 6 R44

D **Step 3**

$$\begin{array}{r} 64 \\ \times\ 6 \\ \hline 384 \\ +\ 44 \\ \hline 428 \end{array}$$

So, the theater must have 7 sections.

Do You Understand?

Convince Me! Suppose each section of the theater has only 45 seats. How many sections would be needed to seat 428 people?

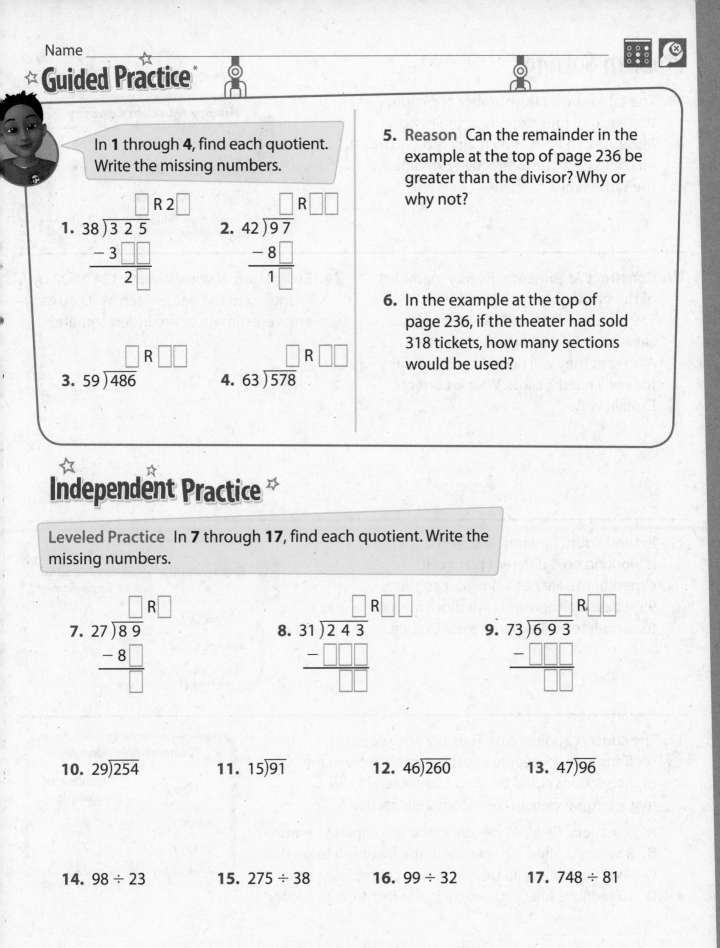

Guided Practice

In **1** through **4**, find each quotient. Write the missing numbers.

1. ☐ R 2☐
   38)3 2 5
   − 3☐☐
   ──────
   2☐

2. ☐ R ☐☐
   42)9 7
   − 8☐
   ────
   1☐

3. ☐ R ☐☐
   59)486

4. ☐ R ☐☐
   63)578

5. **Reason** Can the remainder in the example at the top of page 236 be greater than the divisor? Why or why not?

6. In the example at the top of page 236, if the theater had sold 318 tickets, how many sections would be used?

Independent Practice

Leveled Practice In **7** through **17**, find each quotient. Write the missing numbers.

7. ☐ R ☐
   27)8 9
   − 8☐
   ────
   ☐

8. ☐ R ☐☐
   31)2 4 3
   − ☐☐☐
   ──────
   ☐☐

9. ☐ R ☐☐
   73)6 9 3
   − ☐☐☐
   ──────
   ☐☐

10. 29)254

11. 15)91

12. 46)260

13. 47)96

14. 98 ÷ 23

15. 275 ÷ 38

16. 99 ÷ 32

17. 748 ÷ 81

Problem Solving

18. The table shows the number of people that each of four exhibits at the History Museum can hold. How many groups of 48 could view the Interactive Exhibit at the same time?

History Museum Capacity	
Governor Exhibit	68
Landmark Exhibit	95
Early 1900s Exhibit	85
Interactive Exhibit	260

19. Construct Arguments Twenty members of the photography club will take 559 pictures. They will use memory cards that hold 85 pictures per card. Alan says they will need 6 cards. Jill says they will need 7 cards. Who is correct? Explain why.

20. Estimation If you estimate 124 × 22 by rounding to the nearest ten, will you get an overestimate or an underestimate?

21. Extend Your Thinking A scientist is working on 4 different plant cell experiments. He has a box that contains 95 slides. Are there enough slides for him to complete all 4 experiments? Explain.

Experiment	Number of Slides Needed Per Experiment
Animal Cell	23
Mineral Color	32
Plant Cell	24

22. The concert audience on Tuesday was seated in sections with 75 people in each section. How many of the sections could be filled completely? How many people were in the incomplete section?

A 8 sections filled, 45 people in the incomplete section

B 8 sections filled, 120 people in the incomplete section

C 9 sections filled, 45 people in the incomplete section

D 10 sections filled, 30 people in the incomplete section

Concert Attendance	
Day	Number of People
Monday	750
Tuesday	720
Wednesday	780

Another Look!

Vera needs 237 mini-pizzas for guests at a party. Each package has 42 mini-pizzas. How many packages does Vera need to buy?

> Remember, the number in each group is the divisor.

Step 1

Divide the ones.
Multiply the number of ones by the number of pizzas in each group.

$$
\begin{array}{r}
5 \\
42\overline{)237} \\
210
\end{array}
$$

← 237 ones ÷ 42 pizzas
← 42 × 5 ones = 210 ones

Step 2

Subtract the ones.
Write the remainder.

$$
\begin{array}{r}
5\ R27 \\
42\overline{)237} \\
-\ 210 \\
\hline
27
\end{array}
$$

So, Vera needs to buy 6 packages.

In **1** through **9**, find each quotient. Write the missing numbers.

1. $53\overline{)429}$ □R□

2. $28\overline{)202}$ □R□

3. $12\overline{)83}$ □R□□

4. $51\overline{)489}$ □R□□

5. $46\overline{)979}$ □□R□□

6. $38\overline{)800}$ □□R□

7. $167 \div 17 =$ __ R __

8. $365 \div 52 =$ __ R __

9. $89 \div 30 =$ __ R __

10. Communicate Explain how you know that Mia's answer to the problem shown below has an error.

$$
\begin{array}{r}
8\ \text{R}24 \\
16\overline{)152} \\
-\underline{128} \\
24
\end{array}
$$

11. Connect Which problem will have the greater quotient, 394 ÷ 56 or 394 ÷ 57? Why? Write a word problem that shows why your answer is correct.

12. Number Sense Explain why 0.2 and 0.02 are **NOT** equivalent.

13. ⭐ For every 90 minutes of sleep, a person has one dream stage. Rachel went to bed at 10:00 P.M. and woke up at 5:30 A.M. How many dream stages did she likely have?

A 5
B 6
C 9
D 10

Remember, 1 hour = 60 minutes.

14. Explain Ms. Lopez has $118 for tickets at the Sports Fun Park. She needs to buy 1 adult ticket for $19. How many child tickets can she buy if child tickets cost $12 each? Explain how you found your answer.

15. In Exercise 14, Ms. Lopez changed her plans and decided to purchase another adult ticket and 6 child tickets. How much money will she have left?

16. Extend Your Thinking Jane wants to buy an Internet service plan for 31 days. She wants to pay between $2 and $3 each day. Which plan offers an Internet service plan at a cost between $2 and $3 each day? Explain.

DATA

Connect Global Internet Plans	
Plan Name	**Cost Per Month**
Wired	$49
Fast	$69
Quick	$99
Speedy	$109

Name _____

☆ ☆
Solve & Share

A factory is going to ship 814 stuffed animals. Each of the packing boxes will hold 18 stuffed animals. How many boxes are needed? How many boxes will be filled? *Solve this problem any way you choose.*

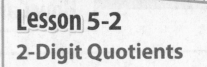

⭐ **TEKS 5.3C** Solve with proficiency for quotients of up to a four-digit dividend by a two-digit divisor using strategies and the standard algorithm. Also 5.3. Mathematical Process Standards 5.1C, 5.1D, 5.1F

Connect You know how to divide when the quotient has one digit. *Show your work!*

Digital Resources at PearsonTexas.com

Solve   Learn   Glossary   Check   Tools   Games

Look Back!

Analyze Relationships How does the number of boxes needed compare to the number of boxes filled?

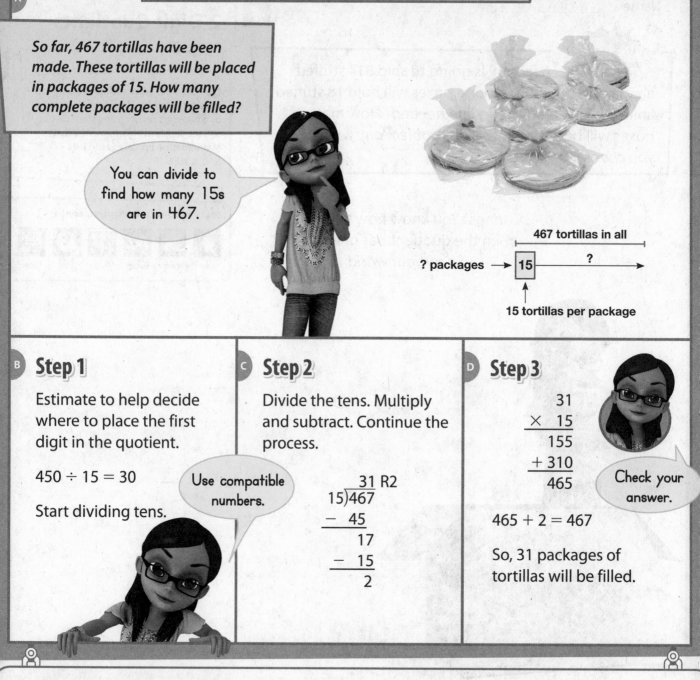

A

So far, 467 tortillas have been made. These tortillas will be placed in packages of 15. How many complete packages will be filled?

You can divide to find how many 15s are in 467.

467 tortillas in all

? packages → 15 ?

15 tortillas per package

B Step 1

Estimate to help decide where to place the first digit in the quotient.

$450 \div 15 = 30$

Start dividing tens.

Use compatible numbers.

C Step 2

Divide the tens. Multiply and subtract. Continue the process.

$$
\begin{array}{r}
31 \text{ R2} \\
15\overline{)467} \\
-\ 45 \\
\hline
17 \\
-\ 15 \\
\hline
2
\end{array}
$$

D Step 3

$$
\begin{array}{r}
31 \\
\times\ 15 \\
\hline
155 \\
+\ 310 \\
\hline
465
\end{array}
$$

Check your answer.

$465 + 2 = 467$

So, 31 packages of tortillas will be filled.

Do You Understand?

Convince Me! In the problem above, how would your estimate be different if 627 tortillas were made? Use your estimate to solve $627 \div 15$.

☆ Guided Practice*

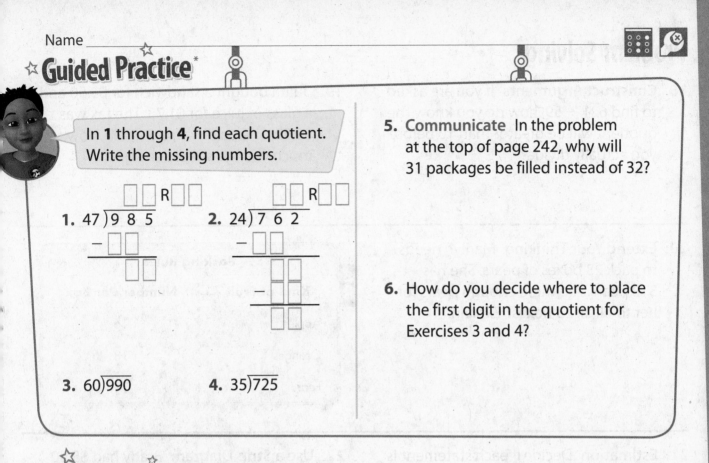

In **1** through **4**, find each quotient. Write the missing numbers.

1. 47)985 □□ R □□
−□□
□□

2. 24)762 □□ R □□
−□□
−□□
□□

3. 60)990

4. 35)725

5. Communicate In the problem at the top of page 242, why will 31 packages be filled instead of 32?

6. How do you decide where to place the first digit in the quotient for Exercises 3 and 4?

Independent Practice ☆

Leveled Practice In **7** through **17**, find each quotient. Write the missing numbers.

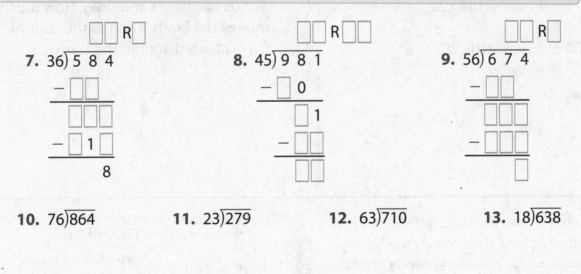

7. 36)584 □□ R □
−□□
□□□
−□1□
8

8. 45)981 □□ R □□
−□0
□1
−□□
□□

9. 56)674 □□ R □
−□□
□□□
−□□□
□

10. 76)864

11. 23)279

12. 63)710

13. 18)638

14. 989 ÷ 13

15. 678 ÷ 27

16. 980 ÷ 45

17. 717 ÷ 31

Problem Solving

18. Construct Arguments If you are asked to find 621 ÷ 59, how do you know the quotient will be greater than 10 before you actually divide?

19. Julita bought a sandwich for $3.50 and a glass of juice for $1.75. The tax was $0.42. She paid with a $10 bill. How much change should she get?

20. Extend Your Thinking Marilyn needs to pack 23 boxes of pears. She has 318 pears. Are there enough pears for her to fill all 23 boxes? Explain.

Packing Rules	
Kind of Fruit	**Number Per Box**
Apples	16
Oranges	18
Pears	14

21. Estimation Decide if each statement is true or false. Explain.

A 710 ÷ 20 is greater than 30.

B 821 ÷ 40 is less than 20.

C 300 ÷ 15 is exactly 20.

22. Use a Strip Diagram Brady had $5.00 when she left the county fair. She spent $11.00 on her ticket, and she bought lunch for $6.00. After lunch, she spent $17.00 on games and rides. How much money did Brady bring to the county fair? Draw a diagram. Then solve.

23. ⭐ The table shows the time needed for different bird eggs to hatch. About how many days does it take for a goose egg to hatch?

A 15 days

B 16 days

C 25 days

D 31 days

1 day equals 24 hours.

Hatching Time for Bird Eggs	
Kind of Bird	**Number of Hours Needed**
Chicken	500
Dove	340
Goose	735
Turkey	675

Name _____

Another Look!

Tamika has 564 tiles. She is making 24 picture frames. Each frame will get the same number of tiles. How many tiles should she put on each frame?

You can estimate to help you decide where the first digit of the quotient should be.

Step 1

Divide the tens.
Multiply the number of tens by the number of groups.

$$\begin{array}{r} 2 \\ 24\overline{)564} \\ -48 \\ \hline 8 \end{array}$$

←56 tens ÷ 24 groups

←24 × 2 tens = 48 tens

Step 2

Divide the ones.
Subtract. Write the remainder.

$$\begin{array}{r} 23\ \text{R}12 \\ 24\overline{)564} \\ -48 \\ \hline 84 \\ -72 \\ \hline 12 \end{array}$$

←84 ones ÷ 24 groups

←24 × 3 ones = 72 ones

Tamika should put 23 tiles on each frame.

In **1** through **9**, find each quotient. Write the missing numbers.

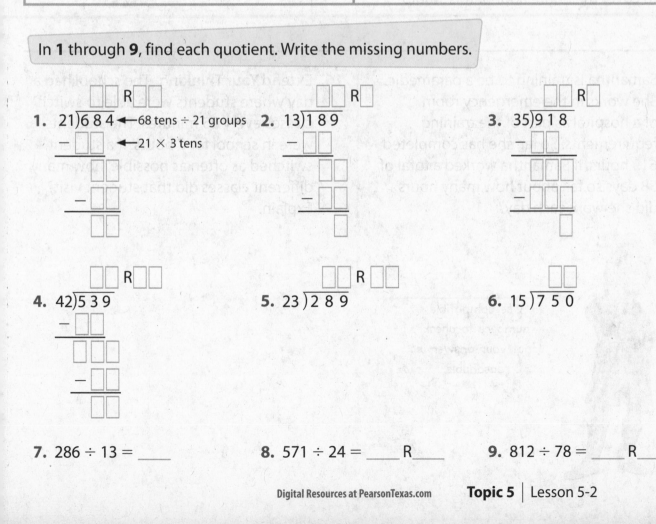

1. 21⟌6 8 4 ←68 tens ÷ 21 groups
   − ←21 × 3 tens

2. 13⟌1 8 9

3. 35⟌9 1 8

4. 42⟌5 3 9

5. 23⟌2 8 9

6. 15⟌7 5 0

7. 286 ÷ 13 = _____

8. 571 ÷ 24 = _____ R_____

9. 812 ÷ 78 = _____ R_____

10. Communicate Alisa said if you have a two-digit divisor and a three-digit dividend, the quotient will always have two digits. Is she correct? Explain.

11. Estimation The total dinner bill at a buffet was $589 for 31 people. About how much did it cost per person? Explain how you estimated.

12. One of the thorny devil lizard's favorite foods is ants. If it ate 45 ants in one minute, about how long would the lizard take to eat 535 ants if it continued eating at the same rate?

A 9 minutes

B 10 minutes

C 12 minutes

D 15 minutes

13. Personal Financial Literacy Leah has saved $26.48. Ted has saved $26.84. Who has saved more?

14. Analyze Information The rubber flooring used in a karate studio comes in square sheets. Each sheet covers 32 square feet. How many sheets are needed to cover the entire floor of this studio?

28 ft | Karate Studio
64 ft

15. Samantha is training to be a paramedic. She works in the emergency room of a hospital as part of the training requirements. So far, she has completed 619 hours. If Samantha worked a total of 58 days so far, about how many hours did she work each day?

16. Extend Your Thinking The school had a day where students were able to switch classes every 25 minutes. The students were in school for 7 hours. If a student switched as often as possible, how many different classes did that student visit? Explain.

Use compatible numbers to check that your answer is reasonable.

Name _____

Solve & Share

Marcia's choir needs to raise $5,375 for its annual trip. Each of the 25 members of the choir will need to contribute equally. About how much money does each person need to raise? *Solve this problem any way you choose.*

⭐ TEKS 5.3C Solve with proficiency for quotients of up to a four-digit dividend by a two-digit divisor using strategies and the standard algorithm. Also 5.3. Mathematical Process Standards 5.1B, 5.1C, 5.1D, 5.1G

Digital Resources at PearsonTexas.com

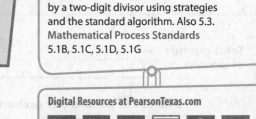

| Solve | Learn | Glossary | Check | Tools | Games |

Use **estimation** to find about how large the quotient will be. *Show your work!*

Look Back!

Number Sense Do you think the exact answer is greater than or less than your estimate? Explain.

How Do You Solve Problems Involving Division of Greater Numbers?

In one season, 14 orchards produced 7,826 pounds of pecans. On average, how many pounds of pecans came from each orchard?

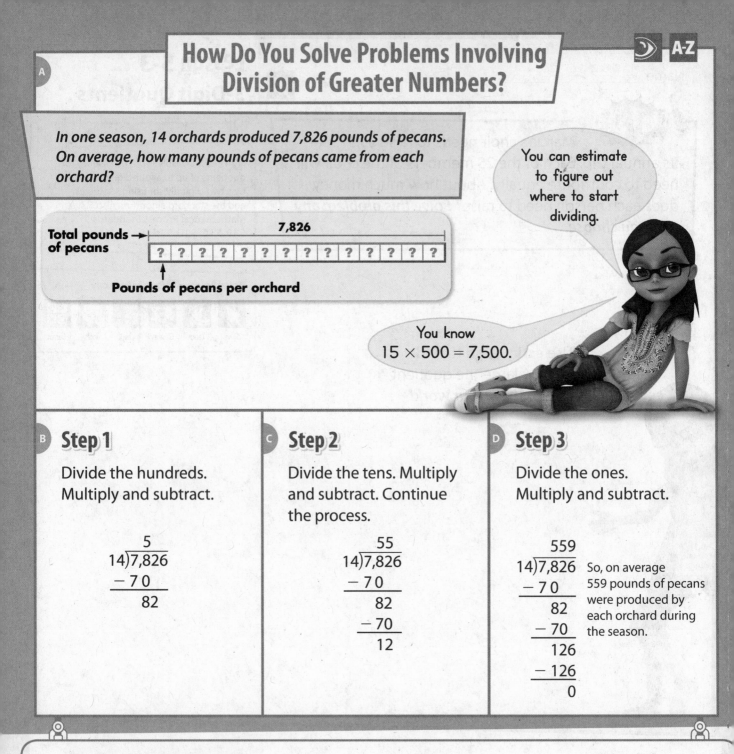

Total pounds of pecans → 7,826

Pounds of pecans per orchard

You can estimate to figure out where to start dividing.

You know
15 × 500 = 7,500.

B **Step 1**

Divide the hundreds. Multiply and subtract.

$$\begin{array}{r} 5 \\ 14\overline{)7{,}826} \\ -70 \\ \hline 82 \end{array}$$

C **Step 2**

Divide the tens. Multiply and subtract. Continue the process.

$$\begin{array}{r} 55 \\ 14\overline{)7{,}826} \\ -70 \\ \hline 82 \\ -70 \\ \hline 12 \end{array}$$

D **Step 3**

Divide the ones. Multiply and subtract.

$$\begin{array}{r} 559 \\ 14\overline{)7{,}826} \\ -70 \\ \hline 82 \\ -70 \\ \hline 126 \\ -126 \\ \hline 0 \end{array}$$

So, on average 559 pounds of pecans were produced by each orchard during the season.

Do You Understand?

Convince Me! If only 11 orchards harvested the 7,826 pounds of pecans, about how many pounds would have come from each orchard?

☆ Guided Practice ☆

In **1** and **2**, find each quotient. Write the missing numbers.

1. 12)2,9 6 4
   — 2 4
     6

2. 39)4,0 9 8

3. **Number Sense** In the example on page 248, if one of the orchards was not able to produce pecans, but the total produced stayed the same, how would the number of pounds produced by each orchard change? Explain.

4. **Estimation** In Exercises 1 and 2, how do you know the first digit of the quotient is in the hundreds?

Independent Practice ☆

Leveled Practice In **5** through **7**, find each quotient. Write the missing numbers.

5. 24)7,4 8 8

6. 43)8,7 8 1

7. 81)9,9 6 3

In **8** through **10**, find each quotient.

8. 17)4,219

9. 52)9,708

10. 28)8,568

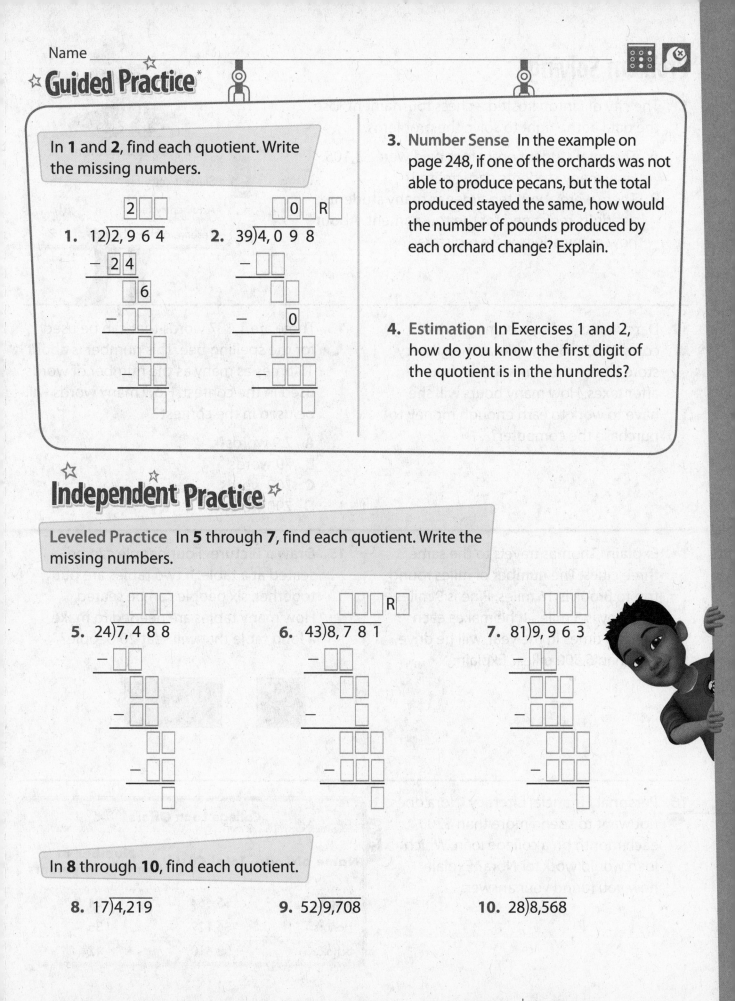

Problem Solving

11. The city of Linton hosted a chess tournament. Use the data at the right to solve the problems.

    A The total student entry fees paid were $3,105. How many students participated?

    B There were about ten times as many students as adults registered for the tournament. About how many adults were registered?

Chess Tournament

Student entry fee	$15
Adult entry fee	$18
Reserve a chess board	$12

---

12. Darci wants to buy a computer that costs $1,236. She works at the grocery store where she earns $11 an hour after taxes. How many hours will she have to work to earn enough money to purchase the computer?

13. There are 1,187 words that can be used for the spelling bee. This number is about 15 times as many as the number of words used in the contest. How many words will be used in the contest?

    A 7.9 words
    B 79 words
    C 709 words
    D 790 words

---

14. **Explain** Thomas travels to the same three cities. The number of miles round trip to Brook is 16 miles, Pine is 9 miles, and Troy is 5 miles. If he makes each trip 220 times in the year, will he drive less than 6,500 miles? Explain.

15. **Draw a Picture** Four people can be seated at a table. If two tables are put together, six people can be seated. How many tables are needed to make a long table that will seat 20 people?

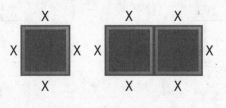

---

16. **Personal Financial Literacy** Nora does not want to spend more than $200 each month on a college loan. Which loan would work for Nora? Explain how you found your answer.

College Loan Offers		
Name of Loan	Total Cost	Number of Monthly Payments
Smart	$5,664	24
Honors	$6,129	36
Scholar	$8,610	42

Name _____

Another Look!

A county has 26 towns. Each town will get an equal share of $8,970 for library use. What amount will each town get?

First, decide where to start dividing.

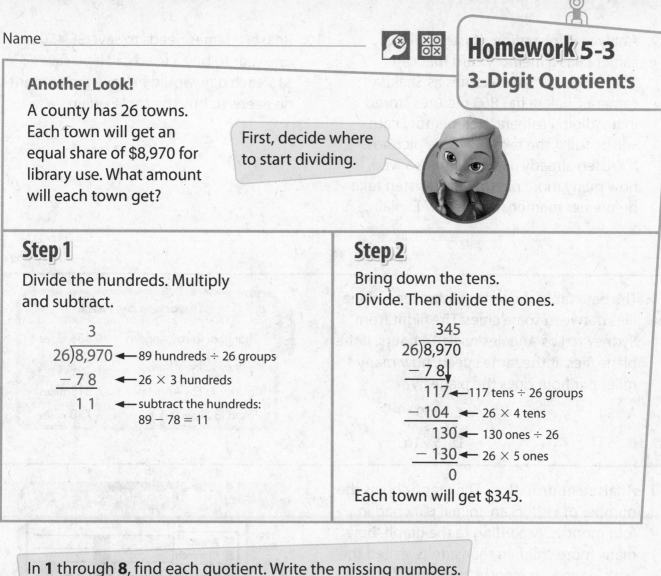

Step 1

Divide the hundreds. Multiply and subtract.

$$
\begin{array}{r}
3 \\
26\overline{)8{,}970} \\
\end{array}
$$
⟵ 89 hundreds ÷ 26 groups

$-\ 78$ ⟵ 26 × 3 hundreds

$1\ 1$ ⟵ subtract the hundreds:
$89 - 78 = 11$

Step 2

Bring down the tens.
Divide. Then divide the ones.

$$
\begin{array}{r}
345 \\
26\overline{)8{,}970} \\
\end{array}
$$

$-\ 78$

117 ⟵ 117 tens ÷ 26 groups

$-\ 104$ ⟵ 26 × 4 tens

130 ⟵ 130 ones ÷ 26

$-\ 130$ ⟵ 26 × 5 ones

0

Each town will get $345.

In **1** through **8**, find each quotient. Write the missing numbers.

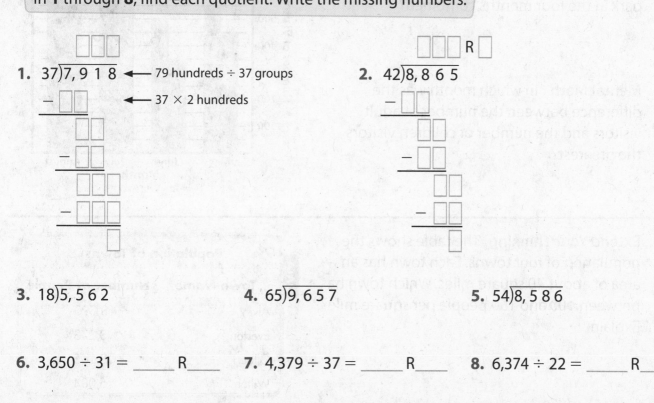

1. $37\overline{)7{,}918}$ ⟵ 79 hundreds ÷ 37 groups

⟵ 37 × 2 hundreds

2. $42\overline{)8{,}865}$

3. $18\overline{)5{,}562}$

4. $65\overline{)9{,}657}$

5. $54\overline{)8{,}586}$

6. $3{,}650 \div 31 =$ _____ R_____

7. $4{,}379 \div 37 =$ _____ R_____

8. $6{,}374 \div 22 =$ _____ R_____

9. **Analyze Information** Kristen's digital camera has a memory card that can hold twice as many pictures as Shakira's camera. Shakira has 863 pictures stored in her digital camera. Her memory card will be full if she takes 37 more pictures. If Kristen already has 59 pictures saved, how many more pictures can Kristen take before her memory card is full? Explain.

10. **Reason** James needs to save $5,450 in one year to buy a used car. If he saves $15 each day, would he save the amount he needs to buy the car? Explain.

11. The data table shows the distances a plane flies between some cities. The flight from Sydney to Los Angeles takes 14 hours. If the plane flies at the same speed, how many miles per hour does the plane fly?

   A 54

   B 537

   C 709

   D 5,216

DATA

Distances by Plane	
Shanghai to Los Angeles	6,438 miles
Sydney to New York	9,926 miles
Sydney to Los Angeles	7,518 miles
Tokyo to New York	6,740 miles

12. **Analyze Information** The graph shows the number of visitors an animal park had in four months. According to the graph, how many more children than adults visited the park in the four months combined?

13. **Mental Math** In which month was the difference between the number of adult visitors and the number of children visitors the greatest?

14. **Extend Your Thinking** The table shows the population of four towns. Each town has an area of about 40 square miles. Which town has between 100 and 150 people per square mile? Explain.

DATA

Population of Towns	
Town Name	**Number of People**
Alvey	8,390
Everton	3,273
Gilbert	8,165
Wilton	5,084

Name _____

Solve & Share

A bakery needs to make a batch of 196 bagels. Each baking sheet holds the same number of bagels. How many baking sheets are needed? **Solve this problem any way you choose.**

⭐ TEKS 5.3C Solve with proficiency for quotients of up to a four-digit dividend by a two-digit divisor using strategies and the standard algorithm. Also 5.3. Mathematical Process Standards 5.1B, 5.1C, 5.1D, 5.1G

Digital Resources at PearsonTexas.com

| Solve | Learn | Glossary | Check | Tools | Games |

You can **estimate** using rounding or compatible numbers. **Show your work!**

18 bagels per sheet

Look Back!

Communicate How did your estimate help you find the quotient?

How Can You Use Estimation to Decide if Your Quotient Is Reasonable?

Orchard workers have grapefruit seedlings to plant in 23 equal rows. How many seedlings will be in each row?

832 grapefruit seedlings

You can use compatible numbers to estimate 832 ÷ 23.

B Step 1

832 is about 800
23 is about 20

$800 ÷ 20 = 40$

The first digit is in the tens place. Start dividing tens.

$$\begin{array}{r} 4 \\ 23\overline{)832} \\ -92 \end{array}$$

The estimate is too high.

C Step 2

Try 3.

$$\begin{array}{r} 3 \\ 23\overline{)832} \\ -69 \\ \hline 14 \end{array}$$

Bring down the ones. Continue dividing.

$$\begin{array}{r} 36\ R4 \\ 23\overline{)832} \\ -69 \\ \hline 142 \\ -138 \\ \hline 4 \end{array}$$

D Step 3

Compare your answer to the estimate.

36 is close to 40. So the answer is reasonable.

There will be 36 grapefruit seedlings in each row.

Do You Understand?

Convince Me! In Step 1 above, how do you know the estimate is too high? Explain.

☆ Guided Practice ☆

1. Estimate 452 ÷ 21.

> Remember to check that your answer is reasonable.

2. Complete.

```
       □□ R□□
  21)4 5 2
    -□□
     □□
    -□□
     □□
```

3. For Exercise 2, how can you use estimation to decide where to place the first digit of the quotient?

4. **Writing to Explain** How can you use estimation to check if a quotient is reasonable?

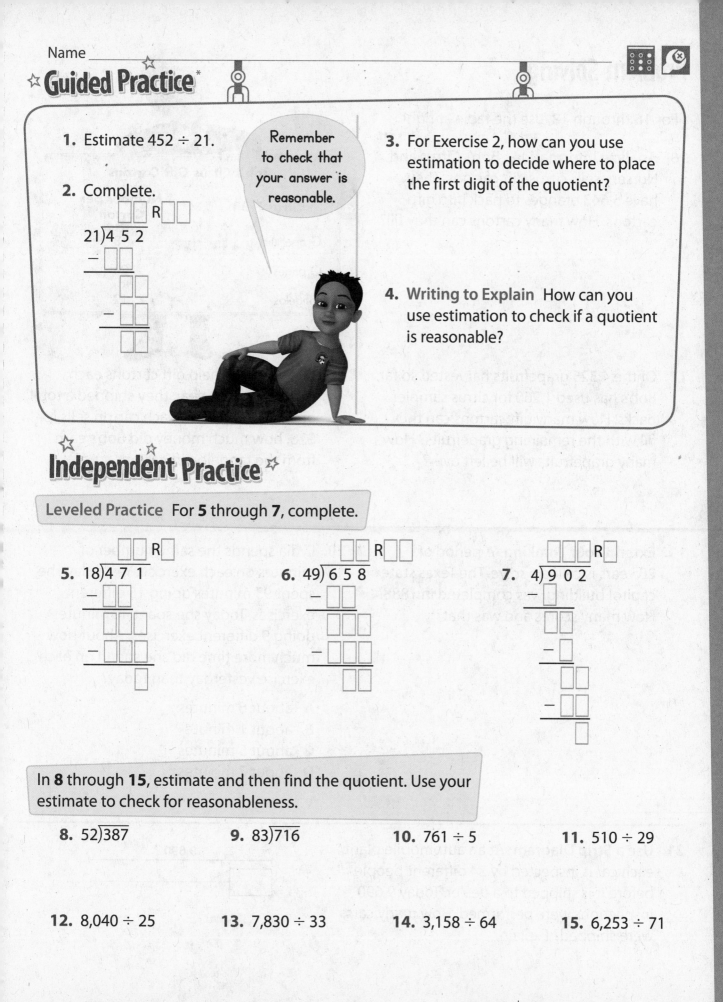

☆ Independent Practice ☆

Leveled Practice For **5** through **7**, complete.

5.
```
     □□ R□
18)4 7 1
  -□□
   □□□
  -□□□
    □
```

6.
```
     □□ R□□
49)6 5 8
  -□□
   □□□
  -□□□
    □□
```

7.
```
      □□□ R□
 4)9 0 2
  -□
   □□
  -□□
    □□
   -□□
     □
```

In **8** through **15**, estimate and then find the quotient. Use your estimate to check for reasonableness.

8. 52)387

9. 83)716

10. 761 ÷ 5

11. 510 ÷ 29

12. 8,040 ÷ 25

13. 7,830 ÷ 33

14. 3,158 ÷ 64

15. 6,253 ÷ 71

Problem Solving

For **16** through **18**, use the table at right.

16. Analyze Information Bob's Citrus and Nursery sells citrus gift cartons. They have 5,643 oranges to pack into gift cartons. How many cartons can they fill?

DATA

Bob's Citrus Gift Cartons

Citrus Fruit	Number per Carton
Grapefruit	18
Oranges	24
Tangelos	12

17. Of the 4,325 grapefruits harvested so far, Bob's has used 1,260 for citrus sampler packs. How many gift cartons can they fill with the remaining grapefruits? How many grapefruits will be left over?

18. Bob's sells tangelo gift cartons each December. Last year, they shipped a total of 3,300 tangelos. If each carton sells for $28, how much money did Bob's earn from the tangelo gift cartons sold?

19. Extend Your Thinking A period of 20 years is called a *score*. The Texas state capitol building was completed in 1888. How many scores ago was that?

20. Lydia spends the same number of minutes on each exercise. Yesterday she spent 93 minutes doing 15 different exercises. Today she spent 48 minutes doing 9 different exercises. About how much more time did she spend on each exercise yesterday than today?

   A about 6 minutes
   B about 1 minute
   C about 5 minutes
   D about 7 minutes

21. Use a Strip Diagram At an automobile plant, each car is inspected by 34 different people before it is shipped to a dealer. Today 9,690 inspections were performed. How many cars were shipped? Explain.

9,690

?

Name _____

Another Look!

At the driving range, golfers can rent buckets of 32 golf balls. The range has a supply of 2,650 golf balls. How many buckets are needed for the balls?

Use compatible numbers to estimate 2,650 ÷ 32. You can use 2,700 ÷ 30 = 90.

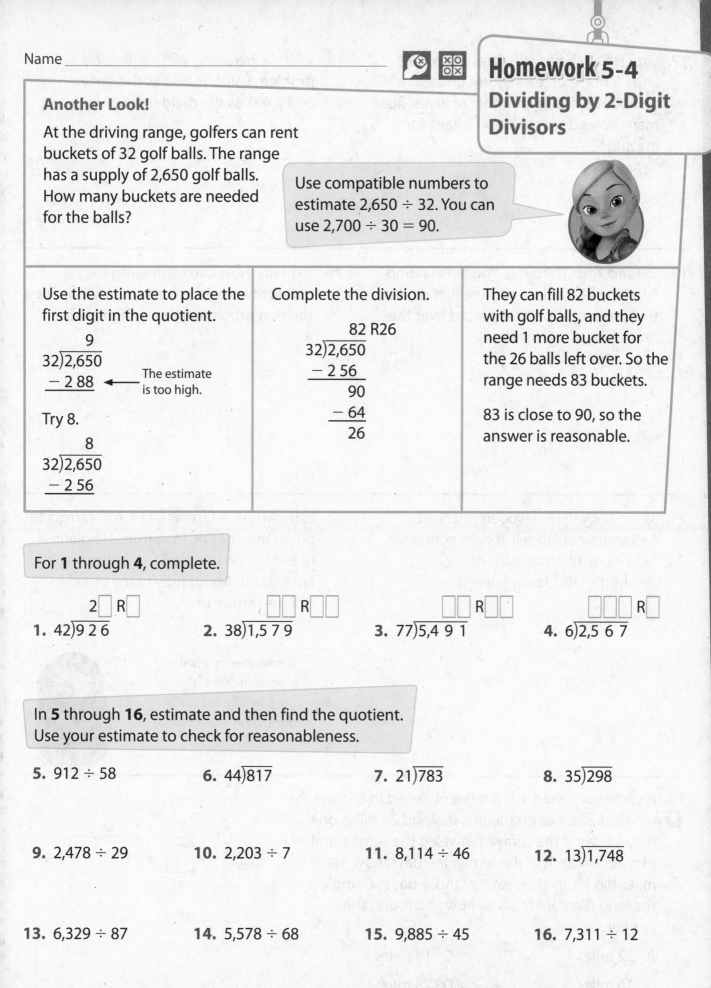

Use the estimate to place the first digit in the quotient.

$$\begin{array}{r} 9 \\ 32\overline{)2,650} \\ -2\,88 \end{array}$$ ← The estimate is too high.

Try 8.

$$\begin{array}{r} 8 \\ 32\overline{)2,650} \\ -2\,56 \end{array}$$

Complete the division.

$$\begin{array}{r} 82\ R26 \\ 32\overline{)2,650} \\ -2\,56 \\ \hline 90 \\ -64 \\ \hline 26 \end{array}$$

They can fill 82 buckets with golf balls, and they need 1 more bucket for the 26 balls left over. So the range needs 83 buckets.

83 is close to 90, so the answer is reasonable.

For 1 through 4, complete.

1. $\begin{array}{r} 2\square\ R\square \\ 42\overline{)9\,2\,6} \end{array}$

2. $\begin{array}{r} \square\square\ R\square\square \\ 38\overline{)1,5\,7\,9} \end{array}$

3. $\begin{array}{r} \square\square\ R\square\square \\ 77\overline{)5,4\,9\,1} \end{array}$

4. $\begin{array}{r} \square\square\square\ R\square \\ 6\overline{)2,5\,6\,7} \end{array}$

In 5 through 16, estimate and then find the quotient. Use your estimate to check for reasonableness.

5. 912 ÷ 58

6. 44)817

7. 21)783

8. 35)298

9. 2,478 ÷ 29

10. 2,203 ÷ 7

11. 8,114 ÷ 46

12. 13)1,748

13. 6,329 ÷ 87

14. 5,578 ÷ 68

15. 9,885 ÷ 45

16. 7,311 ÷ 12

17. Lazy H Ranch has 505 acres of pasture and 79 horses. If each horse grazes on about the same number of acres, how many acres does each horse have for grazing?

18. Write a Problem Write a division problem using the 53 as the divisor and 2,491 as the dividend. Solve.

---

19. Extend Your Thinking You are dividing 3,972 by 41. Explain why the first digit in the quotient should be placed over the tens place of the dividend.

20. Explain How can estimating the quotient help you check your answer to a division problem for reasonableness?

---

21. Jason packed his raspberry harvest in 245 containers to sell. If each container held 45 raspberries, how many raspberries did Jason harvest?

22. Estimation A farmer has 4,700 carrots to put in bunches of 15 carrots. He plans to sell the carrots for $5 per bunch at his farm stand. About how many bunches will the farmer make?

Remember to read a problem carefully. Identify the information you need.

---

23. A caravan crossed 1,378 miles of desert in 85 days. It ⭐ traveled 22 miles on the first day and 28 miles on the second day. If the caravan traveled the same number of miles on each of the remaining days, how many miles did it travel on each of those days? Complete the strip diagram to show how you found the answer.

number of days → [ ]————?————→

A 22 miles   C 18 miles

B 16 miles   D 28 miles

Name _____

★ **Solve & Share** ★

Juno rides his bike twice as far on Sunday as he does on Saturday. How many miles does he ride on Sunday? *Make up missing information to solve this problem.*

How can you formulate a plan to help you solve this problem? *Show your work!*

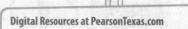

TEKS 5.1B Use a problem-solving model that incorporates analyzing given information, formulating a plan or strategy, determining a solution, justifying the solution, and evaluating the problem-solving process and the reasonableness of the solution. Also, 5.1. Mathematical Process Standards 5.1D, 5.1E

Digital Resources at PearsonTexas.com

| Solve | Learn | Glossary | Check | Tools | Games |

Look Back!

Communicate Add some information to your problem that is not needed to solve it.

What Information Is Needed to Solve a Problem?

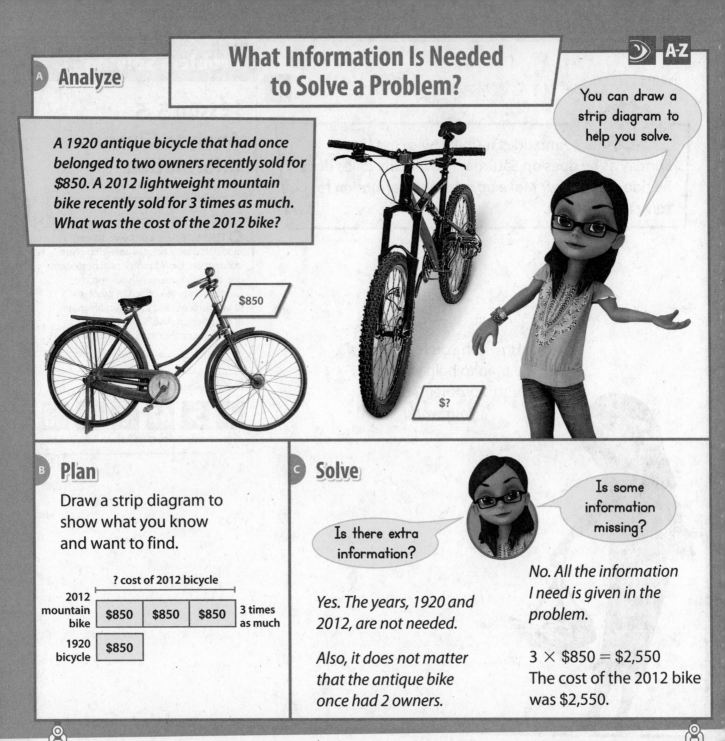

You can draw a strip diagram to help you solve.

A 1920 antique bicycle that had once belonged to two owners recently sold for $850. A 2012 lightweight mountain bike recently sold for 3 times as much. What was the cost of the 2012 bike?

$850

$?

B **Plan**

Draw a strip diagram to show what you know and want to find.

? cost of 2012 bicycle

| 2012 mountain bike | $850 | $850 | $850 | 3 times as much |
| 1920 bicycle | $850 |

C **Solve**

Is there extra information?

Is some information missing?

Yes. The years, 1920 and 2012, are not needed.

Also, it does not matter that the antique bike once had 2 owners.

No. All the information I need is given in the problem.

3 × $850 = $2,550
The cost of the 2012 bike was $2,550.

Do You Understand?

Convince Me! Special high tech wheels for the mountain bike cost $225 each. Replacement wheels for an antique bike cost even more! The antique dealer has $600 to spend on replacement wheels. How much would it cost to buy the replacement wheels?

Can you solve this problem? Explain your thinking.

☆ Guided Practice ☆

For **1** and **2**, decide if each problem has extra or missing information. Solve if possible.

1. An adult male gorilla eats about 40 pounds of food each day. An adult female gorilla eats about half as much. How many pounds of food does an adult male gorilla eat in one week?

2. Lacey is buying dried fruit to feed her pet bird. How much will it cost to feed the bird for one month?

3. Draw a diagram to show what you know and want to find in Problem 1.

4. **Analyze Information** Why is it important to find the extra or missing information before solving a problem?

5. **Represent** Write a real-world problem that does not include all of the information to solve it. Under the problem, write the missing information.

Independent Practice ☆

For **6** through **8**, decide if each problem has extra or missing information. Solve if possible.

6. Eli has played 5 baseball games so far this season. How many runs did he score if he scored 2 runs each game for the first 4 games?

7. Sonja posted 45 band concert flyers in 2 days. Over the next 2 days, Elsie posted 60 flyers, and Frank posted 30 flyers. How many flyers did the 3 students post altogether?

8. A storage room in an electronics store has boxes containing flat-screen TV sets. Each box contains 1 TV set. Each box weighs between 13 pounds and 28 pounds. Estimate the least and greatest total weight of all the boxes.

> You may want to draw a line through information you do not need.

Problem Solving

9. Mrs. Torance has invited 16 people to a party. What information is missing if she wants to serve enough submarine sandwiches at her party?

Each sub feeds 3 children or 2 adults

10. Roses are on sale at the market at 2 for $1.00. Mindy has $20.00. If she buys 16 roses, how much will they cost?

11. **Math and Science** Kim heats a 250-gram sample of water at a steady rate. It takes 3 minutes for the water temperature to increase by 10°C. If the starting temperature is 25°C, how long will it take the water sample to reach 75°C?

12. John and his sister visited Texas State Aquarium in Corpus Christi. There they learned that 1 catfish produces 40 eggs and 1 goldfish produces 20 eggs. How many catfish produce 2,400 eggs?

A 40   **C** 240

B 60   **D** 2,400

13. Sylvia had $23 to spend at the circus. She spent $12.50 on admission. During lunch, she bought a hot dog and a drink for $6.75. How much money did Sylvia have left to spend after lunch?

14. Greg bought a sandwich and a drink at Dunstan's Deli. He paid $4.50. Which sandwich and drink did he buy?

DATA	Dunstan's Deli	
	Chicken	$4.25
	Roast Beef	$3.75
	Tuna	$3.50
	Milk	$0.60
	Juice	$0.75

15. There are 395 guests at a banquet. Of these, 356 are adults and the rest are children. There are 6 rows of tables with 8 tables in each row. Each table can seat 8 people. Are there enough tables to seat all the guests? If not, how many more tables are needed?

16. **Communicate** There are 24 hours in one day. How can you use addition to find the number of hours in one week? How can you use multiplication?

17. **Extend Your Thinking** One decade equals 10 years and one century equals 100 years. Are there more years in 11 decades or 1 century?

Another Look!

A furniture company has a block of birch with a mass of 8,460 kilograms. They plan to cut this wood to make 12 desks of equal size. They also make matching chairs from pine. What will the mass be for each of the smaller blocks of wood?

Is there extra information?

Analyze

What do you know?

- A block of birch has a mass of 8,460 kilograms.
- The wood will be used to make 12 desks.

What are you asked to find?

- The mass of each smaller block of wood.

Plan and Solve

Draw a strip diagram to show what you know and what to find.

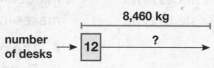

Solve the problem.

$8,460 \div 12 = 705$

Justify and Evaluate

Is your answer correct?

Yes, $705 \times 12 = 8,460$.

Write the answer in a complete sentence.

Each smaller block of birch has a mass of 705 kilograms.

In **1** through **3**, tell what information is extra or what information is missing. Solve if possible.

1. Kaitlyn's painting class meets for 1.25 hours twice a week. She also takes photographs for 3 hours each week. How many hours does Kaitlyn spend in painting class in four weeks?

2. Efrain bought 5 graphic T-shirts and a pair of jeans at the clothing outlet. He spent $50 on the T-shirts. How much did he spend in all?

3. Write a real-world division problem that gives extra information. Underline the extra information. Show how to solve your problem using a strip diagram.

4. It takes 4 hours to drive from Boston to New York. Jordan has a meeting in New York at 2:00 P.M. Can she arrive at her meeting on time?

5. Franco hikes 4 miles each day for 5 days. He carries 100 ounces of water. It takes him 2 hours to hike 4 miles. How many hours does he hike in 5 days?

6. Krista can type 62 words per minute. She wrote an essay by hand in 5 hours, and it is now 4 pages long. Each page has 125 words. She wants to type her essay. About how long will it take Krista to type the essay?

Do you need an exact answer or is an estimate enough?

7. Jorge buys T-shirts for $4 each and paints designs on them. He sells the designed T-shirts for $7 each. What information is needed to find how much profit Jorge makes in one week?

A The price of T-shirts at a store

B The color of the T-shirts that he buys

C The types of designs he draws on the T-shirts

D The number of T-shirts he sells in one week

8. Extend Your Thinking Robert spelled 29 words in his first spelling bee and spelled 23 of them correctly. He spelled 41 words in his second spelling bee and spelled 5 of them incorrectly. In his third spelling bee, he spelled 29 words correctly and 4 words incorrectly. How many words did Robert spell correctly in all? Explain how you found your answer.

9. Zoe is organizing science supplies. She has 162 glass slides to clean, dry, and pack into boxes. Each box can hold 24 glass slides. How many boxes does Zoe need to pack all the glass slides? Draw a strip diagram and write an equation to solve.

Name _____

1. **Mental Math** Shara has 358 pennies. She puts them in stacks of 50. How many stacks can she make? How many pennies are left? How can you use mental math to find the answers?

Applying Math Processes

- How does this problem connect to previous ones?
- What is my plan?
- How can I use tools?
- How can I use number sense?
- How can I communicate and represent my thinking?
- How can I organize and record information?
- How can I explain my work?
- How can I justify my answer?

2. Mr. Davis is driving from New York City to Miami, Florida. The total distance is 1,283 miles. He wants to make the trip in 4 days. If he drives the same distance the first 3 days and 221 miles on the fourth day, how many miles does he drive each day on the first 3 days?

3. **Construct Arguments** Without dividing, explain how you know that the quotient of $146 \div 15$ is less than 10.

4. During a school fundraiser, cheese and pepperoni pizzas were sold. Twice as many cheese pizzas were sold as pepperoni pizzas. If 1,716 pizzas were sold, how many pepperoni pizzas were sold?

5. **Check for Reasonableness** To get ready for a swimming tournament, Jennifer trains for 90 minutes 5 days each week. She does this for 10 weeks. She tells her coach that she will have trained for about 50,000 minutes this way. Is her estimate reasonable? Explain.

6. **Extend Your Thinking** Nathan works the same number of hours each day, 5 days a week. He earns $12 per hour. Last week he earned $420. How many hours does he work each day? Describe two ways to find the answer.

Error Search

Find each problem that is not correct. Change what is wrong and rewrite the problem so it is correct.

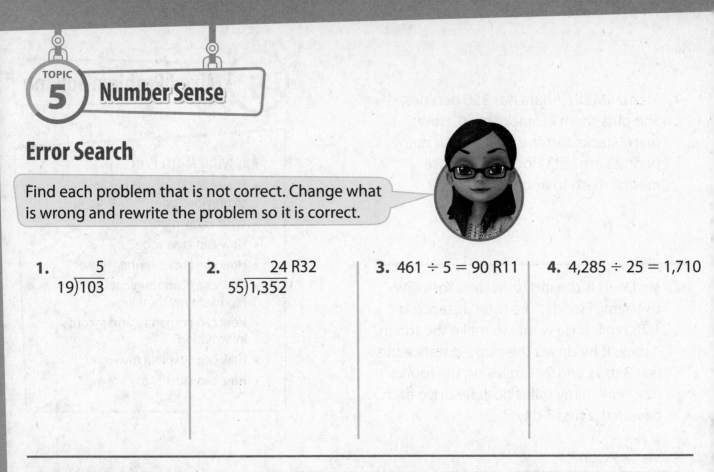

1.   5
       19)103

2.   24 R32
       55)1,352

3. 461 ÷ 5 = 90 R11

4. 4,285 ÷ 25 = 1,710

Target Number

Mental Math Using any numbers from the box as divisors and dividends, list as many division problems equivalent to the Target Number as you can. Numbers in the boxes may be used more than once.

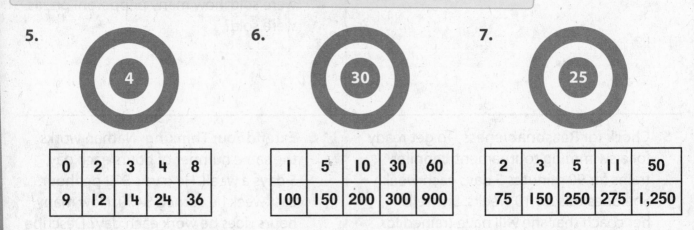

5.

4

0	2	3	4	8
9	12	14	24	36

6.

30

I	5	10	30	60
100	150	200	300	900

7.

25

2	3	5	II	50
75	150	250	275	1,250

Name _____

Set A pages 235–240

Find $18\overline{)139}$.

Step 1 Estimate. How many times can you multiply the divisor to get a product that is close to the dividend?

$7 \times 20 = 140$ ◄— Use 7 as your estimate.

Step 2 Divide the ones. How many ones in 139 can go into each of 18 groups?

$$\begin{array}{r} 7 \\ 18\overline{)139} \\ 126 \end{array} \quad 7 \times 18 = 126$$

Step 3 Subtract. Write the remainder.

$$\begin{array}{r} 7\,R\,13 \\ 18\overline{)139} \\ -126 \\ \hline 13 \end{array}$$

Remember that you can use multiplication to estimate the quotient.

1. $25\overline{)194}$ **2.** $13\overline{)90}$

3. $37\overline{)120}$ **4.** $18\overline{)85}$

5. $14\overline{)73}$ **6.** $49\overline{)216}$

7. $79\overline{)698}$ **8.** $82\overline{)599}$

Set B pages 241–246, 247–252

Find $789 \div 19$.

Estimate first.

$800 \div 20 = 40$.

Divide the tens. Multiply, subtract, and compare.

Bring down the ones. Divide the ones. Multiply, subtract, and compare. Check the quotient with your estimate.

$$\begin{array}{r} 41\,R\,10 \\ 19\overline{)789} \\ -76 \\ \hline 29 \\ -19 \\ \hline 10 \end{array}$$

Remember that you can check your answer by multiplying the quotient by the divisor, and then adding the remainder.

1. $16\overline{)234}$ **2.** $38\overline{)792}$

3. $42\overline{)523}$ **4.** $47\overline{)5,190}$

5. $58\overline{)7,211}$ **6.** $12\overline{)3,549}$

Find 4,321 ÷ 21.

Estimate first to help decide where to place the first digit in the quotient. Use compatible numbers.

Think: 4,000 ÷ 20 = 200

So, the first digit is in the hundreds place.

Divide.

```
        205 R16
   21)4,321
      − 42
        121
      − 105
         16
```

Remember that you can use your estimate to check your answer for reasonableness.

> Estimate and then find each quotient. Check each answer for reasonableness.

1. 612 ÷ 21   **2.** 544 ÷ 57

3. 5,100 ÷ 24   **4.** 1,777 ÷ 88

5. 47)5,198   **6.** 92)3,612

7. 11)1,224   **8.** 26)6,333

Decide if the problem has missing or extra information. Solve if possible.

Kay has 3 folders. Each folder has 6 pockets for subjects. How many sheets of paper are in each folder?

What you know: 3 folders, 6 pockets per folder

What you want to find: How many sheets of paper are in each folder

Can you solve? No, information about the number of sheets of paper is missing.

Remember that some problems have extra information, but can be solved.

> Decide if the problem has missing or extra information. Solve if possible.

1. Mario had $40.20. He went to the store and bought apples, cereal, and bread. How much change did he get back?

2. Alanna bought 6 books. Each book cost $13, and each bookmark cost $2. How much did she spend on books?

Name _____

1. The cost to rent a lodge for a reunion is $975. If 65 people attend and pay the same price, how much does each person pay?

   A $16

   B $15

   C $14

   D $13

2. Shady Rivers summer camp has 188 campers this week. If there are 22 campers to each cabin, what is the fewest number of cabins needed?

   A 7 cabins

   B 8 cabins

   C 9 cabins

   D 10 cabins

3. The table shows how many employees are going to a conference. If 28 employees can sit in each row of chairs, how many rows of chairs will they need?

Group	Number signed up to attend
Accounting	137
Marketing	146
Central Office	41

   A 12 rows

   B 14 rows

   C 54 rows

   D 324 rows

4. The cost of renting a bus is $1,344. If 32 people ride the bus and share the cost equally, what is the cost per person?

   A $10

   B $32

   C $39

   D $42

5. Palm Beach County is the largest county in Florida, with 2,578 square miles. A township is 36 square miles. How many full-size townships would fit in Palm Beach County?

   A 71 townships

   B 72 townships

   C 81 townships

   D 82 townships

6. The table shows the number of students going on a field trip. If one chaperone is needed for every 12 students, how many chaperones are needed?

DATA	Grade	Number of Students
	Fifth Grade	310
	Sixth Grade	305
	Seventh Grade	225

   A 70 chaperones

   B 62 chaperones

   C 60 chaperones

   D 7 chaperones

7. A city has 1,728 law enforcement officers. The officers are divided into equal groups. Which of the following is **NOT** a number of complete groups that can be made?

    A 48 groups

    B 42 groups

    C 36 groups

    D 32 groups

8. Four schools are going on an overnight field trip. There are 220 students in each school. They will sleep 12 to a cabin. What is the fewest number of cabins needed for all the students?

9. Charles burns 4,350 calories hiking 15 miles of the Appalachian Trail. He burns the same number of calories each mile. How many calories does he burn each mile?

10. A company needs to order 400 note pads. If there are 48 note pads in each box, how many boxes does the company need to order?

    A 8 boxes

    B 9 boxes

    C 10 boxes

    D Not here

11. A group of 7 campers has 4 hours to hike to a lighthouse and back before sundown. The lighthouse is 28 meters high. It is located 12 kilometers from camp. How fast do they have to walk?

12. Jessie made 312 mini energy bars. She puts 24 bars in each bag. She plans to sell each bag for $6. How many bags can she make?

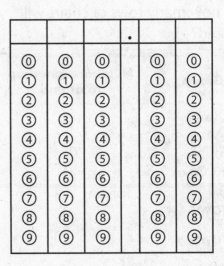

TOPIC 6

Dividing Decimals

Essential Question: What are the standard procedures for estimating and finding quotients involving decimals?

> The thermal energy of an object depends on its temperature and on how many particles it contains.

> A cup of hot cocoa has more thermal energy than a cup of cold milk.

> I can chill with that! Five marshmallows roasting on a stick have more thermal energy than just one! Here's a project about thermal energy.

Math and Science Project: Thermal Energy

Do Research Use the Internet or other sources to learn about thermal energy. Make a list of 3 ways you use thermal energy in your home and at school. Which use is most important to you? Why?

Journal: Write a Report Include what you found. Also in your report:

- Ask each member of your household 3 ways they use thermal energy. Organize your data in a table.

- Draw conclusions from your data. How does your household use thermal energy?

- Make up and solve problems by dividing decimals.

Review What You Know

Vocabulary

Choose the best term from the box.
Write it on the blank.

> • decimal   • divisor
> • dividend   • quotient

1. _____ is the name for the answer to a division problem.

2. A number that is being divided by another number is called the _____.

3. A number that is divided into another number is called the _____.

Whole Number Operations

Find each value.

4. 9,007 − 3,128   **5.** 7,964 + 3,872

6. 35 × 17   **7.** 181 × 42

8. 768 ÷ 6   **9.** 506 ÷ 22

10. 6,357 ÷ 60   **11.** 3,320 ÷ 89

Rounding Decimals

Round each number to the place of the underlined digit.

12. <u>4</u>.3   **13.** <u>1</u>5.7   **14.** 0.3<u>4</u>

15. 9<u>6</u>.5   **16.** 81.<u>2</u>7   **17.** <u>2</u>05.3

Decimals

18. An insect measured 1.25 cm long. Which number is less than 1.25?

   A 1.35   **C** 1.26

   B 1.3   **D** 1.2

19. Explain What decimal does this model represent? Explain.

Decimal Operations

Find each value.

20. 23.7 − 11.82   **21.** 66.8 + 3.64

22. 9 × 1.4   **23.** 3.2 × 7.6

Name _____

Solve & Share

An object is 279.4 centimeters wide. If you divide the object into 10 equal parts, how wide will each part be? **Solve this problem any way you choose.**

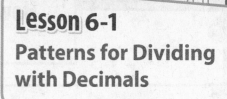

Connect Ideas How can you use what you know about the relationship between multiplication and division to help you?

⬈ TEKS 5.3G Solve for quotients of decimals to the hundredths, up to four-digit dividends and two-digit whole number divisors, using strategies and algorithms, including the standard algorithm. Also, 5.3.
Mathematical Process Standards 5.1B, 5.1C, 5.1F, 5.1G

Digital Resources at PearsonTexas.com

| Solve | Learn | Glossary | Check | Tools | Games |

Look Back!

Number Sense What do you notice about the width of the object and the width of each part?

How Can You Divide Decimals by 10 and 100?

Shondra wants to cut a cloth into 10 strips. All the strips should be exactly the same size. How long will each strip be? How long would each strip be if Shondra cut the cloth in 100 strips?

You can divide to find equal parts of a whole.

89.5 cm

Moving the decimal point to the left decreases the number's value.

Dividing Decimals by 10 and 100

B Find $89.5 \div 10$.

A number divided by 10 is less than the number.

Place value is based on 10, so dividing by 10 gives the same result as moving the decimal point one place to the left.

$89.5 \div 10 = 8.95$

Each cloth strip will be 8.95 centimeters long.

C Find $89.5 \div 100$.

A number divided by 100 is less than the number.

Dividing by 100 gives the same result as moving the decimal point two places to the left.

$89.5 \div 100 = 0.895$

Each cloth strip will be 0.895 centimeters long.

Do You Understand?

Convince Me! Suppose you have a rope that is 94.6 cm long. If you cut the rope into 10 equal sections, how long would each section be? If you cut a rope that was 946 cm long into 100 pieces, how long would each piece be? How are the two quotients you found related?

☆ Guided Practice ☆

In **1** through **6**, use mental math to find each quotient.

1. 370.2 ÷ 10   **2.** 126.4 ÷ 10

3. 725 ÷ 10   **4.** 72.5 ÷ 10

5. 281.4 ÷ 10   **6.** 281.4 ÷ 20

7. Construct Arguments Krista divides a number by 10. She also divides the same number by 50. Which quotient is greater? How can you tell?

8. Number Sense If Shondra wanted to cut the cloth into 50 strips, how wide would each strip be?

Independent Practice ☆

Leveled Practice In **9** through **23**, find each quotient. Use mental math.

9. 2,500 ÷ 10   **10.** 2,020 ÷ 5   **11.** 450 ÷ 50

250 ÷ 10   2,020 ÷ 50   45 ÷ 50

25 ÷ 10   202 ÷ 5   450 ÷ 90

2.5 ÷ 10   202 ÷ 50   45 ÷ 90

12. 136.5 ÷ 10   **13.** 753 ÷ 100   **14.** 890.1 ÷ 10   **15.** 8,567 ÷ 100

16. 864 ÷ 10   **17.** 864 ÷ 20   **18.** 86.4 ÷ 10   **19.** 86.4 ÷ 20

20. 7,700 ÷ 10   **21.** 770 ÷ 10   **22.** 77 ÷ 10   **23.** 7.7 ÷ 10

Problem Solving

For **24** through **26**, use the table.

24. Pacific Middle School posted the winning times at the swim meet. What was the difference between the winning butterfly time and the winning backstroke time?

DATA		
50-yard freestyle	22.17 seconds
100-yard backstroke	53.83 seconds
100-yard butterfly	58.49 seconds

25. The winning time for the 100-yard freestyle race was twice the 50-yard freestyle time. What was the winning time for the 100-yard freestyle?

26. What was the difference between the winning 100-yard freestyle time and the winning butterfly time?

27. ⭐ Michael wrote the equations below. In which equation is n **NOT** equal to 100?

- **A** $1,956 \div n = 19.56$
- **B** $0.477 \times n = 47.7$
- **C** $32 \div n = 3.2$
- **D** $190 \div n = 1.9$

28. A pickup truck carrying 100 identical bricks weighs 6,755 pounds. If the truck weighs 6,240 pounds empty, what is the weight of each brick?

29. Connect The dimensions of a room on a blueprint measure 12 inches long and 10 inches wide. The dimensions of the actual room are 12 times as great. How many feet long and wide is the actual room?

30. Explain Connor divided 7,438 by 100. He said his answer was 743.8. Is this a reasonable answer?

31. Personal Financial Literacy Several years ago, Mrs. Fiero bought 100 shares of a company's stock priced at $91.73 per share. Last week she sold the 100 shares for $116.05 per share. How much money did Mrs. Fiero make on her stock investment?

32. Extend Your Thinking Katie noticed a pattern in the answers for each of the expressions below. What do you notice?

14.6×0.1 $14.6 \div 10$

146×0.01 $146 \div 100$

146×0.001 $146 \div 1,000$

Another Look!

Sanjai has 275 pounds of clay. He uses the clay to make 100 identical bowls. How much clay does he use for each bowl?

To divide by 10, move the decimal point 1 place to the left.

To divide by 100, move the decimal point 2 places to the left.

$275 \div 100 = \textbf{2.75} = 2.75$

Sanjai uses 2.75 pounds of clay for each bowl.

In **1** through **6**, use mental math and patterns to complete each problem.

1. $2,500 \div 10 =$ _____

$250 \div$ _____ $= 25$

_____ $\div 10 = 2.5$

$2.5 \div 10 =$ _____

2. $20 \div$ _____ $= 2$

$20 \div 20 =$ _____

_____ $\div 40 = 0.5$

$20 \div 80 =$ _____

3. _____ $\div 10 = \$675$

$\$675 \div$ _____ $= \$67.50$

$\$6,750 \div 100 =$ _____

_____ $\div 100 = \$6.75$

4. $9,600 \div 10 =$ _____

$960 \div 10 =$ _____

$96 \div 10 =$ _____

$9.6 \div 10 =$ _____

5. $\$800 \div$ _____ $= \$80$

_____ $\div 10 = \$8$

$\$8 \div 10 =$ _____

$\$0.80 \div 10 =$ _____

6. $1,200 \div 30 =$ _____

$120 \div$ _____ $= 4$

_____ $\div 30 = 0.4$

$1.2 \div 30 =$ _____

7. $4 \div 100$

8. $15 \div 50$

9. $450 \div 10$

10. $60 \div 100$

11. $55 \div 10$

12. $9 \div 100$

13. $8,020 \div 100$

14. $150 \div 10$

15. $16 \div 40$

16. $1.8 \div 60$

17. $720 \div 100$

18. $3,500 \div 10$

Remember to insert zeros to the left in the number you divide, if needed.

19. The city has a section of land 3,694.7 feet long. The city wants to make 10 equal-sized garden plots with this land. How long will each garden plot be?

20. Javier plays the saxophone. For 5 days each week, he practices for 1.5 hours. If he does this for 26 weeks, how many total hours will he practice?

21. For her 10-day vacation, Ms. Corrin spent $1,535.50 for air fare and a motel. The air fare was $354. If the motel charged the same amount for each of the 10 nights, how much did each night cost?

22. Explain Lance says that 2,376 ÷ 100 is the same as 2,376 × 0.1. Is he correct? Why or why not?

23. Analyze Information For a party, 10 friends are buying 100 cups, 100 plates, a punchbowl, and 200 balloons. If the friends share the cost equally, how much should each friend contribute?

What steps do you need to solve to find the answer?

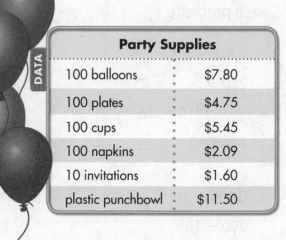

Party Supplies	
100 balloons	$7.80
100 plates	$4.75
100 cups	$5.45
100 napkins	$2.09
10 invitations	$1.60
plastic punchbowl	$11.50

24. Connect A stack of 100 pennies is 6.1 inches tall. A stack of 100 dimes is 5.3 inches tall. How much taller is a stack of 10 pennies than a stack of 10 dimes?

  A 0.08 inch
  B 0.53 inch
  C 0.61 inch
  D 0.8 inch

25. Extend Your Thinking On a large map, the distance from Austin, Texas, to Milwaukee, Wisconsin, is 13.7 inches. The actual distance is about 1,000 miles. What is the distance on the same map from Waco, Texas, to Plano, Texas, if the actual distance is about 100 miles? Round your answer to the nearest tenth.

Name _____

Solve & Share

A 135.8-foot piece of construction material needs to be cut into pieces that are each 16 feet long. About how many pieces can be cut? **Solve this problem any way you choose.**

How can you use what you know about mental math to help you?

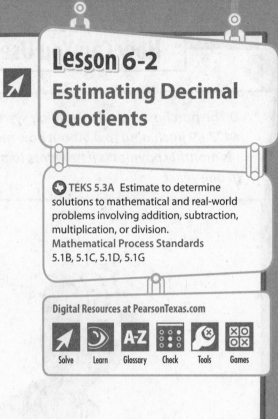

TEKS 5.3A Estimate to determine solutions to mathematical and real-world problems involving addition, subtraction, multiplication, or division. **Mathematical Process Standards 5.1B, 5.1C, 5.1D, 5.1G**

Digital Resources at PearsonTexas.com

Solve   Learn   Glossary   Check   Tools   Games

Look Back!

Number Sense Can you find a different way to estimate the answer for the problem above? Explain.

A

Diego purchased a video gaming system for $473.89 (including tax). About how much are his monthly payments if he wants to pay this off in one year?

You can use division to find equal groups.

B ## One Way

Estimate $473.89 ÷ 12. Use rounding.

To the nearest whole number, 473.89 rounds to 474.

12 rounds to 10.

$473.89 ÷ 12 is about
$474 ÷ 10 = $47.40.

Each monthly payment will be about $47.40.

C ## Another Way

Estimate $473.89 ÷ 12.
Use compatible numbers.

Look for compatible numbers.

$473.89 ÷ 12 is close to
$480 ÷ 12 = $40.

Each monthly payment will be about $40.

You know
48 ÷ 12 = 4.

Do You Understand?

Convince Me! In the example above, which estimate is closer to the exact answer? Tell how you decided.

☆ Guided Practice *

In **1** through **6**, estimate each quotient. Use rounding or compatible numbers.

1. $42 \div 2.8$ **2.** $102 \div 9.6$

3. $48.9 \div 4$ **4.** $72.59 \div 7$

5. $15.4 \div 1.9$ **6.** $44.07 \div 6.3$

7. Number Sense Leo is estimating $53.1 \div 8.4$. Do you think he should use $53 \div 8$ or $54 \div 9$ to estimate? Why?

8. Explain Is each quotient greater than or less than 1? How do you know?

A $0.2 \div 4$

B $1.35 \div 0.6$

Independent Practice ☆

Leveled Practice For **9** and **10**, complete the work and estimate each quotient.

9. Estimate $64.5 \div 12.3$ using rounding.
$$65 \div 10 = \underline{\quad}$$

10. Estimate $64.5 \div 12.3$ using compatible numbers.
$$60 \div 12 = \underline{\quad}$$

In **11** through **19**, estimate each quotient.

11. $7 \div 0.85$ **12.** $9.6 \div 0.91$ **13.** $17.7 \div 3.2$

14. $91.02 \div 4.9$ **15.** $45.64 \div 6.87$ **16.** $821.22 \div 79.4$

17. $22.5 \div 3$ **18.** $15.66 \div 9.3$ **19.** $156.3 \div 14.5$

Problem Solving

20. Number Sense Luci's mother gave her $7.50 to buy 8 spiral notebooks. With tax, the cost of each notebook is $1.05. Does Luci have enough money? Use compatible numbers and estimation to help you decide.

21. Personal Financial Literacy Kerri has a balance of $185 on her credit card. She is charged 15%, or 0.15, times the balance in interest. How much interest does she get charged?

The decimal 0.15 can be represented as 15% or 15 percent.

22. Mauricio scored a total of 34.42 points in five gymnastic events. Which number sentence shows how you could best estimate Mauricio's average score?

A $35 \div 5 = 7$
B $35 \div 7 = 5$
C $30 \div 10 = 3$
D $40 \div 10 = 4$

23. Analyze Information Lei has a car that averages 14.5 miles per gallon while Roman's car averages 28.5 miles per gallon. Use estimation to find how many times as many miles per gallon Roman's car gets compared to Lei's car.

In **24** through **26**, use the table.

24. Which sample from the experiment had the least mass? Which had the lowest temperature?

Sample	Mass	Temperature
1	0.98 g	37.57°C
2	0.58 g	57.37°C
3	0.058 g	75.50°C
4	0.098 g	73.57°C

25. Another experiment was performed on Sample 3 and the temperature recorded was 82.14°C. How many degrees did it change?

26. What is the difference in mass between Sample 1 and Sample 2?

27. Without dividing, how do you know that the quotient of 95.5 ÷ 12 will **NOT** be 14?

28. Extend Your Thinking Write a decimal division problem that has an estimated quotient of 4. Explain how to get that estimate.

© Pearson Education, Inc. 5

Name _____

Another Look!

When estimating with decimal division, you can use rounding or compatible numbers to make your math computation easier.

Estimate 28.4 ÷ 9.5.

One Way		**Another Way**	
Use rounding.		Use compatible numbers.	
28.4 ÷ 9.5	Write the original problem.	28.4 ÷ 9.5	Write the original problem.
↓ ↓		↓ ↓	
28 ÷ 10 = 2.8	Round 28.4 to the nearest whole number. Round 9.5 to 10.	27 ÷ 9 = 3	Use compatible numbers.

In **1** and **2**, complete the work to estimate each quotient.

1. Estimate 52.3 ÷ 11.4 using rounding.

   52.3 ÷ 11.4
   ↓   ↓
   52 ÷ 10 = _____

2. Estimate 52.3 ÷ 11.4 using compatible numbers.

   52.3 ÷ 11.4
   ↓   ↓
   55 ÷ 11 = _____

In **3** through **11**, estimate each quotient.

3. 25.1 ÷ 8

4. 59.67 ÷ 11.1

5. 82.77 ÷ 7.5

6. 496.3 ÷ 98

7. 1.76 ÷ 0.91

8. 13.077 ÷ 7.41

9. 41.3 ÷ 6.76

10. 81.4 ÷ 10.03

11. 384.4 ÷ 88.1

12. Communicate Ms. Barton and three neighbors purchased a snowblower to share. If the snowblower cost $439.20, describe how you can estimate each person's share of the cost.

13. Check for Reasonableness Is 100 a reasonable estimate for 915.25 ÷ 88.22? Explain.

14. Formulate a Plan Hodi is building a birdhouse. Each of the four walls of the birdhouse needs to be 5.5 inches long. Hodi has a piece of board that is 24.5 inches long. Is the board long enough to cut the four walls of the birdhouse? Estimate using compatible numbers.

15. On Monday, 3.11 inches of rain fell and on Tuesday, 0.81 inch of rain fell. On Wednesday, twice as much rain fell as on Tuesday. How much rain fell during the 3-day period?

16. ⭐ Martin is saving for a table and 4 chairs. The table is on sale for $425.75 and each chair is $70.50. About how much money should he save per week to be able to purchase the table and chairs in 8 weeks?

  A About $0.90
  B About $9
  C About $90
  D About $900

Remember to put the decimal point in the right place.

17. Use a Strip Diagram Another store is selling the same table and chairs at a discount. Each chair is $59 and the table is $29.75 less than at the other store. Martin is able to purchase the furniture with credit and pay the store the same amount for 8 weeks. What is his weekly payment amount for the total cost of the furniture?

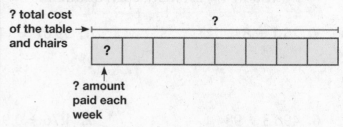

? total cost of the table → and chairs

? amount paid each week

18. Number Sense A veterinarian weighs three cats. The American Shorthair weighs 13.65 pounds. The Persian weighs 13.07 pounds, and the Maine Coon weighs 13.6 pounds. List the cats in order from least to greatest weight.

19. Extend Your Thinking Use estimation to decide which is the better value: 12 pairs of socks for $35.75 or 8 pairs of socks for $31.15. Explain your answer.

Name _____

☆ **Solve & Share** ☆

Chris paid $3.60 for 3 colored pens. Each pen costs the same. How much did each pen cost?

⭐ TEKS 5.3F Represent quotients of decimals to the hundredths, up to four-digit dividends and two-digit whole number divisors, using objects and pictorial models, including area models. Also, 5.3G. Mathematical Process Standards 5.1C, 5.1D, 5.1E, 5.1F, 5.1G

How can you use representations to model dividing a decimal? *Show your work!*

Digital Resources at PearsonTexas.com

Solve Learn Glossary Check Tools Games

Look Back!

Number Sense Without dividing, how do you know that the exact answer to the problem above has to be greater than 1?

How Can You Write a Quotient for a Decimal Dividend?

Three friends received $2.58 for aluminum cans they recycled. They decided to share the money equally. How much will each friend get?

You can divide because the total is being shared equally.

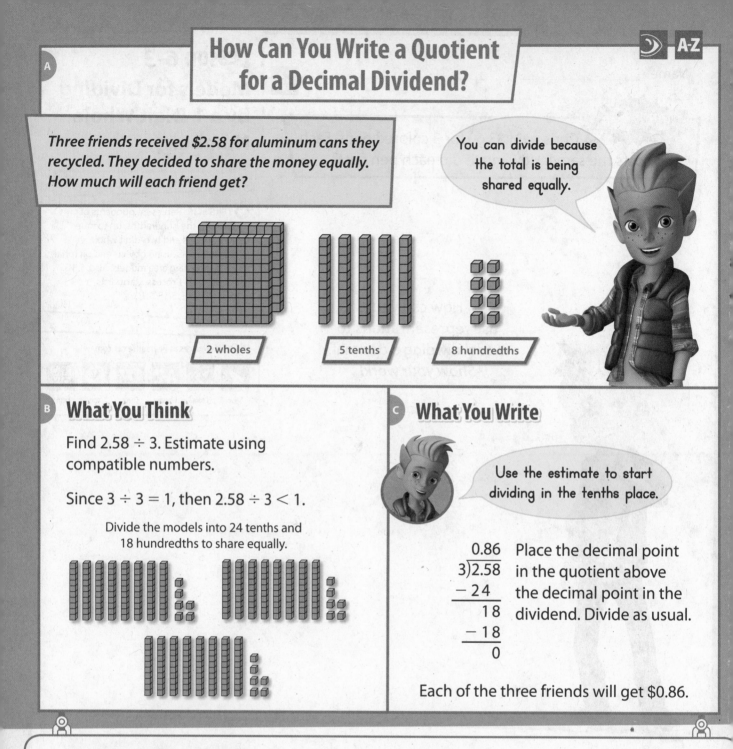

2 wholes

5 tenths

8 hundredths

B What You Think

Find 2.58 ÷ 3. Estimate using compatible numbers.

Since 3 ÷ 3 = 1, then 2.58 ÷ 3 < 1.

Divide the models into 24 tenths and 18 hundredths to share equally.

C What You Write

Use the estimate to start dividing in the tenths place.

```
   0.86
3)2.58
  -24
   18
  -18
    0
```

Place the decimal point in the quotient above the decimal point in the dividend. Divide as usual.

Each of the three friends will get $0.86.

Do You Understand?

Convince Me! The next week 4 friends got $8.24 for the cans they collected. How much money will each friend make? Estimate using compatible numbers and then calculate.

☆ Guided Practice ☆

Use the model to help you complete the division.

1. Use models to help you divide 2.16 ÷ 4. Complete the division calculation.

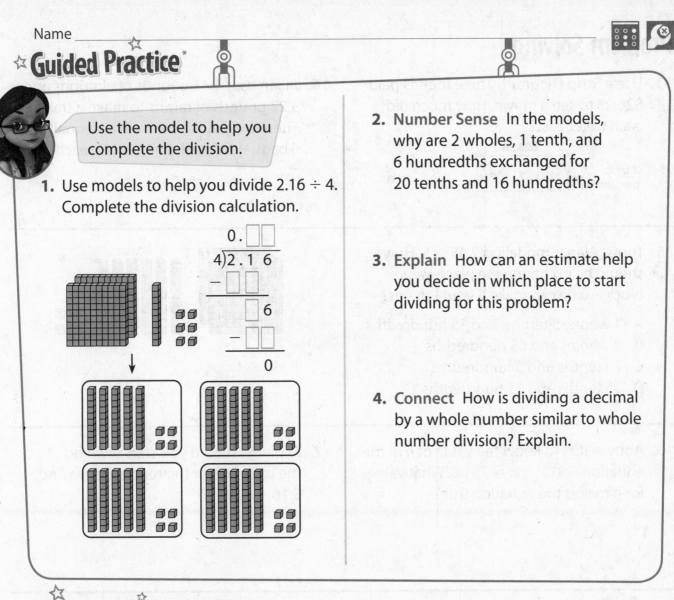

$$
\begin{array}{r}
0.\square\square \\
4\overline{)2.1\ 6} \\
-\square\square \\
\hline
\square\ 6 \\
-\square\square \\
\hline
0
\end{array}
$$

2. Number Sense In the models, why are 2 wholes, 1 tenth, and 6 hundredths exchanged for 20 tenths and 16 hundredths?

3. Explain How can an estimate help you decide in which place to start dividing for this problem?

4. Connect How is dividing a decimal by a whole number similar to whole number division? Explain.

☆ Independent Practice ☆

Leveled Practice In **5** through **12**, use models to help you divide.

5.
$$
\begin{array}{r}
0.4\square \\
3\overline{)1.3\ 5} \\
-\square\square \\
\hline
\square\ 5 \\
-\square\square \\
\hline
\square
\end{array}
$$

6.
$$
\begin{array}{r}
0.\square\square \\
6\overline{)2.7\ 6} \\
-\square\square \\
\hline
\square\ 6 \\
-\square\square \\
\hline
\square
\end{array}
$$

7.
$$
\begin{array}{r}
1.\square\square \\
5\overline{)6.8\ 5} \\
-5 \\
\hline
\square\ 8 \\
-\square\square \\
\hline
\square\ 5 \\
-\square\square \\
\hline
\end{array}
$$

8.
$$
\begin{array}{r}
\square.\square\square \\
4\overline{)5.7\ 2} \\
-\square \\
\hline
\square\square \\
-\square\square \\
\hline
\square\square \\
-\square\square \\
\hline
\square
\end{array}
$$

9. 2.38 ÷ 7

10. 4.71 ÷ 3

11. 1.76 ÷ 8

12. 5.36 ÷ 2

Problem Solving

13. **Use a Strip Diagram** Three friends paid $26.25 to see a movie. How much did each ticket cost?

$26.25

? cost per ticket → | ? | ? | ? |

14. Jillian uses 1.41 pounds of almonds and 3.27 pounds of raisins to make a trail mix. Then she divides the trail mix equally into 6 bags. How much trail mix is in each bag?

15. **Tools** ⭐ Alan is modeling $2.65 \div 5$. How should he exchange the place-value blocks so he can make 5 equal shares?

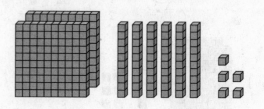

   A 1 whole, 5 tenths, and 15 hundredths
   B 2 wholes and 65 hundredths
   C 26 tenths and 5 hundredths
   D 25 tenths and 15 hundredths

16. Abby wants to know the value of n in the equation $7.913 \times n = 791.3$. What value for n makes the equation true?

17. **Explain** Should you start dividing the ones first or the tenths first to find $5.16 \div 6$? Why?

18. **Justify** There are 264 children going on a field trip. Are 5 buses enough if each bus holds 52 children? Tell how you decided.

Think about what information in the problem you need to compare.

19. **Extend Your Thinking** Ginny earned $49.50 for 6 hours of gardening and $38.60 for 4 hours of babysitting. For which job did she earn more money per hour? How much more per hour did she earn? Explain how you found the answers.

Another Look!

Draw a model to help you find 3.25 ÷ 5.

3 wholes, 2 tenths, and 5 hundredths

↓

32 tenths and 5 hundredths

↓

30 tenths and 25 hundredths

Think about how you can exchange 3 wholes, 2 tenths, and 5 hundredths so you can make 5 equal shares.

What You Show

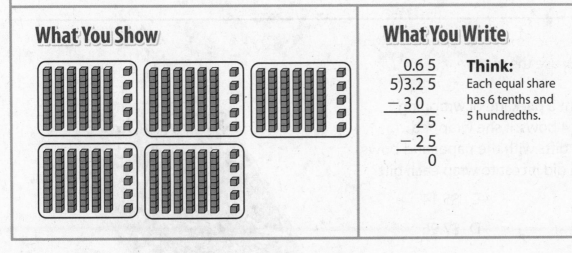

What You Write

$$\begin{array}{r} 0.6\,5 \\ 5\overline{)3.2\,5} \\ -\,3\,0 \\ \hline 2\,5 \\ -\,2\,5 \\ \hline 0 \end{array}$$

Think:
Each equal share has 6 tenths and 5 hundredths.

In **1** through **8**, use models to help you divide.

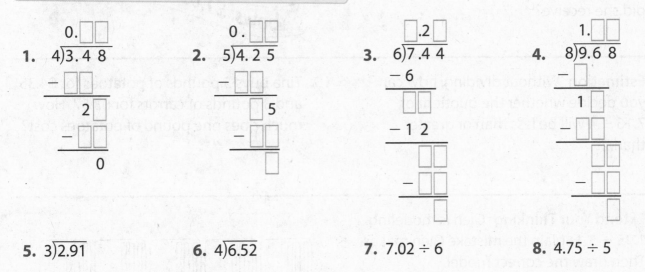

1. 0.☐☐
   4)3.4 8
   − ☐☐
   2☐
   − ☐☐
   0

2. 0.☐☐
   5)4.2 5
   − ☐☐
   ☐5
   − ☐☐
   ☐

3. ☐.2☐
   6)7.4 4
   − 6
   ☐☐
   − 1 2
   ☐☐
   − ☐☐
   ☐

4. 1.☐☐
   8)9.6 8
   − ☐
   1☐☐
   − ☐☐
   ☐☐
   − ☐☐
   ☐

5. 3)2.91

6. 4)6.52

7. 7.02 ÷ 6

8. 4.75 ÷ 5

9. Communicate Janice is dividing 1.92 ÷ 6. Why does she exchange the models shown for 18 tenths and 12 ones?

---

10. Keith has 7.8 ounces of tuna salad. If he makes 3 sandwiches with an equal amount of tuna on each, how much tuna does he put on each one?

11. A newspaper stand sold 1,000 copies of the city newspaper for $1,600. What is the price of one copy?

For **12** and **13**, use the picture.

12. ⭐ Inez bought a package of wrapping paper and 4 bows. If she wrapped 4 identical gifts with the paper and bows, how much did it cost to wrap each gift?

   A $1.99   **C** $5.14

   B $2.01   **D** $7.96

13. Inez paid for the wrapping paper and 4 bows with a $20 bill. How much change did she receive?

$3.76/package

bows: $1.05 each

---

14. Estimation Without dividing, how can you decide whether the quotient of 7.16 ÷ 4 will be less than or greater than 2?

15. Tina buys 5 pounds of potatoes for $4.35 and 3 pounds of carrots for $3.57. How much does one pound of potatoes cost?

---

16. Extend Your Thinking Glen is modeling 1.95 ÷ 5. Explain the mistake Glen makes. Then draw the correct model.

Name _____

☆ ☆
Solve & Share

A concrete mason separated 107.25 pounds of sand evenly into 3 containers. How much sand did he put into each container? *Solve this problem any way you choose.*

⊕ TEKS 5.3G Solve for quotient of decimals to the hundredths, up to four-digit dividends and two-digit whole number divisors, using strategies and algorithms, including the standard algorithm. Mathematical Process Standards 5.1A, 5.1B, 5.1C, 5.1F, 5.1G

How can you **connect ideas** about dividing a decimal by a whole number to what you know about dividing whole numbers? *Show your work!*

Digital Resources at PearsonTexas.com

Solve   Learn   Glossary   Check   Tools   Games

107.25 lb

Look Back!

Justify How can you estimate the answer to the problem above?

How Can You Write a Decimal Quotient When Dividing Whole Numbers?

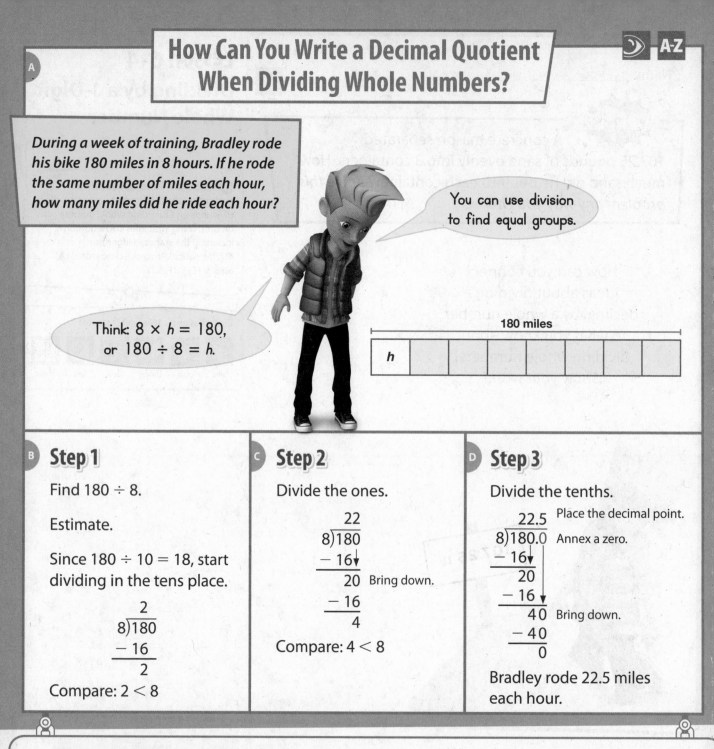

During a week of training, Bradley rode his bike 180 miles in 8 hours. If he rode the same number of miles each hour, how many miles did he ride each hour?

You can use division to find equal groups.

Think: $8 \times h = 180$, or $180 \div 8 = h$.

180 miles

h							

Step 1

Find $180 \div 8$.

Estimate.

Since $180 \div 10 = 18$, start dividing in the tens place.

$$\begin{array}{r} 2 \\ 8\overline{)180} \\ -16 \\ \hline 2 \end{array}$$

Compare: $2 < 8$

Step 2

Divide the ones.

$$\begin{array}{r} 22 \\ 8\overline{)180} \\ -16\downarrow \\ \hline 20 \\ -16 \\ \hline 4 \end{array}$$ Bring down.

Compare: $4 < 8$

Step 3

Divide the tenths.

$$\begin{array}{r} 22.5 \\ 8\overline{)180.0} \\ -16\downarrow \\ \hline 20 \\ -16\downarrow \\ \hline 40 \\ -40 \\ \hline 0 \end{array}$$

Place the decimal point.

Annex a zero.

Bring down.

Bradley rode 22.5 miles each hour.

Do You Understand?

Convince Me! For the problem below, give an example for when you could use compatible numbers to estimate the answer. Explain your thinking.

$5.68 \div 8$

☆ Guided Practice ☆

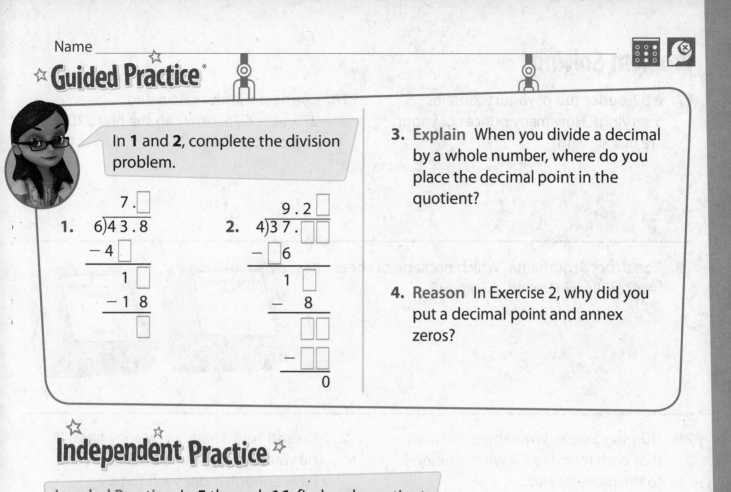

In **1** and **2**, complete the division problem.

1.
```
      7.□
  6)4 3 . 8
   − 4 □
     1 □
   − 1 8
       □
```

2.
```
      9 . 2 □
  4)3 7 . □□
   − □ 6
     1 □
     −   8
       □□
     − □□
          0
```

3. **Explain** When you divide a decimal by a whole number, where do you place the decimal point in the quotient?

4. **Reason** In Exercise 2, why did you put a decimal point and annex zeros?

☆ Independent Practice ☆

Leveled Practice In **5** through **16**, find each quotient.

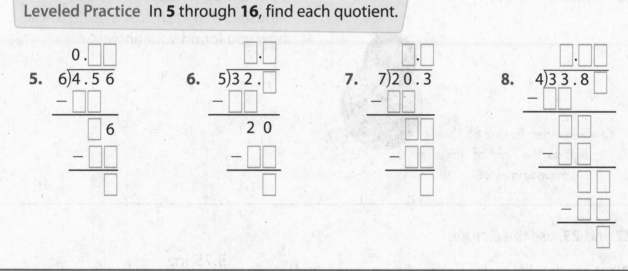

5.
```
    0 . □□
  6)4 . 5 6
  − □□
    □ 6
  − □□
    □
```

6.
```
    □ . □
  5)3 2 . □
  − □□
    2 0
  − □□
    □
```

7.
```
    □ . □
  7)2 0 . 3
  − □□
    □□
  − □□
    □
```

8.
```
    □ . □□
  4)3 3 . 8 □
  − □□
    □ □
  − □ □
    □ □
  − □□
    □
```

9. 19 ÷ 5

10. 7.83 ÷ 3

11. 48.62 ÷ 2

12. 62 ÷ 8

13. 35.5 ÷ 5

14. 100 ÷ 8

15. 1.44 ÷ 9

16. $7.20 ÷ 6

Problem Solving

17. A 32-ounce tub of yogurt contains 5 servings. How many ounces of yogurt are in 1 serving?

18. **Connect** Harriet calculated $27 \div 4 = 6.75$. How can she find $270 \div 4$ without dividing?

19. **Construct Arguments** Which package of cheese has heavier slices? How do you know?

Colby Cheese
6 slices
7.2 ounces

American Cheese
8 slices
7.6 ounces

20. **Number Sense** Write three decimals that each round to 2.7 when rounded to the nearest tenth.

Remember to look at the digit to the right of the rounding place.

21. **Extend Your Thinking** Manny has $75. He wants to buy a tree for $24. Will he have enough money left to buy 4 bushes that each cost $12.25? Show how you found your answer.

In **22** and **23**, use the picture.

22. What are the dimensions of a ⭐ single stamp?

   A 1.1 in. by 0.075 in.
   B 1.1 in. by 0.75 in.
   C 0.22 in. by 0.375 in.
   D 0.11 in. by 0.75 in.

23. In 2012, the total cost of 10 first class letter stamps was $4.50. What was the cost of one stamp?

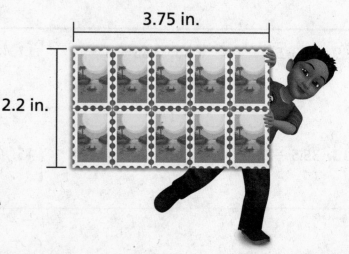

3.75 in.

2.2 in.

Another Look!

The mass of 6 identical gold bracelets is 75 grams. What is the mass of each bracelet?

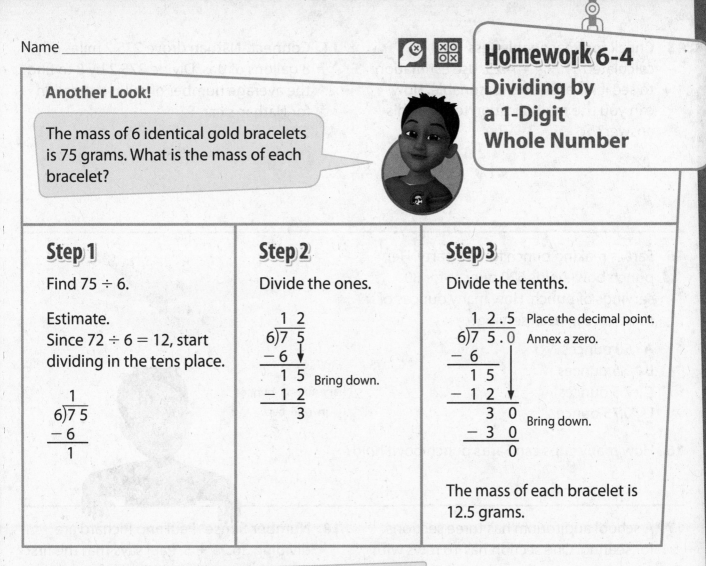

Step 1

Find 75 ÷ 6.

Estimate.
Since 72 ÷ 6 = 12, start dividing in the tens place.

```
   1
6)7 5
 − 6
   1
```

Step 2

Divide the ones.

```
   1 2
6)7 5
 − 6 ↓
   1 5      Bring down.
 − 1 2
     3
```

Step 3

Divide the tenths.

```
   1 2.5     Place the decimal point.
6)7 5.0      Annex a zero.
 − 6 ↓
   1 5
 − 1 2 ↓
     3 0     Bring down.
   − 3 0
       0
```

The mass of each bracelet is 12.5 grams.

Leveled Practice In **1** through **12**, find each quotient.

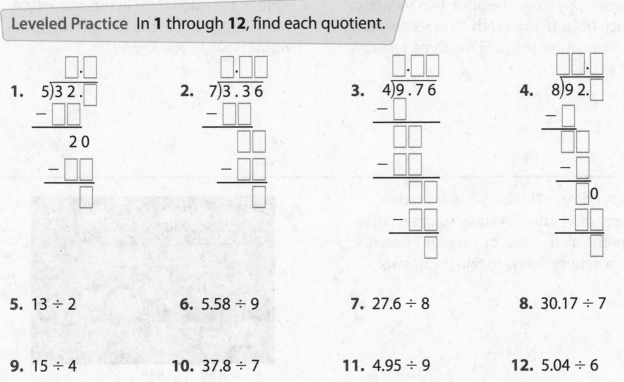

1. 5)3 2.□

2. 7)3 . 3 6

3. 4)9 . 7 6

4. 8)9 2.□

5. 13 ÷ 2

6. 5.58 ÷ 9

7. 27.6 ÷ 8

8. 30.17 ÷ 7

9. 15 ÷ 4

10. 37.8 ÷ 7

11. 4.95 ÷ 9

12. 5.04 ÷ 6

13. **Check for Reasonableness** Ned calculated $17 \div 4 = 4.25$. Use estimation to see if his answer is reasonable. How can you use multiplication to check his answer?

14. **Connect** Nathan drove 275.2 miles on 8 gallons of gas. Divide 275.2 by 8 to find the average number of miles per gallon for Nathan's car.

15. Sara is making punch for her party. Her ⭐ punch bowl holds 600 ounces for 80 servings of punch. How many ounces of punch are in each serving?

A   60 ounces

B   9.5 ounces

C   7.5 ounces

D   0.75 ounce

There are 8 ounces in one cup.

16. How many cups can Sara's punch bowl hold?

17. A school auditorium has three sections for seating. One section has 16 rows with 14 seats per row. The other two sections each have 18 rows with 10 seats per row. How many seats are in the three sections in all?

18. **Number Sense** Paul and Richard are dividing $36.25 \div 5$. Paul says that the first digit of the quotient is in the ones place. Richard says it is in the tens place. Who is right? How do you know?

19. **Extend Your Thinking** Gayle made a baby quilt using 24 equal squares. What are the dimensions of 1 square? Describe two different ways to find the answer.

3 ft

4.5 ft

Name _____

Solve & Share

Stan has a rectangular piece of carpet that has an area of 23.4 square meters. The length is 13 meters, but he needs to find the width. What is the quotient for 23.4 ÷ 13 = n? *Use the picture below to tell how you decided.*

⭐ TEKS 5.3F Represent quotients of decimals to the hundredths, up to four-digit dividends and two-digit whole number divisors, using objects and pictorial models, including area models. Mathematical Process Standards 5.1B, 5.1C, 5.1D, 5.1F, 5.1G

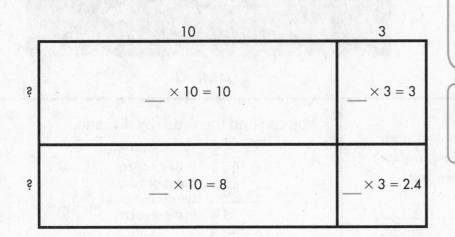

	10	3
?	___ × 10 = 10	___ × 3 = 3
?	___ × 10 = 8	___ × 3 = 2.4

Digital Resources at PearsonTexas.com

Solve   Learn   Glossary   Check   Tools   Games

Connect You can use what you know about multiplication and division.

Look Back!

Estimation How could you estimate the width of the rectangle?

A

Erin's garden has an area of 84.8 square feet. She knows the length is 16 feet. What is the width of the garden shown? Can you solve $84.8 \div 16 = w$?

w

16 ft

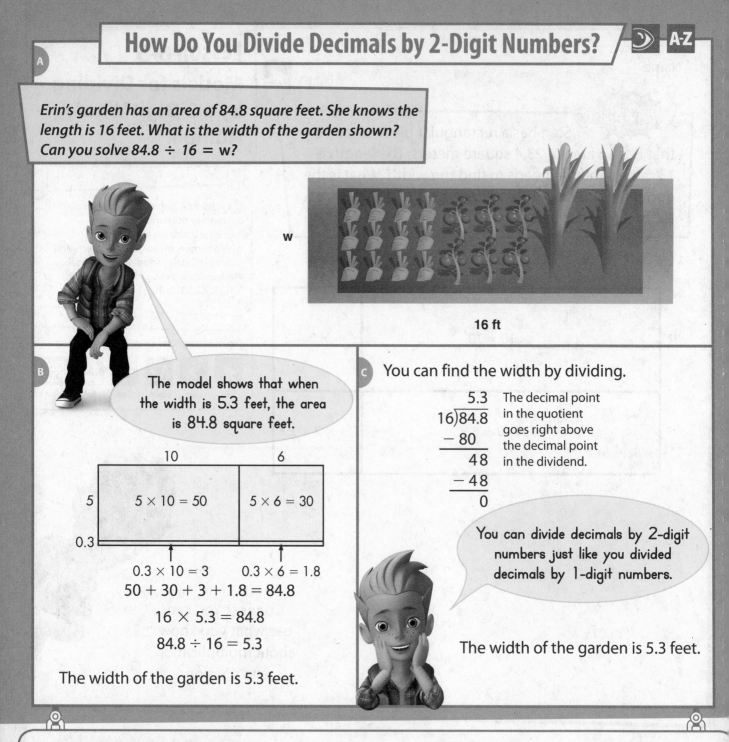

B

The model shows that when the width is 5.3 feet, the area is 84.8 square feet.

	10	6
5	$5 \times 10 = 50$	$5 \times 6 = 30$
0.3		

$0.3 \times 10 = 3$ $0.3 \times 6 = 1.8$

$50 + 30 + 3 + 1.8 = 84.8$

$16 \times 5.3 = 84.8$

$84.8 \div 16 = 5.3$

The width of the garden is 5.3 feet.

C

You can find the width by dividing.

$$\begin{array}{r} 5.3 \\ 16\overline{)84.8} \\ -80 \\ \hline 48 \\ -48 \\ \hline 0 \end{array}$$

The decimal point in the quotient goes right above the decimal point in the dividend.

You can divide decimals by 2-digit numbers just like you divided decimals by 1-digit numbers.

The width of the garden is 5.3 feet.

Do You Understand?

Convince Me! To find the width of the garden above, Amy divided 848 by 16 and got 53. How could she then use estimation to place the decimal point?

☆ **Guided Practice** *

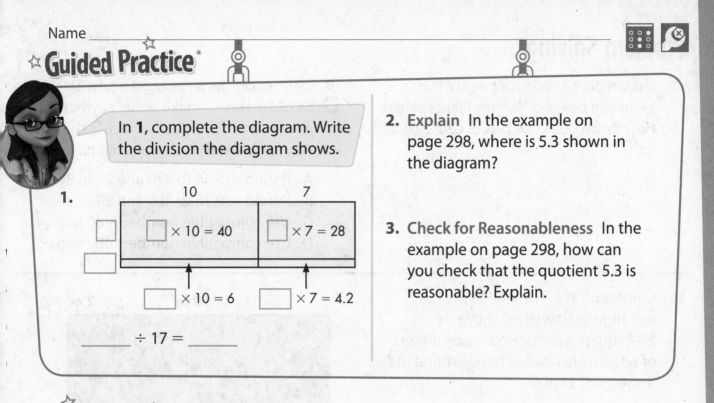

In **1**, complete the diagram. Write the division the diagram shows.

1.

10	7
☐ × 10 = 40	☐ × 7 = 28

☐ × 10 = 6   ☐ × 7 = 4.2

_____ ÷ 17 = _____

2. Explain In the example on page 298, where is 5.3 shown in the diagram?

3. Check for Reasonableness In the example on page 298, how can you check that the quotient 5.3 is reasonable? Explain.

☆ **Independent Practice** ☆

In **4** through **7**, complete each diagram. Write the division the diagram shows.

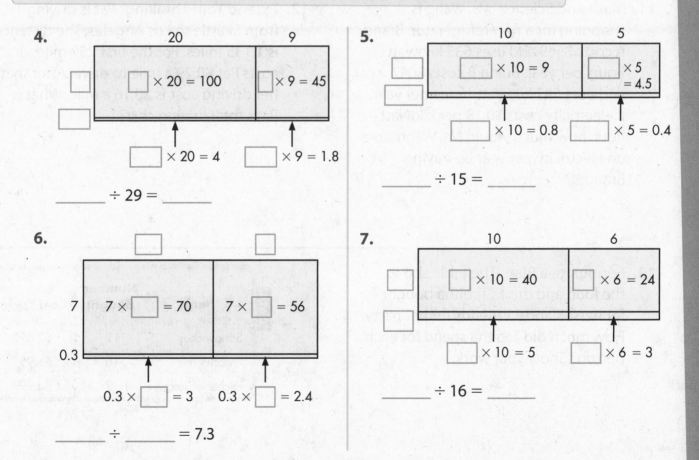

4.

20	9
☐ × 20 = 100	☐ × 9 = 45

☐ × 20 = 4   ☐ × 9 = 1.8

_____ ÷ 29 = _____

5.

10	5
☐ × 10 = 9	☐ × 5 = 4.5

☐ × 10 = 0.8   ☐ × 5 = 0.4

_____ ÷ 15 = _____

6.

☐	☐
7	7 × ☐ = 70	7 × ☐ = 56
0.3		

0.3 × ☐ = 3   0.3 × ☐ = 2.4

_____ ÷ _____ = 7.3

7.

10	6
☐ × 10 = 40	☐ × 6 = 24

☐ × 10 = 5   ☐ × 6 = 3

_____ ÷ 16 = _____

Problem Solving

8. Sharon pays $98.75 for twenty-five 14-ounce boxes of Yummy Flakes cereal. How much does one box of cereal cost?

9. Estimation Javier bought a new TV for $479.76. He will make equal payments each month for 2 years. Which is the best way for Javier to estimate each payment?

   A Round 479.76 to 470 and 24 to 30.

   B Round 479.76 to 480 and 24 to 30.

   C Use compatible numbers 480 and 24.

   D Use compatible numbers 400 and 25.

---

10. Communicate The area of the rectangular flowerbed shown is 20.4 square meters. How many meters of edging are needed to go around the flowerbed? Explain.

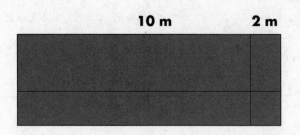

---

11. Math and Science Ms. Wang is shopping for a new refrigerator. Brand A costs $569 and uses 635 kilowatt-hours per year. Brand B costs $647 and uses 582 kilowatt-hours per year. If electricity costs $0.18 per kilowatt-hour, how much would Ms. Wang save on electricity per year by buying Brand B?

12. Extend Your Thinking Pat is driving from Seattle to Los Angeles. The distance is 1,135 miles. For the first 250 miles, it costs Pat $0.29 a mile to drive. After that, her driving cost is $0.16 a mile. What is Pat's total driving cost?

---

13. Formulate a Plan The table shows the food and drinks Tabitha bought for herself and 11 friends for her party. How much did Tabitha spend for each person? Show your work.

Item	Number Bought	Cost Each
Sandwiches	12	$2.89
French Fries	10	$1.99
Pitcher of Juice	2	$4.99

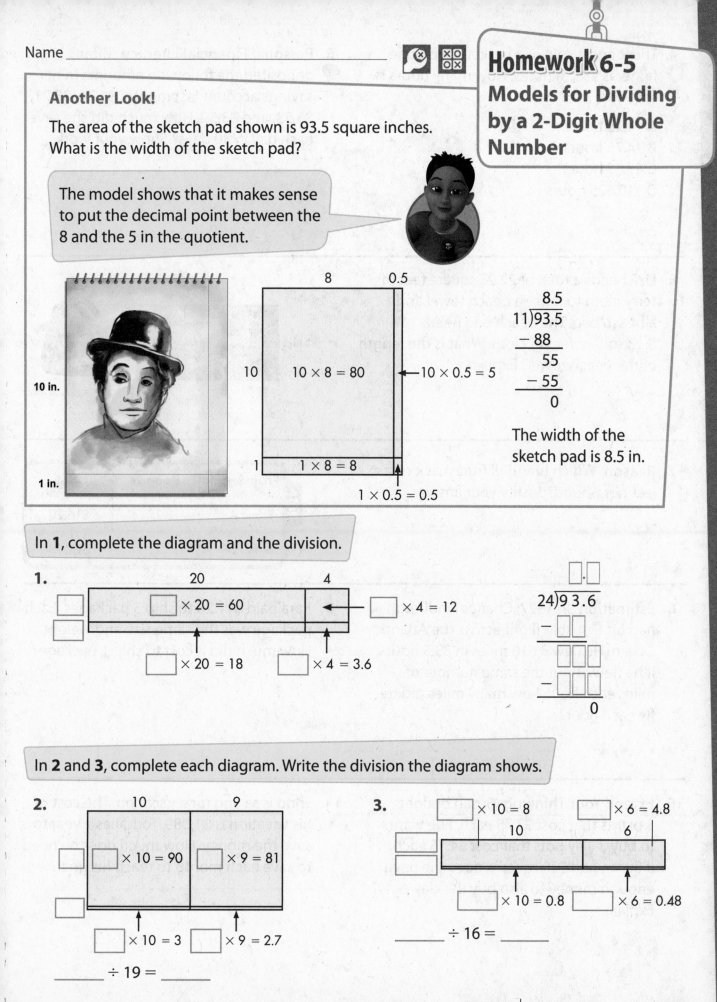

Another Look!

The area of the sketch pad shown is 93.5 square inches. What is the width of the sketch pad?

The model shows that it makes sense to put the decimal point between the 8 and the 5 in the quotient.

8   0.5

10 | 10 × 8 = 80   ← 10 × 0.5 = 5

1 | 1 × 8 = 8

1 × 0.5 = 0.5

$$\begin{array}{r} 8.5 \\ 11{\overline{)93.5}} \\ -88 \\ \hline 55 \\ -55 \\ \hline 0 \end{array}$$

The width of the sketch pad is 8.5 in.

10 in.

1 in.

In **1**, complete the diagram and the division.

1.

20   4

☐ | ☐ × 20 = 60 ← ☐ × 4 = 12

☐ × 20 = 18   ☐ × 4 = 3.6

$$\begin{array}{r} \boxed{}\boxed{}.\boxed{} \\ 24{\overline{)93.6}} \\ -\boxed{} \\ \hline \boxed{} \\ -\boxed{} \\ \hline 0 \end{array}$$

In **2** and **3**, complete each diagram. Write the division the diagram shows.

2.

10   9

☐ | ☐ × 10 = 90   ☐ × 9 = 81

☐ × 10 = 3   ☐ × 9 = 2.7

_____ ÷ 19 = _____

3.

☐ × 10 = 8   ☐ × 6 = 4.8

10   6

☐ × 10 = 0.8   ☐ × 6 = 0.48

_____ ÷ 16 = _____

4. The longest spin of a basketball on one ⭐ finger is 255 minutes. How many hours is that?

    A 4.25 hours

    B 4.75 hours

    C 9.65 hours

    D 10.625 hours

5. Personal Financial Literacy Tiffany deposited the following amounts in her savings account last month: $6.74, $5.21, $5.53, and $3.52. How much did she save each day in 30 days? Show your work.

6. Liza needs a total of 22.23 square feet of terry cloth to make a beach towel and a beach bag. The beach bag needs 5.13 square feet of cloth. What is the length of the beach towel? Explain.

3 feet

7. Reason Which brand of fruit snack costs less per pound? Justify your answer.

Fruit Snack	Pounds	Cost
Brand A	29	$16.20
Brand B	25	$22.25

8. Estimation In 1927, Charles Lindbergh had his first solo flight across the Atlantic Ocean. He flew 3,610 miles in 33.5 hours. If he flew about the same number of miles each hour, how many miles did he fly each hour?

9. Kara paid $11.20 to ship 5 packages. Each package was the same size and weight. How much did it cost to ship 1 package?

10. Extend Your Thinking Susan bought 3 plants that cost $2.75 each. She wants to buy 3 clay pots that cost $4.15 each. If Susan had $20 to start, does she have enough money to also buy the clay pots? Explain.

11. Todd is saving for a vacation. The cost of his vacation is $1,089. Todd has a year to save the money. How much does he need to save each month to reach his goal?

Name _____

Solve & Share

Enrique buys 12 bottles of juice for $25.44. How much does each bottle of juice cost?

TEKS 5.3G Solve for quotients of decimals to the hundredths, up to four-digit dividends and two-digit whole number divisors, using strategies and algorithms, including the standard algorithm. Also 5.3. Mathematical Process Standards 5.1B, 5.1C, 5.1D, 5.1E, 5.1G

You can **select and use tools.** You can use paper and pencil, estimation, and number sense.

Digital Resources at PearsonTexas.com

Solve   Learn   Glossary   Check   Tools   Games

$25.44

JUICE

Look Back!

Construct Arguments Tell how to check your answer.

How Do You Divide Decimals by 2-Digit Whole Numbers?

Cameron has a case of hamburgers. Each hamburger is the same weight. How much does each hamburger weigh?

You can divide decimals by 2-digit numbers just like you divided decimals by 1-digit numbers.

15 Hamburgers
net wt: 3.6 lb

B Step 1

Draw a strip diagram to represent the problem.

3.6 pounds

| h | h | h | h | h | h | h | h | h | h | h | h | h | h | h |

Write an equation to solve.

$15 \times h = 3.6$ or
$3.6 \div 15 = h$

C Step 2

Divide.

$$
\begin{array}{r}
0.24 \\
15\overline{)3.60} \\
-\underline{3\,0} \\
60 \\
-\underline{60} \\
0
\end{array}
$$

The decimal point in the quotient goes right above the decimal point in the dividend.

Remember that $3.6 = 3.60$, so you can annex a zero in the dividend.

Each hamburger weighs 0.24 pound.

Do You Understand?

Convince Me! How could you use estimation to decide where to place the 2 in the quotient above?

☆ Guided Practice*

In **1** and **2**, complete the division problem.

1.

```
      □ . 2 □
 49)3 0 6 . 2 5
  − □ 9 □
      1 □ □
    − 9 8
      □ □ □
      − 2 4 5
          □
```

2.

```
      0 . □ □
 15)1 4 . 4 □
  − □ □ □
        9 □
      − □ 0
          □
```

3. **Construct Arguments** Do you place the decimal point differently when you divide a decimal by a two-digit number than when you divide by a one-digit number? Explain.

4. **Reason** How would you estimate the quotient of $180 ÷ 62$, and in which place would you start dividing?

Independent Practice ☆

Leveled Practice In **5** through **12**, find each quotient.

5.

```
        □ □
 17)7 8 . 2
  − □ □
    □ □ □
  − □ □ □
        0
```

6.

```
          □ □
 40)2 3 2 . 0
  − □ □ □
      □ □ □
    − □ □ □
          0
```

7.

```
        □ . 7 □
 53)3 0 4 . 7 5
  − □ 6 □
        3 □ □
      − 3 7 1
        □ □ □
      − 2 6 5
          □
```

8.

```
      0 . □ □
 18)1 5 . 3 □
  − □ □ □
        9 □
      − □ 0
          □
```

9. 27)91.8

10. 15)3.9

11. 88)396

12. 50)247.5

Problem Solving

13. Formulate a Plan Marty has a fenced ⭐ yard in the shape of a rectangle. Its area is 635.4 square feet. The width of the yard is 18 feet. What is the length of the fence?

    A 101.8 feet

    B 105.6 feet

    C 106.6 feet

    D 141.2 feet

14. How can estimating help you decide in what place to put the first digit in the quotient below?

$47\overline{)112.8}$

15. Construct Arguments Jerry and Hannah solved the same problem two different ways. Are both of their answers correct? Explain why or why not.

16. Use multiplication to check that Hannah's answer is correct. Show your work.

17. Represent Tamika needs 152 cups of lemonade for the picnic. How many gallons of lemonade is that? Write an equation which could be used to find the answer.

Remember, there are 16 cups in a gallon.

18. Extend Your Thinking Julia's dad is using pipe to frame a playhouse for her. He has a total of 64 feet of pipe for the windows. Each window should be 2.5 feet on each side. How many square windows can he make? Tell how you found the answer.

© Pearson Education, Inc. 5

Another Look!

For 18 days, a mail carrier kept track of how many miles she walked on her route each day. She reported a total of 50.4 miles. If her route was the same each day, how many miles did she walk each day? Find 50.4 ÷ 18.

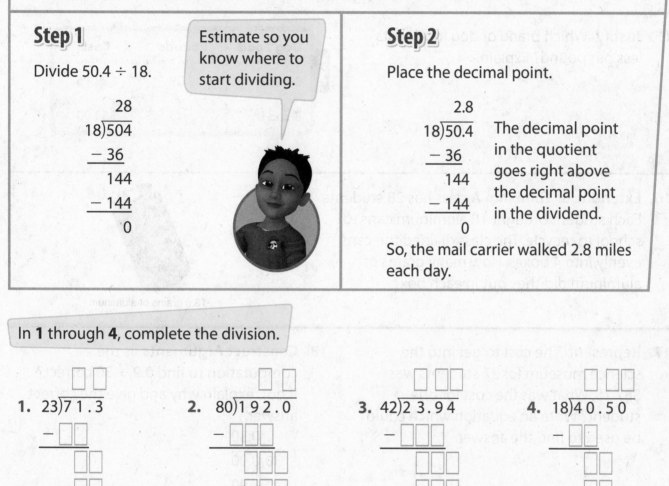

Step 1

Divide 50.4 ÷ 18.

Estimate so you know where to start dividing.

```
      28
18)504
   − 36
     144
   − 144
       0
```

Step 2

Place the decimal point.

```
      2.8
18)50.4
   − 36
     144
   − 144
       0
```

The decimal point in the quotient goes right above the decimal point in the dividend.

So, the mail carrier walked 2.8 miles each day.

In **1** through **4**, complete the division.

1. 23)71.3

2. 80)192.0

3. 42)23.94

4. 18)40.50

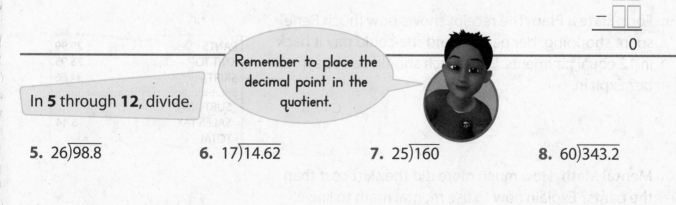

In **5** through **12**, divide.

Remember to place the decimal point in the quotient.

5. 26)98.8

6. 17)14.62

7. 25)160

8. 60)343.2

9. 83.2 ÷ 26

10. 25.6 ÷ 4

11. 90.54 ÷ 18

12. 2.4 ÷ 16

13. Personal Financial Literacy Corey spent $7.58 of his allowance and gave $0.75 to his brother. He saved the rest. His allowance is $10. How much did he save? Show your work.

14. Estimation How might you best estimate the quotient of 352.25 ÷ 33?

A Round 352.25 to 352.

B Round 352.25 to 352 and 33 to 30.

C Round 352.25 to 400 and 33 to 30.

D Use compatible numbers 350 and 35.

15. Justify Which brand of dog food costs less per pound? Explain.

DATA	Dog Food	Pounds	Cost
	Brand A	39	$29.95
	Brand B	45	$50.00

16. Extend Your Thinking A class has 28 students. Each student brought 10 aluminum cans to school to recycle. The class divided the cans evenly into 4 boxes. How many grams of aluminum did they put in each box?

13.6 grams of aluminum

17. Represent The cost to get into the science museum for 27 students was $87.75. What was the cost for one student? Write an equation which could be used to find the answer.

18. Construct Arguments Is the computation to find 0.9 ÷ 30 correct? If not, explain why and give the correct answer.

$$
\begin{array}{r}
0.30 \\
30\overline{)0.90} \\
-90 \\
\hline
0
\end{array}
$$

19. Formulate a Plan The receipt shows how much Rene spent shopping. Her parents said she could pay it back in 12 equal payments. How much should each payment be? Explain.

PANTS	29.99
KNIT TOP	25.95
SKIRT	34.86
SUBTOTAL	
SALES TAX	5.44
TOTAL	

20. Mental Math How much more did the skirt cost than the pants? Explain how to use mental math to solve.

Name _____

☆ **Solve & Share**

How many 6-ounce glasses can you completely fill with 33 ounces of orange juice? Johnny said, "I can fill 5.5 glasses completely." Is Johnny's answer reasonable? Explain. *Solve this problem any way you choose.*

🔷 TEKS 5.1B Use a problem-solving model that incorporates analyzing given information, formulating a plan or strategy, determining a solution, justifying the solution, and evaluating the problem-solving process and the reasonableness of the solution. Also, 5.3G.
Mathematical Process Standards 5.1A, 5.1C, 5.1D, 5.1E, 5.1G

Analyze Information Restate the question in your own words. *Show your work!*

Digital Resources at PearsonTexas.com

Solve	Learn	Glossary	Check	Tools	Games

Look Back!

Check for Reasonableness What does it mean for the answer to a problem to be reasonable? How did you check that your answer is reasonable?

How Can You Check for Reasonableness?

Analyze

Mr. Patel bought 29.5 pounds of shrimp at the fish market. He put the shrimp in 5-pound bags. How many bags can he fill? How many bags does he need in all?

You can draw a strip diagram to represent the problem.

29.5 pounds of shrimp

5

? bags

5 pounds per bag

Answer: 29.5 ÷ 5 = 5.9. So, 5 bags can be filled.

Justify

Is my calculation reasonable?

You can check by using multiplication.

You know that $5 \times 5 = 25$, and $5 \times 0.9 = 4.5$.
$25 + 4.5 = 29.5$

So, 5.9 is reasonable.

Evaluate

Did I answer the right questions?
The question has two parts. Did you answer both of them correctly?

Mr. Patel can put 25 pounds of shrimp in 5 bags. He will need one more bag for the remaining 4.5 pounds of shrimp.

So, the correct answer should be that 5 bags are filled, but 6 bags are needed in all.

Do You Understand?

Convince Me! A bird feeder needs to be refilled every 3 days with 5 cups of seed. A bag of seed holds 22.5 cups. How many bags of seed are needed to fill the feeder for 3 weeks? Brad thinks 2 bags of seed are needed. Is his answer reasonable? Explain.

A-Z

Kes

© Pearson Education, Inc. 5

☆ Guided Practice ☆

In **1** and **2**, look back and check. Tell if the answer is reasonable. Explain why or why not.

1. In the school cafeteria, each table holds 10 students. There are 48 students at lunch. How many tables are needed to seat all of the students?

   Answer: 48 ÷ 10 = 4.8 tables

2. How many 12-ounce servings can the cafeteria make out of 183 ounces of juice?

   Answer: 183 ÷ 12 = 15.25

   They can make 15 servings.

3. How could you use estimation to decide that 5.9 is a reasonable answer for the problem on page 310?

4. **Connect** Write a real-world problem that you can solve by dividing. Give an answer to be checked for reasonableness.

Remember to check that your calculation is correct.

☆ Independent Practice ☆

In **5** and **6**, look back and check. Tell if the answer is reasonable. Explain why or why not.

5. Lionel is buying ice chests to hold 144 bottles of lemonade for a picnic. Each ice chest holds 20 bottles. How many ice chests should he buy?

   Answer: 8 ice chests

6. In math class, Carlos scored 70 points on one quiz and 45 points on another quiz. The sum of his quiz scores was then divided by two. Next, this score was tripled. How many points does Carlos have?

   Answer: 70 + 45 = 115, 115 ÷ 2 = 57.5, 3 × 57.5 = 172.5

   Carlos has 172.5 points.

Problem Solving

7. Jana has 93.75 inches of lace. She is making party invitations that are 4 inches long and 3.5 inches wide. How many party invitations can she decorate with a lace border?

8. Personal Financial Literacy Max is going to borrow money to buy a TV. For one TV he must pay back $438 in 12 months. For the other TV, he must pay back $555 in 15 months. Which TV has lower monthly payments? Explain how you know.

In **9** and **10**, use the picture.

9. Justify Christy wants to buy three polos. Will the total cost be less at Mia's Outlet or Suzy's Store? Justify your answer.

10. Mia's Outlet is having a sale. If Sam buys 3 shirts at the regular price, he will get 2 free shirts. How much will each shirt cost if Sam buys them during the sale?

11. Duane bought 6 plums and 4 peaches. The peaches cost $2.83 in all and the plums cost $0.33 each. Duane paid with a $5 bill. How much change did he receive?

12. Analyze Information Leslie's ceramics class meets for 1.5 hours twice a week, and she spends another 3 hours a week in pottery class. To find how much time Leslie spends doing ceramics each week, identify the hidden question.

A How much time does Leslie spend in ceramics class each week?

B How much time must Leslie practice ceramics per week?

C How long is a ceramics class?

D How many hours are in a day?

Another Look!

How can you justify that your answer is reasonable?

There are 60 students going on a field trip. One chaperone is needed for each 8 students. How many chaperones are needed?

Answer: 60 ÷ 8 = 8.5
8 chaperones

Is my calculation reasonable?

No; 7 × 8 = 56 and 8 × 8 = 64, so the quotient should be between 7 and 8. 60 ÷ 8 = 7.5

Did I answer the right questions?

8 chaperones are needed. The right answer was found, but based on the wrong calculation.

In **1** through **3**, look back and check. Justify why the answer is reasonable or not reasonable.

1. Myrna has 26 daisies. She can plant 3 daisies in each pot. How many pots can she completely fill?

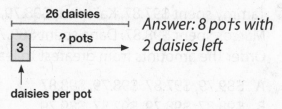

26 daisies

3   ? pots

daisies per pot

Answer: 8 pots with 2 daisies left

2. A wood carver shipped 180 carved animals in boxes that hold 8 animals each. How many boxes did the wood carver need to ship all the animals?

Answer: 180 ÷ 8 = 2.25
The wood carver can fill 2 boxes.

3. Mrs. Goia has 49 students in her art classes. She is ordering art supplies.

A How many cases of pastels does she need to order?

Answer: 17 cases

B How many cases of charcoals does she need to order?

Answer: 8 cases with 1 student left

Art Supplies	
Item	**Number of Students per Case**
Case of pastels	3
Case of paints	4
Case of charcoals	6

DATA

4. Represent Pia needs 100 red beads to make a necklace. She already has 38 red beads. How many more red beads does she need? Write an equation and solve.

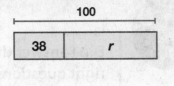

100	
38	r

5. Estimation Bridget sold 62 tickets for a school concert at $3.95 each. About how much money did she collect for all 62 tickets? Show your work.

6. Formulate a Plan Five friends are going to a movie. Three of the friends are 12 years old and the other two are 13 years old. They want to share the cost equally. How much should each friend pay? Explain.

7. Ms. Rashmi plans to serve 1 bottle of water to each of the 28 people who will attend the school fair. There are 6 bottles of water in a case. How many cases of bottled water must she buy?

8. Four friends went to the grocery store. Tammy spent $97.87, Kai spent $98.79, Marcos spent $98.87, Dana spent $89.79. Order the amounts from greatest to least.

A $89.79, $97.87, $98.79, $98.87

B $98.87, $98.79, $97.87, $89.79

C $98.87, $97.87, $98.79, $89.79

D Not here

9. Extend Your Thinking Beatrice has saved $125. Does she have enough money to buy 2 bats and 3 caps if the sales tax is $8.40? Show your work.

Item	Price
Bat	$29.98
Cap	$19.99

DATA

Name _____

1. **Use Tools** Marlon bought 10 gallons of water for a total cost of $14.40. How much did each gallon cost? Use place-value blocks to model the division.

Applying Math Processes

- How does this problem connect to previous ones?
- What is my plan?
- How can I use tools?
- How can I use number sense?
- How can I communicate and represent my thinking?
- How can I organize and record information?
- How can I explain my work?
- How can I justify my answer?

2. **Construct Arguments** Meg says writing 154.2 as 154.20 does not change its value. Explain why you agree or disagree.

3. **Communicate** Explain how to locate 3.33 on the number line.

3.30 ────────────────── 3.40

4. **Use a Strip Diagram** Ben wrote $5.5 - 0.44 = 1.1$. Is his answer reasonable? Use the strip diagram to tell why or why not.

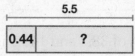

5. **Justify** Jamie and Troy each multiplied 7.025 by 100. Jamie said the answer was 70.25, but Troy said the answer was 702.5. Which student multiplied correctly? How do you know?

6. **Extend Your Thinking** A rancher is selling 240 cows. One third of the cows are sold to a neighboring ranch. Then 50 of the cows are sold to the rancher's brother. How many cows does the rancher have left to sell? Show your work.

You can use patterns to help you place the decimal place correctly.

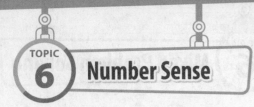

Error Search

Find each problem that is not correct. Circle what is wrong and rewrite the problem so it is correct.

1. $3.56 \div 10 = 35.6$

2. $129.8 \div 100 = 1.298$

3. $0.24 \div 8 = 0.3$

4. $9.15 \div 3 = 3.5$

Reasoning

Write whether each statement is *true* or *false*. If you write *false*, change the numbers or words so that the statement is true.

5. The product of 29.7 and 2.87 is greater than 90.

6. The sum of 38.7 and 149.5 is less 200.

7. The difference between 98.01 and 23.03 is more than 75.

8. The quotient of 25.8 and 5 is less than 5.

9. The product of 239 and 9.8 is greater than 2,400.

10. The difference between 432,093 and 131,081 is greater than 300,000.

Reteaching

Set A pages 273–278

Find 34.05 ÷ 100.

Dividing by 10 means moving the decimal point one place to the left.

Dividing by 100 means moving the decimal point two places to the left.

34.05 ÷ 100 = 0.3405 = 0.3405

Remember that when dividing decimals by 10 or 100, you may need to use one or more zeros as placeholders: 243 ÷ 100 = 2.43.

Use mental math to find each quotient.

1. 34.6 ÷ 10   **2.** 6,483 ÷ 100

3. 148.3 ÷ 10   **4.** 299 ÷ 100

5. 70.7 ÷ 10   **6.** 5,913 ÷ 100

Set B pages 279–284

Estimate 27.3 ÷ 7.1.

Use compatible numbers.

27.3 ÷ 7.1
   ↓   ↓
  28 ÷ 7 = 4

So, 27.3 ÷ 7.1 is about 4.

Remember that compatible numbers are numbers that are easy to compute in your head.

Estimate each quotient.

1. 26.2 ÷ 5   **2.** 49.6 ÷ 7.8

3. 121 ÷ 12.75   **4.** 32.41 ÷ 10.9

Set C pages 285–290, 291–296

Find 1.14 ÷ 3.

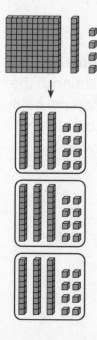

Estimate first.
1.14 ÷ 3 is less than 1, so start dividing in the tenths place.

```
        0.38
    3)1.14
     − 9
      24
    − 24
       0
```

Remember to place the decimal point in the quotient above the decimal point in the dividend. Annex zeros as needed. You may use place-value blocks to help.

1. 6.58 ÷ 7   **2.** 156 ÷ 8

3. Michelle pays $66.85 for a costume pattern and 8 yards of fabric. The pattern costs $4.85. How much does each yard of the fabric cost?

Find 511 ÷ 14.

Estimate first. 500 ÷ 10 = 50, so start dividing in the tens place.

$$
\begin{array}{r}
36.5 \\
14\overline{)511.0} \\
-42 \\
\hline
91 \\
-84 \\
\hline
70 \\
-70 \\
\hline
0
\end{array}
$$

Place the decimal point. Annex a zero.

Remember that you can check your calculation by multiplying the quotient by the divisor.

1. 29.04 ÷ 22 **2.** 144 ÷ 45

3. A 12-ounce bottle of shampoo costs $4.20. A 16-ounce bottle costs $6.88. Which shampoo costs less per ounce? How do you know?

Christine made 60 ounces of jelly. She puts the jelly in 8-ounce jars. How many jars can she fill? How many jars does she need in all?

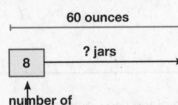

60 ounces

? jars

8

number of ounces per jar

Divide.

$$
\begin{array}{r}
7.5 \\
8\overline{)60.0} \\
-56 \\
\hline
40 \\
-40 \\
\hline
0
\end{array}
$$

She can fill 7 jars, but she needs 8 jars in all.

Use multiplication to check the calculation.
7.5 × 8 = 60

Remember to check the reasonableness of a solution by making sure your calculations are correct, and that you answered the question(s).

1. Ian uses 4 feet of ribbon to wrap each package. How many packages can he wrap with 5.5 yards of ribbon? (Hint: There are 3 feet in a yard.)

2. A painter uses 4 gallons of paint to paint each apartment in a building. If the painter has 45 gallons of paint, how many apartments can be painted completely? How much paint will be left over?

1. Mr. Dodd filled the gas tank on his lawn mower with 3.8 gallons of gas. He mowed his yard 10 times on the same tank of gas. He used the same amount of gas each time he mowed the lawn. How much gas did he use each time the lawn was mowed?

   A 0.038 gallons

   B 0.38 gallons

   C 38 gallons

   D 380 gallons

2. Kimberly scored a total of 35.08 points in four events for her gymnastic competition. If she scored the same amount on each event, how many points did she score on each?

   _____

3. Which quotient does the model Tess made represent?

   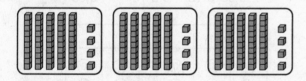

   A 1.35 ÷ 3 = 0.45

   B 1.35 ÷ 3 = 0.54

   C 1.62 ÷ 3 = 0.45

   D Not here

4. The chef at a restaurant bought 37 pounds of salad for $46.25. How much did she pay for each pound of salad?

   A $0.125

   B $1.25

   C $1.30

   D $12.50

5. Which quotient does the model Ruth made represent?

   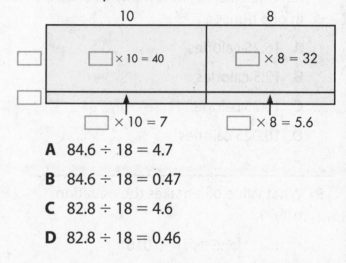

   A 84.6 ÷ 18 = 4.7

   B 84.6 ÷ 18 = 0.47

   C 82.8 ÷ 18 = 4.6

   D 82.8 ÷ 18 = 0.46

6. Toby's faucet dripped a total of 1.92 liters of water in 24 hours. He calculated that the faucet dripped 0.8 liter an hour. Is that calculation reasonable?

   A Yes, 24 × 0.8 = 1.92 so the calculation is correct.

   B Yes, 24 × 24 = 8 so the calculation is correct.

   C No, the calculation is wrong. 1.92 ÷ 24 = 0.08.

   D No, the calculation is wrong. 24 ÷ 1.92 = 12.5.

7. Sue has 93.5 pounds of apples and 9 baskets. She uses compatible numbers to estimate how many pounds of apples to put in each basket. Which of the following estimates does **NOT** use compatible numbers?

A 100 ÷ 10

B 90 ÷ 9

C 90 ÷ 10

D 100 ÷ 9

8. If eight ounces of canned pumpkin have 82 calories, how many calories are in one ounce?

A 16.25 calories

B 12.5 calories

C 10.25 calories

D 10.025 calories

9. What value of *n* makes the equation true?

$$1.6 \div n = 0.016$$

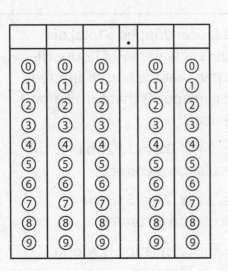

10. Eileen bought 8 roses for $45.50. Which is the best way to estimate the cost of one rose?

A $45 ÷ 5 = $9.00

B $48 ÷ 8 = $6.00

C $45 ÷ 10 = $0.45

D $40 ÷ 8 = $0.50

11. Lou's Diner spent $28.80 on 18 pounds of potatoes. What is the cost for 1 pound of potatoes?

12. What is the missing number in the model?

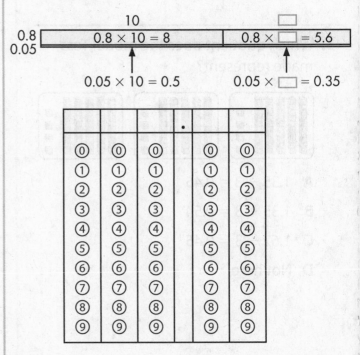

Adding and Subtracting Fractions

Essential Question: How can sums and differences of fractions with unlike denominators be estimated? What is a standard procedure for adding and subtracting fractions with unlike denominators?

A learned trait is a skill or behavior you learn over time. Learned traits are not inherited traits such as eye color.

Cartwheels are a skill that I learned. Wearing a jacket when it's cold is learned behavior.

Score! My learned traits are kicking field goals and drinking lots of water when it's hot. Here's a project about learned traits.

Math and Science Project: Learned Traits

Do Research Use the Internet or other sources to research the term *learned traits*. Make a list of 10 learned traits that you have acquired since you were born. How many are a skill? How many are behaviors? How many of your learned traits did you acquire at school?

Journal: Write a Report Include what you found. Also in your report make a bar graph:

- Label the vertical axis of your bar graph with the numbers 0 through 10.

- Label the horizontal axis with the categories Skill, Behavior, and School.

- Draw bars on the graph. Remember, the height of the bar shows the number.

Review What You Know

Vocabulary

Choose the best term from the box. Write it on the blank.

> - denominator
> - numerator
> - prime number
> - simplest form

1. A _____ has exactly two factors, 1 and itself.

2. The _____ of $\frac{3}{6}$ is $\frac{1}{2}$.

3. The _____ of a fraction tells how many equal parts there are in the whole.

Division

Find each quotient.

4. $12 \div 4$

5. $21 \div 3$

6. $36 \div 2$

7. $48 \div 8$

8. $72 \div 6$

9. $60 \div 15$

10. $52 \div 4$

11. $88 \div 8$

Multiplication

Find each product.

12. 6×7

13. 2×18

14. 15×3

15. 11×5

16. Ms. Rios is setting up an art class for 19 students. She wants each student to have 4 poster sheets. Poster sheets are sold in boxes of 14. Which expression shows the number of boxes of poster sheets she needs for class?

   A $(19 \times 4) - 14$
   B $(19 \times 4) \div 14$
   C $(19 \div 4) \times 14$
   D $(19 \div 4) + 14$

17. Harry has a 42-pound bag and a 18-pound bag of garden soil. If he uses 15 pounds of soil to complete each section of his garden, how many sections can he complete?

Fractions

18. **Writing to Explain** Jamie read $\frac{1}{4}$ of a book for class. Raul read $\frac{3}{4}$ of the same book. Who is closer to reading the whole book? Explain.

My Word Cards

Use the examples for each word on the front of the card to help complete the definitions on the back.

A-Z

prime number

13

factors: 1, 13

composite number

14

factors: 1, 2, 7, 14

numerator

$\frac{1}{4}$ ←— numerator

denominator

$\frac{1}{4}$ ←— denominator

equivalent fractions

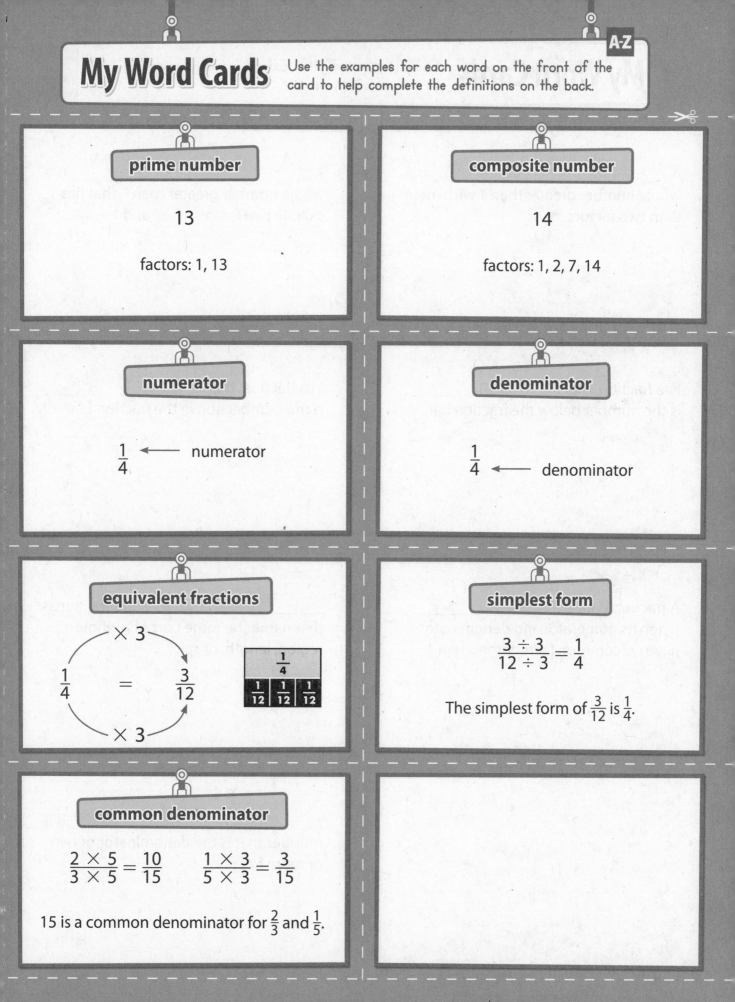

$\frac{1}{4} = \frac{3}{12}$

$\times 3$

$\times 3$

simplest form

$\frac{3 \div 3}{12 \div 3} = \frac{1}{4}$

The simplest form of $\frac{3}{12}$ is $\frac{1}{4}$.

common denominator

$\frac{2 \times 5}{3 \times 5} = \frac{10}{15}$ $\frac{1 \times 3}{5 \times 3} = \frac{3}{15}$

15 is a common denominator for $\frac{2}{3}$ and $\frac{1}{5}$.

My Word Cards

Complete the definition. Extend learning by writing your own definitions.

A _____ is a whole number greater than 1 with more than two factors.

A _____ is a whole number greater than 1 that has exactly two factors, itself and 1.

In a fraction, the _____ is the number below the fraction bar.

In a fraction, the _____ is the number above the fraction bar.

A fraction is in _____ when its numerator and denominator have no common factor other than 1.

_____ are fractions that name the same part of a whole region, length, or set.

A _____ is a number that is the denominator of two or more fractions.

Name _____

Solve & Share

A garden has an area of 24 square units. The length and width of the garden are whole numbers. What dimensions are possible for the garden? *Solve this problem any way you choose.*

⬥ TEKS 5.4A Identify prime and composite numbers. Mathematical Process Standards 5.1C, 5.1D, 5.1G

Number Sense You can use what you know about factors to identify all of the possible garden dimensions. *Show your work!*

Digital Resources at PearsonTexas.com

| Solve | Learn | Glossary | Check | Tools | Games |

Look Back!

Number Sense A rectangular garden has an area of 17 square yards. Its sides are whole numbers of yards. What dimensions are possible?

What Are Prime and Composite Numbers?

Every whole number greater than 1 is either a prime number or a composite number.

On the other hand, a composite number has more than two factors.

A prime number has exactly two factors, 1 and itself.

$1 \times 5 = 5$

The factors of 5 are 1 and 5.

$2 \times 6 = 12$ $3 \times 4 = 12$

The factors of 12 are 1, 2, 3, 4, 6, and 12.

B **Prime or Composite?**

Is 27 a prime number or a composite number?

Use division facts to help you decide.

Since 27 is an odd number, it is **NOT** divisible by 2.

But, $1 \times 27 = 27$ and $3 \times 9 = 27$. So, 1, 3, 9, and 27 are factors of 27.

So, 27 is composite.

C Is 11 prime or composite?

Since 11 is an odd number, it is **NOT** divisible by 2.

It is also **NOT** divisible by 3, 4, 5, 6, 7, 8, 9, or 10.

So, 11 has only two factors, 1 and itself.

The number 11 is prime.

Do You Understand?

Convince Me! Lucero is thinking of a number. The number is greater than 2 and it has 2 as a factor. Is the number prime or composite? Tell how you know.

Name _____

☆ Guided Practice*

In **1** and **2**, list all the factors of each number. Write whether the number is prime or composite.

1. 8

Factors: _____

Prime or Composite? _____

2. 3

Factors: _____

Prime or Composite? _____

3. Reason What factor does every number have in common?

4. List the possible arrays in which you can arrange 18 buttons.

5. Kevin is making a banner with an area of 7 square feet. The width and length of the banner are whole numbers. What are its possible dimensions?

Independent Practice ☆

Leveled Practice In **6** through **13**, list all the factors of each number. Write whether the number is prime or composite.

6. 21

Factors: _____

Prime or Composite? _____

7. 48

Factors: _____

Prime or Composite? _____

8. 13

Factors: _____

Prime or Composite? _____

9. 31

Factors: _____

Prime or Composite? _____

10. 60

Factors: _____

Prime or Composite? _____

11. 108

Factors: _____

Prime or Composite? _____

12. 131

Factors: _____

Prime or Composite? _____

13. 150

Factors: _____

Prime or Composite? _____

*For another example, use Set A on page 381.

Topic 7 | Lesson 7-1

327

Problem Solving

14. Math and Science Eratosthenes was born in Cyrene (now Libya) about 230 B.C. He developed a method for deciding if a number is prime. It is called the Sieve of Eratosthenes because it "strains out" prime numbers from other numbers. Use a hundred chart to find all the prime numbers between 1 and 100.

a Cross out 1. It is not prime or composite.

b Circle 2, the least prime number. Cross out every second number after 2.

c Circle 3, the next prime number. Cross out every third number after 3 (even if it has already been crossed out.)

d Circle 5, and repeat the process.

e Circle 7, and repeat the process.

f Circle all the numbers that have not been crossed out. The numbers that are circled are the prime numbers up to 100.

---

15. The numbers below follow a pattern.

   2   8   32   128   _____

Write an expression that shows one way to find the next number.

16. Communicate Tim says that 1, 4, 7, and 28 are all of the factors of 28. Is he correct? Explain.

---

17. Which expression best represents the table?

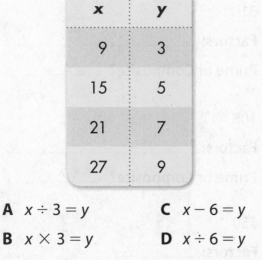

x	y
9	3
15	5
21	7
27	9

A $x \div 3 = y$

B $x \times 3 = y$

C $x - 6 = y$

D $x \div 6 = y$

18. Extend Your Thinking Use the diagrams and explain how they can help you find some factors of 32. List all factors of 32. Write whether 32 is a prime or composite number.

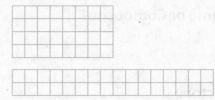

Name _____

Another Look!

Numbers such as 2, 3, 5, 7, and 11 are prime numbers.
A prime number has *only two* factors, itself and 1.
A whole number that has *more than two* factors is
called a composite number.

3 is an example of a prime number.
Its only factors are 1 and 3.

8 is a composite number.
Its factors are 1, 2, 4, and 8.

● ● ● $1 \times 3 = 3$

● ● ● ● ● ● ● ● $1 \times 8 = 8$

● ● ● ●
● ● ● ● $2 \times 4 = 8$

In **1** through **5**, list all the factors of each number.
Write whether the number is prime or composite.

1. 10

Factors: _____

Prime or Composite? _____

Arrays can help you
visualize problems.

Factors You can draw arrays to help. Your
rows must be equal.

2 and 5

● ● ● ● ●
● ● ● ● ●

____ and ____

● ● ● ● ● ● ● ● ● ●

2. 16

Factors: _____

Prime or Composite? _____

3. 23

Factors: _____

Prime or Composite? _____

4. 36

Factors: _____

Prime or Composite? _____

5. 40

Factors: _____

Prime or Composite? _____

6. Explain What are the first 10 prime numbers? Explain why these are prime numbers.

7. Communicate Explain the mistakes in the list of factors for 42 below. List all the correct factors.

1, 2, 4, 6, 7, 12, 24, 42

---

8. A museum wants to use equal rows to arrange the African baskets. Which list shows all the different possible arrangements so that all the rows have the same number? Assume that an arrangement such as 4 × 20 is the same as 20 × 4.

World Cultures Museum	
Exhibit	**Number of Items**
African Baskets	80
Asian Carvings	56
Indian Statues	74

DATA

A 1 × 80; 4 × 20; 8 × 10
B 1 × 80; 2 × 40; 4 × 20; 5 × 16; 8 × 10
C 2 × 40; 5 × 16; 8 × 10
D 2 × 40; 4 × 20; 5 × 16; 8 × 10

---

9. Extend Your Thinking Luz says you can complete a multiplication table to help find most factors of 24. Explain why she is correct. Which factors of 24 would be missing from the table? List all the factors of 24.

X	1	2	3	4	5	6	7	8	9	10	11	12
1	1	2	3	4	5							
2	2	4	6	8	10							
3	3	6	9	12	15							
4	4	8	12	16	20							
5	5	10	15	20	25							
6												
7												
8												
9												
10												
11												
12												

---

10. Extend Your Thinking Mr. Gray wants to find all the different ways to arrange 16 square tiles into a rectangle shape for a wall mural. One way is shown. Draw all the different ways to arrange 16 squares into a rectangle shape. Write the factors for each way.

1 × 16

© Pearson Education, Inc. 5

Solve & Share

Find a fraction that represents the same part of a whole as $\frac{4}{6}$. *Use fraction strips to solve this.*

TEKS 5.3H Represent and solve addition and subtraction of fractions with unequal denominators referring to the same whole using objects and pictorial models and properties of operations. Mathematical Process Standards 5.1A, 5.1D, 5.1E, 5.1G

The fraction strips show equivalent fractions.
$\frac{2}{3} = \frac{4}{6} = \frac{6}{9} = \frac{8}{12}$

1					
$\frac{1}{3}$		$\frac{1}{3}$		$\frac{1}{3}$	
$\frac{1}{6}$	$\frac{1}{6}$	$\frac{1}{6}$	$\frac{1}{6}$	$\frac{1}{6}$	$\frac{1}{6}$
$\frac{1}{9}$ $\frac{1}{9}$ $\frac{1}{9}$ $\frac{1}{9}$ $\frac{1}{9}$ $\frac{1}{9}$				$\frac{1}{9}$ $\frac{1}{9}$ $\frac{1}{9}$	
$\frac{1}{12}$ $\frac{1}{12}$ $\frac{1}{12}$ $\frac{1}{12}$ $\frac{1}{12}$ $\frac{1}{12}$ $\frac{1}{12}$ $\frac{1}{12}$				$\frac{1}{12}$ $\frac{1}{12}$ $\frac{1}{12}$ $\frac{1}{12}$	

Digital Resources at PearsonTexas.com

Solve Learn Glossary Check Tools Games

Create and Use Representations You can show how two fractions are equivalent. *Show your work!*

Look Back!

Communicate How can you show fractions that are equivalent to $\frac{6}{8}$? Name two of those fractions.

How Can You Find Equivalent Fractions?

Fractions that have different numerators and denominators but name the same amount are called equivalent fractions.

The fraction strips show equivalent fractions.
$\frac{2}{3} = \frac{4}{6} = \frac{6}{9} = \frac{8}{12}$

Equivalent is another way of saying "equal".

1		
$\frac{1}{3}$	$\frac{1}{3}$	$\frac{1}{3}$

| $\frac{1}{6}$ | $\frac{1}{6}$ | $\frac{1}{6}$ | $\frac{1}{6}$ | $\frac{1}{6}$ | $\frac{1}{6}$ |

| $\frac{1}{9}$ | $\frac{1}{9}$ | $\frac{1}{9}$ | $\frac{1}{9}$ | $\frac{1}{9}$ | $\frac{1}{9}$ | $\frac{1}{9}$ | $\frac{1}{9}$ | $\frac{1}{9}$ |

| $\frac{1}{12}$ | $\frac{1}{12}$ | $\frac{1}{12}$ | $\frac{1}{12}$ | $\frac{1}{12}$ | $\frac{1}{12}$ | $\frac{1}{12}$ | $\frac{1}{12}$ | $\frac{1}{12}$ | $\frac{1}{12}$ | $\frac{1}{12}$ | $\frac{1}{12}$ |

B One Way

You can multiply both the numerator and the denominator by the same nonzero number.

$$\frac{10 \times 2}{15 \times 2} = \frac{20}{30}$$

$\frac{10}{15}$ and $\frac{20}{30}$ are equivalent fractions.

C Another Way

You can divide the numerator and denominator by the same nonzero number if they can both be divided evenly.

$$\frac{10 \div 5}{15 \div 5} = \frac{2}{3}$$

$\frac{10}{15}$ and $\frac{2}{3}$ are equivalent fractions.

Do You Understand?

Convince Me! Why is multiplying the numerator and the denominator by the same nonzero number the same as multiplying the fraction by 1? Use the calculation above to explain.

☆ **Guided Practice** *

In **1** through **4**, write two fractions that are equivalent to the fraction given. You may use fraction strips to help.

1. $\frac{2}{4}$ $\frac{2 \times 2}{4 \times 2} = \frac{\square}{\square}$ **2.** $\frac{6}{10}$

$\frac{2 \div 2}{4 \div 2} = \frac{\square}{\square}$

3. $\frac{4}{9}$ **4.** $\frac{24}{48}$

5. Reason Explain why $\frac{1}{2}$ of an apple is not equivalent to $\frac{4}{8}$ of a pizza.

6. Why wouldn't you use division to find an equivalent fraction for $\frac{7}{15}$?

☆ **Independent Practice** ☆

Leveled Practice In **7** through **18**, write two fractions that are equivalent to the fraction given.

You may use fraction strips to help.

7. $\frac{3}{12}$ $\frac{3 \times 2}{12 \times 2} = \frac{\square}{\square}$ **8.** $\frac{6}{12}$ $\frac{6 \div 3}{12 \div 3} = \frac{\square}{\square}$ **9.** $\frac{10}{35}$ $\frac{10 \times 2}{35 \times 2} = \frac{\square}{\square}$

$\frac{3 \div 3}{12 \div 3} = \frac{\square}{\square}$ $\frac{6 \div 6}{12 \div 6} = \frac{\square}{\square}$ $\frac{10 \div 5}{35 \div 5} = \frac{\square}{\square}$

10. $\frac{6}{9}$ **11.** $\frac{5}{7}$ **12.** $\frac{9}{10}$

13. $\frac{32}{40}$ **14.** $\frac{28}{36}$ **15.** $\frac{1}{1000}$

16. $\frac{3}{11}$ **17.** $\frac{14}{21}$ **18.** $\frac{27}{36}$

Problem Solving

19. **Explain** Kai says that $\frac{3}{7} = \frac{9}{14}$. Is Kai correct? Explain.

20. **Justify** Jenna claims that no matter how many equivalent fractions are found for any fraction, she can always find one more. Is she right? Explain.

21. **Extend Your Thinking** How can you use equivalent fractions to know that $\frac{43}{200}$ is between $\frac{1}{5}$ and $\frac{1}{4}$?

22. Mr. Morey divided a pizza into 12 equal parts to share among 6 people. Each person got $\frac{2}{12}$ of the pizza. What is an equivalent fraction that names the same amount of pizza that each person got?

23. To complete the repair of the Harper Building, the construction company worked 12 hours each day. How many days did it take for the company to complete the repair of the building?

DATA

Sturdy Construction Company	
Project	Number of Hours to Complete
Cooper Building Repair	3,068
Harper Building Repair	1,445
Library Extension	2,730

24. ⭐ Ace Stationery Supplies buys cartons containing many items and sells individual items from the carton to customers. Which of the following fractions is equivalent to the part of the carton of staplers sold in Week 1?

A $\frac{1}{5}$

B $\frac{1}{6}$

C $\frac{3}{8}$

D $\frac{5}{8}$

DATA

Ace Stationery Supplies Week 1 Sales		
Item	Number of Items Per Full Carton	Number of Items Sold
Box of Staples	30	5
Notebooks	12	4
Pencils	36	18
Staplers	40	15

Homework 7-2
Equivalent Fractions

Another Look!

Vin served $\frac{4}{10}$ of a pan of pasta. What are two equivalent fractions that each name the same part of the pasta served?

> If you use division, make sure both the numerator and the denominator can be divided evenly by the same number.

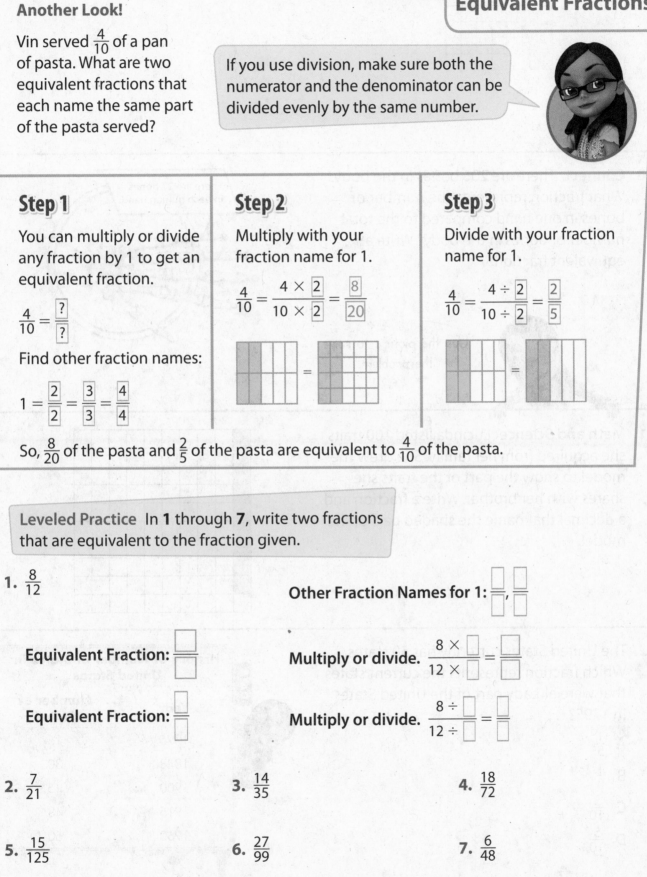

Step 1

You can multiply or divide any fraction by 1 to get an equivalent fraction.

$$\frac{4}{10} = \frac{?}{?}$$

Find other fraction names:

$$1 = \frac{2}{2} = \frac{3}{3} = \frac{4}{4}$$

Step 2

Multiply with your fraction name for 1.

$$\frac{4}{10} = \frac{4 \times 2}{10 \times 2} = \frac{8}{20}$$

Step 3

Divide with your fraction name for 1.

$$\frac{4}{10} = \frac{4 \div 2}{10 \div 2} = \frac{2}{5}$$

So, $\frac{8}{20}$ of the pasta and $\frac{2}{5}$ of the pasta are equivalent to $\frac{4}{10}$ of the pasta.

Leveled Practice In **1** through **7**, write two fractions that are equivalent to the fraction given.

1. $\frac{8}{12}$

Other Fraction Names for 1: $\frac{\square}{\square}$, $\frac{\square}{\square}$

Equivalent Fraction: $\frac{\square}{\square}$

Multiply or divide. $\frac{8 \times \square}{12 \times \square} = \frac{\square}{\square}$

Equivalent Fraction: $\frac{\square}{\square}$

Multiply or divide. $\frac{8 \div \square}{12 \div \square} = \frac{\square}{\square}$

2. $\frac{7}{21}$

3. $\frac{14}{35}$

4. $\frac{18}{72}$

5. $\frac{15}{125}$

6. $\frac{27}{99}$

7. $\frac{6}{48}$

8. Extend Your Thinking How does this diagram help show that $\frac{2}{7} = \frac{8}{28}$?

9. Draw a Picture Draw a grid like the one in Exercise 8 to show that $\frac{5}{6} = \frac{15}{18}$.

10. Connect There are 206 bones in the body. What fraction represents the number of bones in one hand compared to the total number of bones in the body? Write an equivalent fraction.

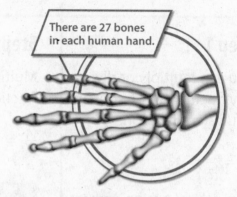

There are 27 bones in each human hand.

Use the picture to solve the problem.

11. Math and Science Lucinda listed 100 traits she acquired from her family. She drew the model to show the part of the traits she shares with her brother. Write a fraction and a decimal that name the shaded part of the model.

12. The United States currently has 50 states. Which fraction represents the current states that were already part of the United States in 1795?

A $\frac{1}{5}$

B $\frac{1}{6}$

C $\frac{3}{10}$

D $\frac{5}{10}$

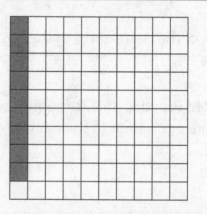

History of Number of States in United States	
Year	**Number of States**
1795	15
1848	30
1900	45
1915	48
1960	50

Name _____

Solve & Share

Two rectangles are divided into equal parts and shaded. Write all of the fractions that name the shaded areas of the rectangles. Then write fractions that name the unshaded areas. **Solve this problem any way you choose.**

TEKS 5.3H Represent and solve addition and subtraction of fractions with unequal denominators referring to the same whole using objects and pictorial models and properties of operations. Mathematical Process Standards 5.1A, 5.1B, 5.1D, 5.1F, 5.1G

Connect Ideas Each rectangle represents 1 whole. You can represent the equal parts as fractions of the whole. **Show your work!**

Digital Resources at PearsonTexas.com

Solve | Learn | Glossary | Check | Tools | Games

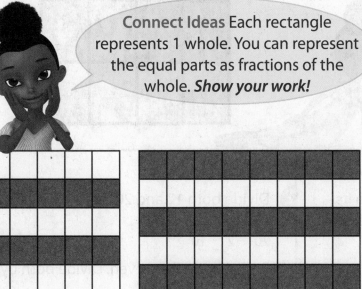

Look Back!

Analyze Relationships Which of your fractions has a numerator and a denominator that cannot be divided evenly by the same whole number other than 1?

How Can You Write a Fraction in Simplest Form?

A stained glass window has 20 panes. Out of 20 sections, 12 are yellow. So $\frac{12}{20}$ of the panes are yellow. Notice how the picture also shows that $\frac{3}{5}$ of the panes are yellow.

The fractions $\frac{12}{20}$ and $\frac{3}{5}$ are equivalent.

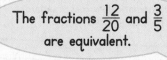

B
A fraction is in simplest form when its numerator and denominator have no common factor other than 1.

To write $\frac{12}{20}$ in simplest form, find a common factor of the numerator and the denominator. Since 12 and 20 are even numbers, they have 2 as a factor.

You can find other common factors by using division facts.

C
Divide both 12 and 20 by 2.

$$\frac{12 \div 2}{20 \div 2} = \frac{6}{10}$$

Both 6 and 10 are even. Divide both by 2.

$$\frac{6 \div 2}{10 \div 2} = \frac{3}{5}$$

Since 3 and 5 have no common factor other than 1, you know that $\frac{3}{5}$ is in simplest form.

Do You Understand?

Convince Me! Look at this stained glass window. What fraction shows the number of green panes out of the total number of panes? How would you write this fraction in simplest form? Tell how you can "see" this fraction in the window.

☆ Guided Practice *

In **1** and **2**, write each fraction in simplest form.

1. $\frac{16}{32}$ $\frac{16 \div 2}{32 \div 2} = \frac{\square}{\square}$

$\frac{8 \div 2}{16 \div 2} = \frac{\square}{\square}$

$\frac{4 \div 2}{8 \div 2} = \frac{\square}{\square}$

$\frac{2 \div 2}{4 \div 2} = \frac{\square}{\square}$

2. $\frac{30}{40}$ $\frac{30 \div 2}{40 \div 2} = \frac{\square}{\square}$

$\frac{15 \div 5}{20 \div 5} = \frac{\square}{\square}$

3. In the stained glass window pattern at the top of page 338, what fraction in simplest form names the green tiles?

4. **Reason** Can a fraction with an even numerator and an even denominator be in simplest form? Why or why not?

☆ Independent Practice ☆

Leveled Practice In **5** through **19**, write each fraction in simplest form.

> How can you tell when a fraction is in simplest form?

5. $\frac{33}{77}$ $\frac{33 \div 11}{77 \div 11} = \frac{\square}{\square}$

6. $\frac{16}{20}$ $\frac{16 \div 2}{20 \div 2} = \frac{\square}{\square}$

$\frac{8 \div \square}{10 \div \square} = \frac{\square}{\square}$

7. $\frac{30}{40}$ $\frac{30 \div 10}{40 \div 10} = \frac{\square}{\square}$

8. $\frac{10}{14}$

9. $\frac{10}{15}$

10. $\frac{12}{100}$

11. $\frac{18}{21}$

12. $\frac{42}{48}$

13. $\frac{99}{121}$

14. $\frac{14}{49}$

15. $\frac{36}{81}$

16. $\frac{24}{40}$

17. $\frac{22}{110}$

18. $\frac{32}{168}$

19. $\frac{13}{39}$

Problem Solving

20. Explain How do you know that $\frac{55}{80}$ is not in simplest form?

21. Extend Your Thinking Can you assume that any fraction is in simplest form if either the numerator or denominator is a prime number? Explain.

22. Connect Write a fraction in simplest form that names the shaded part of the figure.

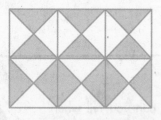

23. Mrs. Lok is planning a 600-mile trip. Her car has an 18-gallon gas tank and gets 29 miles per gallon. Will 1 tank full of gas be enough for the trip? How do you know?

24. Analyze Information It takes 73 days for an egg of a bearded dragon lizard to hatch. What fraction in simplest form represents the part of a year, in days, it takes for the egg to hatch? Complete the diagram below.

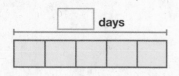

Remember, there are 365 days in 1 year.

25. Mayflies can live at the bottom of lakes for 2 to 3 years before they become winged adults. A mayfly is $\frac{4}{10}$ of an inch long. Which of the following fractions is $\frac{4}{10}$ in simplest form?

A $\frac{1}{6}$

B $\frac{1}{4}$

C $\frac{2}{5}$

D $\frac{8}{20}$

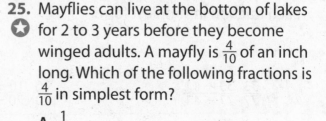

Find a common factor of 4 and 10.

Another Look!

In a survey, $\frac{15}{40}$ of the people said they have a pet. What is the simplest form of the fraction?

> You have found the simplest form when no other number, except 1, is a factor of both the numerator and denominator.

Step 1

If both the numerator and denominator are even numbers, you can divide both by 2.

$$\frac{15}{40} = \frac{?}{?}$$

The numerator, 15, is odd, so you cannot divide both by 2.

Step 2

Find another fraction name for 1 that can evenly divide both the numerator and denominator.

If you can, use basic facts to help.

$$1 = \frac{5}{5} \qquad \begin{array}{l}15 \div 5 \text{ is a basic fact.}\\ 40 \div 5 \text{ is a basic fact.}\end{array}$$

Step 3

Divide with your fraction name for 1.

$$\frac{15}{40} \quad \frac{15 \div \boxed{5}}{40 \div \boxed{5}} = \frac{3}{8}$$

Check that you cannot divide both any further, except by the number 1.

So, $\frac{3}{8}$ is the simplest form of $\frac{15}{40}$.

In **1** through **15**, write each fraction in simplest form.

1. $\frac{16}{40}$ $\quad \frac{16 \div \boxed{}}{40 \div \boxed{}} = \frac{\boxed{}}{\boxed{}}$

2. $\frac{6}{42}$ $\quad \frac{6 \div \boxed{}}{42 \div \boxed{}} = \frac{\boxed{}}{\boxed{}}$

3. $\frac{26}{36}$ $\quad \frac{26 \div \boxed{}}{36 \div \boxed{}} = \frac{\boxed{}}{\boxed{}}$

4. $\frac{14}{21}$

5. $\frac{55}{60}$

6. $\frac{34}{42}$

7. $\frac{63}{70}$

8. $\frac{21}{49}$

9. $\frac{4}{15}$

10. $\frac{40}{72}$

11. $\frac{18}{33}$

12. $\frac{36}{45}$

13. $\frac{10}{35}$

14. $\frac{25}{75}$

15. $\frac{16}{60}$

16. Communicate Jana writes that $\frac{19}{28}$ of the students in her class are wearing sneakers. Explain how you can tell that $\frac{19}{28}$ is in simplest form.

17. Reason A polygon has a perimeter of 36 inches. Each side of the polygon is exactly 12 inches long. What is the name of the polygon that is described?

18. Analyze Information Bicyclist Mike Hall rode around the world in 91 days. What fraction in simplest form represents the part of a year, in weeks, he took to complete this ride?

HINTS: 1 week = 7 days;
1 year = 52 weeks

19. Personal Financial Literacy Kurt wants to save $38 in 8 weeks. How much does he need to save each week?

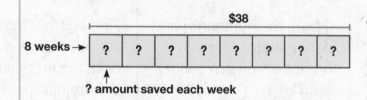

$38

8 weeks →

? amount saved each week

20. Tia asked people to choose how they prefer to get their news. Which fraction, in simplest form, represents the number of votes for newspaper?

A $\frac{1}{28}$

B $\frac{7}{20}$

C $\frac{7}{25}$

D $\frac{7}{100}$

Where do you prefer to get your news?	
News Source	**Number of Votes**
Internet	43
Magazine	8
Newspaper	28
Radio	9
Television	12

DATA

21. Extend Your Thinking The entire area of Earth's surface is 510 million square kilometers. What is a good estimate of the area of Earth's surface that is covered by water? Explain how you got your answer.

DATA

Geography Facts About Earth
Amount of Earth's Surface Covered by Water, about $\frac{7}{10}$
Highest Point, Mt. Everest, 8,848 meters
Number of Continents, 7
Total Land Area, about 149 million square kilometers

Solve & Share

Jack needs about $1\frac{1}{2}$ yards of string. He has three pieces of string that are different lengths. Without finding the exact amount, which two pieces should he choose to get closest to $1\frac{1}{2}$ yards of string? **Solve this problem any way you choose.**

You can use **estimation** to find the answer. **Show your work!**

TEKS 5.3A Estimate to determine solutions to mathematical and real-world problems involving addition, subtraction, multiplication, or division. Mathematical Process Standards 5.1B, 5.1C, 5.1D, 5.1G

Digital Resources at PearsonTexas.com

Solve   Learn   Glossary   Check   Tools   Games

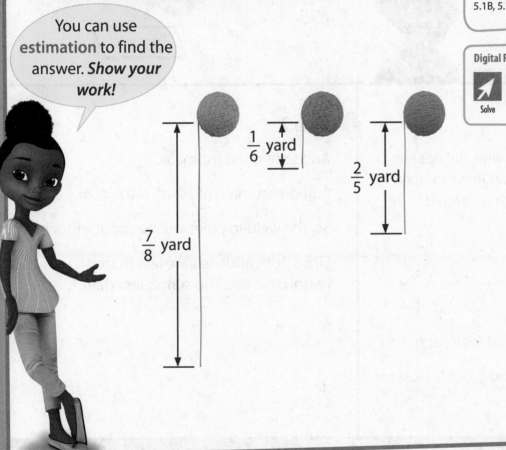

$\frac{1}{6}$ yard

$\frac{2}{5}$ yard

$\frac{7}{8}$ yard

Look Back!

Mental Math How can a number line help you estimate each fraction?

A

Mr. Fish is welding together 2 copper pipes to repair a leak. He will use the pipes shown. Is the new pipe closer to $\frac{1}{2}$ foot or 1 foot long? Explain.

Estimate the sum $\frac{1}{6} + \frac{5}{12}$ to find about how long the combined pipes will be.

$\frac{5}{12}$ foot long

$\frac{1}{6}$ foot long

You can add to find the sum.

B

Step 1

Replace each fraction with the nearest half or whole. A number line can make it easy to decide if each fraction is closest to 0, $\frac{1}{2}$, or 1.

$$\frac{1}{6} \qquad \frac{5}{12}$$

0 $\qquad$ $\frac{1}{2}$ $\qquad$ 1

$\frac{1}{6}$ is between 0 and $\frac{1}{2}$, but is closer to 0.

$\frac{5}{12}$ is also between 0 and $\frac{1}{2}$, but is closer to $\frac{1}{2}$.

C

Step 2

Add to find the estimate.

A good estimate of $\frac{1}{6} + \frac{5}{12}$ is $0 + \frac{1}{2}$, or $\frac{1}{2}$.

So, the welded pipes will be about $\frac{1}{2}$ foot long.

Since both addends are less than $\frac{1}{2}$, it is reasonable that the sum is less than 1.

Do You Understand?

Convine Me! Nolini says that if the denominator is more than twice the numerator, the fraction can always be replaced with 0. Is she correct? Give an example in your explanation.

☆ Guided Practice ☆

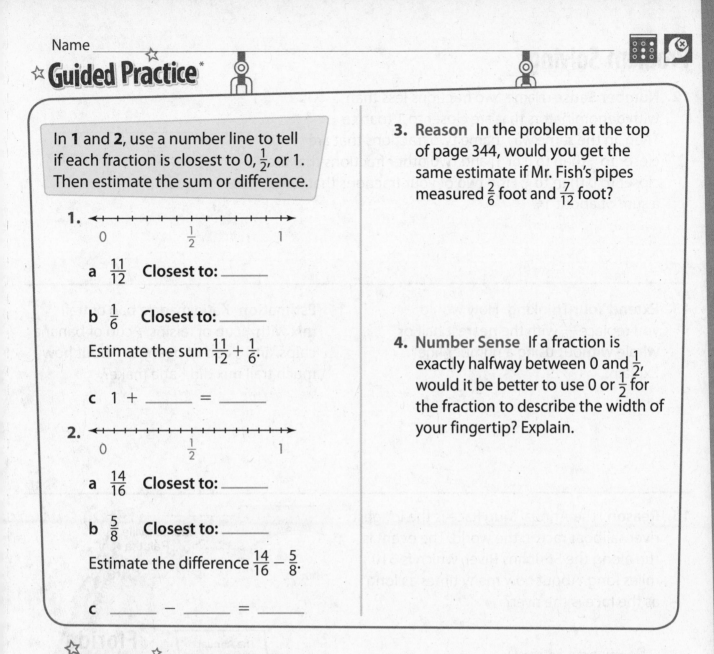

In **1** and **2**, use a number line to tell if each fraction is closest to 0, $\frac{1}{2}$, or 1. Then estimate the sum or difference.

1.

0        $\frac{1}{2}$ 1

a $\frac{11}{12}$ **Closest to:** _____

b $\frac{1}{6}$ **Closest to:** _____

Estimate the sum $\frac{11}{12} + \frac{1}{6}$.

c $1 +$ _____ $=$ _____

2.

0        $\frac{1}{2}$ 1

a $\frac{14}{16}$ **Closest to:** _____

b $\frac{5}{8}$ **Closest to:** _____

Estimate the difference $\frac{14}{16} - \frac{5}{8}$.

c _____ $-$ _____ $=$ _____

3. Reason In the problem at the top of page 344, would you get the same estimate if Mr. Fish's pipes measured $\frac{2}{6}$ foot and $\frac{7}{12}$ foot?

4. Number Sense If a fraction is exactly halfway between 0 and $\frac{1}{2}$, would it be better to use 0 or $\frac{1}{2}$ for the fraction to describe the width of your fingertip? Explain.

☆ Independent Practice ☆

Leveled Practice In **5**, use a number line to tell if each fraction is closest to 0, $\frac{1}{2}$, or 1.

In **6** through **11**, estimate the sum or difference by replacing each fraction with 0, $\frac{1}{2}$, or 1.

5.

0        $\frac{1}{2}$ 1

a $\frac{3}{4}$ **Closest to:** _____

b $\frac{5}{12}$ **Closest to:** _____

Estimate the difference $\frac{3}{4} - \frac{5}{12}$.

c _____ $-$ _____ $=$ _____

6. $\frac{9}{10} + \frac{5}{6}$

7. $\frac{11}{18} - \frac{2}{9}$

8. $\frac{1}{16} + \frac{2}{15}$

9. $\frac{24}{25} - \frac{1}{9}$

10. $\frac{3}{36} + \frac{1}{10}$

11. $\frac{37}{40} - \frac{26}{50}$

Problem Solving

12. **Number Sense** Name two fractions less than 1 with denominators that are closer to 1 than to $\frac{1}{2}$. Then, in the same way, name two fractions that are closer to $\frac{1}{2}$ than to 0 or 1, and two other fractions that are closer to 0 than to $\frac{1}{2}$. Find two of your fractions that have a sum of about $1\frac{1}{2}$.

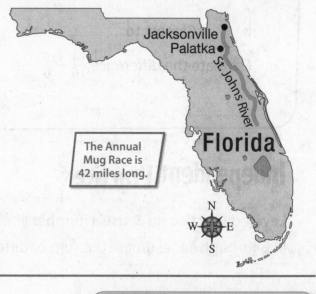

13. **Extend Your Thinking** How would you replace $\frac{27}{50}$ with the nearest half or whole without using a number line? Explain.

14. **Estimation** Katie made a bag of trail mix with $\frac{1}{2}$ cup of raisins, $\frac{3}{5}$ cup of banana chips, and $\frac{3}{8}$ cup of peanuts. About how much trail mix did Katie make?

15. **Reason** The Annual Mug Race is the longest river sailboat race in the world. The event is run along the St. Johns River, which is 310 miles long. About how many times as long as the race is the river?

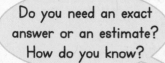

Do you need an exact answer or an estimate? How do you know?

The Annual Mug Race is 42 miles long.

Jacksonville
Palatka
St. Johns River

Florida

N W E S

16. ⭐ Ms. Dell is using the recipe to make play dough for her art class. Which of the following equations gives the best estimate of how many more cups, c, of flour than salt is used in the recipe?

A $1 - \frac{1}{2} = c$ **C** $\frac{1}{2} + \frac{1}{2} = c$

B $\frac{1}{2} - \frac{1}{2} = c$ **D** $1 + \frac{1}{2} = c$

Play Dough Recipe

Ingredient	Amount
Flour	$\frac{3}{4}$ cup
Food Color	2–3 drops
Salt	$\frac{3}{8}$ cup
Vegetable Oil	$\frac{1}{16}$ cup
Water	$\frac{3}{4}$ cup

DATA

346

Another Look!

Estimate $\frac{10}{12} - \frac{4}{9}$.

For an odd denominator, split it evenly to get the halfway number. If you split 9 between 2 people, each person gets 4 and a half.

Step 1

You can use halfway numbers to help decide if a fraction is closest to 0, to $\frac{1}{2}$, or to 1.

Is $\frac{10}{12}$ closest to 0, $\frac{1}{2}$, or 1?

Find the halfway number between 0 and the denominator:

0 1 2 3 4 5 **6** 7 8 9 10 11 **12**

6 is halfway between 0 and 12.

Step 2

Decide if the numerator is about the same as the halfway number, closer to 0, or to 12.

$\frac{10}{12}$

0 1 2 3 4 5 6 7 8 9 **10** 11 12

0      $\frac{1}{2}$ 1

10 is closest to 12.

So, $\frac{10}{12}$ is closest to 1.

Step 3

If the numerator is close to the halfway number, it is closest to $\frac{1}{2}$.

$\frac{4}{9}$

0 1 2 3 4 $4\frac{1}{2}$ 5 6 7 8 9

0      $\frac{1}{2}$ 1

4 is closest to $4\frac{1}{2}$.

So, $\frac{4}{9}$ is closest to $\frac{1}{2}$.

$\frac{10}{12} - \frac{4}{9}$ is about $\frac{1}{2}$.

In **1** through **7**, estimate each sum or difference by replacing each fraction with 0, $\frac{1}{2}$, or 1.

1.

0      $\frac{1}{2}$ 1

$\frac{4}{18} + \frac{3}{7}$

$\frac{4}{18}$ **Closest to:** _____

$\frac{3}{7}$ **Closest to:** _____

Estimate:

_____ + _____ = _____

2. $\frac{8}{15} + \frac{2}{5}$

3. $\frac{17}{21} - \frac{2}{10}$

4. $\frac{8}{10} + \frac{4}{9}$

5. $\frac{12}{15} - \frac{3}{7}$

6. $\frac{15}{20} + \frac{7}{8}$

7. $\frac{8}{14} - \frac{4}{10}$

8. **Communicate** Sam and Lou need a total of 1 foot of wire for a science project. Sam's wire measured $\frac{8}{12}$-foot long. Lou's wire measured $\frac{7}{8}$-foot long. Do they have enough wire for the science project? Explain.

9. **Explain** Katya measured the growth of a plant seedling. The seedling grew $\frac{1}{3}$ inch by the end of the first week. The seedling grew another $\frac{5}{6}$ inch by the end of the second week. About how much did the seedling grow in the first 2 weeks? Explain how you made your estimate.

10. **Analyze Information** A scientist measured the amount of rain that fell in a town during one month. How much more rainfall was there in Week 4 than in Week 1?

March Rainfall	
Week	Millimeters
1	2.6
2	3.329
3	4.06
4	4.075

DATA

11. **Extend Your Thinking** Jack is growing Red Wiggler worms to help make compost. He measured the lengths of two young worms. The 10-day old worm is $\frac{10}{12}$ inch long. The 20-day old worm is $1\frac{4}{6}$ inches long. About how much longer is the 20-day old worm than the 10-day old worm? Explain how you found your estimate.

You can use the number line.

0      $\frac{1}{2}$ 1 $1\frac{1}{2}$ 2

12. Elena is using the recipe to make two batches of granola. Which of the following is **NOT** a reasonable estimate of the total number of cups of seeds and nuts she will need?

  A 1 cup

  B 2 cups

  C 3 cups

  D $3\frac{1}{2}$ cups

13. About how many cups of pumpkin seeds, rolled oats, and walnuts does Elena's recipe use? Explain how you decided.

Granola Recipe	
Ingredient	Amount
Honey	$\frac{1}{4}$ cup
Peanuts	$\frac{3}{4}$ cup
Pumpkin Seeds	$\frac{1}{8}$ cup
Rolled Oats	4 cups
Sunflower Seeds	$\frac{1}{8}$ cup
Walnuts	$\frac{2}{3}$ cup

DATA

☆ Solve & Share ☆

Sue wants $\frac{1}{2}$ of a rectangular pan of cornbread. Dena wants $\frac{1}{3}$ of the same pan of cornbread. How should you cut the cornbread so that each of the girls gets the size portion she wants? **Solve this problem any way you choose.**

⭐ TEKS 5.3H Represent and solve addition and subtraction of fractions with unequal denominators referring to the same whole using objects and pictorial models and properties of operations. Mathematical Process Standards 5.1A, 5.1C, 5.1D, 5.1E, 5.1F, 5.1G

Create and Use Representations You can draw a picture to represent the pan as 1 whole. Then solve. **Show your work!**

Digital Resources at PearsonTexas.com

Solve   Learn   Glossary   Check   Tools   Games

Look Back!

Justify Is there more than one way to divide the pan of cornbread into equal-sized parts? Explain how you know.

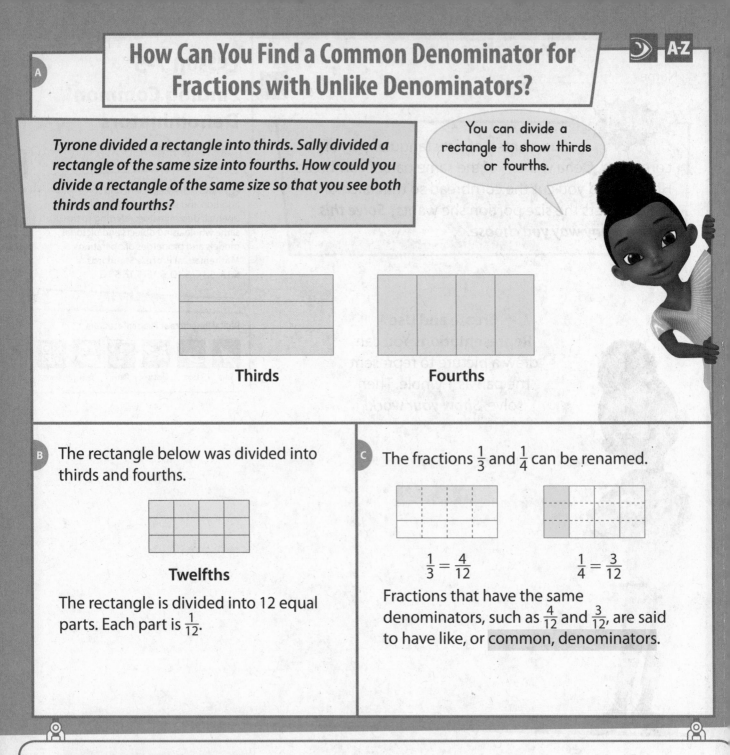

How Can You Find a Common Denominator for Fractions with Unlike Denominators?

A

Tyrone divided a rectangle into thirds. Sally divided a rectangle of the same size into fourths. How could you divide a rectangle of the same size so that you see both thirds and fourths?

You can divide a rectangle to show thirds or fourths.

Thirds

Fourths

B The rectangle below was divided into thirds and fourths.

Twelfths

The rectangle is divided into 12 equal parts. Each part is $\frac{1}{12}$.

C The fractions $\frac{1}{3}$ and $\frac{1}{4}$ can be renamed.

$$\frac{1}{3} = \frac{4}{12}$$

$$\frac{1}{4} = \frac{3}{12}$$

Fractions that have the same denominators, such as $\frac{4}{12}$ and $\frac{3}{12}$, are said to have like, or **common, denominators.**

Do You Understand?

Convince Me! Draw rectangles like the ones above to find fractions equivalent to $\frac{2}{5}$ and $\frac{1}{3}$ that have the same denominator.

350

© Pearson Education, Inc. 5

Another Example

How can you use multiples to find a common denominator?

Find a common denominator for $\frac{7}{12}$ and $\frac{5}{6}$. Then rename each fraction.

One Way

Multiply the denominators: $12 \times 6 = 72$.

Rename both fractions so they have a common denominator of 72.

$$\frac{7}{12} = \frac{7 \times 6}{12 \times 6} = \frac{42}{72} \qquad \frac{5}{6} = \frac{5 \times 12}{6 \times 12} = \frac{60}{72}$$

So, $\frac{42}{72}$ and $\frac{60}{72}$ is one way to name $\frac{7}{12}$ and $\frac{5}{6}$ with a common denominator.

Another Way

Check to see if one denominator is a multiple of the other.

You know that 12 is a multiple of 6.

$$\frac{5}{6} = \frac{5 \times 2}{6 \times 2} = \frac{10}{12}$$

So, $\frac{7}{12}$ and $\frac{10}{12}$ is another way to name $\frac{7}{12}$ and $\frac{5}{6}$ with a common denominator.

☆ Guided Practice *

In **1** and **2**, find a common denominator for each pair of fractions.

1. $\frac{3}{8}$ and $\frac{2}{3}$

2. $\frac{1}{6}$ and $\frac{1}{3}$

3. How many twelfths are in each $\frac{1}{3}$ section of Tyrone's rectangle, and how many twelfths are in each $\frac{1}{4}$ section of Sally's rectangle?

Independent Practice ☆

In **4** through **7**, find a common denominator for each pair of fractions. Then rename each fraction.

4. $\frac{2}{5}$ and $\frac{1}{6}$

5. $\frac{1}{3}$ and $\frac{4}{5}$

6. $\frac{5}{8}$ and $\frac{3}{4}$

7. $\frac{3}{10}$ and $\frac{3}{8}$

Problem Solving

8. Communicate Explain any mistakes in the renaming of the fractions below. Show the correct renaming.

$$\frac{3}{4} = \frac{9}{12} \qquad \frac{2}{3} = \frac{6}{12}$$

9. Extend Your Thinking For keeping business records, every three months of a year is called a quarter. How many months are equal to three-quarters of a year? Explain how you found your answer.

10. Represent Nelda baked two kinds of pasta in pans. Each pan was the same size. She sliced one pan of pasta into 6 equal pieces. She sliced the other pan into 8 equal pieces. How can the pans of pasta now be sliced so that 24 people can have an equal share of each kind of pasta? Draw on the pictures to show your work. If Nelda has served $\frac{1}{8}$ of a pan of 24 pieces so far, how many pieces has she served?

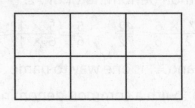

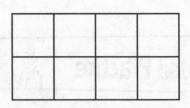

11. Number Sense What is the price of premium gasoline rounded to the nearest dollar? rounded to the nearest dime? rounded to the nearest penny?

Gasoline Prices	
Grade	**Price (per gallon)**
Regular	$4.199
Premium	$4.409
Diesel	$5.019

12. ⭐ Pam will walk the Lily Pond Trail and the Windy Lake Trail. Which of the following fraction pairs names the lengths of each trail she will walk using a common denominator?

A $\frac{3}{8}$ and $\frac{7}{8}$ **C** $\frac{18}{24}$ and $\frac{42}{24}$

B $\frac{12}{16}$ and $\frac{14}{16}$ **D** $\frac{24}{32}$ and $\frac{21}{32}$

Pine Park Trails	
Trail Name	**Length**
Frog Path	$\frac{2}{3}$ mile
Lily Pond	$\frac{3}{4}$ mile
Pinecone Way	$\frac{8}{10}$ mile
Windy Lake	$\frac{7}{8}$ mile

Another Look!

Rename $\frac{4}{10}$ and $\frac{3}{8}$ using a common denominator.

> **Remember:** A multiple is a product of the number and any other nonzero whole number.

Step 1

Find a common denominator for $\frac{4}{10}$ and $\frac{3}{8}$.

List multiples of the denominators 10 and 8. Then look for a common multiple.

10: 10, 20, 30, 40

8: 8, 16, 24, 32, 40

The number 40 can be used as the common denominator.

Step 2

Rename $\frac{4}{10}$ and $\frac{3}{8}$ using 40 as the common denominator.

Multiply the numerator and denominator by the same nonzero numbers.

$\frac{4}{10}$ $\frac{4 \times 4}{10 \times 4} = \frac{16}{40}$ $\frac{3}{8}$ $\frac{3 \times 5}{8 \times 5} = \frac{15}{40}$

So, $\frac{16}{40}$ and $\frac{15}{40}$ are another way to name $\frac{4}{10}$ and $\frac{3}{8}$ using a common denominator.

In **1** through **9**, find a common denominator for each pair of fractions. Then rename each fraction.

1. $\frac{1}{3}$ and $\frac{4}{9}$

$\frac{1}{3}$ **Rename:** _____

$\frac{4}{9}$ **Rename:** _____

$\frac{1}{3}$ **Multiples of the denominator:** _____

$\frac{4}{9}$ **Multiples of the denominator:** _____

Common Denominator: _____

Multiply. $\frac{1 \times \square}{3 \times \square} = \frac{\square}{\square}$ $\frac{4 \times \square}{9 \times \square} = \frac{\square}{\square}$

---

2. $\frac{3}{4}$ and $\frac{2}{5}$

3. $\frac{4}{7}$ and $\frac{2}{3}$

4. $\frac{1}{2}$ and $\frac{7}{11}$

5. $\frac{5}{12}$ and $\frac{3}{5}$

6. $\frac{3}{4}$ and $\frac{11}{16}$

7. $\frac{6}{7}$ and $\frac{1}{5}$

8. $\frac{9}{15}$ and $\frac{4}{9}$

9. $\frac{5}{6}$ and $\frac{8}{21}$

10. **Explain** On the Dell River, a boat will pass the Colby drawbridge and then the Wave drawbridge. Rename each of the two drawbridge opening times. Use the number of minutes in an hour as a common denominator. Then rename each opening time using another common denominator. Explain how you found your answers.

   HINT: 60 minutes = 1 hour

Dell River Drawbridge Openings	
Bridge Name	**Time of Opening**
Asher Cross	On the hour
Colby	On the $\frac{3}{4}$ hour
Rainbow	On the $\frac{2}{3}$ hour
Red Bank	On the $\frac{1}{4}$ hour
Wave	On the $\frac{1}{6}$ hour

11. **Extend Your Thinking** Phil baked two kinds of pies. Each pie pan was the same size. He served $\frac{1}{2}$ of the blueberry pie. He served $\frac{1}{4}$ of the apple pie. If each pie had 8 pieces to start, what fraction in eighths of the apple pie did he serve? How many more pieces of the blueberry pie than the apple pie did he serve?

12. **Connect** Shelly is trying to improve her running time for a track race. She ran the first race in 43.13 seconds. In the second race, she had a time of 43.1 seconds. She ran the third race in 43.07 seconds. If this pattern continues, how many seconds will Shelly run in the fourth race?

13. Jamal is studying plant growth in Juneau, Alaska, and Yuma, Arizona. Which of the following fraction pairs names the amounts of sunny days each year for the two cities using a common denominator?

   A $\frac{6}{48}$ and $\frac{24}{48}$ 　　 C $\frac{8}{24}$ and $\frac{6}{24}$

   B $\frac{6}{48}$ and $\frac{16}{48}$ 　　 D $\frac{3}{24}$ and $\frac{16}{24}$

City	Sunny Days Each Year
Del Rio, Texas	$\frac{1}{3}$ year
Juneau, Alaska	$\frac{1}{8}$ year
Lewiston, Idaho	$\frac{1}{4}$ year
Rochester, New York	$\frac{1}{6}$ year
Yuma, Arizona	$\frac{2}{3}$ year

14. **Connect** Alicia measured $\frac{1}{4}$ yard of the Blue Diamonds fabric and $\frac{5}{6}$ yard of the Yellow Bonnets fabric to make a quilt. Rename each length of fabric. Use the number of inches in a yard as a common denominator.

   HINT: 1 yard = 3 feet; 1 foot = 12 inches

   How many inches equal 1 yard?

© Pearson Education, Inc. 5

Name _____

Solve & Share

Over the weekend, Eleni ate $\frac{1}{4}$ box of cereal, and Freddie ate $\frac{3}{8}$ of the same box. What portion of the box of cereal did they eat in all? *Use or draw fraction strips to help solve the problem.*

TEKS 5.3H Represent and solve addition and subtraction of fractions with unequal denominators referring to the same whole using objects and pictorial models and properties of operations. Also 5.3K.
Mathematical Process Standards 5.1B, 5.1D, 5.1F, 5.1G

Digital Resources at PearsonTexas.com

Solve   Learn   Glossary   Check   Tools   Games

Formulate a Plan You can use fraction strips to represent adding fractions. *Show your work!*

Look Back!

Justify What steps did you take to solve this problem?

How Can You Add Fractions with Unlike Denominators?

Alex rode his scooter from his house to the park. Later, he rode from the park to baseball practice. How far did Alex ride?

You can add to find the total distance that Alex rode his scooter.

$\frac{1}{2}$ mile

$\frac{1}{3}$ mile

Step 1

Change the fractions to equivalent fractions with a common, or like, denominator.

1	
$\frac{1}{2}$	$\frac{1}{3}$

Multiples of 2: 2, 4, 6, 8, 10, 12, . . .

Multiples of 3: 3, 6, 9, 12, . . .

The number 6 is a common multiple of 2 and 3, so $\frac{1}{2}$ and $\frac{1}{3}$ can both be rewritten with a common denominator of 6.

Step 2

Write the equivalent fractions.

1				
$\frac{1}{2}$			$\frac{1}{3}$	
$\frac{1}{6}$	$\frac{1}{6}$	$\frac{1}{6}$	$\frac{1}{6}$	$\frac{1}{6}$

$$\frac{1}{2} \overset{\times 3}{\underset{\times 3}{=}} \frac{3}{6} \qquad \frac{1}{3} \overset{\times 2}{\underset{\times 2}{=}} \frac{2}{6}$$

Step 3

Add the numerators. Simplify if necessary.

$$\begin{array}{r} \frac{1}{2} = \frac{3}{6} \\ + \frac{1}{3} = \frac{2}{6} \\ \hline \frac{5}{6} \end{array}$$

Alex rode his scooter $\frac{5}{6}$ mile.

Do You Understand?

Convince Me! In the example above, would you get the same sum if you used 12 as the common denominator? Explain.

Another Example

You can use properties of operations to add fractions with different denominators.

Commutative Property of Addition	Associative Property of Addition	Identity Property of Addition

Example: $\frac{5}{8} + \frac{1}{4} = \frac{1}{4} + \frac{5}{8}$

$\frac{5}{8} + \frac{2}{8} = \frac{2}{8} + \frac{5}{8}$

Check: $\frac{7}{8} = \frac{7}{8}$ ✔

Example: $\frac{1}{8} + \left(\frac{1}{4} + \frac{1}{2}\right) = \left(\frac{1}{8} + \frac{1}{4}\right) + \frac{1}{2}$

Check: $\frac{1}{8} + \frac{3}{4} = \frac{3}{8} + \frac{1}{2}$,

$\frac{1}{8} + \frac{6}{8} = \frac{3}{8} + \frac{4}{8}$ and $\frac{7}{8} = \frac{7}{8}$ ✔

Example: $\frac{5}{6} + \frac{0}{3} = \frac{5}{6}$

Check: $\frac{5}{6} = \frac{5}{6}$ ✔

☆ Guided Practice *

In **1**, find the sum. Use properties of operations to help. Simplify, if necessary.

1. $\frac{1}{2} + \frac{1}{4} = \frac{\square}{\square} + \frac{\square}{\square} = \frac{\square}{\square}$

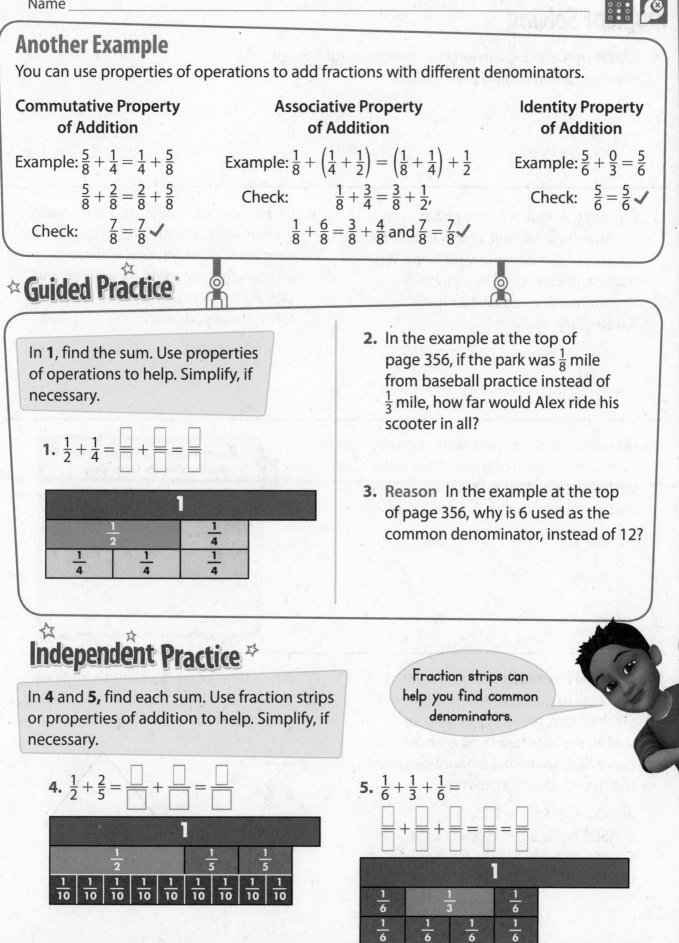

2. In the example at the top of page 356, if the park was $\frac{1}{8}$ mile from baseball practice instead of $\frac{1}{3}$ mile, how far would Alex ride his scooter in all?

3. **Reason** In the example at the top of page 356, why is 6 used as the common denominator, instead of 12?

☆ Independent Practice ☆

In **4** and **5**, find each sum. Use fraction strips or properties of addition to help. Simplify, if necessary.

4. $\frac{1}{2} + \frac{2}{5} = \frac{\square}{\square} + \frac{\square}{\square} = \frac{\square}{\square}$

5. $\frac{1}{6} + \frac{1}{3} + \frac{1}{6} =$

$\frac{\square}{\square} + \frac{\square}{\square} + \frac{\square}{\square} = \frac{\square}{\square} = \frac{\square}{\square}$

Fraction strips can help you find common denominators.

Problem Solving

6. Communicate Explain why the denominator 6 is not changed when adding the fractions.

$$\frac{3}{6} = \frac{3}{6}$$
$$+\frac{1}{3} = \frac{2}{6}$$
$$\overline{\frac{5}{6}}$$

7. Connect About $\frac{1}{10}$ of the bones in your body are in your skull. Your hands have about $\frac{1}{4}$ of the bones in your body. What fraction of the bones in your body are in your hands and skull? Simplify, if necessary.

8. Of 36 chemical elements, 2 are named for women scientists and 25 are named for places. What fraction of these 36 elements is named for women and places? Write your answer in simplest form. Show your work.

9. Connect Roger made a table showing how he spends his time in one day. What is the total part of the day that Roger spends sleeping and on the computer? Simplify, if necessary.

DATA

Amount of Time Spent on Activates in One Day	
Activity	**Part of Day**
Work	$\frac{1}{3}$ day
Sleep	$\frac{3}{8}$ day
Meals	$\frac{1}{8}$ day
Computer	$\frac{1}{6}$ day

10. Personal Financial Literacy A girls' club sold hats to raise money. They ordered 500 hats that cost $5.15 each. They sold all the hats for $18.50 each. Which expression shows the amount of money the club made after expenses?

A $500 \times (18.50 + 5.15)$
B $(500 \times 18.50) + (500 \times 5.15)$
C $(500 \times 5.15) - (500 \times 18.50)$
D $500 \times (18.50 - 5.15)$

11. If two sides of an isosceles triangle each measure $\frac{1}{4}$ ft, and the third side measures $\frac{3}{8}$ ft, what is the perimeter of the triangle?

A $\frac{5}{8}$ ft
B $\frac{7}{8}$ ft
C $\frac{7}{16}$ ft
D $\frac{7}{32}$ ft

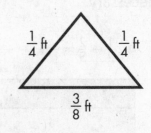

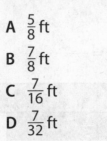

Another Look!

Find $\frac{1}{6} + \frac{5}{8}$ in simplest form.

Remember: A multiple is a product of the number and any other nonzero whole number.

Step 1

List multiples of the denominators.

Look for a multiple that is the same in both lists. Choose the least one.

6: 6, 12, 18, 24, 30, 36, 42, 48
8: 8, 16, 24, 32, 40, 48

24 and 48 are common multiples of 6 and 8. 24 is the lesser of the two.

Step 2

Rename each fraction using the common multiple as the denominator.

$\frac{1}{6}$ $\frac{1 \times 4}{6 \times 4} = \frac{4}{24}$

$\frac{5}{8}$ $\frac{5 \times 3}{8 \times 3} = \frac{15}{24}$

Step 3

Add with your renamed fractions.

$\frac{4}{24} + \frac{15}{24} = \frac{19}{24}$

Check that you cannot divide both the numerator and denominator any further, except by 1.

So, $\frac{1}{6} + \frac{5}{8} = \frac{19}{24}$ in simplest form.

In **1** through **4**, find each sum. Simplify, if necessary.

1. $\frac{1}{2} + \frac{1}{6}$

   Least multiple that is the same: _____

   Add using renamed fractions:

   ____ + ____ = ____

   Simplify.

   $\frac{\Box \div 2}{\Box \div 2} = \frac{\Box}{\Box}$

2. $\frac{1}{9} + \frac{5}{6}$

   Least multiple that is the same: _____

   Add using renamed fractions:

   ____ + ____ = ____

3. $\frac{4}{5} + \frac{1}{15}$

   Least multiple that is the same: _____

   Add using renamed fractions:

   ____ + ____ = ____

4. $\frac{2}{8} + \frac{1}{2}$

   Least multiple that is the same: _____

   Add using renamed fractions:

   ____ + ____ = ____

   Simplify

   $\frac{\Box \div 2}{\Box \div 2} = \frac{\Box}{\Box}$

5. **Draw a Picture** In the morning before school, Janine spends $\frac{1}{10}$ hour making the bed, $\frac{1}{5}$ hour getting dressed, $\frac{1}{2}$ hour eating breakfast. What is the total fraction of an hour, in simplest form, she spends doing the activities? Complete the drawing of fraction strips to show the solution.

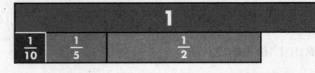

1		
$\frac{1}{10}$	$\frac{1}{5}$	$\frac{1}{2}$

6. **Math and Science** Hair color is an inherited trait. In Marci's family, her mother has brown hair. Her father has blond hair. The family has 6 children in all. Of the 6 children, $\frac{1}{3}$ of them have blond hair, $\frac{1}{6}$ of them have red hair, and $\frac{1}{2}$ of them have brown hair. In simplest form, what fraction of the children has red or brown hair?

7. Abdul bought a loaf of bread for $1.59 and a package of cheese for $2.69. How much did Abdul spend? Complete the diagram below.

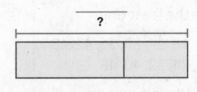

8. Marcus is making a picture frame. He buys two Type A wood pieces and two Type B wood pieces. Which of the following is the total length, in simplest form, of the wood pieces he bought?

A $\frac{2}{5}$ foot   C $\frac{1}{6}$ foot

B $\frac{5}{6}$ foot   D $\frac{5}{12}$ foot

Wood Frame Pieces	
Type	**Length**
A	$\frac{1}{6}$ foot
B	$\frac{1}{4}$ foot
C	$\frac{3}{4}$ foot

9. **Extend Your Thinking** Robert wants to walk one mile for his exercise each day. He made a table to show the distance from his home to each of four different places. What is the total distance, in simplest form, from home to the store and back home, and from home to the library and back home? If Robert walks this total distance, will he walk one mile? Explain how you found your answer.

Walking Distances from Home to Each Place	
Place	**Distance**
Bank	$\frac{1}{5}$ mile
Library	$\frac{1}{10}$ mile
Park	$\frac{1}{2}$ mile
Store	$\frac{1}{4}$ mile

Name _____

☆ ☆
Solve & Share

Rose bought a length of copper pipe. She used $\frac{1}{2}$ yard to repair the shower. How much pipe does she have left? *Solve this problem any way you choose.*

⭐ TEKS 5.3H Represent and solve addition and subtraction of fractions with unequal denominators referring to the same whole using objects and pictorial models and properties of operations. Also, 5.3K. Mathematical Process Standards 5.1A, 5.1C, 5.1D, 5.1G

$\frac{4}{6}$ yard

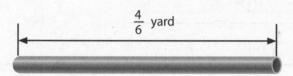

Digital Resources at PearsonTexas.com

Solve   Learn   Glossary   Check   Tools   Games

You can use **mental math** to rename $\frac{1}{2}$ and $\frac{4}{6}$ as fractions with like denominators. *Show your work!*

Look Back!

Connect How is adding fractions with unlike denominators similar to subtracting fractions with unlike denominators?

How Can You Subtract Fractions with Unlike Denominators?

Linda used $\frac{1}{4}$ yard of the fabric she bought for a sewing project. How much fabric did she have left?

You can use subtraction to find how much fabric was left.

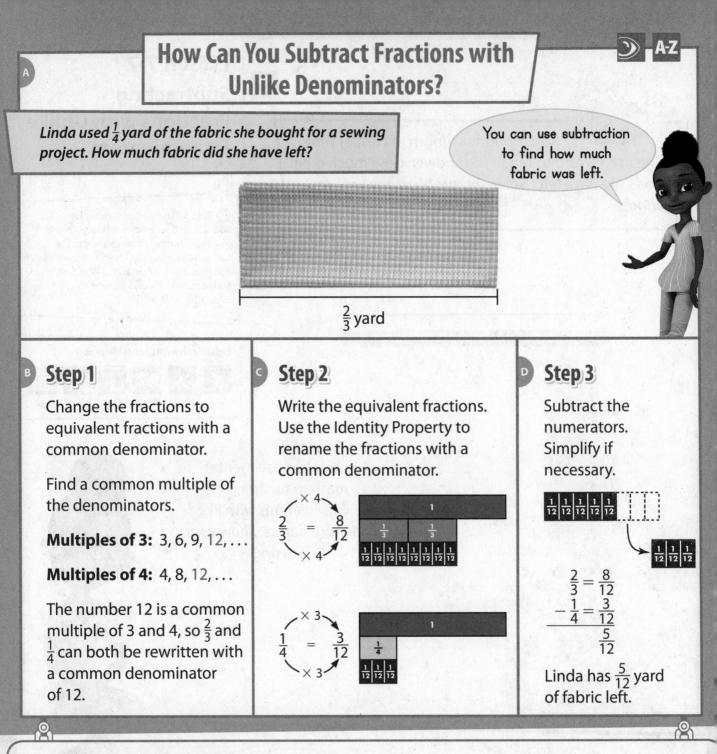

$\frac{2}{3}$ yard

B Step 1

Change the fractions to equivalent fractions with a common denominator.

Find a common multiple of the denominators.

Multiples of 3: 3, 6, 9, 12, ...

Multiples of 4: 4, 8, 12, ...

The number 12 is a common multiple of 3 and 4, so $\frac{2}{3}$ and $\frac{1}{4}$ can both be rewritten with a common denominator of 12.

C Step 2

Write the equivalent fractions. Use the Identity Property to rename the fractions with a common denominator.

$\frac{2}{3} \overset{\times 4}{\underset{\times 4}{=}} \frac{8}{12}$

$\frac{1}{4} \overset{\times 3}{\underset{\times 3}{=}} \frac{3}{12}$

D Step 3

Subtract the numerators. Simplify if necessary.

$$\begin{array}{r} \frac{2}{3} = \frac{8}{12} \\ - \frac{1}{4} = \frac{3}{12} \\ \hline \frac{5}{12} \end{array}$$

Linda has $\frac{5}{12}$ yard of fabric left.

Do You Understand?

Convince Me! Suppose Linda had $\frac{2}{3}$ of a yard of fabric and told Sandra that she used $\frac{3}{4}$ of a yard. Sandra says this is not possible. Do you agree? Explain your answer.

Another Example

On page 357 you used properties of operations to add fractions with unequal denominators. You can also use properties of operations to represent subtraction of fractions with unequal denominators.

Use properties of operations to solve $\frac{2}{3} - \frac{1}{6}$.

$$\frac{2}{3} - \frac{1}{6} = \frac{4}{6} - \frac{1}{6}$$

$$\frac{4}{6} - \frac{1}{6} = \left(\frac{1}{6} + \frac{1}{6} + \frac{1}{6} + \frac{1}{6}\right) - \frac{1}{6}$$

$$\frac{4}{6} - \frac{1}{6} = \left(\frac{1}{6} + \frac{1}{6} + \frac{1}{6}\right) + \left(\frac{1}{6} - \frac{1}{6}\right)$$

$$\frac{4}{6} - \frac{1}{6} = \frac{3}{6} + 0$$

$$\frac{3}{6} = \frac{3}{6} = \frac{1}{2}$$

☆ Guided Practice *

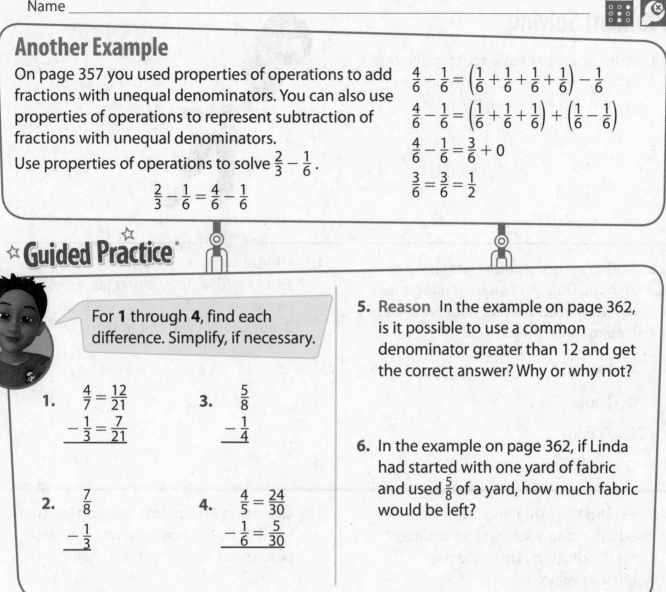

For **1** through **4**, find each difference. Simplify, if necessary.

1.
$$\frac{4}{7} = \frac{12}{21}$$
$$-\frac{1}{3} = \frac{7}{21}$$

3.
$$\frac{5}{8}$$
$$-\frac{1}{4}$$

2.
$$\frac{7}{8}$$
$$-\frac{1}{3}$$

4.
$$\frac{4}{5} = \frac{24}{30}$$
$$-\frac{1}{6} = \frac{5}{30}$$

5. **Reason** In the example on page 362, is it possible to use a common denominator greater than 12 and get the correct answer? Why or why not?

6. In the example on page 362, if Linda had started with one yard of fabric and used $\frac{5}{8}$ of a yard, how much fabric would be left?

☆ Independent Practice ☆

Leveled Practice In **7** through **12**, find each difference. Simplify, if necessary.

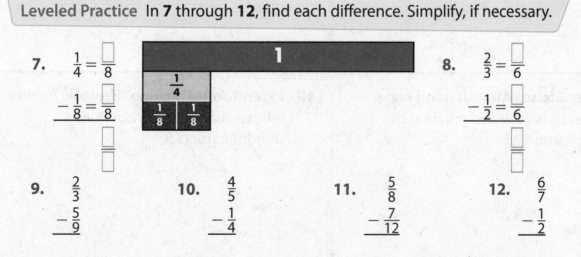

7.
$$\frac{1}{4} = \frac{\square}{8}$$
$$-\frac{1}{8} = \frac{\square}{8}$$
$$\frac{\square}{\square}$$

8.
$$\frac{2}{3} = \frac{\square}{6}$$
$$-\frac{1}{2} = \frac{\square}{6}$$
$$\frac{\square}{\square}$$

9.
$$\frac{2}{3}$$
$$-\frac{5}{9}$$

10.
$$\frac{4}{5}$$
$$-\frac{1}{4}$$

11.
$$\frac{5}{8}$$
$$-\frac{7}{12}$$

12.
$$\frac{6}{7}$$
$$-\frac{1}{2}$$

Problem Solving

13. Write a number sentence to name the difference between the location of Point *A* and Point *B* on the ruler.

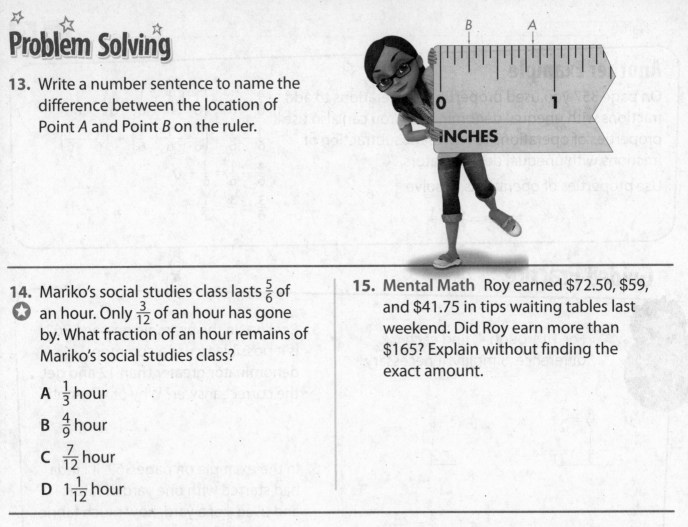

14. Mariko's social studies class lasts $\frac{5}{6}$ of an hour. Only $\frac{3}{12}$ of an hour has gone by. What fraction of an hour remains of Mariko's social studies class?

A $\frac{1}{3}$ hour

B $\frac{4}{9}$ hour

C $\frac{7}{12}$ hour

D $1\frac{1}{12}$ hour

15. Mental Math Roy earned $72.50, $59, and $41.75 in tips waiting tables last weekend. Did Roy earn more than $165? Explain without finding the exact amount.

16. Extend Your Thinking Write an addition and a subtraction equation for the diagram. Then find the missing value.

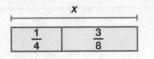

17. Construct Arguments Why do fractions need to have a common denominator before you add or subtract them?

18. Number Sense Without using paper and pencil, how would you find the sum of 9.8 and 2.6?

19. Extend Your Thinking Find two fractions whose difference is $\frac{1}{5}$ but neither denominator is 5.

Another Look!

Beth wants to exercise for $\frac{4}{5}$ hour. So far, she has exercised for $\frac{2}{3}$ hour. What fraction of an hour does she have left to exercise?

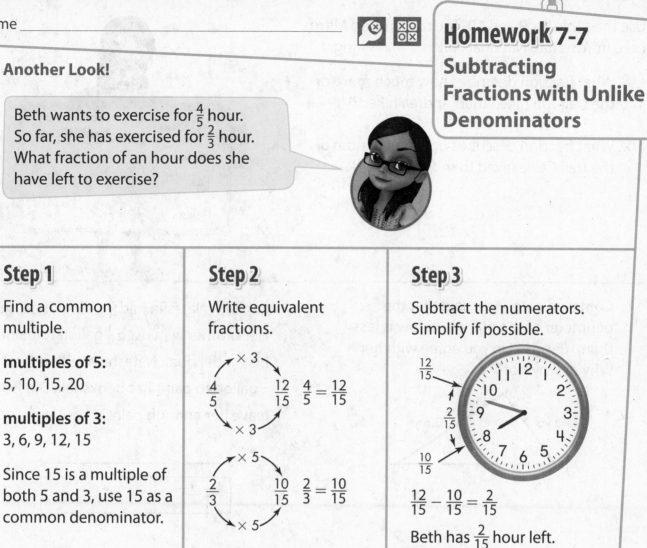

Step 1

Find a common multiple.

multiples of 5:
5, 10, 15, 20

multiples of 3:
3, 6, 9, 12, 15

Since 15 is a multiple of both 5 and 3, use 15 as a common denominator.

Step 2

Write equivalent fractions.

$\frac{4}{5}$ ×3 → $\frac{12}{15}$ $\frac{4}{5} = \frac{12}{15}$

$\frac{2}{3}$ ×5 → $\frac{10}{15}$ $\frac{2}{3} = \frac{10}{15}$

Step 3

Subtract the numerators. Simplify if possible.

$$\frac{12}{15} - \frac{10}{15} = \frac{2}{15}$$

Beth has $\frac{2}{15}$ hour left.

In **1** through **8**, find each difference. Simplify, if necessary.

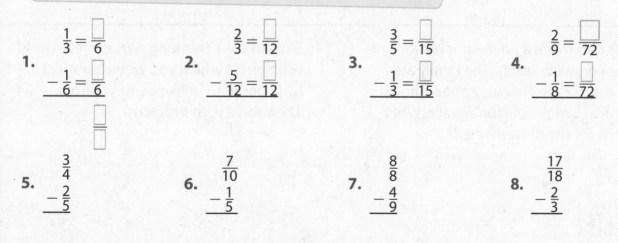

1. $\frac{1}{3} = \frac{\square}{6}$
   $-\frac{1}{6} = \frac{\square}{6}$
   $\frac{\square}{\square}$

2. $\frac{2}{3} = \frac{\square}{12}$
   $-\frac{5}{12} = \frac{\square}{12}$

3. $\frac{3}{5} = \frac{\square}{15}$
   $-\frac{1}{3} = \frac{\square}{15}$

4. $\frac{2}{9} = \frac{\square}{72}$
   $-\frac{1}{8} = \frac{\square}{72}$

5. $\frac{3}{4}$
   $-\frac{2}{5}$

6. $\frac{7}{10}$
   $-\frac{1}{5}$

7. $\frac{8}{8}$
   $-\frac{4}{9}$

8. $\frac{17}{18}$
   $-\frac{2}{3}$

Use the table for **9** and **10**. The trail around Mirror Lake in Yosemite National Park is 5 miles long.

9. What fraction describes how much more of the trail Jon hiked than Andrea hiked?

10. What fraction describes how much more of the trail Callie hiked than Jon hiked?

DATA	Hiker	Fraction of Trail Hiked
	Andrea	$\frac{2}{5}$
	Jon	$\frac{1}{2}$
	Callie	$\frac{4}{5}$

11. **Communicate** Amy said that the perimeter of the triangle below is less than 10 yards. Do you agree with her? Why or why not?

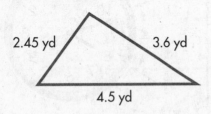

2.45 yd   3.6 yd
4.5 yd

12. **Explain** Natasha had $\frac{7}{8}$ gallon of paint. Her brother Ivan used $\frac{1}{4}$ gallon to paint his model boat. Natasha needs at least $\frac{1}{2}$ gallon to paint her bookshelf. Did Ivan leave her enough paint?

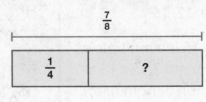

13. Paul's dad made a turkey pot pie for ⭐ dinner on Wednesday. The family ate $\frac{4}{8}$ of the pie. On Thursday after school, Paul ate $\frac{2}{16}$ of the pie for a snack. What fraction of the pie remained?

   A $\frac{1}{4}$ pie

   B $\frac{3}{8}$ pie

   C $\frac{5}{8}$ pie

   D $\frac{11}{16}$ pie

14. **Extend Your Thinking** Write a real-world problem in which you would subtract fractions with unlike denominators. Then solve your problem.

© Pearson Education, Inc. 5

Name _____

Solve & Share

Tyler and Dean ordered pizza. Tyler ate $\frac{1}{2}$ of the pizza and Dean ate $\frac{1}{3}$ of the pizza. How much of the pizza was eaten, and how much is left over? **Solve this problem any way you choose.**

🔷 **TEKS 5.3K** Add and subtract positive rational numbers fluently.
Mathematical Process Standards
5.1A, 5.1B, 5.1C, 5.1D, 5.1G

Digital Resources at PearsonTexas.com

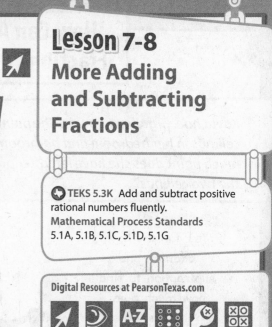

Solve	Learn	Glossary	Check	Tools	Games

You can use **number sense** to help you solve this problem. **Show your work!**

Look Back!

Check for Reasonableness How can you check that your answer is reasonable?

How Can Adding and Subtracting Fractions Help You Solve Problems?

Kayla had $\frac{9}{10}$ gallon of paint. She painted the ceilings in her bedroom and bathroom. How much paint does she have left after painting the two ceilings?

$\frac{2}{3}$ gallon

$\frac{1}{5}$ gallon

You can use both addition and subtraction to find how much paint she has left.

BEDROOM

BATHROOM

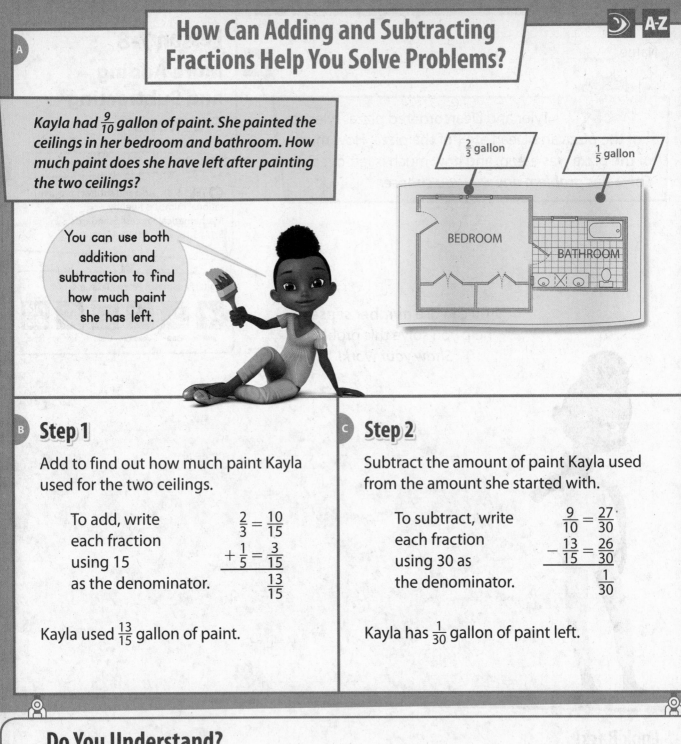

B Step 1

Add to find out how much paint Kayla used for the two ceilings.

To add, write each fraction using 15 as the denominator.

$$\frac{2}{3} = \frac{10}{15}$$
$$+\frac{1}{5} = \frac{3}{15}$$
$$\frac{13}{15}$$

Kayla used $\frac{13}{15}$ gallon of paint.

C Step 2

Subtract the amount of paint Kayla used from the amount she started with.

To subtract, write each fraction using 30 as the denominator.

$$\frac{9}{10} = \frac{27}{30}$$
$$-\frac{13}{15} = \frac{26}{30}$$
$$\frac{1}{30}$$

Kayla has $\frac{1}{30}$ gallon of paint left.

Do You Understand?

Convince Me! For the problem above, tell how you would use estimation to check the answer for reasonableness.

☆ Guided Practice ☆

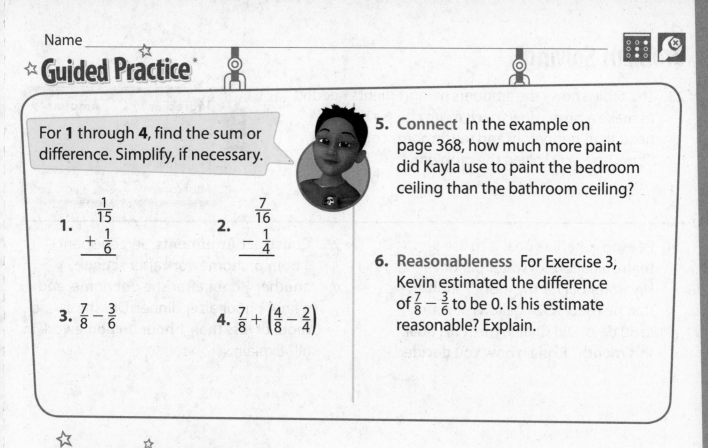

For **1** through **4**, find the sum or difference. Simplify, if necessary.

1.
$$\frac{1}{15}$$
$$+\ \frac{1}{6}$$

2.
$$\frac{7}{16}$$
$$-\ \frac{1}{4}$$

3. $\frac{7}{8} - \frac{3}{6}$

4. $\frac{7}{8} + \left(\frac{4}{8} - \frac{2}{4}\right)$

5. **Connect** In the example on page 368, how much more paint did Kayla use to paint the bedroom ceiling than the bathroom ceiling?

6. **Reasonableness** For Exercise 3, Kevin estimated the difference of $\frac{7}{8} - \frac{3}{6}$ to be 0. Is his estimate reasonable? Explain.

☆ Independent Practice ☆

For **7** through **22**, find the sum or difference. Simplify, if necessary.

7.
$$\frac{4}{50}$$
$$+\ \frac{3}{5}$$

8.
$$\frac{2}{3}$$
$$-\ \frac{7}{12}$$

9.
$$\frac{9}{10}$$
$$+\ \frac{2}{100}$$

10.
$$\frac{4}{9}$$
$$+\ \frac{1}{4}$$

11. $\frac{13}{15} - \frac{1}{3}$

12. $\frac{7}{16} + \frac{3}{8}$

13. $\frac{2}{5} + \frac{1}{4}$

14. $\frac{1}{7} + \frac{1}{2}$

15. $\frac{1}{2} - \frac{3}{16}$

16. $\frac{7}{8} - \frac{2}{3}$

17. $\frac{11}{12} - \frac{4}{6}$

18. $\frac{7}{18} + \frac{5}{9}$

19. $\left(\frac{7}{8} + \frac{1}{12}\right) - \frac{1}{2}$

20. $\left(\frac{11}{18} - \frac{4}{9}\right) + \frac{1}{6}$

21. $\frac{13}{14} - \left(\frac{1}{2} + \frac{2}{7}\right)$

22. $\frac{1}{6} + \left(\frac{11}{15} - \frac{7}{10}\right)$

Problem Solving

23. The table shows the amounts of ingredients needed to make a pizza. How much more cheese do you need than pepperoni and mushrooms combined? Show how you solved the problem.

Ingredient	Amount
Cheese	$\frac{3}{4}$ c
Pepperoni	$\frac{1}{3}$ c
Mushrooms	$\frac{1}{4}$ c

24. Reason Charlie's goal is to use less than 50 gallons of water per day. His water bill for the month showed that he used 1,524 gallons of water in 30 days. Did Charlie meet his goal this month? Explain how you decided.

25. Construct Arguments Jereen spent $\frac{1}{4}$ hour on homework after school, another $\frac{1}{2}$ hour after she got home, and a final $\frac{1}{3}$ hour after dinner. Did she spend more or less than 1 hour on homework in all? Explain.

26. Joel made some muffins. He gave $\frac{1}{4}$ of the muffins to a neighbor. He took $\frac{3}{8}$ of the muffins to school. What fraction of the muffins is left?

A $\frac{4}{12}$ **C** $\frac{5}{12}$

B $\frac{3}{8}$ **D** $\frac{8}{8}$

27. Extend Your Thinking Find two fractions whose sum is $\frac{2}{3}$ but neither denominator is 3.

28. Explain Carl has three lengths of cable, $\frac{5}{6}$ yard long, $\frac{1}{4}$ yard long, and $\frac{2}{3}$ yard long. If he uses 1 yard of cable, how much cable will he have left? Explain how you found your answer.

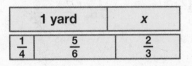

1 yard		x
$\frac{1}{4}$	$\frac{5}{6}$	$\frac{2}{3}$

29. Reason Anna writes the decimal 0.15. Bryan says he can write a decimal smaller than Anna's using the digits 1 and 5. Is he correct?

Another Look!

Carla wants to make a Veggie Toss using eggplant, green peppers, spring onions, and mushrooms. Besides the eggplant, how many pounds of the other ingredients does she need in all? Use data from the recipe.

Veggie Toss Recipe

Eggplant	$\frac{3}{4}$ pound (lb)
Green peppers	$\frac{1}{3}$ pound (lb)
Spring onions	$\frac{1}{4}$ pound (lb)
Mushrooms	$\frac{3}{8}$ pound (lb)

Use what you know about adding and subtracting fractions to solve problems.

Step 1

List the amounts of green peppers, spring onions, and mushrooms. Then, find a common denominator and rename each fraction.

$$\left(\frac{1}{3} + \frac{1}{4}\right) + \frac{3}{8} = \left(\frac{8}{24} + \frac{6}{24}\right) + \frac{9}{24}$$

Step 2

Add the renamed fraction amounts. Simplify, if necessary.

$$\frac{14}{24} + \frac{9}{24} = \frac{23}{24}$$

Carla needs $\frac{23}{24}$ pound of the other veggies in all.

For **1** through **12**, find the sum or difference. Simplify, if necessary.

1. $\frac{1}{12} + \frac{7}{9}$

2. $\frac{4}{18} + \frac{2}{9}$

3. $\frac{1}{3} + \frac{1}{5}$

4. $\frac{5}{15} + \frac{3}{5}$

5. $\frac{1}{2} - \left(\frac{1}{8} + \frac{1}{8}\right)$

6. $\frac{3}{4} + \left(\frac{1}{4} - \frac{1}{6}\right)$

7. $\left(\frac{1}{2} + \frac{3}{20}\right) - \frac{2}{20}$

8. $\left(\frac{2}{5} + \frac{1}{5}\right) - \frac{3}{10}$

9. $\frac{3}{4} - \frac{5}{8}$

10. $\frac{2}{3} - \frac{2}{7}$

11. $\frac{12}{15} - \frac{1}{6}$

12. $\frac{5}{9} - \frac{3}{8}$

13. The table shows the amounts of two ingredients Tara used to make a snack mix. She ate $\frac{5}{8}$ cup of the snack mix for lunch. How much of the mix is left? Show how you solved.

Ingredient	Amount
Rice Crackers	$\frac{3}{4}$ c
Pretzels	$\frac{2}{3}$ c

14. A plumber is fitting a water pipe that is $\frac{3}{4}$ foot long on to a water pipe that is $\frac{2}{12}$ foot long. How long will the finished pipe be?

A $\frac{11}{12}$ foot

B $\frac{8}{16}$ foot

C $\frac{2}{12}$ foot

D 1 foot

15. Carl has three lengths of cable, $\frac{3}{6}$ yard long, $\frac{1}{4}$ yard long, and $\frac{1}{3}$ yard long. Which two pieces together make a length of $\frac{20}{24}$ yard?

16. **Communicate** A kitten's heartbeat can be as fast as 240 beats per minute. To find the number of times a kitten's heart beats in 30 seconds, Aiden says divide 240 by 30. Do you agree with him? Why or why not?

17. **Number Sense** Explain how you know the quotients 540 ÷ 90 and 5,400 ÷ 900 are equal without doing any computation.

18. **Extend Your Thinking** Write an addition and subtraction equation for the diagram. Then find the missing value.

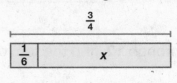

19. Jorge counted the number of spots of each color on his dog. Which fraction, in simplest form, shows the spots that are black compared to all the spots? Use the table.

Color	Number of Spots
Black	8
White	13
Gray	3

20. Samantha is making soup. To make the broth, she combines $\frac{2}{5}$ cup of vegetable stock and $\frac{2}{3}$ cup of chicken stock. Boiling the broth causes $\frac{1}{4}$ cup of the liquid to evaporate. How much broth is left after it is boiled? Show how you solved.

Name _____

Solve & Share

Michelle rode her bike $\frac{3}{4}$ mile on Thursday, $\frac{6}{8}$ mile on Friday, and $\frac{1}{2}$ mile on Saturday. How far did she ride her bike in all? *Solve this problem any way you choose.*

⭐ TEKS 5.1D Communicate mathematical ideas, reasoning, and their implications using multiple representations, including symbols, diagrams, graphs, and language as appropriate. Also, 5.3H. **Mathematical Process Standards** 5.1B, 5.1C, 5.1D, 5.1E, 5.1F, 5.1G

Digital Resources at PearsonTexas.com

Solve   Learn   Glossary   Check   Tools   Games

You can use a strip diagram to help you **communicate** a mathematical idea. *Show your work!*

Look Back!

Communicate How much farther did Michelle ride her bike on Thursday than on Friday?

How Can You Use a Strip Diagram to Solve a Problem?

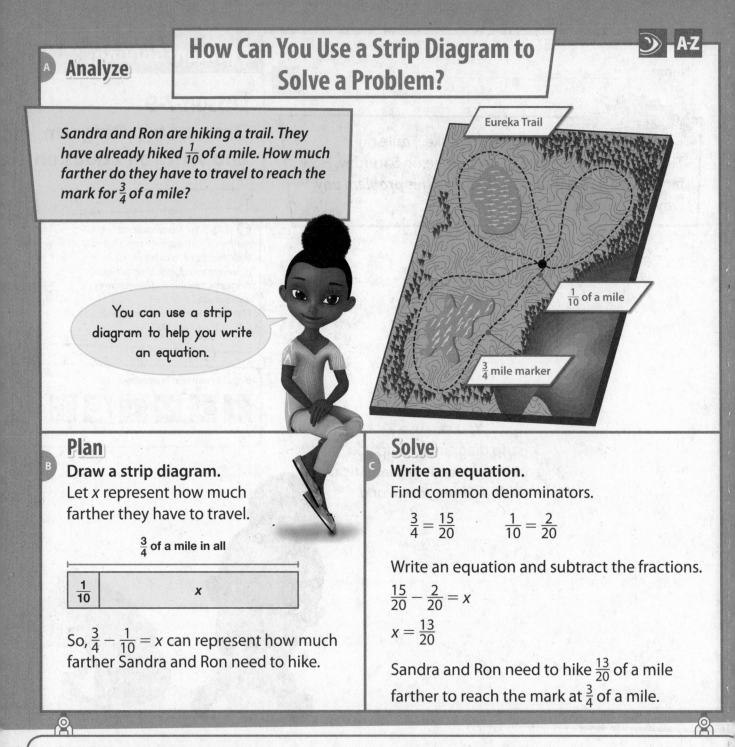

Sandra and Ron are hiking a trail. They have already hiked $\frac{1}{10}$ of a mile. How much farther do they have to travel to reach the mark for $\frac{3}{4}$ of a mile?

Eureka Trail

$\frac{1}{10}$ of a mile

$\frac{3}{4}$ mile marker

You can use a strip diagram to help you write an equation.

Plan

B

Draw a strip diagram.

Let x represent how much farther they have to travel.

$\frac{3}{4}$ of a mile in all

$\frac{1}{10}$	x

So, $\frac{3}{4} - \frac{1}{10} = x$ can represent how much farther Sandra and Ron need to hike.

Solve

C

Write an equation.

Find common denominators.

$$\frac{3}{4} = \frac{15}{20} \qquad \frac{1}{10} = \frac{2}{20}$$

Write an equation and subtract the fractions.

$$\frac{15}{20} - \frac{2}{20} = x$$

$$x = \frac{13}{20}$$

Sandra and Ron need to hike $\frac{13}{20}$ of a mile farther to reach the mark at $\frac{3}{4}$ of a mile.

Do You Understand?

Convince Me! The total length of a short hike is $\frac{4}{5}$ mile. How much of the hike remains after traveling $\frac{3}{10}$ mile? Show how you know. Use a strip diagram or write an equation.

✰ Guided Practice*

For **1**, complete the strip diagram and write an equation to solve.

1. Hannah ran $\frac{1}{3}$ of a mile. David ran $\frac{1}{6}$ of a mile. How much farther did Hannah run than David?

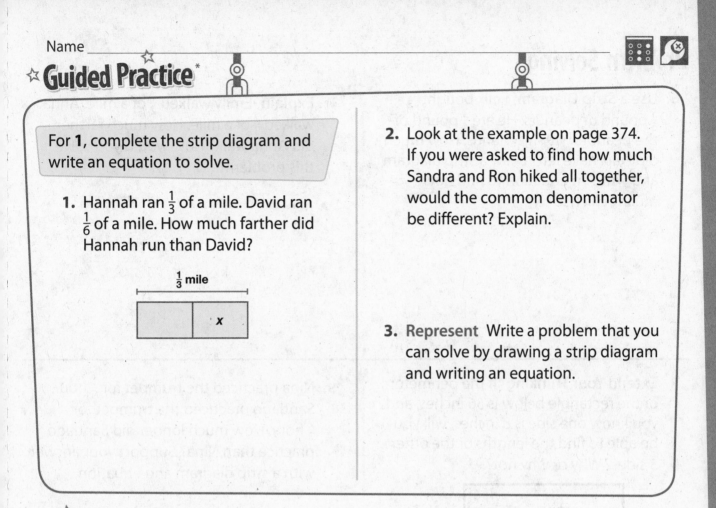

$\frac{1}{3}$ mile

2. Look at the example on page 374. If you were asked to find how much Sandra and Ron hiked all together, would the common denominator be different? Explain.

3. **Represent** Write a problem that you can solve by drawing a strip diagram and writing an equation.

Independent Practice ✰

For **4** and **5**, label the parts of a strip diagram and write an equation to solve.

4. Steve connected a wire extension that is $\frac{3}{8}$ foot long to another wire that is $\frac{1}{2}$ foot long. How long is the wire with the extension?

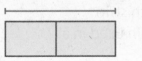

5. The smallest female spider measures about $\frac{1}{2}$ millimeter (mm) in length. The smallest male spider measures about $\frac{2}{5}$ mm in length. How much longer is the female spider than the male spider?

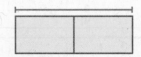

Problem Solving

6. Use a Strip Diagram Felix bought $\frac{5}{6}$ pound of peanuts. He ate $\frac{3}{4}$ pound of the peanuts with his friends. How much did Felix have left? Draw a strip diagram and write an equation to find how much Felix had left.

7. Explain Emily walked $\frac{1}{2}$ of a mile. Anna walked $\frac{2}{3}$ of a mile. How much farther did Anna walk? How would you solve this problem?

8. Extend Your Thinking If the perimeter of the rectangle below is 56 inches, and you know one side is 8 inches, will you be able to find the lengths of the other 3 sides? Why or why not?

8 inches

9. Nina practiced the trumpet for $\frac{1}{6}$ hour. Santiago practiced the trumpet for $\frac{2}{3}$ hour. How much longer did Santiago practice than Nina? Support your answer with a strip diagram and equation.

10. Justin used $\frac{3}{4}$ pound of broccoli to make a stir-fry and $\frac{9}{10}$ pound of broccoli to make cheddar and broccoli soup. Which strip diagram can be used to find how much broccoli Justin used in all?

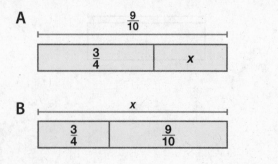

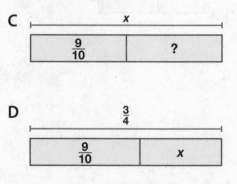

Name _____

Another Look!

You can draw a strip diagram and write an equation to help you solve real-world problems.

Read and Understand

Pippa filled $\frac{1}{8}$ of a jar with blue stones, $\frac{1}{4}$ of the jar with yellow stones, and $\frac{1}{2}$ of the jar with purple stones. How much of the jar is filled?

What do I know? Pippa filled $\frac{1}{8}$, $\frac{1}{4}$, and $\frac{1}{2}$ of a jar.

What am I asked to find?
How much of the jar is filled with stones?

Plan

Draw a strip diagram and write an equation.

	x	
$\frac{1}{8}$	$\frac{1}{4}$	$\frac{1}{2}$

$\frac{1}{8} + \frac{1}{4} + \frac{1}{2} = x$

Solve

Find equal fractions and add. Simplify if you need to.

$\frac{1}{8} + \frac{1}{4} + \frac{1}{2} = \frac{1}{8} + \frac{2}{8} + \frac{4}{8} = \frac{7}{8}$

$x = \frac{7}{8}$

Pippa filled the jar $\frac{7}{8}$ full of stones.

For **1** through **3**, draw a strip diagram and write an equation to solve.

1. Joel walked $\frac{2}{5}$ of a mile to the store, $\frac{3}{10}$ of a mile to the library, and $\frac{1}{20}$ of a mile to the post office. Let $x =$ the total distance Joel walked. How far did he walk?

2. Midge walked $\frac{7}{8}$ mile Monday and $\frac{4}{5}$ mile Tuesday. Let $x =$ how much farther she walked on Monday. How much farther did Midge walk on Monday?

3. Glenda wrote $\frac{1}{7}$ of her paper on Monday, $\frac{1}{14}$ of her paper on Tuesday, and $\frac{2}{28}$ of her paper on Wednesday. She said she wrote more than half of her paper. Is she correct? Why or why not?

4. Ned caught $\frac{1}{3}$ pound of fish. Sarah caught $\frac{5}{12}$ pound of fish.
⭐ Jessa caught $\frac{1}{6}$ pound of fish. Which strip diagram shows how to find how many pounds of fish they caught in all?

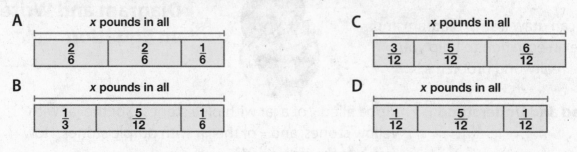

A x pounds in all
| $\frac{2}{6}$ | $\frac{2}{6}$ | $\frac{1}{6}$ |

B x pounds in all
| $\frac{1}{3}$ | $\frac{5}{12}$ | $\frac{1}{6}$ |

C x pounds in all
| $\frac{3}{12}$ | $\frac{5}{12}$ | $\frac{6}{12}$ |

D x pounds in all
| $\frac{1}{12}$ | $\frac{5}{12}$ | $\frac{1}{12}$ |

5. **Use a Strip Diagram** Jamie bought $\frac{5}{8}$ pound of wheat flour. He also bought $\frac{1}{4}$ pound of rice flour. How much flour did he buy? Draw a strip diagram and write an equation to solve.

6. **Use a Strip Diagram** Katie is $\frac{3}{5}$ of the way to Brianna's house. Larry is $\frac{7}{10}$ of the way to Brianna's house. How much closer to Brianna's house is Larry? Draw a strip diagram and write an equation to solve.

7. **Extend Your Thinking** Jack's dog has a rectangular pen. The length is two feet longer than the width. The width is 6 feet. What is the perimeter of the pen?

What do you need to know in order to find the perimeter?

8. **Construct Arguments** Sal has 8 comic books and 4 detective books. His sister says $\frac{2}{3}$ of his books are comic books. Sal says that $\frac{8}{12}$ of his books are comic books. Who is correct? Explain.

9. **Math and Science** Meteorologists use fractions to describe the amount of cloud cover. The table shows four types. How would you describe clouds covering $\frac{3}{7}$ of the sky? $\frac{7}{8}$ of the sky?

Cloud Cover	
Word	**Fraction**
clear	0 to $\frac{1}{10}$
scattered	$\frac{1}{10}$ to $\frac{5}{10}$
broken	$\frac{5}{10}$ to $\frac{9}{10}$
overcast	$\frac{9}{10}$ to $\frac{10}{10}$

Name _____

For **1** and **2**, use the data table.

1. Bruce feeds his horse 4 carrots, 4.9 kilograms of oats, and 5.8 kilograms of alfalfa hay each day. What is the total cost to feed his horse each day?

Horse Feed Costs	
Oats	$0.40/kg
Alfalfa Hay	$0.20/kg
Carrots	$0.17/carrot

DATA

2. **Number Sense** What is the cost of a carrot rounded to the nearest ten cents?

Applying Math Processes

- How does this problem connect to previous ones?
- What is my plan?
- How can I use tools?
- How can I use number sense?
- How can I communicate and represent my thinking?
- How can I organize and record information?
- How can I explain my work?
- How can I justify my answer?

3. **Explain** The distance of a bus trip from Columbus, Ohio, to Washington, D.C., is 418 miles. If a bus travels at 60 miles per hour, can the bus complete the trip in 7 hours? Explain.

4. **Construct Arguments** A season of gymnastics classes costs $617.49, including tax. Marsha estimates that saving about $50 each month for 1 year will give her enough money to pay for a season of classes. Will her estimate work? Explain.

5. Sofia hiked $2\frac{5}{8}$ miles on Saturday and $3\frac{3}{4}$ miles on Sunday. Use the Identity Property to rename the mixed numbers with a common denominator. Then find how many total miles she hiked.

6. **Analyze Information** How much more rain was there in August than in June?

Month	Rain (in Inches)
May	3.48
June	3.16
July	3.92
August	4.07

DATA

A 0.91 inch   **C** 4.07 inches

B 1.91 inches   **D** 7.23 inches

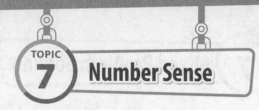

Error Search

Find each problem that is not correct. Explain what is wrong and rewrite the problem so it is correct.

1. 231 ÷ 6

```
      3.85
  6)231.0
  − 18
     51
   − 48
      30
    − 30
       0
```

2. 197.75 ÷ 7

```
       28.25
   7)197.75
   − 14
      57
    − 56
      17
    − 14
      35
    − 35
       0
```

3. 57.06 ÷ 18

```
       3.107
  18)57.06
   − 54
      30
    − 18
     126
   − 126
       0
```

4. 6.3 ÷ 35

```
       1.8
  35)6.30
   − 35
     280
   − 280
       0
```

Compatible Numbers

Mental Math Draw loops around two or more numbers next to each other, across or down, with a product of 5 or 10. Look for compatible numbers (numbers that are easy to compute with mentally).

5. Find products of 5.

0.5	10	2	0.25	5
0.1	50	5	20	1
0.2	0.1	0.5	1.25	2.5
25	25	0.3	4	2
0.4	2	5	4	0.25

6. Find products of 10.

2	0.5	20	0.25	0.5
5	0.2	50	40	40
0.3	5	4	0.5	0.5
50	2	0.2	0.5	6
0.8	0.2	5	0.5	20

Set A pages 325–330

Is 6 a prime or composite number?

A prime number is a whole number with no other factors besides 1 and itself.

A composite number is a number that is not prime; it has factors other than 1 and itself.

Factors of 6: 1 and 6, and 2 and 3

The number 6 is composite.

Is 47 a prime or composite number?

Since the only factors of 47 are 1 and 47, it is a prime number.

Remember that a prime number is a whole number greater than 1, and has only two factors, 1 and itself.

Classify each as prime or composite.

1. 11
2. 15
3. 18
4. 19
5. 27
6. 33
7. 200
8. 555

Set B pages 331–336, 337–342

Write $\frac{21}{36}$ in simplest form.

To express a fraction in simplest form, find an equivalent fraction with the least numerator and denominator possible. Divide the numerator and denominator by common factors until the only common factor is 1.

$\frac{21 \div 3}{36 \div 3} = \frac{7}{12}$

Remember to make sure there is no number other than 1 that can divide the numerator and denominator evenly.

Write each fraction in simplest form.

1. $\frac{45}{60}$
2. $\frac{32}{96}$
3. $\frac{24}{30}$
4. $\frac{42}{49}$

Set C pages 343–348

Estimate $\frac{7}{12} - \frac{1}{8}$.

Estimate the difference by replacing each fraction with 0, $\frac{1}{2}$, or 1.

Step 1 $\frac{7}{12}$ is close to $\frac{6}{12}$. Round $\frac{7}{12}$ to $\frac{1}{2}$.

Step 2 $\frac{1}{8}$ is close to 0. Round $\frac{1}{8}$ to 0.

Step 3 $\frac{1}{2} - 0 = \frac{1}{2}$

$\frac{7}{12} - \frac{1}{8}$ is about $\frac{1}{2}$.

Remember that you can use a number line to find if a fraction is closest to 0, $\frac{1}{2}$, or 1.

Estimate each sum or difference.

0      $\frac{1}{2}$ 1

1. $\frac{2}{3} + \frac{5}{6}$
2. $\frac{7}{8} - \frac{5}{12}$
3. $\frac{1}{8} + \frac{1}{16}$
4. $\frac{5}{8} - \frac{1}{6}$

Find a common denominator for $\frac{4}{9}$ and $\frac{1}{3}$. Then rename each fraction.

Step 1 Multiply the denominators:

$9 \times 3 = 27$, so 27 is a common denominator.

Step 2 Rename the fractions:

$$\frac{4}{9} \times \frac{3}{3} = \frac{12}{27} \qquad \frac{1}{3} \times \frac{9}{9} = \frac{9}{27}$$

So, $\frac{12}{27}$ and $\frac{9}{27}$.

Remember you can check to see if one denominator is a multiple of the other. Since 9 is a multiple of 3, another common denominator for the fractions $\frac{4}{9}$ and $\frac{1}{3}$ is 9.

1. $\frac{3}{5}$ and $\frac{7}{10}$

2. $\frac{5}{6}$ and $\frac{7}{18}$

3. $\frac{3}{7}$ and $\frac{1}{4}$

Find $\frac{5}{6} - \frac{3}{4}$.

Step 1 Find common multiples of 6 and 4.

The least common multiple is 12, so use 12 as the common denominator.

Step 2 Use the Identity Property to write equivalent fractions.

$$\frac{5}{6} = \frac{5 \times 2}{6 \times 2} = \frac{10}{12} \qquad \frac{3}{4} = \frac{3 \times 3}{4 \times 3} = \frac{9}{12}$$

Step 3 Subtract. Simplify, if necessary.

$$\frac{10}{12} - \frac{9}{12} = \frac{1}{12}$$

Remember to multiply the numerator and denominator by the same number when writing an equivalent fraction.

1. $\frac{2}{5} + \frac{3}{10}$　　2. $\frac{1}{9} + \frac{5}{6}$

3. $\frac{3}{4} - \frac{5}{12}$　　4. $\frac{7}{8} - \frac{2}{3}$

5. Teresa spends $\frac{1}{3}$ of her day at school. She spends $\frac{1}{12}$ of her day eating meals. What is the total part of the day that Teresa spends at school and eating meals? Simplify, if necessary.

Tina and Andy are building a model airplane. Tina built $\frac{1}{3}$ of the model, and Andy built $\frac{1}{5}$. How much more has Tina built than Andy?

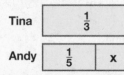

Tina	$\frac{1}{3}$	
Andy	$\frac{1}{5}$	x

Find a common denominator and subtract.

$$\frac{1}{3} = \frac{5}{15} \qquad \frac{1}{5} = \frac{3}{15} \qquad \text{So, } x = \frac{5}{15} - \frac{3}{15} = \frac{2}{15}$$

Tina built $\frac{2}{15}$ more of the model than Andy.

Remember to draw a strip diagram to help you write an equation.

1. Bonnie ran $\frac{1}{4}$ of a mile. Olga ran $\frac{1}{8}$ of a mile. How far did they run in all?

2. Use your strip diagram to write and solve an equation to find how much farther Bonnie ran.

© Pearson Education, Inc. 5

Name _____

1. The table shows water fowl that Henry counted at the lake. Which of the following fractions represents the fraction, in simplest form, of the water fowl that are Mallards?

Water Fowl Type	Number
Canadian geese	5
Cranes	3
Mallards	12

DATA

A $\frac{3}{5}$

B $\frac{8}{12}$

C $\frac{3}{2}$

D $\frac{5}{3}$

2. Pam is writing the prime numbers between 1 and 20. Which of the following is **NOT** one of Pam's numbers?

A 11

B 15

C 17

D 19

3. Sandra drove for $\frac{1}{3}$ hour to get to the store. Then she drove $\frac{1}{5}$ hour to get to the library. What fraction of an hour, in simplest form, did Sandra drive in all?

A $\frac{2}{3}$

B $\frac{8}{15}$

C $\frac{10}{15}$

D $\frac{16}{30}$

4. Cecil wrote the fraction $\frac{4}{6}$. Susie wants to write an equivalent fraction. Which of the following could be her fraction?

A $\frac{2}{3}$

B $\frac{6}{9}$

C $\frac{8}{12}$

D All of the above.

5. Benjamin and his sister shared a large sandwich. Benjamin ate $\frac{3}{5}$ of the sandwich and his sister ate $\frac{1}{10}$ of the sandwich. Which is the best way to estimate how much more Benjamin ate than his sister?

A $\frac{1}{2} - 0 = \frac{1}{2}$

B $\frac{1}{2} - \frac{1}{2} = 0$

C $1 - 0 = 1$

D All of the above

6. Roger has $\frac{5}{12}$ of a jar of blackberry jam and $\frac{3}{8}$ of a jar of strawberry jam. Which pair of fractions renames $\frac{5}{12}$ and $\frac{3}{8}$ using a common denominator?

A $\frac{5}{12}$ and $\frac{3}{12}$

B $\frac{10}{16}$ and $\frac{6}{16}$

C $\frac{10}{24}$ and $\frac{12}{24}$

D $\frac{10}{24}$ and $\frac{9}{24}$

7. Of the balls in Luke's garage, $\frac{1}{3}$ are basketballs and $\frac{1}{15}$ are soccer balls. What fraction of the balls, in simplest form, are either basketballs or soccer balls?

A $\frac{2}{5}$ C $\frac{6}{15}$

B $\frac{4}{15}$ D $\frac{12}{30}$

10. Mica read $\frac{1}{6}$ of a book on Monday and $\frac{3}{8}$ on Tuesday. Susan read $\frac{5}{6}$ of the same book. How much more of the book has Susan read than Mica?

A $\frac{14}{24}$ C $\frac{7}{12}$

B $\frac{8}{24}$ D $\frac{7}{24}$

8. The strip diagram below shows the fractional parts of a pizza eaten by Pablo and Jaime. Use the strip diagram to write an equation representing how you would find the total amount of pizza eaten.

? pizza eaten

$\frac{1}{3}$	$\frac{1}{4}$

11. Nikolai says that the fraction $\frac{16}{28}$ can be written in simplest form as $\frac{1}{2}$. Is he correct? If not, explain how you can write the fraction in simplest form.

9. Teri and her friends bought a party-size sandwich that was $\frac{7}{9}$ yard long. They ate $\frac{1}{3}$ of a yard of the sandwich. Teri wrote the part of the sandwich that was left as a fraction in simplest form. What is the numerator of this fraction?

12. Rhys is studying for a math test. A review problem lists the numbers 9, 16, 21, 47, and 52. Which of these numbers is a prime number?

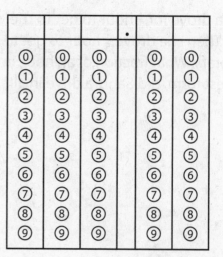

Adding and Subtracting Mixed Numbers

Essential Questions: How can sums and differences of mixed numbers be estimated? What is a standard procedure for adding and subtracting mixed numbers?

Did you know that the fossil of the oldest known flying mammal — a bat — was found in Wyoming?

Fossil evidence shows that around 50 million years ago, Earth's climate was warm and land and oceans were filled with life.

Make no bones about it! You can find fossils of ancient animals today! Here's a project about fossils!

Math and Science Project: Fossils Tell Story

Do Research Use the Internet or other sources to find out more about fossils. What are fossils? How and where do we find them? What do they tell us about the past? What can they tell us about the future? Pay particular attention to fossils from the Eocene epoch.

Journal: Write a Report Include what you found. Also in your report:

- Describe a fossil that you have seen or would like to find.

- Tell if there are any fossils where you live.

- Make up and solve addition and subtraction problems with mixed numbers about fossils.

Name _____

Review What You Know

Vocabulary

Choose the best term from the box. Write it on the blank.

- composite number
- common multiple
- common denominator
- prime number

1. A _____ is a whole number greater than 1 that has exactly two factors, itself and 1.

2. A _____ is a number that is a multiple of two or more numbers.

3. A _____ is a whole number greater than 1 with more than 2 factors.

Comparing Fractions

Compare. Write $>$, $<$, or $=$ for each $\bigcirc$.

4. $\frac{5}{25} \bigcirc \frac{2}{5}$ **5.** $\frac{12}{27} \bigcirc \frac{6}{9}$

6. $\frac{11}{16} \bigcirc \frac{2}{8}$ **7.** $\frac{2}{7} \bigcirc \frac{1}{5}$

8. Liam bought $\frac{5}{8}$ pound of cherries. Harrison bought more cherries than Liam. Which could be the amount of cherries that Harrison bought?

A $\frac{1}{2}$ pound   **C** $\frac{2}{3}$ pound

B $\frac{2}{5}$ pound   **D** $\frac{3}{5}$ pound

Properties of Operations

9. Use properties of operations to fill in the blanks.

a. $\frac{3}{8} + \frac{2}{3} = \underline{\quad} + \frac{3}{8}$

b. $\left(\frac{1}{2} + \frac{1}{6}\right) + \frac{3}{4} = \frac{1}{2} + \left(\underline{\quad} + \frac{3}{4}\right)$

c. $\frac{3}{4} + \underline{\quad} = \frac{3}{4}$

10. Use properties of operations to explain how you know $\frac{1}{2} + \frac{1}{3}$ is the same as $\frac{1}{3} + \frac{1}{2}$.

11. Use properties of operations to find $\frac{1}{2} - \frac{1}{8}$. Fill in the blanks.

$\frac{1}{2} - \frac{1}{8}$

$\frac{4}{8} - \frac{1}{8} = \left(\frac{1}{8} + \frac{1}{8} + \frac{1}{8} + \underline{\quad}\right) - \frac{1}{8}$

$\frac{4}{8} - \frac{1}{8} = \left(\frac{1}{8} + \frac{1}{8} + \underline{\quad}\right) + \left(\frac{1}{8} - \underline{\quad}\right)$

$\frac{4}{8} - \frac{1}{8} = \frac{3}{8} + \underline{\quad} = \underline{\quad}$

My Word Cards

Use the examples for each word on the front of the card to help complete the definitions on the back.

A-Z

proper fraction

$$\frac{2}{3}$$

improper fraction

$$\frac{5}{3}$$

mixed number

$$1\frac{2}{3}$$

benchmark fraction

$$\frac{1}{4}, \frac{1}{3}, \frac{1}{2}, \frac{2}{3}, \frac{3}{4}$$

My Word Cards

Complete the definition. Extend learning by writing your own definitions.

A(n) _____ is a fraction whose numerator is greater than or equal to its denominator.

A(n) _____ is a fraction less than 1; its numerator is less than its denominator.

Common fractions used for estimating, such as $\frac{1}{4}$, $\frac{1}{3}$, $\frac{1}{2}$, $\frac{2}{3}$, and $\frac{3}{4}$ are called

_____.

A number that has a whole-number part and a fractional part is called a

_____.

☆ ☆
Solve & Share

Use what you know about fractions between 0 and 1 to give the fraction for each of the points A, B, C, and D. *Tell how you decided.*

⬥ TEKS 5.3H Represent and solve addition and subtraction of fractions with unequal denominators referring to the same whole using objects and pictorial models and properties of operations. Mathematical Process Standards 5.1A, 5.1C

```
      A          B               C               D
  ←─┼──┴──┼──┼──┴──┼──┼──┼──┼──┼──┴──┼──┼──┼──┼──┴──┼──→
    0     1        2        3        4        5
```

Digital Resources at PearsonTexas.com

Solve   Learn   Glossary   Check   Tools   Games

How can you use **number sense** to name a point on a number line? *Show your work!*

Look Back!

Connect Can you give an example of when you would describe a quantity that is more than 1 but less than 2?

How Can You Represent Quantities That Are Greater Than or Equal to 1?

A-Z

Jenny and Tyler are baking bread. How do the measurements they use relate to fractions and mixed numbers?

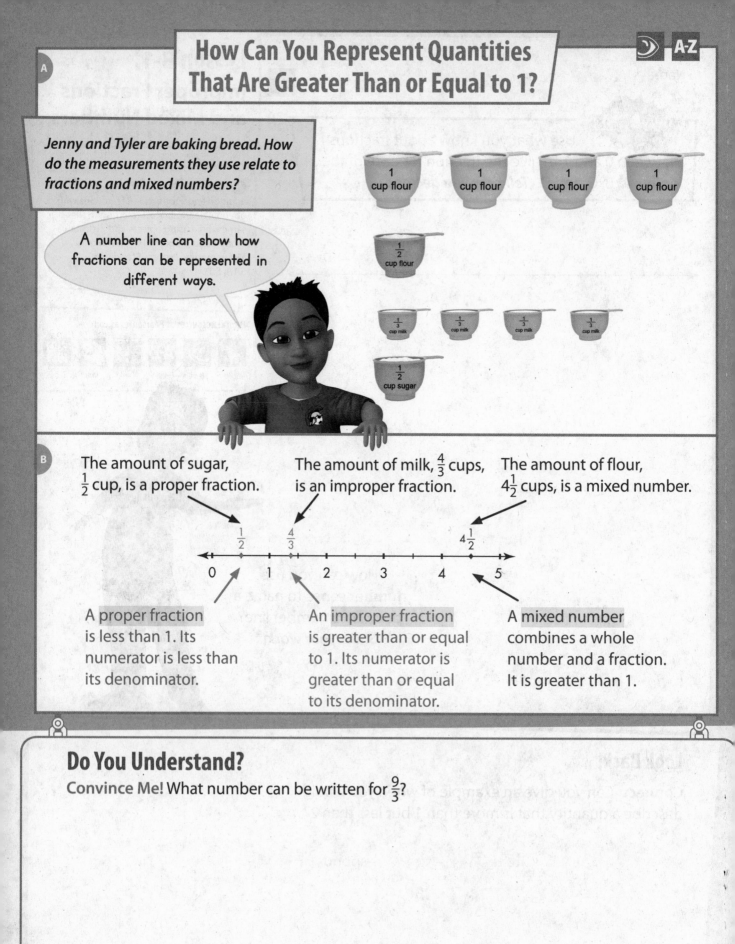

A number line can show how fractions can be represented in different ways.

1 cup flour 1 cup flour 1 cup flour 1 cup flour

$\frac{1}{2}$ cup flour

$\frac{1}{3}$ cup milk $\frac{1}{3}$ cup milk $\frac{1}{3}$ cup milk $\frac{1}{3}$ cup milk

$\frac{1}{2}$ cup sugar

B

The amount of sugar, $\frac{1}{2}$ cup, is a proper fraction.

The amount of milk, $\frac{4}{3}$ cups, is an improper fraction.

The amount of flour, $4\frac{1}{2}$ cups, is a mixed number.

A proper fraction is less than 1. Its numerator is less than its denominator.

An improper fraction is greater than or equal to 1. Its numerator is greater than or equal to its denominator.

A mixed number combines a whole number and a fraction. It is greater than 1.

Do You Understand?

Convince Me! What number can be written for $\frac{9}{3}$?

Another Example

How do you write an improper fraction as a mixed number?

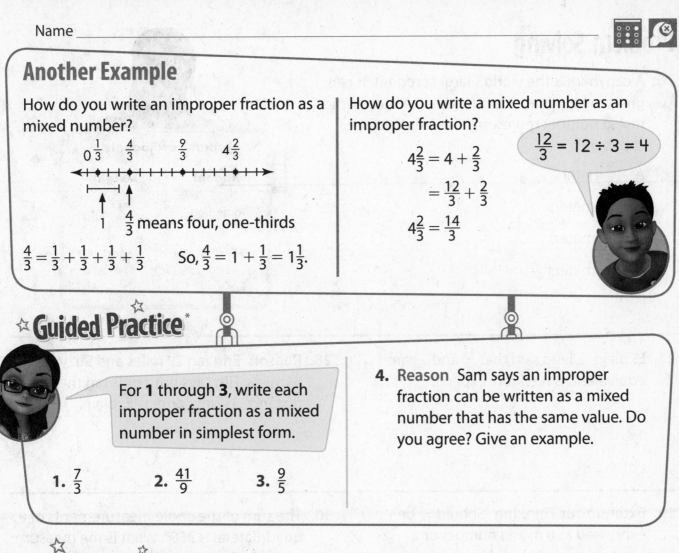

$\frac{4}{3}$ means four, one-thirds

$\frac{4}{3} = \frac{1}{3} + \frac{1}{3} + \frac{1}{3} + \frac{1}{3}$ So, $\frac{4}{3} = 1 + \frac{1}{3} = 1\frac{1}{3}$.

How do you write a mixed number as an improper fraction?

$4\frac{2}{3} = 4 + \frac{2}{3}$

$= \frac{12}{3} + \frac{2}{3}$

$4\frac{2}{3} = \frac{14}{3}$

$\frac{12}{3} = 12 \div 3 = 4$

☆ Guided Practice *

For **1** through **3**, write each improper fraction as a mixed number in simplest form.

1. $\frac{7}{3}$ 2. $\frac{41}{9}$ 3. $\frac{9}{5}$

4. **Reason** Sam says an improper fraction can be written as a mixed number that has the same value. Do you agree? Give an example.

Independent Practice ☆

For **5** through **20**, write each fraction in simplest form.

5. $\frac{38}{7}$ 6. $\frac{14}{8}$ 7. $\frac{8}{3}$ 8. $\frac{42}{6}$

9. $\frac{17}{5}$ 10. $\frac{21}{9}$ 11. $\frac{31}{4}$ 12. $\frac{19}{2}$

13. $1\frac{1}{8}$ 14. $4\frac{2}{3}$ 15. $3\frac{1}{11}$ 16. $5\frac{3}{5}$

17. $2\frac{7}{12}$ 18. $8\frac{1}{4}$ 19. $6\frac{1}{7}$ 20. $3\frac{5}{9}$

For **21** through **25**, write the letter that corresponds to each number.

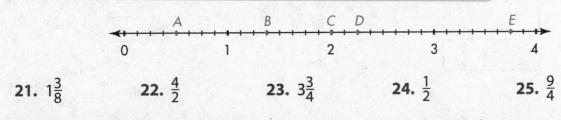

21. $1\frac{3}{8}$ 22. $\frac{4}{2}$ 23. $3\frac{3}{4}$ 24. $\frac{1}{2}$ 25. $\frac{9}{4}$

Problem Solving

26. A capybara is the world's largest rodent. It can grow to be $\frac{7}{10}$ meter longer than a nutria. Which mixed number represents the length of the capybara?

A $1\frac{3}{5}$ meters

B $1\frac{3}{10}$ meters

C $2\frac{9}{10}$ meters

D $1\frac{1}{10}$ meters

Lengths of Rodents	
Rodent	**Length**
Prairie Dog	$\frac{3}{10}$ m
Gopher	$\frac{1}{4}$ m
Nutria	$\frac{3}{5}$ m

27. Explain Diego said that $\frac{13}{4}$ and $2\frac{1}{4}$ are equivalent. Is he right? Explain.

28. Reason Erin ran $2\frac{3}{5}$ miles and Suzy ran $\frac{23}{5}$ miles. Tim says both girls ran the same distance. Is Tim correct? Explain.

29. Extend Your Thinking Should $\frac{15}{15}$ be expressed as a mixed number or a whole number? How do you know?

30. The sum of the angle measurements of a quadrilateral is 360°. What is the measure of the fourth angle in the quadrilateral shown below?

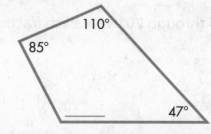

110°
85°
47°

31. Math and Science A paleontologist finds two fossil bones. Bone A is $\frac{1}{2}$ meter long. Bone B is $\frac{2}{5}$ meter longer than Bone A. How long is Bone B? Complete the strip diagram to solve.

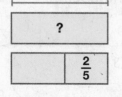

?

	$\frac{2}{5}$

32. Sarah and Jason both earn $9 for each hour they work. Last week, Sarah's pay was $85.50. Jason worked 3 times as many hours last week as Sarah. How much money did Jason make last week?

392

Name _____

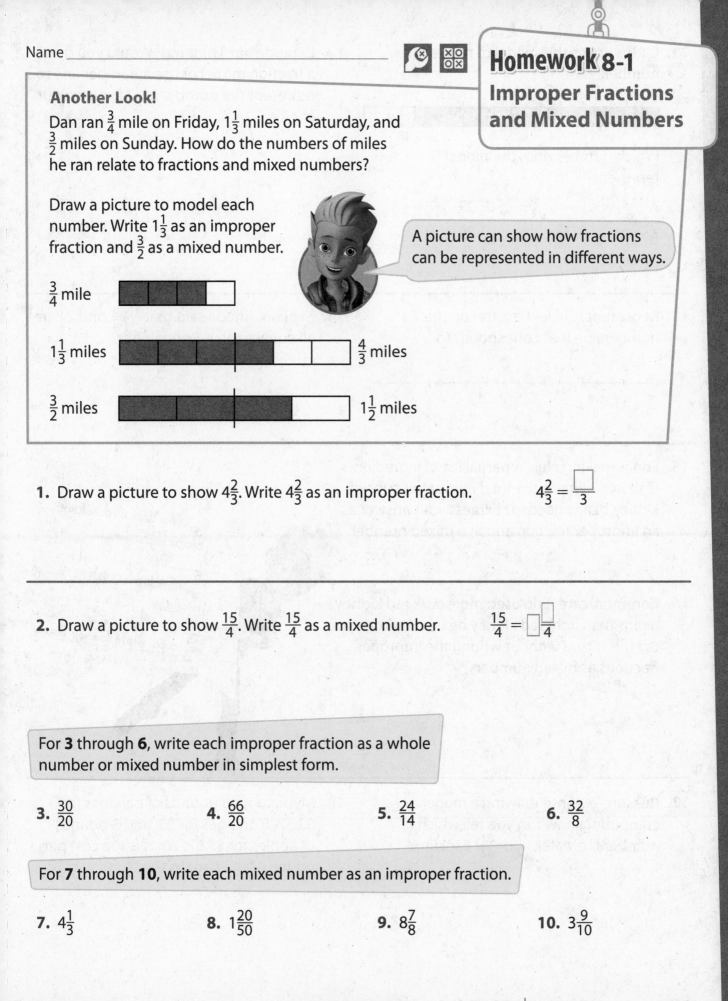

Homework 8-1
Improper Fractions and Mixed Numbers

Another Look!

Dan ran $\frac{3}{4}$ mile on Friday, $1\frac{1}{3}$ miles on Saturday, and $\frac{3}{2}$ miles on Sunday. How do the numbers of miles he ran relate to fractions and mixed numbers?

Draw a picture to model each number. Write $1\frac{1}{3}$ as an improper fraction and $\frac{3}{2}$ as a mixed number.

A picture can show how fractions can be represented in different ways.

$\frac{3}{4}$ mile

$1\frac{1}{3}$ miles $\frac{4}{3}$ miles

$\frac{3}{2}$ miles $1\frac{1}{2}$ miles

1. Draw a picture to show $4\frac{2}{3}$. Write $4\frac{2}{3}$ as an improper fraction. $4\frac{2}{3} = \frac{\square}{3}$

2. Draw a picture to show $\frac{15}{4}$. Write $\frac{15}{4}$ as a mixed number. $\frac{15}{4} = \square\frac{\square}{4}$

For **3** through **6**, write each improper fraction as a whole number or mixed number in simplest form.

3. $\frac{30}{20}$ 4. $\frac{66}{20}$ 5. $\frac{24}{14}$ 6. $\frac{32}{8}$

For **7** through **10**, write each mixed number as an improper fraction.

7. $4\frac{1}{3}$ 8. $1\frac{20}{50}$ 9. $8\frac{7}{8}$ 10. $3\frac{9}{10}$

11. Carlos draws this model to represent a number. ⭐

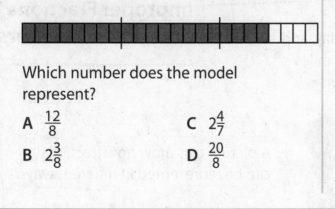

Which number does the model represent?

A $\frac{12}{8}$ C $2\frac{4}{7}$

B $2\frac{3}{8}$ D $\frac{20}{8}$

12. Extend Your Thinking Would you draw a fraction model or use a number line to represent the number $32\frac{5}{8}$? Explain your choice.

---

13. Represent Circle the letter on the number line that corresponds to $\frac{27}{5}$.

```
        F      A C        B     D  E
    <--+--+--+--+--+--+--+--+--+--+--+-->
       4           5           6
```

14. Explain Rhoda said that $\frac{10}{4}$, $\frac{5}{2}$, and $2\frac{1}{2}$ are all equivalent. Is Rhoda right?

---

15. Erin is making chili. A partial list of ingredients is shown. What is the total number of cups of kidney beans needed? Express your answer as an improper fraction and as a mixed number.

16. Communicate Erin used more dark red kidney beans than light red kidney beans. How can you tell this is true without writing the improper fractions as mixed numbers?

> **Chili**
>
> $\frac{7}{3}$ cups dark red kidney beans
>
> $\frac{5}{3}$ cups light red kidney beans
>
> $\frac{3}{2}$ cups white kidney beans

---

17. Reason Without drawing a model or computing, how can you tell which number is greater, $\frac{71}{72}$ or $\frac{63}{62}$? Explain.

18. Myrna buys 3 pounds of bananas for $2.37, 6 oranges for $3, and 3 pounds of apples for $5.67. What is the cost per pound of the bananas?

Name _____

Solve & Share

Alex has 5 cups of strawberries. He wants to use $1\frac{6}{8}$ cups of strawberries for a fruit salad and $3\frac{1}{2}$ cups for jam. Does Alex have enough strawberries to make both recipes? *Solve this problem any way you choose.*

TEKS 5.3A Estimate to determine solutions to mathematical and real-world problems involving addition, subtraction, multiplication, or division.
Mathematical Process Standards 5.1A, 5.1B, 5.1C, 5.1D

Digital Resources at PearsonTexas.com

Solve   Learn   Glossary   Check   Tools   Games

Estimation You can estimate because you just need to know if Alex has enough. *Show your work!*

Look Back!

Number Sense Does it make sense to use 1 and 3 to estimate if Alex has enough strawberries? Explain.

What Are Some Ways to Estimate?

Jamila's mom wants to make a size 10 dress and jacket. About how many yards of fabric does she need?

Estimate the sum $2\frac{1}{4} + 1\frac{5}{8}$ to find how many yards of fabric she needs.

DATA

Fabric Required (in yards)		
	Size 10	Size 14
Dress	$2\frac{1}{4}$	$2\frac{7}{8}$
Jacket	$1\frac{5}{8}$	$2\frac{1}{4}$

B One Way

Use a number line to round fractions and mixed numbers to the nearest whole number.

$1\frac{5}{8}$ rounds to 2 $2\frac{1}{4}$ rounds to 2

$$\begin{array}{ccccccc} 1 & \frac{1}{2} & \frac{5}{8} & 2 & \frac{1}{4} & \frac{1}{2} & 3 \end{array}$$

So, $2\frac{1}{4} + 1\frac{5}{8} \approx 2 + 2$, or 4.

Jamila's mom needs about 4 yards of fabric.

C Another Way

Use $\frac{1}{2}$ as a benchmark fraction.

Replace each fraction with the nearest $\frac{1}{2}$ unit.

$1\frac{5}{8}$ is close to $1\frac{1}{2}$.

$2\frac{1}{4}$ is halfway between 2 and $2\frac{1}{2}$.

You can replace $2\frac{1}{4}$ with $2\frac{1}{2}$.

So, $2\frac{1}{4} + 1\frac{5}{8}$ is about $2\frac{1}{2} + 1\frac{1}{2} = 4$.

Do You Understand?

Convince Me! In Part C above, why does it make sense to replace $2\frac{1}{4}$ with $2\frac{1}{2}$ rather than 2?

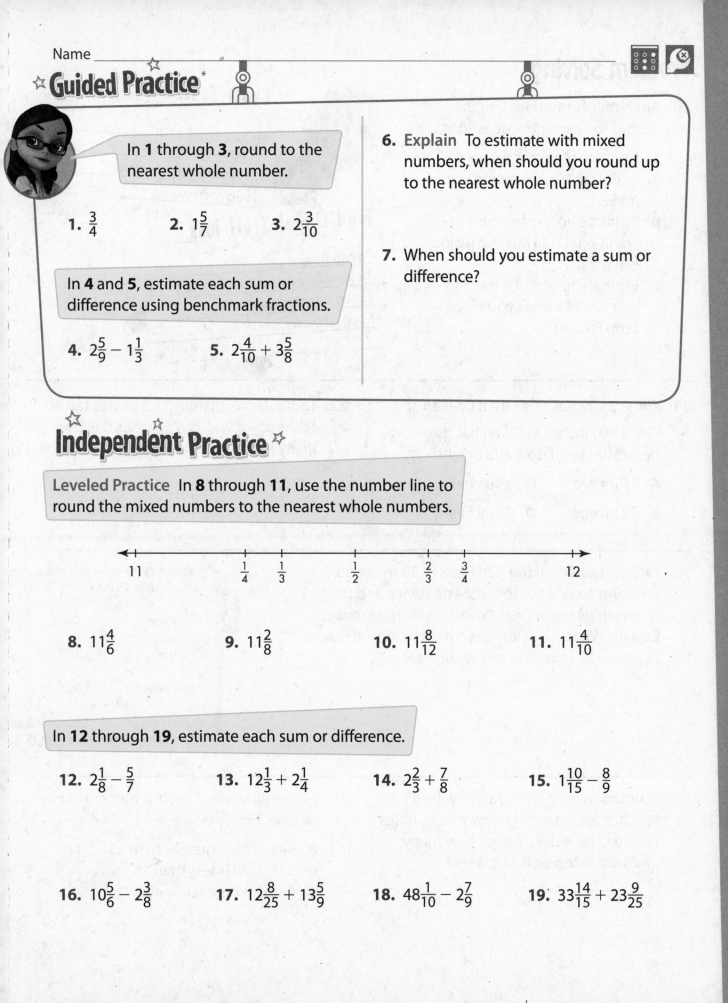

☆ Guided Practice *

In **1** through **3**, round to the nearest whole number.

1. $\frac{3}{4}$

2. $1\frac{5}{7}$

3. $2\frac{3}{10}$

In **4** and **5**, estimate each sum or difference using benchmark fractions.

4. $2\frac{5}{9} - 1\frac{1}{3}$

5. $2\frac{4}{10} + 3\frac{5}{8}$

6. **Explain** To estimate with mixed numbers, when should you round up to the nearest whole number?

7. When should you estimate a sum or difference?

Independent Practice ☆

Leveled Practice In **8** through **11**, use the number line to round the mixed numbers to the nearest whole numbers.

8. $11\frac{4}{6}$

9. $11\frac{2}{8}$

10. $11\frac{8}{12}$

11. $11\frac{4}{10}$

In **12** through **19**, estimate each sum or difference.

12. $2\frac{1}{8} - \frac{5}{7}$

13. $12\frac{1}{3} + 2\frac{1}{4}$

14. $2\frac{2}{3} + \frac{7}{8}$

15. $1\frac{10}{15} - \frac{8}{9}$

16. $10\frac{5}{6} - 2\frac{3}{8}$

17. $12\frac{8}{25} + 13\frac{5}{9}$

18. $48\frac{1}{10} - 2\frac{7}{9}$

19. $33\frac{14}{15} + 23\frac{9}{25}$

Problem Solving

20. Analyze Information Use the recipes to answer the questions.

  a Estimate how many cups of Fruit Trail Mix the recipe can make.

  b Estimate how many cups of Traditional Trail Mix the recipe can make.

  c Estimate how much trail mix you would have if you made both recipes.

Fruit Trail Mix
- $\frac{1}{2}$ cup raisins
- $\frac{3}{8}$ cup sunflower seeds
- 1 cup unsalted peanuts
- $\frac{1}{4}$ cup coconut

Traditional Trail Mix
- $1\frac{1}{3}$ cup raisins
- 1 cup sunflower seeds
- $1\frac{3}{4}$ cup unsalted peanuts
- 1 cup cashews

---

21. Kim is $3\frac{5}{8}$ inches taller than Colleen. If Kim is $60\frac{3}{4}$ inches tall, which is the best estimate of Colleen's height?

  A 57 inches   **C** 63 inches

  B 59 inches   **D** 64 inches

22. Today, Dina's plant is 12.5 inches tall. Yesterday it was 11.75 inches tall. How many inches did the plant grow?

---

23. Extend Your Thinking Cal has $12.50 to spend. He wants to ride the roller coaster twice and the Ferris wheel once. Does Cal have enough money? Explain. What are 3 possible combinations of rides Cal can take using the money he has?

Ride Prices	
Ride	**Cost**
Carousel	$3.75
Ferris Wheel	$4.25
Roller Coaster	$5.50

DATA

---

24. Estimation Last week Jason walked $3\frac{1}{4}$ miles each day for 3 days and $4\frac{5}{8}$ miles each day for 4 days. About how many miles did Jason walk last week?

25. Reason Decide if each statement is *true* or *false*. Explain.

  a $945 \div 40$ is greater than 25.

  b $315 \div 20$ is less than 15.

  c $440 \div 11$ is exactly 40.

Name _____

Another Look!

Kyra has $4\frac{1}{8}$ yards of red ribbon and $7\frac{2}{3}$ yards of blue ribbon. About how many yards of ribbon does she have?

Round both numbers to the nearest whole number. Then add or subtract.

To round mixed numbers:
If the fractional part is greater than or equal to $\frac{1}{2}$, round up. If the fractional part is less than $\frac{1}{2}$, drop the fraction and use the whole number.

Estimate $4\frac{1}{8} + 7\frac{2}{3}$.

$4\frac{1}{8}$ rounds down to 4.

$7\frac{2}{3}$ rounds up to 8.

$4 + 8 = 12$

So, $4\frac{1}{8} + 7\frac{2}{3}$ is about 12.

Kyra has about 12 yards of ribbon.

In **1** through **8**, round to the nearest whole number.

1. $8\frac{5}{6}$ **2.** $13\frac{8}{9}$ **3.** $43\frac{1}{3}$ **4.** $6\frac{6}{7}$

5. $7\frac{40}{81}$ **6.** $29\frac{4}{5}$ **7.** $88\frac{2}{4}$ **8.** $20\frac{3}{10}$

In **9** through **17**, estimate each sum or difference.

9. $7\frac{1}{9} + 8\frac{2}{5}$ **10.** $14\frac{5}{8} - 3\frac{7}{10}$ **11.** $2\frac{1}{4} + 5\frac{1}{2} + 10\frac{3}{4}$

12. $11\frac{3}{5} - 4\frac{1}{12}$ **13.** $9 + 3\frac{11}{14} + 5\frac{1}{9}$ **14.** $15\frac{6}{7} - 12\frac{2}{10}$

15. $3\frac{2}{5} + 6\frac{5}{7}$ **16.** $20\frac{1}{3} - 9\frac{1}{2}$ **17.** $25\frac{7}{8} + 8\frac{7}{12}$

18. Robert says his better long jump was about 1 foot farther than May's better long jump. Is he correct? Explain.

Participant	Event	Distance
Robert	Long Jump	**1.** $6\frac{5}{12}$ ft **2.** $5\frac{2}{3}$ ft
	Softball Throw	$62\frac{1}{5}$ ft
May	Long Jump	**1.** $4\frac{2}{3}$ ft **2.** $4\frac{3}{4}$ ft
	Softball Throw	$71\frac{7}{8}$ ft

DATA

19. If the school record for the softball throw is 78 feet, about how much farther must Robert throw the ball to match the record?

A 15 feet **C** 18 feet

B 16 feet **D** 20 feet

20. About how much farther is May's softball throw than Robert's softball throw?

21. Daniel has 3 vegetable gardens. Each garden has room for 25 rows of plants with 18 plants in each row. What is the greatest number of plants that Daniel can grow in his garden?

22. Use a Strip Diagram Six people are sharing the rental cost for a cabin. If the cabin costs $525 to rent, how much does each person pay? Use the strip diagram to solve.

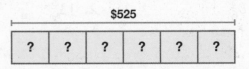
$525
| ? | ? | ? | ? | ? | ? |

23. Extend Your Thinking Consider the sum of $\frac{3}{5} + \frac{3}{4}$. First, round each fraction and estimate the sum. Then, add the two fractions using a common denominator and round the result. Which is closer to the actual sum?

24. Connect To make one batch of granola, Linda mixes 1 pound of oat flakes, 6 ounces of walnuts, 5 ounces of raisins, and 4 ounces of sunflower seeds. How many total pounds of granola does one batch make?

Remember:
1 pound = 16 ounces.

☆ ☆
Solve & Share

Tory is cutting bread loaves into fourths. She needs to wrap up $3\frac{3}{4}$ loaves to take to a luncheon and $1\frac{2}{4}$ loaves for a bake sale. How many loaves does Tory need to wrap in all for the luncheon and the bake sale? *Use a model to solve this problem.*

⬢ TEKS 5.3H Represent and solve addition and subtraction of fractions with unequal denominators referring to the same whole using objects and pictorial models and properties of operations. Also, 5.3K.
Mathematical Process Standards 5.1B, 5.1C, 5.1E, 5.1G

Digital Resources at PearsonTexas.com

Solve   Learn   Glossary   Check   Tools   Games

Create and Use Representations You can use fraction strips to model adding mixed numbers. *Show your work!*

Look Back!

Number Sense How can you estimate the sum above?

How Can You Model Addition of Mixed Numbers?

Bill has 2 boards he will use to make picture frames. What is the total length of the boards Bill has to make picture frames?

$2\frac{5}{12}$ feet

$1\frac{11}{12}$ feet

You can use addition to find the total length of the boards.

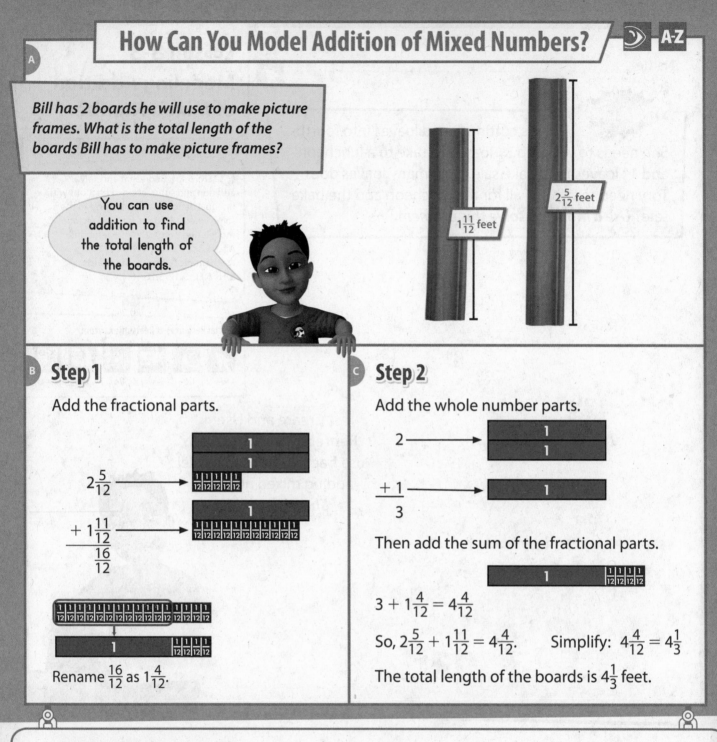

B **Step 1**

Add the fractional parts.

$2\frac{5}{12}$

1
1

$\frac{1}{12}\frac{1}{12}\frac{1}{12}\frac{1}{12}\frac{1}{12}$

$+ 1\frac{11}{12}$

1

$\frac{1}{12}\frac{1}{12}\frac{1}{12}\frac{1}{12}\frac{1}{12}\frac{1}{12}\frac{1}{12}\frac{1}{12}\frac{1}{12}\frac{1}{12}\frac{1}{12}$

$\frac{16}{12}$

$\frac{1}{12}\frac{1}{12}\frac{1}{12}\frac{1}{12}\frac{1}{12}\frac{1}{12}\frac{1}{12}\frac{1}{12}\frac{1}{12}\frac{1}{12}\frac{1}{12}\frac{1}{12}\frac{1}{12}\frac{1}{12}\frac{1}{12}\frac{1}{12}$

| 1 | $\frac{1}{12}\frac{1}{12}\frac{1}{12}\frac{1}{12}$ |

Rename $\frac{16}{12}$ as $1\frac{4}{12}$.

C **Step 2**

Add the whole number parts.

2

1
1

$+ 1$

1

3

Then add the sum of the fractional parts.

| 1 | $\frac{1}{12}\frac{1}{12}\frac{1}{12}\frac{1}{12}$ |

$3 + 1\frac{4}{12} = 4\frac{4}{12}$

So, $2\frac{5}{12} + 1\frac{11}{12} = 4\frac{4}{12}$.   Simplify: $4\frac{4}{12} = 4\frac{1}{3}$

The total length of the boards is $4\frac{1}{3}$ feet.

Do You Understand?

Convince Me! Suppose Bill's boards were $2\frac{11}{12}$ feet and $1\frac{5}{12}$ feet.
What would be the total length of these two boards? Show your work.

☆ Guided Practice*

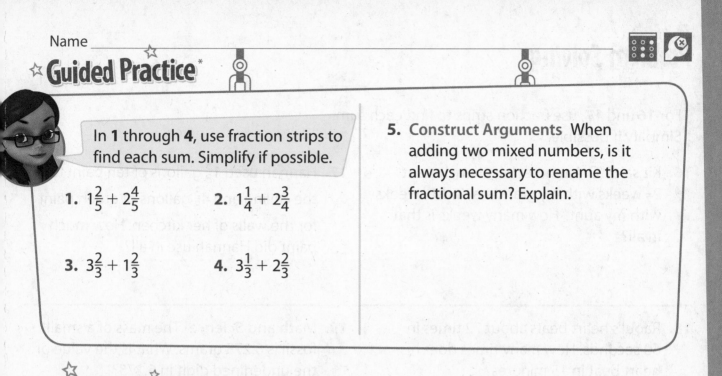

In **1** through **4**, use fraction strips to find each sum. Simplify if possible.

1. $1\frac{2}{5} + 2\frac{4}{5}$ **2.** $1\frac{1}{4} + 2\frac{3}{4}$

3. $3\frac{2}{3} + 1\frac{2}{3}$ **4.** $3\frac{1}{3} + 2\frac{2}{3}$

5. Construct Arguments When adding two mixed numbers, is it always necessary to rename the fractional sum? Explain.

Independent Practice ☆

Leveled Practice In **6** and **7**, use each model to find the sum. Simplify if possible.

6. Charles used $1\frac{2}{3}$ cups of walnuts and $2\frac{2}{3}$ cups of cranberries to make breakfast bread. How many cups of walnuts and cranberries did he use in all?

7. Mary worked $2\frac{3}{4}$ hours on Monday and $1\frac{3}{4}$ hours on Tuesday. How many hours did she work in all on Monday and Tuesday?

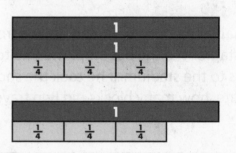

In **8** through **15**, use fraction strips to find each sum. Simplify if possible.

8. $2\frac{3}{5} + 1\frac{3}{5}$ **9.** $4\frac{5}{12} + 1\frac{7}{12}$ **10.** $4\frac{9}{10} + 3\frac{7}{10}$ **11.** $5\frac{3}{4} + 2\frac{3}{4}$

12. $1\frac{7}{8} + 3\frac{5}{8}$ **13.** $2\frac{1}{2} + 1\frac{1}{2}$ **14.** $3\frac{2}{5} + 3\frac{4}{5}$ **15.** $2\frac{7}{12} + 1\frac{7}{12}$

Problem Solving

For **16** and **17**, use fraction strips to find each sum. Simplify if possible.

16. Kit said, "On summer vacation, I spent $2\frac{4}{7}$ weeks with my grandma and $1\frac{6}{7}$ weeks with my aunt." How many weeks is that in all?

17. Hannah used $1\frac{5}{8}$ gallons of tan paint for the ceiling and $4\frac{3}{8}$ gallons of green paint for the walls of her kitchen. How much paint did Hannah use in all?

18. Raoul's heart beats about 72 times in 60 seconds. How many times does his heart beat in 15 minutes?

19. Math and Science The mass of a small fossil is 6.275 grams. What is the value of the underlined digit in 6.2$\underline{7}$5?

   A 7 ones   **C** 7 hundredths

   B 7 tenths   **D** 7 thousandths

For **20** and **21**, use the map at the right. Each unit represents one block.

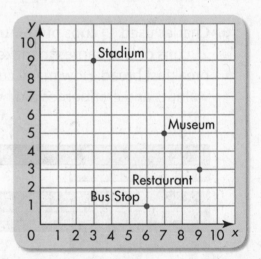

20. Ben left the museum and walked 4 blocks to his next destination. What was Ben's destination?

21. Analyze Information Ben walked from the restaurant to the bus stop. Then he took the bus to the stadium. If he took the shortest route, how many blocks did Ben travel?

22. Extend Your Thinking Dara is making granola bars. The recipe calls for $1\frac{2}{3}$ cups of brown sugar for the bars and $1\frac{1}{3}$ cups of brown sugar for the topping. Dara has $3\frac{1}{4}$ cups of brown sugar. Does she have enough brown sugar to make the granola bars and the topping? Explain.

You can use fraction strips or a number line to compare amounts.

Name_____

Another Look!

Draw a model to add $1\frac{7}{8} + 2\frac{3}{8}$.

> Remember to simplify the sum of mixed numbers, if possible.

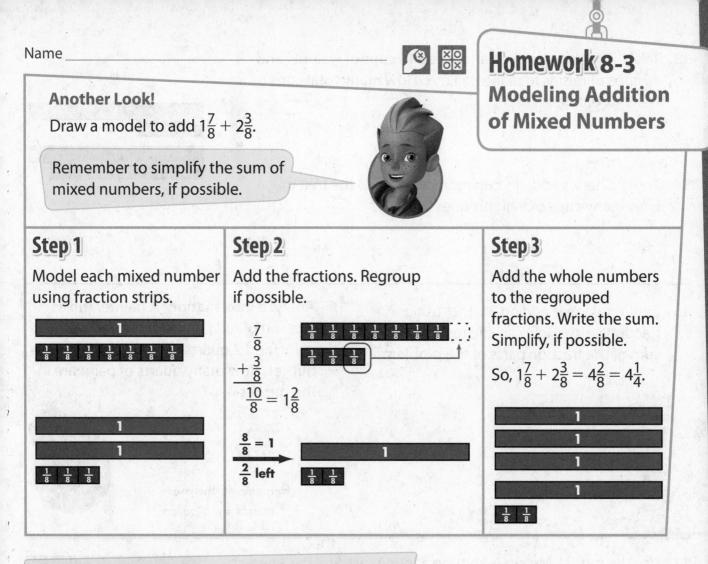

Step 1

Model each mixed number using fraction strips.

Step 2

Add the fractions. Regroup if possible.

$$\frac{7}{8}$$
$$+\frac{3}{8}$$
$$\frac{10}{8} = 1\frac{2}{8}$$

$$\frac{8}{8} = 1$$
$$\frac{2}{8} \text{ left}$$

Step 3

Add the whole numbers to the regrouped fractions. Write the sum. Simplify, if possible.

So, $1\frac{7}{8} + 2\frac{3}{8} = 4\frac{2}{8} = 4\frac{1}{4}$.

In **1** through **12**, use fraction strips to find each sum. Simplify if possible.

1. $3\frac{1}{2} + 1\frac{1}{2}$

2. $2\frac{5}{12} + 4\frac{3}{12}$

3. $3\frac{3}{4} + 3\frac{3}{4}$

4. $2\frac{5}{8} + 4\frac{3}{8}$

5. $5\frac{2}{6} + 3\frac{5}{6}$

6. $2\frac{2}{4} + 6\frac{3}{4}$

7. $3\frac{2}{8} + 4\frac{7}{8}$

8. $4\frac{5}{12} + 5\frac{7}{12}$

9. $2\frac{3}{8} + 4\frac{5}{8}$

10. $6\frac{2}{4} + 7\frac{3}{4}$

11. $4\frac{5}{8} + 6\frac{7}{8}$

12. $2\frac{4}{12} + 4\frac{5}{12}$

13. Tools Use the model. Charles used $1\frac{3}{8}$ cups of walnuts and $1\frac{7}{8}$ cups of raisins to make trail mix. How many total cups of trail mix did he make?

14. Tools Charles added $\frac{5}{8}$ cup more walnuts to the trail mix. How many cups of trail mix does he have?

---

15. Explain Jane is adding $3\frac{2}{3} + 2\frac{2}{3}$ using fraction strips. How can she rename the sum of the fraction parts of the problem?

16. Analyze Information A painter mixes $\frac{1}{4}$ gallon of red paint, 3 quarts of yellow paint, and 2 quarts of white paint in a bucket. How many quarts of paint are in the bucket?

Remember, there are 4 quarts in 1 gallon.

---

17. ★ Use the model. Megan is knitting a long scarf. She has knitted $2\frac{7}{12}$ feet so far. She needs to knit another $2\frac{11}{12}$ feet to complete the scarf. Which of the following expressions can Megan use to find the length in feet of the completed scarf?

A $2\frac{7}{12} + 2\frac{11}{12}$

C $7\frac{1}{12} + 11\frac{1}{12}$

B $2\frac{5}{12} + 2\frac{7}{12}$

D $4 + \frac{11}{12}$

---

18. Mental Math Lori went to the movies. She spent $9.50 for a movie ticket, $5.50 for a box of popcorn, and $2.25 for a drink. How much did Lori spend in all? Show your work.

19. Extend Your Thinking Kayla walked $1\frac{1}{4}$ miles from home to school. Then she walked $1\frac{3}{4}$ from school to the store. Finally she walked $2\frac{1}{4}$ miles from the store to the library. How many miles did Kayla walk to get from school to the library? Use fraction strips to help.

Name _____

Solve & Share

Joaquin used $1\frac{1}{2}$ cups of whole-wheat flour and $1\frac{2}{3}$ cups of buckwheat flour in a recipe. How much flour did he use in all? *Solve any way you choose.*

⭐ TEKS 5.3K Add and subtract positive rational numbers fluently. Also, 5.3H. Mathematical Process Standards 5.1A, 5.1B, 5.1D, 5.1F

Digital Resources at PearsonTexas.com

Solve   Learn   Glossary   Check   Tools   Games

Connect
Use what you know about adding fractions. *Show your work!*

FLOUR

Look Back!

Communicate How is adding mixed numbers with unlike denominators the same as adding fractions with unlike denominators? How is it different?

How Can You Add Mixed Numbers?

A

Rhoda mixed $1\frac{1}{2}$ cups of sand with $2\frac{2}{3}$ cups of potting mixture to prepare soil for her cactus plants. After mixing them together, how many cups of soil does Rhoda have?

You can use addition to find the total amount of soil.

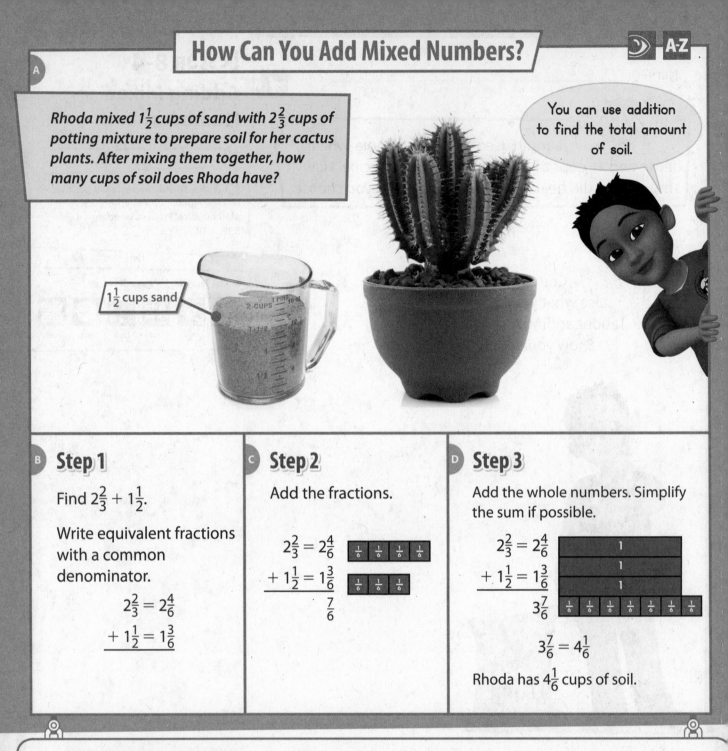

$1\frac{1}{2}$ cups sand

B **Step 1**

Find $2\frac{2}{3} + 1\frac{1}{2}$.

Write equivalent fractions with a common denominator.

$$2\frac{2}{3} = 2\frac{4}{6}$$
$$+ 1\frac{1}{2} = 1\frac{3}{6}$$

C **Step 2**

Add the fractions.

$$2\frac{2}{3} = 2\frac{4}{6}$$
$$+ 1\frac{1}{2} = 1\frac{3}{6}$$
$$\frac{7}{6}$$

D **Step 3**

Add the whole numbers. Simplify the sum if possible.

$$2\frac{2}{3} = 2\frac{4}{6}$$
$$+ 1\frac{1}{2} = 1\frac{3}{6}$$
$$3\frac{7}{6}$$

$$3\frac{7}{6} = 4\frac{1}{6}$$

Rhoda has $4\frac{1}{6}$ cups of soil.

Do You Understand?

Convince Me! Kyle used 9 as an estimate for $3\frac{1}{6} + 5\frac{7}{8}$. He added and got $9\frac{1}{24}$ for the actual sum. Is his answer reasonable? Explain.

☆ Guided Practice ☆

For **1** through **4**, estimate and then find each sum. Check for reasonableness.

1. $\quad 1\frac{7}{8} = 1\frac{\square}{8}$

$\quad + 1\frac{1}{4} = 1\frac{\square}{8}$

2. $\quad 2\frac{2}{5} = 2\frac{\square}{30}$

$\quad + 5\frac{5}{6} = 5\frac{\square}{30}$

3. $4\frac{1}{9} + 1\frac{1}{3}$

4. $6\frac{5}{12} + 4\frac{5}{8}$

5. Reason How is adding mixed numbers like adding fractions and whole numbers?

6. Look back at Exercise 2. Why is the denominator 30 used in the equivalent fractions?

☆ Independent Practice ☆

Leveled Practice For **7** through **18**, estimate and then find each sum. Check for reasonableness.

Remember, fractions need to have a common, or like, denominator before they can be added.

7. $\quad 3\frac{1}{6} = 3\frac{\square}{6}$

$\quad + 5\frac{2}{3} = 5\frac{\square}{6}$

8. $\quad 11\frac{1}{2} = 11\frac{\square}{10}$

$\quad + 10\frac{3}{5} = 10\frac{\square}{10}$

9. $\quad 9\frac{3}{16} = 9\frac{3}{16}$

$\quad + 7\frac{5}{8} = 7\frac{\square}{\square}$

10. $\quad 5\frac{6}{7} = 5\frac{\square}{\square}$

$\quad + 8\frac{1}{14} = 8\frac{1}{14}$

11. $4\frac{1}{10} + 6\frac{1}{2}$

12. $9\frac{7}{12} + 4\frac{3}{4}$

13. $5 + 3\frac{1}{8}$

14. $8\frac{3}{4} + 7\frac{3}{4}$

15. $2\frac{3}{4} + 7\frac{3}{5}$

16. $3\frac{8}{9} + 8\frac{1}{2}$

17. $1\frac{7}{12} + 2\frac{3}{8}$

18. $3\frac{11}{12} + 9\frac{1}{16}$

Problem Solving

19. Use the map to find the answer.

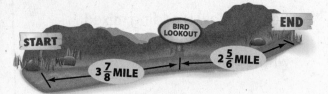

START   BIRD LOOKOUT   END

$3\frac{7}{8}$ MILE $2\frac{5}{6}$ MILE

a What is the distance from the start to the end of the trail?

b Louise walked from the start of the trail to the bird lookout and back. Did she walk a longer or shorter distance than if she had walked from the start of the trail to the end? Explain.

c Another day, Louise walked from the start of the trail to the end. At the end, she realized she forgot her binoculars at the bird lookout. She walked from the end of the trail to the bird lookout and back. What is the total distance she walked?

20. Extend Your Thinking Cameron's cat eats 4 ounces of dry cat food and 2 ounces of wet cat food twice a day. Dry food comes in 5-pound bags. Wet food comes in 6-ounce cans.

a How many cans of wet food should he buy to feed his cat for a week?

b How many ounces of wet cat food will be left over at the end of the week?

c How many days can he feed his cat from a 5-pound bag of dry food?

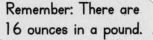

Remember: There are 16 ounces in a pound.

21. A male Parson's chameleon can be up to $23\frac{1}{2}$ inches long. It can extend its tongue up to $35\frac{1}{4}$ inches to catch its food. What is the total length of a male Parson's chameleon when its tongue is fully extended?

22. Arnie skated $1\frac{3}{4}$ miles from home to the lake. He skated $1\frac{1}{3}$ miles around the lake and then skated back home. How many miles did he skate in all?

A $2\frac{1}{12}$ miles   **C** $4\frac{5}{6}$ miles

B $3\frac{1}{12}$ miles   **D** $4\frac{5}{12}$ miles

23. Number Sense Julia bought 12 bags of cucumber seeds. Each bag contains 42 seeds. If she plants one-half of the seeds, how many seeds does she have left?

24. Check for Reasonableness John added $2\frac{7}{12}$ and $5\frac{2}{3}$ and got $7\frac{1}{4}$ as the sum. Is John's answer reasonable? Explain.

Name _____

Another Look!

Randy played soccer for $2\frac{5}{6}$ hours. Then he did homework for $1\frac{3}{4}$ hours. How many hours did he spend on the two activities?

Before you add, you need to write equivalent fractions.

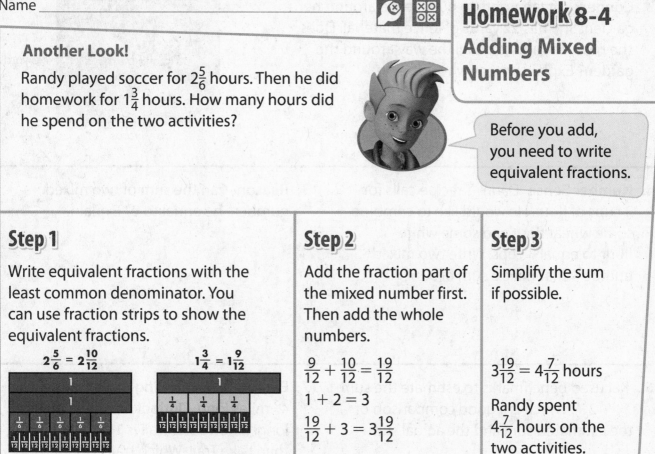

Step 1

Write equivalent fractions with the least common denominator. You can use fraction strips to show the equivalent fractions.

$2\frac{5}{6} = 2\frac{10}{12}$ $1\frac{3}{4} = 1\frac{9}{12}$

Step 2

Add the fraction part of the mixed number first. Then add the whole numbers.

$\frac{9}{12} + \frac{10}{12} = \frac{19}{12}$

$1 + 2 = 3$

$\frac{19}{12} + 3 = 3\frac{19}{12}$

Step 3

Simplify the sum if possible.

$3\frac{19}{12} = 4\frac{7}{12}$ hours

Randy spent $4\frac{7}{12}$ hours on the two activities.

In **1** through **12**, find each sum. Simplify if possible.

Remember to estimate and check that your answer is reasonable.

1. $2\frac{5}{6} = 2\frac{\square}{12}$

    $+ 3\frac{1}{4} = 3\frac{\square}{12}$

2. $1\frac{3}{8}$

    $+ 6\frac{3}{4}$

3. $5\frac{2}{5}$

    $+ 4\frac{1}{2}$

4. $10\frac{1}{3} + \frac{7}{9}$

5. $3\frac{1}{4} + 6\frac{2}{3}$

6. $2\frac{1}{2} + 2\frac{1}{6}$

7. $3\frac{7}{8} + 5\frac{2}{3}$

8. $4\frac{5}{6} + 9\frac{5}{9}$

9. $15\frac{1}{3} + 1\frac{5}{12}$

10. $12\frac{3}{4} + 6\frac{3}{8}$

11. $14\frac{7}{10} + 3\frac{3}{5}$

12. $8\frac{5}{8} + 7\frac{7}{16}$

13. **Connect** Tirzah wants to put a fence around her garden. She has 22 yards of fence material. Does she have enough to go all the way around the garden? Explain why or why not.

Tirzah's garden $4\frac{2}{3}$ yards

$6\frac{3}{4}$ yards

14. **Number Sense** Danny's recipe calls for 3 cups of flour. He would like to combine some wheat flour and some white flour to equal 3 cups. Write two mixed numbers that have a sum of 3.

15. **Reason** Can the sum of two mixed numbers be equal to 2? Explain.

16. Kai used benchmarks to estimate the sum ⭐ $7\frac{7}{8} + 2\frac{11}{12}$. Which is a good comparison of the estimated sum and the actual sum?

   A Estimated $<$ actual
   B Actual $=$ estimated
   C Actual $>$ estimated
   D Estimated $>$ actual

17. **Extend Your Thinking** Lake Trail is $4\frac{3}{5}$ miles long. Outlook Trail is $5\frac{5}{6}$ miles long. Pinewoods Trail is $1\frac{3}{10}$ miles longer than Lake Trail. Which trail is longer, Pinewoods Trail or Outlook Trail? Explain.

Use the data table for **18–20**.

18. Joan reads that an average elephant's brain is $3\frac{4}{10}$ kilograms greater than an average man's brain. How many kilograms is an average elephant's brain?

DATA

Vital Organ Measures		
Average woman's brain	$1\frac{3}{10}$ kg	$2\frac{4}{5}$ lb
Average man's brain	$1\frac{2}{5}$ kg	3 lb
Average human heart	$\frac{3}{10}$ kg	$\frac{7}{10}$ lb

19. What is the total mass of an average man's brain and heart in kilograms (kg)?

20. What is the total weight of an average woman's brain and heart in pounds (lb)?

Name _____

Solve & Share

Clara and Erin volunteered at an animal shelter a total of $9\frac{5}{6}$ hours. Clara worked for $4\frac{1}{6}$ hours. How many hours did Erin work? *You can use fraction strips to solve this problem.*

TEKS 5.3H Represent and solve addition and subtraction of fractions with unequal denominators referring to the same whole using objects and pictorial models and properties of operations. Also, 5.3K. Mathematical Process Standard 5.1C, 5.1D, 5.1F, 5.1G

Digital Resources at PearsonTexas.com

Solve   Learn   Glossary   Check   Tools   Games

Connect Ideas How can you use what you know about adding mixed numbers to help you subtract mixed numbers? *Show your work!*

Look Back!

Estimation How can you estimate the difference for the problem above?

How Can You Model Subtraction of Mixed Numbers?

James needs $1\frac{11}{12}$ inches of pipe to repair a small part of a bicycle frame. He has a pipe that is $2\frac{5}{12}$ inches long. Does he have enough pipe left over to fix a $\frac{3}{4}$-inch piece of frame on another bike?

You can use subtraction to compare numbers.

$2\frac{5}{12}$ inches

$1\frac{11}{12}$ inches

?

B Step 1

Model the number you are subtracting from, $2\frac{5}{12}$.

If the fraction you will be subtracting is greater than the fraction of the number you model, rename 1 whole.

Since $\frac{11}{12} > \frac{5}{12}$, rename 1 whole as $\frac{12}{12}$.

C Step 2

Use your renamed model to cross out the number that you are subtracting, $1\frac{11}{12}$.

There are $\frac{6}{12}$ left.

So, $2\frac{5}{12} - 1\frac{11}{12} = \frac{6}{12}$.   Simplify: $\frac{6}{12} = \frac{1}{2}$

James will have $\frac{1}{2}$ inch of pipe left. He does not have enough for the other bike.

Do You Understand?

Convince Me! Use fraction strips to find $5\frac{1}{4} - 2\frac{3}{4}$.

☆ Guided Practice *

In **1** through **4**, use fraction strips to find each difference. Simplify, if possible.

1. $4\frac{2}{3} - 2\frac{1}{3}$

2. $4\frac{1}{4} - 3\frac{3}{4}$

3. $5\frac{3}{6} - 2\frac{5}{6}$

4. $5\frac{2}{5} - 3\frac{4}{5}$

5. Construct Arguments When subtracting two mixed numbers, is it always necessary to rename one of the wholes? Explain.

Independent Practice ☆

In **6** and **7**, use each model to find the difference.

6. Terrell lives $2\frac{5}{6}$ blocks away from his best friend. His school is $4\frac{1}{6}$ blocks away in the same direction. If he stops at his best friend's house first, how much farther do they have to walk to school?

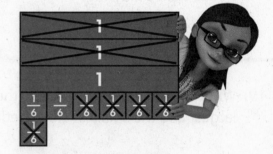

7. Tina bought $3\frac{1}{2}$ pounds of turkey and $2\frac{1}{4}$ pounds of cheese. She used $1\frac{3}{4}$ pounds of cheese to make macaroni and cheese. How many pounds of cheese does she have left?

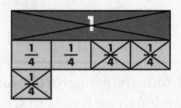

In **8** through **15**, use fraction strips to find each difference. Simplify, if possible.

8. $12\frac{3}{8} - 9\frac{5}{8}$

9. $8\frac{1}{3} - 7\frac{2}{3}$

10. $13\frac{7}{9} - 10\frac{8}{9}$

11. $3\frac{1}{4} - 2\frac{3}{4}$

12. $6\frac{7}{12} - 3\frac{11}{12}$

13. $4\frac{3}{5} - 1\frac{1}{5}$

14. $4\frac{3}{10} - 3\frac{7}{10}$

15. $6\frac{4}{9} - 4\frac{2}{9}$

Problem Solving

16. Kit said, "On my summer vacation, I spent $2\frac{4}{7}$ weeks with my grandma and $1\frac{6}{7}$ weeks with my aunt."

How many weeks longer did Kit spend with her grandmother than with her aunt?

17. Alyssa used $1\frac{2}{3}$ gallons of white paint for the ceiling of her kitchen and $1\frac{2}{3}$ gallons of white paint for her bedroom. She used $3\frac{2}{3}$ gallons of green paint for the walls of her kitchen and $1\frac{3}{4}$ gallons of yellow paint for the walls of her bedroom. How much more green paint did Alyssa use than white paint?

A $\frac{1}{3}$ gallon   **C** 1 gallon.

B $\frac{2}{3}$ gallon   **D** 2 gallons

For **18** and **19**, use the table at the right.

18. How many inches longer is a Hercules beetle than a ladybug?

19. What is the difference between the largest and the smallest stag beetles?

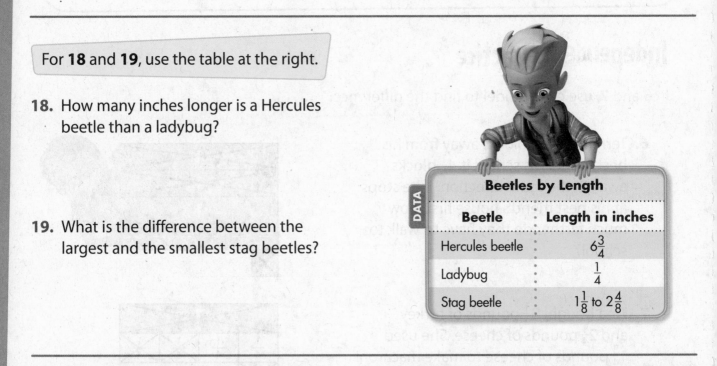

Beetles by Length

Beetle	Length in inches
Hercules beetle	$6\frac{3}{4}$
Ladybug	$\frac{1}{4}$
Stag beetle	$1\frac{1}{8}$ to $2\frac{4}{8}$

DATA

---

20. Extend Your Thinking Nicole, Tasha, Maria, and Joan each walk to school from home. Nicole walks $1\frac{13}{15}$ miles. Tasha walks $2\frac{1}{15}$ miles. Maria walks $1\frac{7}{15}$ miles. Joan walks $2\frac{2}{15}$ miles. How can you find how much farther Joan walks to school than Maria?

21. Use a Strip Diagram Stan needs 90 more points to get a passing grade in class. He already has 6 points. If each book report is worth 7 points, what is the fewest number of book reports Stan can do and still pass the class?

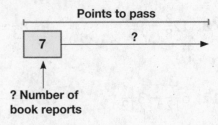

Points to pass

| 7 | ? |

? Number of book reports

Another Look!

Draw a model to subtract $2\frac{1}{5} - 1\frac{2}{5}$.

Remember to simplify your answer, if possible.

Step 1	**Step 2**
Model the number you are subtracting from, $2\frac{1}{5}$.	Rename $2\frac{1}{5}$ as $1\frac{6}{5}$. Cross out one whole and $\frac{2}{5}$ to show subtracting $1\frac{2}{5}$.

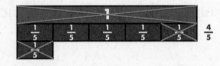

Express the part of the model that is not crossed out as a fraction or mixed number.
So, $2\frac{1}{5} - 1\frac{2}{5} = \frac{4}{5}$.

In **1** through **12**, use fraction strips to find each difference. Simplify, if possible.

1. $6\frac{1}{8} - 3\frac{5}{8}$ **2.** $4 - 1\frac{1}{2}$

3. $5\frac{1}{3} - 3\frac{2}{3}$ **4.** $7\frac{4}{10} - 4\frac{7}{10}$

5. $12\frac{1}{8} - 11\frac{7}{8}$ **6.** $9\frac{3}{5} - 2\frac{2}{5}$

7. $8\frac{3}{12} - 2\frac{5}{12}$ **8.** $12\frac{1}{3} - 5\frac{2}{3}$ **9.** $9\frac{7}{10} - 6\frac{9}{10}$

10. $3\frac{4}{5} - 1\frac{2}{5}$ **11.** $7\frac{1}{4} - 3\frac{3}{4}$ **12.** $10\frac{2}{7} - 7\frac{5}{7}$

13. Tools Use the model to find the difference.

$3\frac{1}{5} - 1\frac{4}{5}$

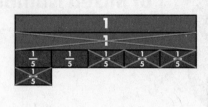

14. Jerome's rain gauge showed that $13\frac{9}{10}$ centimeters (cm) of rain fell last month. This month, the rain gauge measured $15\frac{3}{10}$ centimeters. How many more centimeters of rain fell this month?

A $29\frac{1}{5}$ cm   C $2\frac{2}{5}$ cm

B $15\frac{3}{10}$ cm   D $1\frac{2}{5}$ cm

15. Extend Your Thinking You are subtracting $8\frac{3}{5} - 6\frac{4}{5}$. Do you need to rename $8\frac{3}{5}$? If so, explain how you rename it to subtract. Then find the difference.

16. Explain Danny said 12.309 rounded to the nearest tenth is 12.4. Is Danny correct? Explain.

17. Personal Financial Literacy Lilly bought 3 plants. Each plant cost $4.59. Lilly received $6.23 in change. How much money did Lilly give the cashier?

18. Darius arrived at a ballgame at 4:15. He waited in line for $5\frac{1}{2}$ minutes. Jason arrived $12\frac{1}{2}$ minutes later than Darius and waited in line for $6\frac{1}{2}$ minutes. What time did Jason get admitted to the ballgame?

19. Math and Science Fossils show that insects were much larger around 300 million years ago than today. The table at the right shows some of the wing lengths found from fossils. How much longer is the wing length of the dragonfly than the wing length of the fly?

DATA	Insect	Wing Length
	Dragonfly	19.5 cm
	Grasshopper	16.7 cm
	Fly	9.85 cm

☆ ☆
Solve & Share

Evan is walking $2\frac{1}{8}$ miles to his aunt's house. He has already walked $\frac{3}{4}$ mile. How much farther does he have to go? *Solve this problem any way you choose.*

TEKS 5.3K Add and subtract positive rational numbers fluently. Also, 5.3H. Mathematical Process Standards 5.1C, 5.1D, 5.1E, 5.1F, 5.1G

Digital Resources at PearsonTexas.com

| Solve | Learn | Glossary | Check | Tools | Games |

Connect Use what you know about subtracting fractions. *Show your work!*

Look Back!

Number Sense Jon said, "Changing $\frac{3}{4}$ to $\frac{6}{8}$ makes this easy." What do you think Jon meant?

How Can You Subtract Mixed Numbers?

A golf ball measures about $1\frac{2}{3}$ inches across the center. What is the difference between the distance across the center of the hole and the golf ball?

$4\frac{1}{4}$ inches

You can use objects like fraction strips to solve subtraction problems.

Use Objects.

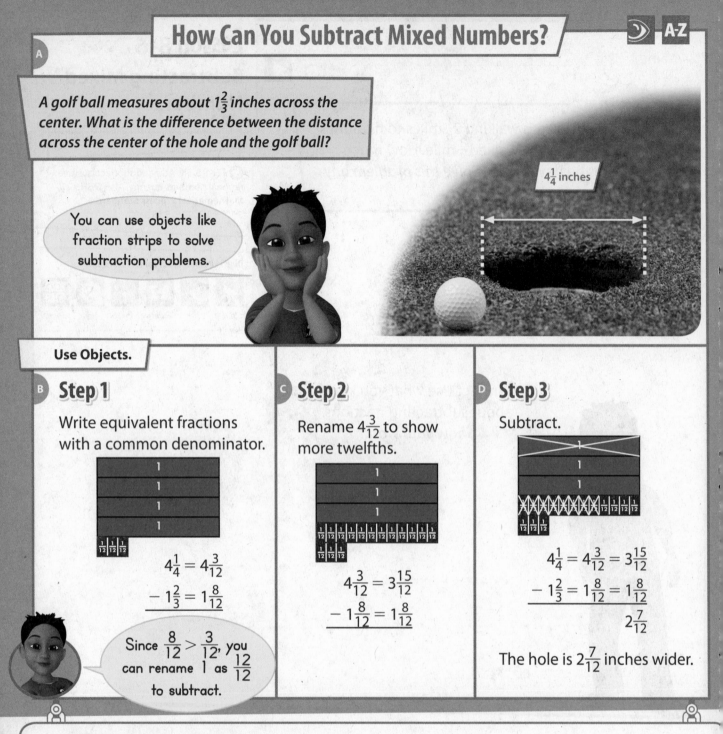

B ## Step 1

Write equivalent fractions with a common denominator.

$$4\frac{1}{4} = 4\frac{3}{12}$$
$$-1\frac{2}{3} = 1\frac{8}{12}$$

Since $\frac{8}{12} > \frac{3}{12}$, you can rename 1 as $\frac{12}{12}$ to subtract.

C ## Step 2

Rename $4\frac{3}{12}$ to show more twelfths.

$$4\frac{3}{12} = 3\frac{15}{12}$$
$$-1\frac{8}{12} = 1\frac{8}{12}$$

D ## Step 3

Subtract.

$$4\frac{1}{4} = 4\frac{3}{12} = 3\frac{15}{12}$$
$$-1\frac{2}{3} = 1\frac{8}{12} = 1\frac{8}{12}$$
$$\overline{\phantom{-1\frac{2}{3}} \quad 2\frac{7}{12}}$$

The hole is $2\frac{7}{12}$ inches wider.

Do You Understand?

Convince Me! Estimate the answer for $8\frac{1}{3} - 3\frac{3}{4}$. Tell how you got your estimate. Susi subtracted and found the actual difference to be $5\frac{7}{12}$. Is her answer reasonable? Explain.

Another Example

Sometimes you may have to rename a whole number to subtract.
Find the difference of $6 - 2\frac{3}{8}$.

$$6 \longrightarrow \text{rename} \longrightarrow 5\frac{8}{8}$$
$$- 2\frac{3}{8} \qquad\qquad\qquad - 2\frac{3}{8}$$
$$\qquad\qquad\qquad\qquad\qquad 3\frac{5}{8}$$

☆ Guided Practice*

Estimate and then find each difference.
Check for reasonableness.

1. $7\frac{2}{3} = 7\frac{\square}{6} = 6\frac{\square}{6}$
   $- 3\frac{5}{6} = 3\frac{\square}{6} = 3\frac{\square}{6}$

2. $5 = \square\frac{\square}{4}$
   $- 2\frac{3}{4} = 2\frac{3}{4}$

3. $6\frac{3}{10} - 1\frac{4}{5}$

4. $9\frac{1}{3} - 4\frac{3}{4}$

5. In Exercise 2, why do you need to rename the 5?

6. **Reason** In the exercise on page 420, could two golf balls fall into the hole at the same time? Explain your reasoning.

Independent Practice ☆

For **7** through **18**, estimate and then find each difference.
Check for reasonableness.

Remember to check your answer for reasonableness by comparing it to the estimate.

7. $8\frac{1}{4} = 8\frac{\square}{8} = 7\frac{\square}{8}$
   $- 2\frac{7}{8} = 2\frac{\square}{8} = 2\frac{\square}{8}$

8. $3\frac{1}{2} = 3\frac{\square}{6}$
   $- 1\frac{1}{3} = 1\frac{\square}{6}$

9. $4\frac{1}{8}$
   $- 1\frac{1}{2}$

10. 6
    $- 2\frac{4}{5}$

11. $6\frac{1}{3} - 5\frac{2}{3}$

12. $9\frac{1}{2} - 6\frac{3}{4}$

13. $8\frac{3}{16} - 3\frac{5}{8}$

14. $7\frac{1}{2} - \frac{7}{10}$

15. $15\frac{1}{6} - 4\frac{3}{8}$

16. $13\frac{1}{12} - 8\frac{1}{4}$

17. $6\frac{1}{3} - 2\frac{3}{5}$

18. $10\frac{5}{12} - 4\frac{7}{8}$

*For another example, see Set F on page 441.

Problem Solving

19. Use a Strip Diagram The average weight of a basketball is $21\frac{1}{10}$ ounces. The average weight of a baseball is $5\frac{1}{4}$ ounces. How many more ounces does the basketball weigh?

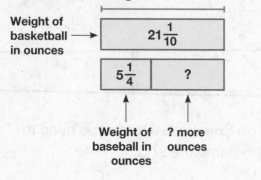

Weight of basketball in ounces → $21\frac{1}{10}$

$5\frac{1}{4}$ | ?

Weight of baseball in ounces ? more ounces

20. The smallest mammals on Earth are the bumblebee bat and the Etruscan pygmy shrew. The length of a bumblebee bat is $1\frac{9}{50}$ inches. The length of an Etruscan pygmy shrew is $1\frac{21}{50}$ inches. How much smaller is the bat than the shrew?

A $\frac{6}{25}$ inch C $1\frac{6}{25}$ inches

B $\frac{12}{25}$ inch D $1\frac{19}{25}$ inches

21. Construct Arguments How are the parallelogram and the rectangle alike? How are they different?

22. Extend Your Thinking Sam used the model to find $2\frac{5}{12} - 1\frac{7}{12}$. Did Sam model the problem correctly? Explain. If not, show how the problem should have been modeled and find the difference.

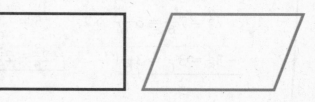

23. Juan and his sister Sally are walking home from school. After walking $2\frac{5}{8}$ miles, Juan stops at the park. He then walks $1\frac{1}{4}$ miles home. After walking $1\frac{3}{8}$ miles, Sally stops at the store before continuing home. How many miles did Sally walk after leaving the store?

24. Personal Financial Literacy Kelly's older sister bought a computer for $598. She must pay $71.72 interest. She has 12 equal monthly payments. How much is each payment? Tell how you found the answer.

Name _____

Another Look!

The Plainville Zoo has had elephants for $2\frac{2}{3}$ years. The zoo has had zebras for $1\frac{1}{2}$ years. How many more years has the zoo had elephants?

Remember: You may need to find a common denominator to subtract.

Step 1

Write equivalent fractions with a common denominator. You can use fraction strips.

$$2\frac{2}{3} = 2\frac{4}{6}$$

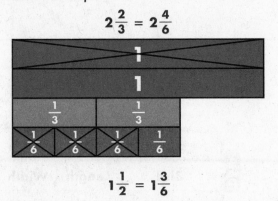

$$1\frac{1}{2} = 1\frac{3}{6}$$

Step 2

Find the difference $2\frac{4}{6} - 1\frac{3}{6}$. Subtract the fractions. Then subtract the whole numbers. Simplify the difference, if possible.

$$\frac{4}{6} - \frac{3}{6} = \frac{1}{6} \qquad\qquad 2 - 1 = 1$$

So, $2\frac{2}{3} - 1\frac{1}{2} = 1\frac{1}{6}$.

The zoo has had the elephants $1\frac{1}{6}$ years longer.

In **1** through **9**, find each difference. Simplify, if possible.

1. $4\frac{3}{5} = 4\frac{\square}{15}$
   $- 2\frac{1}{3} = 2\frac{\square}{15}$

2. 5
   $- 3\frac{5}{6}$

3. $10\frac{5}{8}$
   $- 5\frac{3}{4}$

4. $5\frac{6}{7}$
   $- 1\frac{1}{2}$

5. 3
   $- 1\frac{3}{4}$

6. $6\frac{5}{6}$
   $- 5\frac{1}{2}$

7. $7\frac{3}{10} - 2\frac{1}{5}$

8. $9\frac{2}{3} - 6\frac{1}{2}$

9. $8\frac{1}{4} - \frac{7}{8}$

10. Reason To find the difference of $7 - 3\frac{5}{12}$, how do you rename the 7?

11. Robyn ran $5\frac{3}{4}$ miles last week. She ran $4\frac{1}{10}$ miles this week. How many more miles did she run last week?

12. Extend Your Thinking Explain why it is necessary to rename $4\frac{1}{4}$ to subtract $\frac{3}{4}$ from it.

13. Estimation Every week, Malik spends $5\frac{2}{15}$ hours doing his math homework and $2\frac{13}{20}$ hours doing his science homework. Estimate how much more time Malik spends on his math homework.

Use the table for **14** through **16**. The table shows the length and width of different bird eggs.

14. How much longer is the Canada goose egg than the raven egg?

Egg Sizes in Inches (in.)		
Bird	**Length**	**Width**
Canada goose	$3\frac{2}{5}$	$2\frac{3}{10}$
Robin	$\frac{3}{4}$	$\frac{3}{5}$
Turtle dove	$1\frac{1}{5}$	$\frac{9}{10}$
Raven	$1\frac{9}{10}$	$1\frac{3}{10}$

DATA

15. How much wider is the turtle dove egg than the robin egg?

16. Which shows the birds ordered from smallest ⭐ egg to largest egg?

A Canada goose, Raven, Robin, Turtle dove
B Robin, Turtle dove, Raven, Canada goose
C Robin, Raven, Canada goose, Turtle dove
D Canada goose, Raven, Turtle dove, Robin

How can you compare fractions with unlike denominators?

Name _____

☆ **Solve & Share** ☆

Tim has 15 feet of wrapping paper. He uses $4\frac{1}{3}$ feet for his daughter's present and $5\frac{3}{8}$ feet for his niece's present. How much wrapping paper does Tim have left? *Solve this problem any way you choose.*

⭐ TEKS 5.3K Add and subtract positive rational numbers fluently. Also, 5.3H. Mathematical Process Standards 5.1C, 5.1D, 5.1G

Digital Resources at PearsonTexas.com

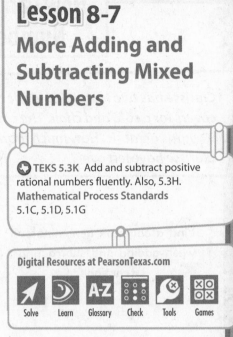

| Solve | Learn | Glossary | Check | Tools | Games |

Reason Can you find the hidden question to solve in this problem? *Show your work!*

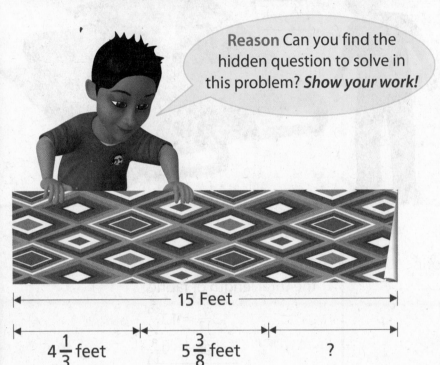

|←——————— 15 Feet ———————→|

$4\frac{1}{3}$ feet $5\frac{3}{8}$ feet   ?

Look Back!

Justify How could you have estimated the amount of wrapping paper that is left for the problem above?

How Can Adding and Subtracting Mixed Numbers Help You Solve Problems?

Clarisse has two lengths of fabric to make covers for a sofa and chair. The covers require $9\frac{2}{3}$ yards of fabric. How much fabric will Clarisse have left over?

Find a common denominator when adding and subtracting fractions.

$7\frac{5}{6}$ yards

$5\frac{3}{4}$ yards

Step 1
B

Add to find out how much fabric Clarisse has in all.

$$5\frac{3}{4} = 5\frac{9}{12}$$
$$+ 7\frac{5}{6} = 7\frac{10}{12}$$
$$12\frac{19}{12} = 13\frac{7}{12}$$

Clarisse has $13\frac{7}{12}$ yards of fabric in all.

Step 2
C

Subtract the amount she will use from the total length of fabric.

$$13\frac{7}{12} = 12\frac{19}{12}$$
$$- \ 9\frac{2}{3} = \ 9\frac{8}{12}$$
$$3\frac{11}{12}$$

Clarisse will have $3\frac{11}{12}$ yards of fabric left over.

Do You Understand?

Convince Me! Clarisse has $14\frac{3}{4}$ yards of fabric to cover another sofa and chair. The new sofa will need $9\frac{1}{6}$ yards of fabric. The new chair will need $4\frac{1}{3}$ yards of fabric. Estimate to decide if Clarisse has enough fabric. How much fabric will she have left over?

Name _____

In **1** through **3**, find the sum or difference.

1. $5\frac{1}{9}$
$\quad -2\frac{2}{3}$

2. $2\frac{1}{4}$
$\quad +8\frac{2}{3}$

3. $6\frac{7}{25}$
$\quad -3\frac{9}{50}$

In **4** through **7**, simplify each expression.

4. $4\frac{3}{5} + 11\frac{2}{15}$

5. $8\frac{2}{3} - 3\frac{3}{4}$

6. $\left(7\frac{2}{3} + 3\frac{4}{5}\right) - 1\frac{4}{15}$

7. $8\frac{2}{5} - \left(3\frac{2}{3} + 2\frac{3}{5}\right)$

8. **Number Sense** In the example on page 426, why do you add before you subtract?

9. **Construct Arguments** In the example on page 426, does Clarisse have enough fabric left over to make two cushions that each use $2\frac{1}{3}$ yards of fabric? Explain.

Independent Practice ☆

In **10** through **14**, find each sum or difference.

10. $9\frac{1}{3}$
$\quad -4\frac{1}{6}$

11. $12\frac{1}{4}$
$\quad -9\frac{3}{5}$

12. $6\frac{3}{5}$
$\quad +1\frac{3}{25}$

13. $3\frac{4}{9}$
$\quad +2\frac{2}{3}$

14. $5\frac{31}{75}$
$\quad -3\frac{2}{25}$

In **15** through **20**, simplify each expression.

15. $\left(2\frac{5}{8} + 2\frac{1}{2}\right) - 4\frac{2}{3}$

16. $\left(5\frac{3}{4} + 1\frac{5}{6}\right) - 6\frac{7}{12}$

17. $4\frac{3}{5} + \left(8\frac{1}{5} - 7\frac{3}{10}\right)$

18. $\left(13 - 10\frac{1}{3}\right) + 2\frac{2}{3}$

19. $\left(2\frac{1}{2} + 3\frac{1}{4}\right) - 1\frac{1}{4}$

20. $2\frac{3}{14} + \left(15\frac{4}{7} - 6\frac{3}{4}\right)$

Problem Solving

The table shows the body lengths and maximum jump lengths for different frog species. For **21** through **23**, use the table. Simplify answers, if possible.

Frog Species	Body Length (cm)	Maximum Jump (cm)
Bullfrog	$20\frac{3}{10}$	$213\frac{1}{2}$
Leopard frog	$12\frac{1}{2}$	$162\frac{1}{2}$
South African sharp-nosed frog	$7\frac{3}{5}$	$334\frac{2}{5}$

21. How much longer is the maximum jump of a South African sharp-nosed frog than the maximum jump of a leopard frog?

22. Rounded to the nearest whole number, how many centimeters long is a bullfrog?

23. Extend Your Thinking Which frog jumps about 10 times its body length? Explain how you found your answer.

---

24. Estimation Use the number line to estimate to the nearest $\frac{1}{2}$ or whole.

1    $1\frac{1}{2}$ 2 $2\frac{1}{2}$ 3

a Estimate the sum of $2\frac{3}{8} + 1\frac{1}{12}$.

b Estimate the difference of $2\frac{1}{8} - 1\frac{9}{10}$.

25. Which is 6.245 rounded to the nearest hundredth?

  A 6.0

  B 6.2

  C 6.24

  D 6.25

26. Number Sense Which number is **NOT** a common denominator of $\frac{7}{15}$ and $\frac{3}{5}$?

  A 15

  B 30

  C 45

  D 55

Another Look!

A park ranger had $4\frac{1}{8}$ cups of birdseed. He bought $6\frac{1}{4}$ more cups of birdseed. Then he filled the park's bird feeders, using $2\frac{1}{2}$ cups of birdseed. How much birdseed is left?

You can write and simplify an expression to solve the problem: $\left(4\frac{1}{8} + 6\frac{1}{4}\right) - 2\frac{1}{2}$

> Always perform operations in parentheses first.

Step 1	Add the mixed numbers in parentheses first. Find a common denominator.	$4\frac{1}{8} + 6\frac{1}{4}$ ↓ ↓ $4\frac{1}{8} + 6\frac{2}{8} = 10\frac{3}{8}$
Step 2	Subtract $2\frac{1}{2}$ from the sum you found. Find a common denominator.	$10\frac{3}{8} - 2\frac{1}{2}$ ↓ ↓ $10\frac{3}{8} - 2\frac{4}{8}$ You can't subtract $\frac{4}{8}$ from $\frac{3}{8}$.
Step 3	Rename if possible.	$9\frac{11}{8} - 2\frac{4}{8} = 7\frac{7}{8}$

So, there are $7\frac{7}{8}$ cups of birdseed left.

> Remember to rename your answer if necessary.

In **1** through **9**, simplify each expression.

1. $\left(5\frac{1}{2} + 2\frac{3}{4}\right) - 3\frac{1}{2}$

2. $10\frac{5}{16} - \left(5\frac{1}{4} + 2\frac{9}{16}\right)$

3. $5\frac{3}{8} + \left(6\frac{3}{4} - 4\frac{1}{8}\right)$

4. $\frac{6}{9} + \frac{5}{18} + 1\frac{3}{6}$

5. $1\frac{4}{10} + 1\frac{3}{20} + 1\frac{1}{5}$

6. $\left(4\frac{2}{3} + 1\frac{1}{6}\right) - 1\frac{5}{6}$

7. $\left(3\frac{3}{8} - 1\frac{1}{5}\right) + 1\frac{7}{8}$

8. $1\frac{6}{7} + \left(4\frac{13}{14} - 3\frac{1}{2}\right)$

9. $10\frac{5}{8} - \left(4\frac{3}{4} + 2\frac{5}{8}\right)$

10. Reason Joel is $2\frac{1}{2}$ inches shorter than Carlos. Carlos is $1\frac{1}{4}$ inches taller than Dan. If Dan is $58\frac{1}{4}$ inches tall, how many inches tall is Joel?

11. Estimation Tina harvested $4\frac{1}{8}$ pounds of tomatoes, $3\frac{2}{3}$ pounds of peppers, and $5\frac{1}{2}$ pounds of strawberries from her garden. About how many pounds in all did she harvest?

12. Suzy spent $6\frac{7}{8}$ days working on her English paper, $3\frac{1}{6}$ days doing her science project, and $1\frac{1}{2}$ days studying for her math test. How many more days did Suzy spend on her English paper and math test combined than on her science project?

13. Which of the following has a sum of 10?

A $1\frac{2}{3} + 3\frac{5}{12} + 4\frac{3}{4}$

B $3\frac{1}{3} + 3\frac{1}{4} + 3\frac{5}{12}$

C $2\frac{3}{8} + 5\frac{1}{2} + 1\frac{1}{4}$

D $5\frac{1}{4} + 1\frac{7}{8} + 3\frac{7}{8}$

14. Extend Your Thinking Veronica is buying cubed cheese from Mr. Sand's deli. She asks for $1\frac{3}{4}$ pounds. When Mr. Sand places some cheese in a container and weighs it, the scale shows $1\frac{1}{4}$ pounds. The container weighs $\frac{1}{16}$ pound. How many more pounds of cheese would Mr. Sand need to add to the scale to get the amount that Veronica asked for? Explain how you solved the problem.

Find the hidden question to solve this problem.

15. Math and Science At a museum, Jenny learned about a fossil that was three billion, four hundred million years old. Write the fossil's age in standard form and expanded form.

16. Four students raised $264 for a charity by washing cars. The students received $8 for each car they washed. How many cars did they wash?

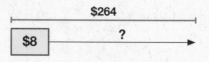

★ ☆ ★
Solve & Share

Juan biked $1\frac{1}{10}$ miles to his friend Mike's house and then to school. He biked $2\frac{7}{10}$ miles in all. What is the distance from Mike's house to school? *Draw a strip diagram to solve this problem.*

⊙ TEKS 5.1D Communicate mathematical ideas, reasoning, and their implications using multiple representations, including symbols, diagrams, graphs, and language as appropriate. Also, 5.3K.
Mathematical Process Standards
5.1A, 5.1B, 5.1C, 5.1D, 5.1F

Digital Resources at PearsonTexas.com

↗	👁	A-Z	⠿	✗	⊠
Solve	Learn	Glossary	Check	Tools	Games

Select and Use Tools
You can use a strip diagram to help you write an equation to solve a problem. *Show your work!*

Look Back!

Connect How does a strip diagram help you write an equation to solve the problem?

Analyze

How Can You Write an Equation to Solve a Multi-Step Problem?

Yori has two dog-sitting jobs. Each day she walks $\frac{3}{10}$ of a mile to get to her first job. Then she walks to her second job. How far is it from Yori's first job to her second job?

You can draw a strip diagram to help you write an equation.

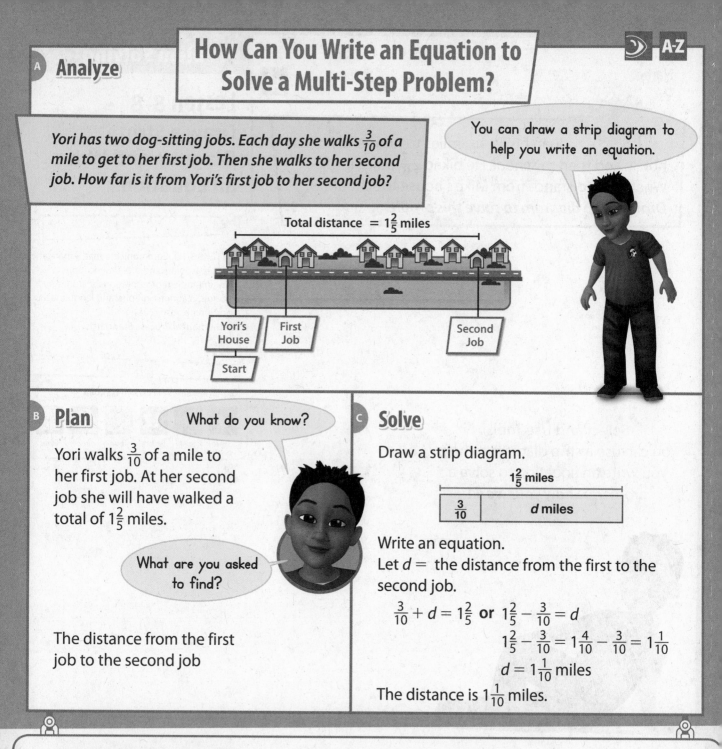

Total distance $= 1\frac{2}{5}$ miles

Yori's House | First Job | Second Job

Start

B ## Plan

What do you know?

Yori walks $\frac{3}{10}$ of a mile to her first job. At her second job she will have walked a total of $1\frac{2}{5}$ miles.

What are you asked to find?

The distance from the first job to the second job

C ## Solve

Draw a strip diagram.

$1\frac{2}{5}$ miles

| $\frac{3}{10}$ | d miles |

Write an equation.
Let $d =$ the distance from the first to the second job.

$$\frac{3}{10} + d = 1\frac{2}{5} \text{ or } 1\frac{2}{5} - \frac{3}{10} = d$$

$$1\frac{2}{5} - \frac{3}{10} = 1\frac{4}{10} - \frac{3}{10} = 1\frac{1}{10}$$

$$d = 1\frac{1}{10} \text{ miles}$$

The distance is $1\frac{1}{10}$ miles.

Do You Understand?

Convince Me! Write a real-world problem that uses addition or subtraction of fractions with like denominators. Draw a strip diagram and write an equation to solve your problem.

☆ Guided Practice ☆

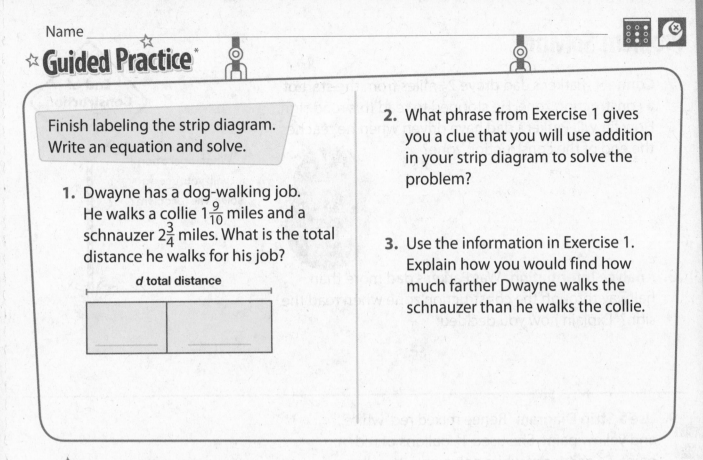

Finish labeling the strip diagram. Write an equation and solve.

1. Dwayne has a dog-walking job. He walks a collie $1\frac{9}{10}$ miles and a schnauzer $2\frac{3}{4}$ miles. What is the total distance he walks for his job?

d total distance

2. What phrase from Exercise 1 gives you a clue that you will use addition in your strip diagram to solve the problem?

3. Use the information in Exercise 1. Explain how you would find how much farther Dwayne walks the schnauzer than he walks the collie.

Independent Practice ☆

In **4** and **5**, draw a strip diagram and write an equation. Then solve.

4. If Jessie hikes all 3 trails, how far will she hike?

Trails and Distances

⬉ Wing Trail $2\frac{3}{4}$ mi

⬆ Sunset Trail $1\frac{7}{8}$ mi

⬈ Ridge Trail $1\frac{1}{3}$ mi

5. Kent only wants to hike Wing Trail. How much farther will Jessie hike than Kent?

6. How much longer is the Wing Trail than the Ridge Trail?

Problem Solving

7. Connect Parker's dad drove $2\frac{1}{3}$ miles from the start of a construction zone. He stopped to read this road sign. How far will Parker's dad have driven when he reaches the end of the construction zone?

End of Construction $1\frac{3}{4}$ mi

What operation will you use to solve the problem?

8. Analyze Information Was Parker's dad more than halfway through the construction zone when read the sign? Explain how you decided.

---

9. Use a Strip Diagram Renee mixed red, white, and yellow paint. She used $1\frac{2}{3}$ gallons of red paint, $5\frac{5}{6}$ gallons of white paint, and $2\frac{1}{2}$ gallons of yellow paint. How many gallons of paint did Renee mix in all?

---

10. Communicate In many cases, a baby's weight at birth is equal to one half his or her weight at age one. Explain how to estimate the weight of a baby at birth if this baby weighs 18 pounds at age one.

---

11. ⭐ Last year, Mr. Kline's fifth-grade class planted a longleaf pine sapling that was $1\frac{5}{12}$ feet tall. Now the sapling is $3\frac{1}{4}$ feet tall. How many feet did the sapling grow from last year?

A $1\frac{1}{2}$ feet

B $1\frac{5}{6}$ feet

C $2\frac{1}{2}$ feet

D $3\frac{3}{12}$ feet

12. Extend Your Thinking Gene says that the two circles below show the same amount. Do you agree? Write a good math explanation to support your decision.

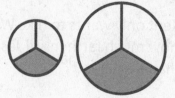

Another Look!

A jeweler has a strand of gold wire that is $1\frac{3}{8}$ inches. He cuts off $\frac{3}{4}$ inch of the wire to make a loop. How long is the remaining piece of wire?

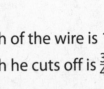

Always identify what you know and what you are asked to find first.

Read and Understand

What do you know?

The length of the wire is $1\frac{3}{8}$ inches.

The length he cuts off is $\frac{3}{4}$ inch.

What are you trying to find?

The length of the wire that is left over

Plan and Solve

Draw a strip diagram to show what you know.

$1\frac{3}{8}$ in.

| $\frac{3}{4}$ in. | x in. |

Write an equation.
Let $x =$ the length of wire left over.

$$1\frac{3}{8} - \frac{3}{4} = x$$

Solve the problem.

$$1\frac{3}{8} - \frac{6}{8} = \frac{11}{8} - \frac{6}{8} = \frac{5}{8}$$

Write the answer in a sentence.

The remaining wire is $\frac{5}{8}$ inch long.

Look Back and Check

Is your answer correct?

Yes, $\frac{3}{4} + \frac{5}{8} = \frac{6}{8} + \frac{5}{8} = \frac{11}{8} = 1\frac{3}{8}$

From his house, Jason rode his bike $1\frac{1}{3}$ miles to the post office. He then rode in the same direction to the park, which is $\frac{1}{4}$ of a mile from the post office. How far did Jason ride?

1. At the right, draw a strip diagram to represent the problem.
   Let $x =$ the distance Jason rode from his house to the park.

2. Write an equation that represents this distance.
   Then solve for x.

3. Mr. Flanders drives $1\frac{2}{3}$ miles to school and $1\frac{2}{3}$ miles home each day. He also drives an extra $2\frac{2}{7}$ miles to go to the gym. How many miles does he drive in one day?

4. Alison is making a 16-inch necklace. The first $4\frac{1}{4}$ inches are filled with red beads and another $8\frac{3}{8}$ inches are filled with blue beads. The rest has white beads. How many inches are filled with white beads?

5. Which of these mixed numbers, when added to $2\frac{1}{3}$, will give you a sum greater than six?

A $3\frac{1}{2}$ C $3\frac{7}{12}$

B $3\frac{5}{12}$ D $3\frac{3}{4}$

6. Extend Your Thinking Dennis says that $1\frac{1}{2}$, $1\frac{2}{4}$, and $1\frac{3}{6}$ are all equivalent. Is he correct? Draw a picture and explain your answer.

7. Math and Science In England, a 6-year-old girl found a fossil that is one hundred sixty million years old. Which number is greater than one hundred sixty million?

A 16,500,322

B 106,385,225

C 161,000,956

D 116,300,034

8. Use a Strip Diagram Cristoff practices playing his guitar for $1\frac{1}{2}$ hours each weekday. He practices this amount of time plus an additional $1\frac{1}{2}$ hours on Sundays. Let $x =$ the number of hours Cristoff practices on Sundays. Draw a strip diagram and write an equation to find the number of hours he practices on Sundays.

9. Stewart drew the triangle shown, with all three sides having the same length. Judith drew the square shown. Which figure has the greater perimeter, the triangle or the square?

$2\frac{1}{6}$ in.

$1\frac{5}{8}$ in.

Remember, *perimeter* is the measure of the distance around a figure.

Name _____

1. **Mental Math** Simone made 206 bookmarks to sell at a craft fair. Each bookmark sells for $2.50. If Simone sells all the bookmarks, how much money will she make? Explain how you used mental math to solve the problem.

Applying Math Processes

- How does this problem connect to previous ones?
- What is my plan?
- How can I use tools?
- How can I use number sense?
- How can I communicate and represent my thinking?
- How can I organize and record information?
- How can I explain my work?
- How can I justify my answer?

2. Darlene is putting a new tiled floor in her kitchen. The floor is in the shape of a rectangle 10 feet long and 8 feet wide. If each tile measures 1 foot by 1 foot, how many tiles does Darlene need to buy?

   A 18 tiles **C** 80 tiles
   B 38 tiles **D** 108 tiles

3. **Analyze Information** Use the table. Lenny walked Rattlesnake Trail and Winding Way Trail. Jillian walked Stone Throw Trail and Winding Way Trail.

Trail Lengths	
Trail Name	**Length (miles)**
Rattlesnake	$3\frac{1}{4}$
Winding Way	$5\frac{2}{3}$
Stone Throw	$4\frac{3}{4}$

DATA

Who walked the greater distance? How many more miles did that person walk?

4. **Extend Your Thinking** Three friends went out to dinner. The bill for their meal is shown. One person has lemonade, one has iced tea, and one has juice. If they share the cost of the pizza and the $4 tip equally, how much does each person owe? Explain.

Joe's Pizza Palace	
Pizza	$12.50
Lemonade	$ 2.00
Iced Tea	$ 1.50
Juice	$ 3.25

DATA

5. **Connect** Sammy plants 5 tulip beds. Each bed has 15 rows with 11 tulips in each row. Sammy has 652 tulip bulbs. How many more bulbs does he need?

6. **Estimation** In the equation $2\frac{3}{8} + x = 5\frac{1}{2}$, estimate the value of x.

Error Search

Find each problem that is not correct.
Change the answer so it is correct.

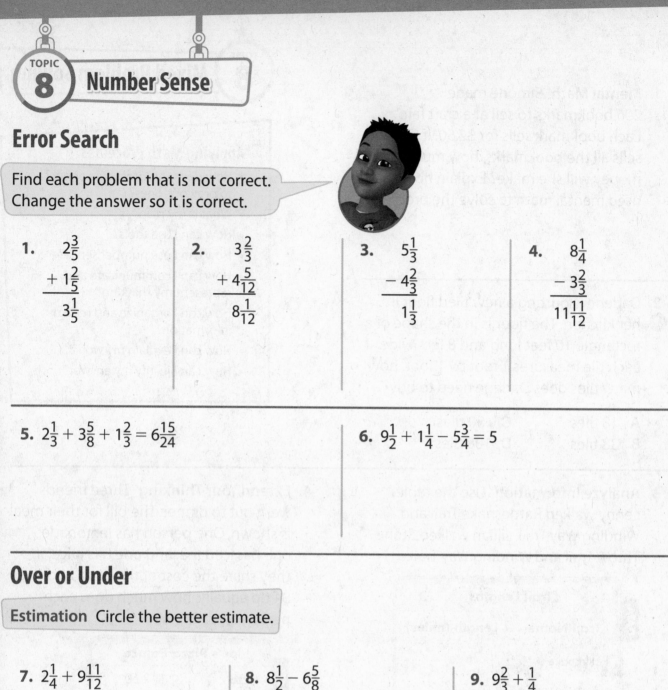

1. $2\frac{3}{5}$
    $+ 1\frac{2}{5}$
    $\overline{3\frac{1}{5}}$

2. $3\frac{2}{3}$
    $+ 4\frac{5}{12}$
    $\overline{8\frac{1}{12}}$

3. $5\frac{1}{3}$
    $- 4\frac{2}{3}$
    $\overline{1\frac{1}{3}}$

4. $8\frac{1}{4}$
    $- 3\frac{2}{3}$
    $\overline{11\frac{11}{12}}$

5. $2\frac{1}{3} + 3\frac{5}{8} + 1\frac{2}{3} = 6\frac{15}{24}$

6. $9\frac{1}{2} + 1\frac{1}{4} - 5\frac{3}{4} = 5$

Over or Under

Estimation Circle the better estimate.

7. $2\frac{1}{4} + 9\frac{11}{12}$

    over 12
    under 12

8. $8\frac{1}{2} - 6\frac{5}{8}$

    over 2
    under 2

9. $9\frac{2}{3} + \frac{1}{4}$

    over 10
    under 10

10. $15\frac{1}{3} + 3\frac{3}{4} + 5\frac{1}{12}$

    over 25
    under 25

11. $12\frac{11}{12} - 2\frac{2}{3}$

    over 10
    under 10

12. $2\frac{1}{8} + 4\frac{1}{12} - 1\frac{1}{2}$

    over 5
    under 5

13. $1\frac{1}{2}$
    $+ 5\frac{3}{4}$

    over 7
    under 7

14. $19\frac{1}{8}$
    $+ 1\frac{5}{12}$

    over 21
    under 21

15. $13\frac{1}{12}$
    $- 11\frac{1}{2}$

    over 2
    under 2

Set A | pages 389–394

Reteaching

Write $\frac{19}{3}$ as a mixed number.

- Divide the numerator by the denominator.

$$\begin{array}{r} 6\,R1 \\ 3\overline{)19} \end{array}$$

- Write the remainder as a fraction in simplest form.

$$\frac{19}{3} = 6\frac{1}{3}$$

Write $9\frac{5}{8}$ as an improper fraction.

$$9\frac{5}{8} = 9 + \frac{5}{8} \text{ and } 9 + \frac{5}{8} = \frac{72}{8} + \frac{5}{8}$$

So, $9\frac{5}{8} = \frac{77}{8}$.

Remember to always write the answer in simplest form.

Write each improper fraction as a mixed number or whole number.

1. $\frac{16}{6}$ 2. $\frac{24}{9}$ 3. $\frac{9}{2}$

Write each as an improper fraction.

4. $4\frac{5}{9}$ 5. $2\frac{7}{11}$ 6. $8\frac{5}{7}$

7. $5\frac{1}{3}$ 8. $10\frac{4}{5}$ 9. $8\frac{8}{11}$

10. $6\frac{3}{8}$ 11. $3\frac{4}{7}$ 12. $9\frac{7}{8}$

Set B | pages 395–400

Estimate $5\frac{1}{3} + 9\frac{9}{11}$.

Compare fractions to $\frac{1}{2}$ to round to the nearest whole number.

Round fractions that are less than $\frac{1}{2}$ to the nearest lesser whole number.

$5\frac{1}{3}$ rounds to 5.

Round fractions greater than or equal to $\frac{1}{2}$ to the nearest greater whole number.

$9\frac{9}{11}$ rounds to 10.

So, $5\frac{1}{3} + 9\frac{9}{11} \approx 5 + 10 = 15$.

Remember that you can also use benchmark fractions such as $\frac{1}{4}, \frac{1}{3}, \frac{1}{2}, \frac{2}{3}$, and $\frac{3}{4}$ to help you estimate.

Round to the nearest whole number.

1. $2\frac{9}{10}$ 2. $9\frac{19}{20}$ 3. $6\frac{2}{7}$

Estimate each sum or difference.

4. $3\frac{1}{4} - 1\frac{1}{2}$ 5. $5\frac{2}{9} + 4\frac{11}{13}$

6. $2\frac{3}{8} + 5\frac{3}{5}$ 7. $9\frac{3}{7} - 6\frac{2}{5}$

8. $8\frac{5}{6} - 2\frac{1}{2}$ 9. $7\frac{3}{4} + 5\frac{1}{8}$

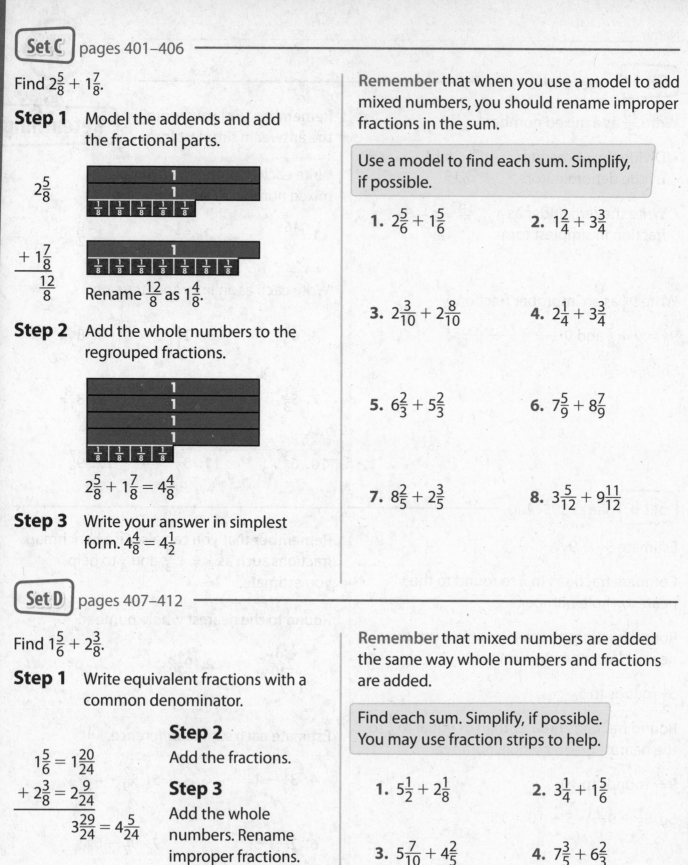

Find $2\frac{5}{8} + 1\frac{7}{8}$.

Step 1 Model the addends and add the fractional parts.

$2\frac{5}{8}$

| 1 |
| 1 |
| $\frac{1}{8}$ | $\frac{1}{8}$ | $\frac{1}{8}$ | $\frac{1}{8}$ | $\frac{1}{8}$ |

$+ 1\frac{7}{8}$

| 1 |
| $\frac{1}{8}$ | $\frac{1}{8}$ | $\frac{1}{8}$ | $\frac{1}{8}$ | $\frac{1}{8}$ | $\frac{1}{8}$ | $\frac{1}{8}$ |

$\frac{12}{8}$ Rename $\frac{12}{8}$ as $1\frac{4}{8}$.

Step 2 Add the whole numbers to the regrouped fractions.

| 1 |
| 1 |
| 1 |
| 1 |
| $\frac{1}{8}$ | $\frac{1}{8}$ | $\frac{1}{8}$ | $\frac{1}{8}$ |

$2\frac{5}{8} + 1\frac{7}{8} = 4\frac{4}{8}$

Step 3 Write your answer in simplest form. $4\frac{4}{8} = 4\frac{1}{2}$

Remember that when you use a model to add mixed numbers, you should rename improper fractions in the sum.

Use a model to find each sum. Simplify, if possible.

1. $2\frac{5}{6} + 1\frac{5}{6}$ 2. $1\frac{2}{4} + 3\frac{3}{4}$

3. $2\frac{3}{10} + 2\frac{8}{10}$ 4. $2\frac{1}{4} + 3\frac{3}{4}$

5. $6\frac{2}{3} + 5\frac{2}{3}$ 6. $7\frac{5}{9} + 8\frac{7}{9}$

7. $8\frac{2}{5} + 2\frac{3}{5}$ 8. $3\frac{5}{12} + 9\frac{11}{12}$

Find $1\frac{5}{6} + 2\frac{3}{8}$.

Step 1 Write equivalent fractions with a common denominator.

Step 2 Add the fractions.

$1\frac{5}{6} = 1\frac{20}{24}$
$+ 2\frac{3}{8} = 2\frac{9}{24}$
$\overline{ 3\frac{29}{24} = 4\frac{5}{24}}$

Step 3

Add the whole numbers. Rename improper fractions. Simplify the sum.

Remember that mixed numbers are added the same way whole numbers and fractions are added.

Find each sum. Simplify, if possible. You may use fraction strips to help.

1. $5\frac{1}{2} + 2\frac{1}{8}$ 2. $3\frac{1}{4} + 1\frac{5}{6}$

3. $5\frac{7}{10} + 4\frac{2}{5}$ 4. $7\frac{3}{5} + 6\frac{2}{3}$

5. $8\frac{5}{9} + 9\frac{1}{3}$ 6. $2\frac{5}{12} + 3\frac{3}{4}$

Set E pages 413–418

Find $2\frac{1}{6} - 1\frac{5}{6}$.

Step 1 Model the number you are subtracting from, $2\frac{1}{6}$. Since $\frac{5}{6} > \frac{1}{6}$, rename 1 whole as $\frac{6}{6}$.

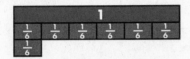

Step 2 Use your renamed model to cross out the number you are subtracting, $1\frac{5}{6}$.

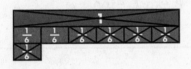

$$2\frac{1}{6} - 1\frac{5}{6} = \frac{2}{6}$$

Step 3 Write the answer in simplest form: $\frac{2}{6} = \frac{1}{3}$

Remember that the difference is the part of the model that is not crossed out.

Use a model to find each difference. Simplify, if possible.

1. $15\frac{3}{5} - 3\frac{4}{5}$ 2. $6\frac{3}{4} - 5\frac{1}{4}$

3. $4\frac{1}{3} - 1\frac{2}{3}$ 4. $12\frac{1}{4} - 7\frac{2}{4}$

5. $9\frac{7}{10} - 3\frac{9}{10}$ 6. $5\frac{5}{8} - 3\frac{1}{8}$

Set F pages 419–424

Find $5\frac{1}{5} - 3\frac{1}{2}$.

Step 1 Write equivalent fractions with a common denominator.

Step 2

$5\frac{1}{5} = 5\frac{2}{10} = 4\frac{12}{10}$

$- 3\frac{1}{2} = 3\frac{5}{10} = 3\frac{5}{10}$

$\phantom{- 3\frac{1}{2} = 3\frac{5}{10} = }1\frac{7}{10}$

Rename $5\frac{2}{10}$ to show more tenths.

Step 3

Subtract the fractions. Subtract the whole numbers. Simplify the difference.

Remember that subtracting mixed numbers may require renaming.

Find each difference. Simplify, if possible. You may use fraction strips to help.

1. $7\frac{5}{6} - 3\frac{2}{3}$ 2. $2\frac{3}{5} - 1\frac{1}{2}$

3. $5\frac{2}{3} - 4\frac{5}{6}$ 4. $9 - 3\frac{3}{8}$

5. $3\frac{1}{9} - 1\frac{1}{3}$ 6. $6\frac{1}{4} - 3\frac{2}{5}$

7. $9\frac{1}{4} - 2\frac{5}{8}$ 8. $4 - 1\frac{2}{5}$

Gil has two lengths of wallpaper, $2\frac{3}{4}$ yards and $1\frac{7}{8}$ yards long. He used some and now has $1\frac{5}{6}$ yards left. How many yards of wallpaper did Gil use?

Step 1

Add to find the total amount of wallpaper Gil has.

$$2\frac{3}{4} = 2\frac{18}{24}$$
$$+\ 1\frac{7}{8} = 1\frac{21}{24}$$
$$\overline{\ 4\frac{5}{8}}$$

Step 2

Subtract to find the amount of wallpaper Gil used.

$$4\frac{5}{8} = 3\frac{39}{24}$$
$$-\ 1\frac{5}{6} = 1\frac{20}{24}$$
$$\overline{\ 2\frac{19}{24}}$$

Gil used $2\frac{19}{24}$ yards of wallpaper.

Remember when you add or subtract mixed numbers, rename the fractional part to have a common denominator.

Simplify each expression.

1. $\left(2\frac{1}{6} + 3\frac{3}{4}\right) - 1\frac{5}{12}$

2. $\left(4\frac{4}{5} + 7\frac{1}{3}\right) - 1\frac{7}{15}$

3. $\left(8\frac{3}{8} - 4\frac{5}{6}\right) + 1\frac{11}{24}$

4. $2\frac{9}{25} + 2\frac{9}{50} + 2\frac{1}{100}$

Sophie and Ryan picked apples. Sophie picked $3\frac{1}{2}$ pounds of apples. Ryan picked $4\frac{5}{8}$ pounds of apples. How many more pounds of apples did Ryan pick than Sophie?

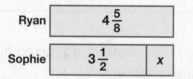

Write an equation. Let x represent how many more pounds of apples Ryan picked.

$$3\frac{1}{2} + x = 4\frac{5}{8} \text{ or } x = 4\frac{5}{8} - 3\frac{1}{2}$$

Find a common denominator and subtract.

$$4\frac{5}{8} = 4\frac{5}{8}$$
$$-\ 3\frac{1}{2} = 3\frac{4}{8}$$
$$\overline{\ 1\frac{1}{8}}$$

Ryan picked $1\frac{1}{8}$ pounds more apples than Sophie.

Remember that a strip diagram can help you write an addition or a subtraction equation.

Draw a picture and write an equation to solve.

1. Justin jogs $3\frac{2}{5}$ miles every morning. He jogs $4\frac{6}{10}$ miles every evening. How many miles does he jog every day?

2. Last year Mia planted a tree that was $5\frac{11}{12}$ feet tall. This year the tree is $7\frac{2}{3}$ feet tall. How many feet did the tree grow?

Name _____

1. George used $1\frac{3}{4}$ pounds of Swiss cheese and $2\frac{1}{8}$ pounds of cheddar cheese to make a large cheesy-chicken casserole. Which expression is the best estimate for the number of pounds of cheese he used?

A $2 + 2$ C $2 + 3$

B $1 + 2$ D $1 + 3$

2. Yao drank $\frac{11}{4}$ bottles of water during a soccer game. What is this number expressed as a mixed number?

A $3\frac{1}{4}$

B $2\frac{3}{4}$

C $2\frac{1}{2}$

D $2\frac{1}{4}$

3. Lee drew the model shown below to solve a math problem. Which expression does Lee's model show?

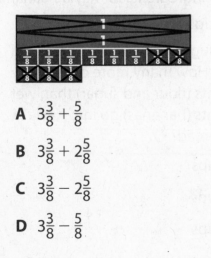

A $3\frac{3}{8} + \frac{5}{8}$

B $3\frac{3}{8} + 2\frac{5}{8}$

C $3\frac{3}{8} - 2\frac{5}{8}$

D $3\frac{3}{8} - \frac{5}{8}$

4. Marie needs $2\frac{1}{4}$ yards of fabric. She already has $1\frac{3}{8}$ yards. How many more yards of fabric does she need?

A $\frac{1}{8}$ yard

B $\frac{3}{4}$ yard

C $\frac{7}{8}$ yard

D Not here

5. The Jacobys went on a 600-mile trip. On the first day they drove $5\frac{2}{3}$ hours, and on the second day they drove $4\frac{3}{5}$ hours. How many hours did they drive during the first two days?

A $10\frac{4}{15}$ hours

B 10 hours

C $9\frac{19}{30}$ hours

D $9\frac{4}{15}$ hours

6. Hasan has $2\frac{7}{8}$ pages of his English paper written and $4\frac{5}{6}$ of his science paper written. He drew the model below to find the total number of pages he has written so far. Which equation does **NOT** match the model?

	x	
$2\frac{7}{8}$		$4\frac{5}{6}$

A $x - 2\frac{7}{8} = 4\frac{5}{6}$

B $x = 2\frac{7}{8} + 4\frac{5}{6}$

C $x = 4\frac{5}{6} - 2\frac{7}{8}$

D $x - 4\frac{5}{6} = 2\frac{7}{8}$

7. Rick made a paper football that was $1\frac{1}{6}$ inches long. Carly made one that was $\frac{5}{6}$ of an inch long. How much longer was Rick's paper football than Carly's?

A $\frac{1}{3}$ in.

B $\frac{1}{6}$ in.

C $1\frac{1}{3}$ in.

D 2 in.

8. Diego measured $\frac{18}{8}$ cups of flour. Which mixed number is equivalent to $\frac{18}{8}$?

A $1\frac{8}{10}$

B $2\frac{1}{8}$

C $2\frac{1}{4}$

D 3

9. Veata used the model below to find the sum of two mixed numbers. What is the sum?

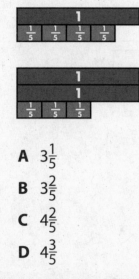

A $3\frac{1}{5}$

B $3\frac{2}{5}$

C $4\frac{2}{5}$

D $4\frac{3}{5}$

10. Aisha is remodeling her kitchen. She is using square tiles like the one shown below. The square below has sides that are $1\frac{1}{4}$ inches long. What is the perimeter of one tile?

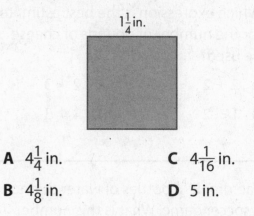

$1\frac{1}{4}$ in.

A $4\frac{1}{4}$ in. C $4\frac{1}{16}$ in.

B $4\frac{1}{8}$ in. D 5 in.

11. To estimate the sum of two fractions, Carla rounds one fraction to 3 and the other fraction to 7. Which is the fraction she rounds to 3?

A $2\frac{5}{8}$

B $2\frac{11}{30}$

C $3\frac{4}{6}$

D $3\frac{7}{9}$

12. The main ingredients for Kayla's banana bread recipe are $2\frac{1}{3}$ cups of flour, $\frac{3}{4}$ cup of sugar, and $1\frac{1}{2}$ cups of mashed bananas. How many more cups of dry ingredients (flour and sugar) than wet ingredients (bananas) go into Kayla's banana bread?

A $1\frac{7}{12}$ cups

B $2\frac{7}{12}$ cups

C $3\frac{7}{12}$ cups

D $4\frac{7}{12}$ cups

Name _____

13. Mark is making a small frame in the shape of an equilateral triangle with the dimensions shown below. What is the perimeter of the frame?

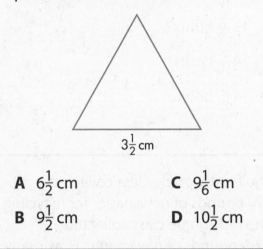

$3\frac{1}{2}$ cm

A $6\frac{1}{2}$ cm   **C** $9\frac{1}{6}$ cm

B $9\frac{1}{2}$ cm   **D** $10\frac{1}{2}$ cm

14. A baker uses food coloring to color cake batter. He needs $4\frac{1}{8}$ ounces of green food coloring. The baker only has $2\frac{3}{8}$ ounces. How much more green food coloring does he need?

A $1\frac{2}{3}$ ounces

B $1\frac{3}{4}$ ounces

C $1\frac{5}{8}$ ounces

D $2\frac{3}{4}$ ounces

15. Which of the following is **NOT** a name for the model?

A $2\frac{1}{2}$

B $2\frac{2}{4}$

C $\frac{10}{4}$

D $\frac{8}{10}$

16. Simplify the expression $12\frac{1}{2} - \left(4\frac{3}{4} + 5\frac{2}{3}\right)$.

A $1\frac{2}{3}$

B $1\frac{3}{4}$

C $2\frac{2}{3}$

D $2\frac{1}{12}$

17. Claude has downloaded $1\frac{7}{8}$ albums to his computer and $2\frac{3}{8}$ albums to his cell phone. How many albums has he downloaded so far?

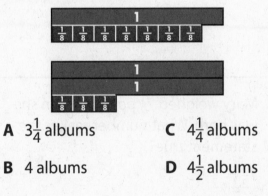

A $3\frac{1}{4}$ albums   **C** $4\frac{1}{4}$ albums

B 4 albums   **D** $4\frac{1}{2}$ albums

18. Last week, Brandon spent $4\frac{3}{4}$ hours on homework. He studied for a math test for $1\frac{1}{3}$ hours on Tuesday. On Thursday, he worked on a science project for $2\frac{5}{12}$ hours. How much time did Brandon spend on schoolwork in all last week?

A $6\frac{1}{2}$ hours   **C** $8\frac{1}{2}$ hours

B $7\frac{1}{2}$ hours   **D** $8\frac{1}{2}$ hours

19. A recipe for fruit salad calls for $2\frac{2}{3}$ cups of pineapple, $2\frac{3}{4}$ cups of strawberries, and $1\frac{1}{4}$ cups of kiwi. About how many cups of fruit salad will the recipe make?

A 5 cups

B 7 cups

C 8 cups

D 10 cups

20. A pelican has a wingspan of $8\frac{1}{5}$ feet. An eagle has a wingspan of $6\frac{2}{3}$ feet. How much longer is the wingspan of a pelican?

21. Mary weighed $7\frac{1}{2}$ pounds when she was born. What number makes the statement true?

$$7\frac{1}{2} = \frac{\blacksquare}{2}$$

22. Gilberto worked $3\frac{1}{4}$ hours on Thursday, $4\frac{2}{5}$ hours on Friday, and $6\frac{1}{2}$ hours on Saturday. How many hours did he work in all during the three days?

A $13\frac{1}{10}$ hours

B $13\frac{3}{20}$ hours

C $14\frac{1}{10}$ hours

D $14\frac{3}{20}$ hours

23. The fourth-grade class collected $27\frac{5}{8}$ pounds of newspaper for recycling. The fifth-grade class collected $32\frac{9}{16}$ pounds of newspaper. How many more pounds of newspaper did the fifth-grade class collect?

24. Dawson says that when you simplify the expression $\left(2\frac{4}{10} + 8\frac{4}{5}\right) - 3\frac{1}{5}$ you get a whole number. What whole number do you get?

446

Glossary

A

acute angle An angle whose measure is between 0° and 90°.

acute triangle A triangle whose angles are all acute angles.

Addition Property of Equality The same number can be added to both sides of an equation and the sides remain equal.

additive pattern A pattern in which corresponding values are related by addition.

algebraic expression A mathematical phrase involving a variable or variables, numbers, and operations.
Example: x − 3

angle A figure formed by two rays that have the same endpoint.

area The number of square units needed to cover a surface or figure.

array A way of displaying objects in rows and columns.

Associative Property of Addition Addends can be regrouped and the sum remains the same.
Example: 1 + (3 + 5) = (1 + 3) + 5

Associative Property of Multiplication Factors can be regrouped and the product remains the same.
Example: 2 × (4 × 10) = (2 × 4) × 10

attribute A characteristic of a shape.

axis (plural: axes) Either of two lines drawn perpendicular to each other in a graph.

B

balance The amount of money in a person's account.

balanced budget A budget in which the total amount of money spent, saved, and shared equals total income.

bar graph A graph that uses bars to show and compare data.

base (of a polygon) The side of a polygon to which the height is perpendicular.

base (of a solid) The face of a solid that is used to name the solid.
Base

benchmark fraction Common fractions used for estimating, such as $\frac{1}{4}, \frac{1}{3}, \frac{1}{2}, \frac{2}{3},$ and $\frac{3}{4}$.

brackets The symbols [and] that are used to group numbers or variables in mathematical expressions.

breaking apart A mental math method used to rewrite a number as the sum of numbers to form an easier problem.

budget A plan for how much income will be received and how it will be spent.

capacity The volume of a container measured in liquid units.

categorical data Data that can be divided into groups.

Celsius (°C) A unit of measure for temperature in the metric system.

centimeter (cm) A metric unit of length. 100 centimeters equal 1 meter.

circle A closed plane figure made up of all the points that are the same distance from a given point.

common denominator A number that is the denominator of two or more fractions.

common multiple A number that is a multiple of two or more numbers.

Commutative Property of Addition The order of addends can be changed and the sum remains the same. *Example:* $3 + 7 = 7 + 3$

Commutative Property of Multiplication The order of factors can be changed and the product remains the same. *Example:* $3 \times 5 = 5 \times 3$

compatible numbers Numbers that are easy to compute with mentally.

compensation Adjusting a number to make a computation easier and balancing the adjustment by changing another number.

composite number A whole number greater than 1 with more than two factors.

composite shape A figure made up to two or more shapes.

coordinate grid A grid that is used to plot and name points in a plane using an ordered pair of numbers.

coordinates The two numbers in an ordered pair.

corresponding Matching terms in a pattern.

credit a. Money put into a person's account. **b.** Buying something now, but paying for it later.

cube A solid figure with six identical squares as its faces.

cubic unit The volume of a cube that measures 1 unit on each edge.

cup (c) A customary unit of capacity. 1 cup = 8 fluid ounces

customary units of measure Units of measure that are used in the United States.

D

data Collected information.

debit Money taken out of a person's account.

decimal A number with one or more places to the right of a decimal point.

degree (°) A unit of measure for angles. Also, a unit of measure for temperature.

denominator The number below the fraction bar in a fraction.

deposit Money put into a person's account.

difference The result of subtracting one number from another.

digits The symbols used to show numbers: 0, 1, 2, 3, 4, 5, 6, 7, 8, 9.

discrete data Data where only whole numbers are possible.

Distributive Property Multiplying a sum (or difference) by a number is the same as multiplying each number in the sum (or difference) by the number and adding (or subtracting) the products.
Example: $3 \times (10 + 4) = (3 \times 10) + (3 \times 4)$

dividend The number to be divided.

divisible A number is divisible by another number if there is no remainder after dividing.

Division Property of Equality Both sides of an equation can be divided by the same nonzero number and the sides remain equal.

divisor The number by which another number is divided.
Example: In $32 \div 4 = 8$, 4 is the divisor.

dot plot A display of responses along a number line with dots used to indicate the number of times a response occurred.

E

edge A line segment where two faces meet in a solid figure.

←Edge

elapsed time The amount of time between the beginning of an event and the end of the event.

equation A number sentence that uses an equal sign to show that two expressions have the same value.
Example: $9 + 3 = 12$

equilateral triangle A triangle whose sides all have the same length.

equivalent decimals Decimals that name the same amount.
Example: $0.7 = 0.70$

equivalent fractions Fractions that name the same part of a whole region, length, or set.

estimate To give an approximate value rather than an exact answer.

evaluate To find the value of an expression when a variable is replaced by a number.

expanded form A way to write a number that shows the place value of each digit. *Example:* 3,000 + 500 + 60 + 2

expenses The amount of money spent.

face A flat surface of a solid figure.

←Face

factors Numbers that are multiplied to get a product.

Fahrenheit (°F) A unit of measure for temperature in the customary system.

fluid ounce (fl oz) A customary unit of capacity equal to 2 tablespoons.

foot (ft) A customary unit of length equal to 12 inches.

formula A rule that uses symbols to relate two or more quantities.

fraction A symbol, such as $\frac{2}{3}$, $\frac{5}{1}$, or $\frac{8}{5}$, used to describe one or more parts of a whole that is divided into equal parts. A fraction can name a part of a whole, a part of a set, a location on a number line, or a division of whole numbers.

frequency table A table used to show the number of times each response occurs in a set of data.

gallon (gal) A unit for measuring capacity in the customary system. 1 gallon = 4 quarts.

gram (g) A metric unit of mass. One gram is equal to 1,000 milligrams.

greater than symbol (>) A symbol that points away from a greater number or expression. *Example:* 450 > 449

gross income The total amount of money a person earns.

height of a polygon The length of a segment from one vertex of a polygon perpendicular to its base.

height of a solid In a prism the perpendicular distance between the top and bottom bases of the figure.

hexagon A polygon with 6 sides.

hundredth One part of 100 equal parts of a whole.

Identity Property of Addition The sum of any number and zero is that number.

Identity Property of Multiplication The product of any number and 1 is that number.

improper fraction A fraction whose numerator is greater than or equal to its denominator.

income Money earned from doing work.

inch (in.) A customary unit of length. 12 inches = 1 foot

input-output table A table that uses a rule to relate one set of numbers to another set of numbers.

intersecting lines Lines that pass through the same point.

interval (on a graph) The difference between consecutive numbers on an axis of a graph.

inverse operations Operations that undo each other. *Example:* Adding 6 and subtracting 6 are inverse operations.

isosceles triangle A triangle with two sides of the same length.

kilogram (kg) A metric unit of mass. One kilogram is equal to 1,000 grams.

kilometer (km) A metric unit of length. One kilometer is equal to 1,000 meters.

less than symbol (<) A symbol that points towards a lesser number or expression.
Example: 305 < 320

line A straight path of points that goes on forever in two directions.

line graph A graph that connects points to show how data change over time.

line of symmetry The line on which a figure can be folded so that both halves are the same.

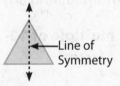

Line of Symmetry

line segment Part of a line having two endpoints.

liter (L) A metric unit of capacity. One liter is equal to 1,000 milliliters.

mass The measure of the quantity of matter in an object.

meter (m) A metric unit of length. One meter is equal to 1,000 millimeters.

metric units of measure Units of measure commonly used by scientists.

mile (mi) A customary unit of length equal to 5,280 feet.

milligram (mg) A metric unit of mass. 1,000 milligrams equal 1 gram.

milliliter (mL) A metric unit of capacity. 1,000 milliliters equal 1 liter.

millimeter (mm) A metric unit of length. 1,000 millimeters equal 1 meter.

mixed number A number that has a whole-number part and a fraction part.

multiple The product of a given whole number and any other whole number.

multiple of 10 A number that has 10 as a factor.

Multiplication Property of Equality Both sides of an equation can be multiplied by the same nonzero number and the sides remain equal.

multiplicative inverse (reciprocal) Two numbers whose product is one.

multiplicative pattern A pattern in which corresponding values are related by multiplication.

net income The amount of money a person receives after deductions are taken from gross income.

numerator The number above the fraction bar in a fraction.

numerical data Data involving numbers including measurement data.

numerical expression A mathematical phrase that contains numbers and at least one operation. *Example:* 325 + 50

obtuse angle An angle whose measure is between 90° and 180°.

135°

obtuse triangle A triangle in which one angle is an obtuse angle.

octagon A polygon with 8 sides.

order of operations The order in which operations are done in calculations. Work inside parentheses and brackets is done first. Then multiplication and division are done in order from left to right, and finally addition and subtraction are done in order from left to right.

ordered pair A pair of numbers used to locate a point on a coordinate grid.

origin The point where the two axes of a coordinate plane intersect. The origin is represented by the ordered pair (0, 0).

ounce (oz) A customary unit of weight. 16 ounces equal 1 pound.

outlier A value that is much greater or much less than the other values in a data set.

overestimate An estimate that is greater than the actual answer.

parallel lines In a plane, lines that never cross and stay the same distance apart.

parallel sides Sides in a polygon that are the same distance apart at every point.

parallelogram A quadrilateral with both pairs of opposite sides parallel.

parentheses The symbols (and) used to group numbers or variables in mathematical expressions.
Example: 3(15 − 7)

partial products Products found by breaking one of two factors into ones, tens, hundreds, and so on, and then multiplying each of these by the other factor.

pentagon A polygon with 5 sides.

perfect square A number that is the product of a counting number multiplied by itself.

perimeter The distance around a figure.

period In a number, a group of three digits, separated by commas, starting from the right.

perpendicular lines Two lines that intersect to form square corners or right angles.

pint (pt) A customary unit of capacity equal to 2 cups.

place value The position of a digit in a number that is used to determine the value of the digit.
Example: In 5,318, the 3 is in the hundreds place. So, the 3 has a value of 300.

plane An endless flat surface.

point An exact location in space.

polygon A closed plane figure made up of line segments.

pound (lb) A customary unit of weight equal to 16 ounces.

prime number A whole number greater than 1 that has exactly two factors, itself and 1.

prism A solid figure with two identical parallel bases and faces that are parallelograms.

product The number that is the result of multiplying two or more factors.

proper fraction A fraction less than 1; its numerator is less than its denominator.

protractor A tool used to measure and draw angles.

pyramid A solid figure with a base that is a polygon whose faces are triangles with a common vertex.

Q

quadrilateral A polygon with 4 sides.

quart (qt) A customary unit of capacity equal to 2 pints.

quotient The answer to a division problem.

R

ray Part of a line that has one endpoint and extends forever in one direction.

reciprocal A given number is a reciprocal of another number if the product of the numbers is one. *Example:* The numbers $\frac{1}{8}$ and $\frac{8}{1}$ are reciprocals because $\frac{1}{8} \times \frac{8}{1} = 1$.

rectangle A parallelogram with four right angles.

rectangular prism A solid figure with 6 rectangular faces.

regular polygon A polygon that has sides of equal length and angles of equal measure.

remainder The amount that is left after dividing a number into equal parts.

rhombus A parallelogram with all sides the same length.

right angle An angle whose measure is 90°.

right triangle A triangle in which one angle is a right angle.

rounding A process that determines which multiple of 10, 100, 1,000, and so on, a number is closest to.

S

sample A representative part of a larger group.

scale (in a graph) A series of numbers at equal intervals along an axis on a graph.

scalene triangle A triangle in which no sides have the same length.

scatterplot A graph that shows paired data values.

sequence A set of numbers that follows a pattern.

sides (of an angle) The two rays that form an angle.

sides of a polygon The line segments that form a polygon.

simplest form A fraction in which the only common factor of the numerator and denominator is one.

solid figure (also: solid) A figure that has three dimensions (length, width, and height).

solution The value of the variable that makes the equation true.

square A rectangle with all sides the same length.

square unit A square with sides one unit long used to measure area.

standard form A common way of writing a number with commas separating groups of three digits starting from the right. *Example:* 3,458,901

stem-and-leaf plot A way to organize numerical data using place value.

straight angle An angle measuring 180°.

strip diagram A tool used to help understand and solve word problems. It is also known as a bar diagram or a tape diagram.

Subtraction Property of Equality The same number can be subtracted from both sides of an equation and the sides remain equal.

sum The result of adding two or more addends.

survey A question or questions used to gather information.

symmetric A figure is symmetric if it can be folded on a line to form two halves that fit exactly on top of each other.

tablespoon (tbsp) A customary unit of capacity. 2 tablespoons = 1 fluid ounce

taxes Money people pay to support the government.

tenth One of ten equal parts of a whole.

terms Numbers in a sequence or variables, such as *x* and *y*, in an algebraic expression.

thousandth One of 1,000 equal parts of a whole.

three-dimensional shape A solid with three dimensions that has volume, such as a rectangular prism.

ton (T) A customary unit of weight equal to 2,000 pounds.

trapezoid A quadrilateral that has exactly one pair of parallel sides.

trend A relationship between two sets of data that shows up as a pattern in a graph, including scatterplots.

triangle A polygon with 3 sides.

underestimate An estimate that is less than the actual answer.

unknown A symbol or letter, such as *x*, that represents a number in an expression or equation.

unit fraction A fraction with a numerator of 1.

V

value (of a digit) The number a digit represents, which is determined by the position of the digit. See also *place value*.

variable A letter, such as *n*, that represents a number in an expression or an equation.

vertex (plural: vertices) **a.** The common endpoint of the two rays in an angle. **b.** A point at which two sides of a polygon meet. **c.** The point at which three or more edges meet in a solid figure.

volume The number of cubic units needed to fill a solid figure.

W

weight A measure of how light or how heavy something is.

whole numbers The numbers 0, 1, 2, 3, 4, and so on.

word form A way to write a number using words.

X

x-axis A horizontal number line on a coordinate grid.

x-coordinate The first number in an ordered pair, which names the distance to the right or left from the origin along the *x*-axis.

Y

y-axis A vertical number line on a coordinate grid.

y-coordinate The second number in an ordered pair, which names the distance up or down from the origin along the *y*-axis.

yard (yd) A customary unit of length equal to 3 feet.

Z

Zero Property of Multiplication The product of any number and 0 is 0.